PENGUIN HANDBOOKS

REDRESS FOR SUCCESS

Dana Shilling is a graduate of Harvard Law School and a member of
the New York bar. She owns her own business, Plaintext, which spe-
cializes in "plain English" forms for consumers, lawyers, doctors, and
other professionals. She is the author of *Fighting Back: A Consumer's
Guide for Getting Satisfaction, Including Plaintext Form Letters to
Rip Out When You're Ripped Off* and *Be Your Own Boss* (available
in Penguin).

REDRESS
FOR
SUCCESS

USING THE LAW TO ENFORCE YOUR RIGHTS AS A WOMAN

DANA SHILLING

PENGUIN BOOKS

PENGUIN BOOKS

Viking Penguin Inc., 40 West 23rd Street,
New York, New York 10010, U.S.A.
Penguin Books Ltd, Harmondsworth,
Middlesex, England
Penguin Books Australia Ltd, Ringwood,
Victoria, Australia
Penguin Books Canada Limited, 2801 John Street,
Markham, Ontario, Canada L3R 1B4
Penguin Books (N.Z.) Ltd, 182–190 Wairau Road,
Auckland 10, New Zealand

First published in simultaneous hardcover and paperback editions by
Viking and in Penguin Books 1985
Published simultaneously in Canada

LIBRARY OF CONGRESS CATALOGING IN PUBLICATION DATA
Shilling, Dana.
Redress for success.
Includes index.
1. Women—Legal status, laws, etc.—United States—Popular works.
2. Sex discrimination in employment—Law and legislation—
United States—Popular works.
3. Sex discrimination against women—Law and legislation—United States—
Popular works.   I. Title.
[KF478.Z9S4 1985b]   346.7301′34
ISBN 0 14 00.8419 3   347.306134   85-6447

The case histories in this book are intended to be illustrative
of the types of problems women may face and of the legal principles
which may be brought to bear in order to assist women in such circumstances.
To the extent that the case histories are not drawn from publicly
available documents or court decisions, they are composites
of situations in which women find themselves. Since they are composites
they do not represent actual situations involving any specific person.

Printed in the United States of America by
R. R. Donnelley & Sons Company,
Harrisonburg, Virginia
Set in Caledonia
Designed by Sharen DuGoff Egana

CONTENTS

Contents

REDRESS FOR SUCCESS

INTRODUCTION
THE HORSE, THE RABBIT, AND THE REAL PROBLEM THREE-STEP

Is the glass half-empty or half-full? A century and a half ago, women were excluded from virtually all paying occupations, women couldn't vote or hold office, and married women couldn't make contracts or hold property. Today, in general, employed women earn far less than employed men; over a lifetime, women with college degrees can expect to earn less than men with high school diplomas; women are underrepresented in virtually every job that is agreeable, interesting, prestigious, or well paid, and overrepresented in low-paid, dead-end "pink collar" jobs. The personal and career sacrifices demanded of mothers are much greater than those fathers have to make. Nobody knows if the ERA will ever pass or if it will be done in by a terror of unisex toilets. So which deserves more attention: the very significant improvement in the legal status of women, or the very significant injustices that remain to be redressed?

If I may be permitted to sound like a politician for a moment, *both* are important; so long as one injustice remains, our job isn't finished. It's important for women to know our history, including legal history (if only to know when we're well off), and to understand both the way things used to be and the process of change. Some of the changes were responses to sociological and economic change, others the result of the raised consciousness (or response to pressure) of legislators and judges. The methods that worked in the past—voter registration, lobbying, and litigation—can work again. This book is partially an (incomplete) legal history and largely a discussion of the state of the law as of the time I wrote it. My objective is to explain what various statutes and judicial (though not necessarily judicious) decisions say, and how those rules can be used to attain your objectives.

I wish that I could detect well-defined patterns and describe them to you, so you would have a few simple maxims to predict judges' or legislators' response to a given problem. But things don't work that way. American law began with English "common law," a body of unwritten principles supplemented and interpreted by judges' decisions. The Constitution and the Bill of Rights were inspired in large part by a desire to change certain unwanted aspects of the British legal system (censorship and searches for subversive materials, for instance) and to keep the central government from becoming too powerful. It's arguable whether this last aim was achieved, but certainly the individual state governments have a great deal of power. Each of the states has its own code of laws and its own court system and its own administrative agencies. The federal government, of course, has a code of laws, a court system, and administrative agencies. So for a given question, there may be no answer (assuming the legal system has not dealt with the question yet), one answer (possible, but unlikely) or a multitude of answers (perhaps three different answers from five federal courts, eleven slightly different responses from twenty state courts, and a fistful of agency rulings saying something else again). At times I can give a straightforward description of a legal principle; more often, I have to explain that some states tackle the question one way, some another, or describe the various legal theories that different courts have evolved.

And why, you may ask, am I telling you all this? Well, knowledge for its own sake is good, and in this book I'm talking about fundamental and therefore fascinating issues of power, money, and sex. If all you know is what you read in the papers, your knowledge of legal issues will be fragmentary and often erroneous. As no one explains to you the finer points of employment discrimination litigation, legal issues related to birth control, or credit discrimination, you probably won't know if you have a triable (suitable for trial in court) case until it's too late for you to bring the case to court. Even if you hire a lawyer, your lawyer may not give you all the available information, or may not really alert you to what you can expect in terms of time, money, and annoyance. If nothing else, I'd like to give you a respect for the complexity of the issues lawyers deal with every day. I can't predict the success with which you can press any individual claim you have, but I can give you a general idea of the place(s) where you might negotiate or litigate, whom you could take action against, and what you'll have to prove to succeed. Much can be accomplished, both for the individual plaintiff and for society as a whole, but it's never easy: both the legal system and the climate around it make sure that every step of the way must be fought, and every inch of ground gained defended.

THE "REAL PROBLEM" TECHNIQUE

Some funny things have happened on the road to equality. Very often, the prospect of "equality" offered to women is like the legendary horse and rabbit pie, made in equal proportions: one horse, one rabbit. Men get most of the money in this society, and most of the attention. Just after the news and entertainment media discovered feminism, they discovered that men had been deprived of the privileges of crying and being supported. Just after the media discovered that women don't enjoy being raped, they discovered that rapists were lonely, confused guys, warped by rejecting mothers and/or wives, and that the husbands and lovers of rape victims suffer photogenic guilt, pain, and repulsion. Just after the media discovered incestuous abuse of young women, they discovered that men who rape their daughters are equally confused, conflicted pussycats who need psychological help. Publicity about wife-beating leads to the excavation of a few beaten husbands and a solemn pronouncement that the "real problem" is "domestic violence" or "spouse abuse."

I learned about the real problem three-step in September of 1983. The *New York Times* op-ed page ran an article by a Moral Majority sympathizer explaining that the "real problem" wasn't right-wing censorship but left-wing censorship. Left-wing censorship was defined as the tendency of bookstores to push Bibles and other religious books to the back of the shop.

The real problem three-step works like this: first, you focus on a complaint by an aggrieved group that you think is unjustified, or that you think is justified but which you can't or have no intention of doing anything about. Then you identify one or more members of the aggrieved group who don't meet your standards of proper conduct. Then you announce that the "real problem" either afflicts all of society or is caused or perpetrated by the aggrieved group. Step one: women protest the unavailability of good, affordable child care. Step two (pick one): some women are very poor mothers/some women want to be full-time homemakers/I don't want to pay for adequate child care/I don't want some ambitious bitch taking my job. Step three: the real problem isn't the lack of child care, but women's unwillingness to be good mothers/spend their entire salary on child care/quit their jobs so men can take the jobs/work a full day at a paid job and the equivalent at an unpaid one.

The legal system isn't entirely immune from this kind of thinking. Legislators and judges have restricted the flow of alimony much more than employers have increased the flow of income to woman employees. Child custody has come full circle. In the rare nineteenth-century divorce cases, custody would automatically be awarded to the father in all except the most dramatic cases of unfitness. Later, it became almost as automatic to award custody of children of "tender years" to their mother, unless she was demonstrably unfit. Today, as men clamor for the emotional rewards of femininity (free expression of emotion, tenderness, and nurturing) without surrendering any of the privileges of machismo, many divorce cases involve bitter custody battles, and it isn't unheard of for a judge to award custody to the father even if there is no allegation that the mother is unfit.

Similarly, a number of cases vindicate the rights of men to whatever miserable bits of advantage women have managed to pick up. Consider cases like these (and see page 18 if the citations—the numbers given after the names—are confusing): *Frontiero v. Richardson,* 411 U.S. 677 (1973), states that if wives of servicemen are entitled to allowances, husbands of servicewomen are entitled to similar allowances without proving dependency; *Weinberger v. Wiesenfeld,* 420 U.S. 636 (1975), is a similar ruling concerning Social Security benefits for widowers and children of working women; and *Orr v. Orr,* 440 U.S. 268 (1979), requires that alimony be available to men on the same terms as to women. Just as the existence of laws against racial discrimination implies the existence of suits by white people for "reverse discrimination," the existence of laws against sex discrimination means that men will come out of the woodwork demanding jobs, promotion, reinstatement, back pay—and attention.

This book is written from a feminist perspective (of which there is approximately one per feminist). Mine is summed up by the Spanish proverb, "Take what you want and pay for it, says God." In my mind, feminism means the right of every women to carry out any choice she makes for which she is qualified and for which she is willing to accept responsibility. (The same is true of men, of course but because I identify particularly with women, I am especially interested in equality of opportunity and reward for women.)

This book is also written from a lawyer's perspective. It's about legal rights and the rituals necessary for enforcing and extending them. Most of the research was done at the law library and by interviewing lawyers with particular kinds of expertise. (As you'll see, I do quote from an occasional newspaper article, if it happened to drift across my vision.) No time has been spent in trying to convince you that rape, sex discrimination, sexual harassment, or sterilization abuse are bad, or why women are entitled to basic human rights, or to quantify any particular atrocity. One incident is too many, and any woman who suffers these forms of victimization needs help.

All of these propositions seem to me to be laughably self-evident, though I know they're controversial in some quarters. If you agree with me that women *have* rights, and that these rights deserve legal protection, the next step is to learn the particular techniques available.

Naturally one book isn't enough to turn you into a lawyer. Indeed, as thousands of law school graduates find out every year, a law school education isn't enough to get you past the bar exam or teach you to represent clients. The alleged purpose of law school is to teach a previously healthy person to "think like a lawyer." My purpose here is to give you that perspective, so you'll be aware of some of the major legal issues in women's rights. I've covered the *public* legal issues, what might be described as "woman against the system." I haven't covered certain issues that are of great interest and importance to many women. Domestic relations questions—things like custody, support, division of property on divorce—are mentioned only in passing. There are several reasons for this. For one thing, most women have at least some sensitivity to, and knowledge of, these issues, and other material is available. I'd like to come back and treat them at the length they need, in another book. But most important, these are issues not only of women's rights but of men's rights. An employer accused of discrimination probably has access to sophisticated legal talent; parents involved in a custody dispute, or a divorcing couple trying to make one insufficient income stretch to support two households, are less likely to have this help.

Law isn't, as it's often thought to be, boring and irrelevant; knowledge of law can save your hide, and ignorance of law can help you dig a pit from which it's difficult or impossible to extricate yourself. The law itself is fascinating, perverse, and beautiful. Studying this exotic creature is always interesting and sometimes vital. This book isn't precisely a do-it-yourself manual. The point isn't to bring your own lawsuits without a lawyer, but to make an intelligent decision about whether you have a legally enforceable grievance at all, and to be an informed client. If you do consult a lawyer, this book aims to inform you about the strategies that can be used and which is likely to be best for you. Many of these decisions are legitimately up to the client. Some lawyers take complete control of a case and make all the decisions—because they're pressed for time, feel insecure in their professional role and threatened if clients ask for information or give suggestions; because they're paternalistic; or because they really believe that an untrained human being is incapable of understanding the mysteries of the law. (Every profession tends to deify itself and create rituals for rendering its operations incomprehensible.) Because it's the client and not the lawyer who has been injured in the first place, and because the entire process is nominally for the client's benefit, I don't think much of this approach.

I wrote this book to introduce women (and men, children, larger primates, and other bookbuyers) to the law affecting women's rights. The scope is fairly wide and the coverage is fairly technical. This book isn't a "Women's Guide to the Law" in the sense of a watered-down synopsis, designed for people the author doesn't think are very bright. Although I haven't covered all the issues, or given quite as many citations as I would have given if I were writing for my fellow lawyers, I have used the same standards of intellectual rigor. The arguments I make are legal arguments, backed up by cases and statutes: the same reasoning process and data I would use in a brief or law review article. If I say that four states have a law of a particular kind, I'll tell you which states I mean and give you citations so you can look it up for yourself or casually mention it in a conversation with your lawyer. (Should you happen to *be* a lawyer, the citations give you a chance to test the accuracy and timeliness of my work, and are a jumping-off place for your own research.)

Because I think women *can* learn about their legal rights in a fair degree of technical detail, and because I think this information is important, I have also provided some basic (and to some degree oversimplified) information about legal reasoning and the legal system. Of course I recognize that my immodesty is only slightly less than Milton's in trying to justify God's ways to Man. At any rate this attempt to explain the law's ways to Woman is a faster read than *Paradise Lost,* and has more jokes. It doesn't have Doré illustrations, but perhaps if sales are encouraging this deficiency can be compensated for in future editions. (Lawbooks are seldom illustrated, though Melvin Belli's *Modern Trials* has singularly repulsive photographs of accident scenes and victims—enough to put you off your feed for a week.)

A ruefully true *New Yorker* cartoon shows a lawyer telling a potential client, "You have a pretty good case. How much justice can you afford?" There are some undoubted wrongs that law can't right; no legal system can stop people from hating each other or force them to behave decently. All it can do is penalize people who get caught doing certain classes of things. Some grievances fall within the law, but it's not really worthwhile to pursue them, because the cost of redress is greater than anything that can be obtained (including the subjective rewards of revenge). So the first step in enforcing any legal right is to find out what, if anything, can be done within the legal system. Maybe the problem is the province of an administrative agency, who at the very least will whine at the malefactor and force it to fill out reams of time-consuming forms. If this is impossible, or unsatisfactory, it may be necessary to file suit, but only *after* all private means of dispute resolution have failed, and *if* the problem fits into one or more legally recognized "causes of action" and if (big if) there is both a reasonable chance of winning and a reasonable chance of getting a meaningful settlement or damages. A worthwhile resolution could include lots of money and/or a (believable) promise of a change in policy—for example, an effort to promote more women, or opening a training program or varsity team to women. Because any litigation is a lot of work, time-consuming, and expensive, the plaintiff had better either have a reasonable belief that the game is worth the candle or be willing to back a long shot.

PRECEDENT

American law works (if it works at all) by precedent and analogy. If a question has already been decided by someone with authority to make the decision (Congress, the state legislature, an administrative agency, the Supreme Court, or a local state or federal court), the next time the question comes up, that answer is very likely to be repeated. The legal term for this is *stare decisis,* Latin for "stand by the decision." This general principle—the legal version of the law of inertia—isn't always applied. Sometimes the underlying law changes: a statute is declared unconstitutional, or the Supreme Court changes its collective mind about something; a law is amended, or a new law passed. If a court wants to go against precedent, or if a lawyer is trying to play down an unfavorable precedent, they will *distinguish* the two situations: find (or confect) enough difference between the two situations to avoid applying the troublesome precedent to the case at hand. For example, the rules of an English gentlemen's club specified, "No dogs may enter the club premises at any time. Any animal leading a blind person is a cat."

If there is no precedent or the precedent is an uncomfortable one, the analogies come into play. One kind of contract case is compared to another kind of contract case; suits brought by women against the drug companies whose products gave them cancer are compared to other drug lawsuits.

When a lawyer has to draft (research and write) a document or argue a case, she has to find out the facts (or her client's version of the facts) and look up the statutes, administrative rulings, and cases that apply. Then she has to write up the document to advance her client's interests (consistent with what is legally permitted and what negotiations with the other party will let her client get away with). If the lawyer represents the client in a lawsuit, she has to find precedents and analogies to make an argument for her client's side.

One of the fascinating things about the law is that there are usually at least two sides to every question, and a colorable (passably plausible) argument can be made for each. Therefore, *conflicts of authority* are frequent. Court A and Court B answer the same question, dealing with the same facts, in different ways, or Court A changes its position over time. Each lawyer's job is to convince the court to adopt the authority favorable to her client's side. Everyone has to listen to the United States Supreme Court; courts usually listen to their own prior pronouncements (unless they find some way to distinguish an uncomfortable case or announce an out-and-out change of direction); lower state courts listen to the higher state courts of their state, and may or may not listen to federal courts; lower federal courts listen to the federal courts immediately above them and may listen to other federal appeals courts.

BALANCE OF POWERS

Remember all that boring stuff in eighth-grade civics about the three branches of government? It's still boring, but it's relevant here. The legislative branch (Congress and the state legislatures) makes laws. The judicial branch (the courts) interprets the statutes, clears up ambiguities, answers unanswered questions (and sometimes unasked questions—"ju-dicial activism" is a controversial activity involving judge-made law), and occasionally tosses out a statute on the grounds that it's unconstitutional, vague, or ambiguous. When that happens, the legislature can change the statute to conform, change the Constitution, or hope that the whole thing will blow over when another court overrules the one that eighty-sixed the statute. The executive branch includes the President, the various gover-nors, and mayors. Most important for this book, it includes the various administrative agencies that are supposed to dig in and actually enforce the law. As you'll see as you progress through this book, the regulations of the Equal Employment Opportunity Commission (EEOC), Food and Drug Administration (FDA) and other federal agencies are exceedingly important.

Overall, "the law" or "the legal system" is an interaction between these three branches. "The law" keeps changing (though not necessarily pro-gressing), and to understand a particular situation and decide what can be done legally, clients and lawyers must understand the relevant trends in each of the three branches. (The law changes faster than books can be printed; I finished the basic research for this one in July 1984 and couldn't update the text—even for "stop the presses" information—any later than March 1985. So don't send me a nasty letter commenting adversely on my ignorance of later developments.)

COURTS AND COURT SYSTEMS

Once a decision is made to take the case to court, however, the court system becomes the most important of the three branches. Most of the legal research will center on finding persuasive court cases to quote, and the case must be conducted in accordance with the applicable rules of "civil procedure" or "criminal procedure" for the court that is chosen. (See "Some Categories," below.)

There are two separate court systems in the United States (state courts and federal courts) and two basic kinds of courts in each system (trial courts and appeals courts). A case can be brought in state court unless for some reason the case is forbidden (for instance, Title VII—the federal law for-bidding employment discrimination—cases can only be brought in federal court; a person or organization can't be sued in a particular state's courts unless he, she, or it has some meaningful connection with that state). The federal courts are "courts of limited jurisdiction": cases can only be brought in federal court if there is some specific authority for bringing them there. (More of this in "Jurisdiction," below.)

Each state has its own court system. At the bottom are "trial" or "lower" courts. Some states, such as New York, have several kinds of lower courts for different kinds of case. The trial court will consider both the facts of the case and the applicable laws. In most state trial courts, the case will be decided by a jury unless the defendant (in a criminal case) or both sides (in a civil case) agree to waive it. There's no hard-and-fast rule, but generally a plaintiff with an easily explained, pathetic case would prefer a jury and hope for a large verdict; one with a highly technical case, involving difficult factual or legal questions, would prefer a judge, on the theory that a jury might toss out a case it didn't understand. However, it has often been questioned whether state lower-court judges are a form of intelligent life.

In a jury trial, the judge decides the questions of law (whether a particular piece of evidence is admissible or not), and the jury decides questions of fact (for example, which car crossed the yellow line). The jury decides which party wins on which points and the damages to be awarded to the winner(s). In a "court" trial (trial before a judge, without a jury) the judge decides everything. Technically speaking, anything a jury decides is a "verdict"; a judge makes a "decision."

An unhappy litigant may be able to appeal the case to a higher, appeals court. In most states, the appeals court (or highest appeals court) is called the Supreme Court; New York, with characteristic perversity, calls a court in the middle of the system the Supreme Court, and the highest court is called the Court of Appeals. Maryland's highest state court is also called the Court of Appeals; Maine and Massachusetts' highest state courts are called the Supreme Judicial Court, and West Virginia's is the Supreme Court of Appeals. In a state like New York, with a lot of judicial business, there will be several layers of appeals courts; a dissatisfied litigant can keep appealing until her case is thrown out or until she gets sick and tired of the whole business. Appeals courts don't have juries and don't hear witnesses or see evidence. Appeals judges read the transcript (record of testimony and exhibits in the trial) and listen to arguments by lawyers. The issue before an appeals court is generally not the facts of the case (whether A's negligence injured B, whether C robbed D's liquor store on the night of April 9) but whether there was something wrong with the trial: a biased judge or jury, say, or a completely inaccurate interpretation of the law. An appeals court can *affirm* the lower court (agree that it was right), *reverse* or *overrule* it (say that it was wrong), *reverse* and *remand* (send it back to the lower court with orders to do it right this time) or *affirm in part, reverse in part* (say that the lower court was right about some things, wrong about others; the reversal may include a remand).

There are three levels of run-of-the-mill federal courts (and special-purpose courts like the Tax Court). The lower courts are called District Courts. There are ninety-one District Courts; each state has at least one, and states with more litigation have two, three, or four. Some cases in the District Court can be tried by juries; others (for example, Title VII employment discrimination cases) can't be. Whether a District Court lit-

igant is entitled to a jury depends on the ancestry of the case. Cases that
are considered legal (roughly, those descended from the kinds of cases
that were tried in medieval English royal courts, typically involving money
damages) are usually entitled to juries; those considered equitable (equally
roughly, offspring of cases tried in ecclesiastical courts, usually involving
orders to someone to do something or stop doing something) usually aren't.
Go figure it.

The next step up is the Court of Appeals. The United States is divided
into thirteen Circuits, each with a Court of Appeals. The First Circuit
takes appeals from the District Courts of Massachusetts, Maine, New
Hampshire, and Rhode Island; the Second Circuit from New York, Vermont, and Connecticut. The Third Circuit covers Pennsylvania, New Jersey, and Delaware; the Fourth handles Virginia, West Virginia, Maryland,
North and South Carolina; the Fifth deals with Mississippi, Louisiana,
and Texas cases. (Admittedly this is a geographical jump; until 1980, the
Fifth Circuit included Alabama, Georgia, and Florida, but these were split
off to form the Eleventh Circuit.) Tennessee, Kentucky, Ohio, and Michigan are in the Sixth Circuit, Illinois, Wisconsin, and Indiana in the Seventh. North and South Dakota, Nebraska, Minnesota, Iowa, Missouri, and
Arkansas are in the Eighth Circuit. The Ninth Circuit (the Second and
Ninth are probably the most prestigious Circuits) covers Washington,
Montana, Oregon, Idaho, California, Nevada, Arizona, Alaska, and
Hawaii. The Tenth Circuit handles appeals from the District Courts of
Wyoming, Utah, Colorado, New Mexico, Kansas, and Oklahoma. There
is a D.C. Circuit, covering the District of Columbia as a place; most cases
against federal agencies are heard here. The other Circuit is called the
Federal Circuit and handles certain recondite federal cases (e.g., customs
and patent appeals). Most Court of Appeals cases are heard by a three-
judge panel; like state appeals courts, they examine a written record rather
than having trials with a full cast of characters.

At the top are Warren Burger and the Supremes. Cases can get to the
Supreme Court by two main routes: *appeal* and *certiorari. Certiorari* is
Latin for "made surer"—that is, the situation is made surer, or clarified,
by sending the record of the case to the Supreme Court. A case can only
be appealed if it falls into certain categories, and if both the case and the
parties trying to appeal it meet the specified legal criteria. Appeal cases
can include cases in which a District Court declares a federal law unconstitutional, a Court of Appeals or District Court three-judge panel declares
a state statute unconstitutional, a state's highest court finds a federal law
unconstitutional or *upholds* a state law whose constitutionality is challenged. However, once a case is appealed and all the criteria are met, the
Supreme Court *must* hear the case.

Any party disgruntled by a Court of Appeals decision or displeased with
a state's highest court if a state or federal law is challenged, or anyone

allegedly deprived of a right granted by a federal law, can petition the Supreme Court for *certiorari;* the Supreme Court decides which of these cases it will hear ("cert. granted") and which it won't ("cert. denied"— I've always wanted to open up a bar for lawyers called the Cert Den). The Supreme Court can test state laws against the Constitution, but can't handle purely state-law questions that have no federal implications. Some cases are more likely to be granted cert. than others—cases in which there is a conflict between Circuits, cases involving conflicting or unanswered questions of federal law, for instance. But naturally the Supreme Court rejects the overwhelming majority of the petitions—it's a long, long way to *certiorari.*

JURISDICTION

"Jurisdiction" is a philosophical, or rather theological, concept in law— rather like the Immaculate Conception for Catholicism. It's possible to doubt it or have another opinion about the matter, but only in another religion.

"Jurisdiction" is a particular court's right to hear a particular case. As I mentioned before, a state court has jurisdiction to hear any case—includ- ing a case involving federal laws—that it isn't specifically forbidden to hear. Federal courts have limited jurisdiction, and can hear only two kinds of cases: *diversity* cases (involving citizens of different states, if the amount at stake is over $10,000) and federal question cases (arising under the Constitution, a federal law, or a treaty). If a potential plaintiff has both state and federal claims against one or more defendants, she can bring separate cases in state and federal court; bring the whole mess in state court (if the federal claims are of a type confined to federal court, she would have to forget about the federal claims); or introduce the matter in federal court, which will take jurisdiction of the state law claims (the process is called "pendent jurisdiction"—of which more on page 66). There are several factors involved in choosing between state and federal courts: the length of time it will take the case to get to court, and the relative sophistication (federal courts are usually more sophisticated) of the possible courts, for example.

Volumes can be (and have been) written about the interpretation of each of these seemingly simple propositions. For example, it's been settled that a corporation is a citizen of the state in which it has been incorporated and the state in which it has its principal place of business (so a corporation can be a citizen of two different states). A person who is a citizen of Colorado and has at least a $10,000 hassle with a corporation chartered in Delaware with headquarters in California can bring a diversity suit in federal court, but a citizen of Delaware or California can't. The rule is "complete diversity": no matter how many parties are involved, no plaintiff can be a citizen of the same state as any defendant. (It isn't entirely certain why the Founding Fathers thought of diversity jurisdiction in the first place; maybe they were afraid that state courts would slam outside plaintiffs automatically, without bothering to listen to the facts of the case.)

That's one aspect of jurisdiction ("subject-matter jurisdiction"). The other aspect is jurisdiction over the person ("personal" or "in personam jurisdiction"). For example, there's no point in suing a dead person, since the court can neither subpoena him nor impose any further sanctions on him—though there may be some point in suing his estate. Governments can be sued only if they agree to be ("sovereign immunity"). More to the point for our purposes here, a corporation can probably be sued in the state or federal courts of any state in which it does business and can very likely be sued in any state in which its products do damage. (This is called "long-arm jurisdiction," as in the long arm of the law, but one shudders to imagine "short-arm jurisdiction.") But a suit can only be brought in a court which has both subject-matter jurisdiction and personal jurisdiction over all the defendants.

Venue is a related but less serious problem: venue is the question of which of several possible courts the case should be brought in. For example, a case brought in the Eastern District of New York might really belong in the Southern District of New York. Sometimes there'll be a motion for change of venue in a criminal case on the grounds that there is prejudice against the defendant (he's a Neo-Nazi and the case is in Brighton Beach; the local newspapers have printed several articles describing the defendant as a mad killer, etc.). If a court lacks jurisdiction, it simply can't hear a case; but a court that isn't necessarily the best venue can hear a case if the defendant agrees not to make a fuss about it. (As the plaintiff made the decision in the first place about where to sue, she can't complain about it.)

The simplest case has one plaintiff and one defendant. A plaintiff can also have grievances against several defendants: suppose a woman suffers sexual harassment at work and is fired for complaining to the union and the Equal Employment Opportunity Commission (EEOC). The possible defendants include the immediate supervisor who harassed her, the top brass who let him get away with it, the corporation that employed her, the union officials, and the union itself. (No, you can't sue the EEOC for doing a lousy job of protecting your rights—that possibility has been anticipated and eliminated by federal law.)

More than one plaintiff can sue the same defendant or defendants: everyone injured in a plane crash, or all women injured by a particular model of IUD sold in Massachusetts, for example. In the federal courts and some state courts, suits with multiple plaintiffs or defendants can be brought as *class actions* under certain circumstances. I say "under certain circumstances" because class actions involve some of the knottiest questions of civil procedure.

SOME CATEGORIES

Civil procedure is the system of arranging the way civil cases will be brought and dealt with; *criminal procedure* serves the same function for criminal cases. Together, they make up *procedural* law. On the other hand, *substantive* law deals with the underlying rights and obligations of citizens toward one another and to the state. As you've guessed, the distinction between substantive and procedural law isn't hard and fast. The distinction matters because when a federal court handles a diversity case, it follows federal procedure (following the Federal Rules of Civil Procedure, Appellate Procedure, and Evidence), but applies state substantive law. The law of which state? Well, there's a legal discipline called "choice of law" that hassles with that, but the basic rule is that the state where the harm occurred—if you can define that—is the state whose laws will apply. (Though there are few simple answers in law, there are hordes of general principles, each with exceptions hanging off it like piglets on a sow. No wonder lawyers are hard-pressed to give a straight answer about anything; one was asked what color a nearby barn was and responded, "It's red on this side.")

The major areas of law include contract law, tort law, and their offspring, products liability law (to be discussed at great length in Chapter VII, "Women's Health Issues"), civil procedure, criminal procedure, administrative law (law relating to administrative agencies such as the EEOC, their powers and their liabilities), tax law, commercial and business law, and family law. Some of these areas will be highlighted in this book. Employment discimination and sexual harassment bring up subtle questions of civil procedure and tort law; the important issues in products liability include identifying the defendant and proper timing of the suit; victims of rape and domestic violence need to know something about criminal procedure. This book is organized into sections, each dealing with the substantive law on a particular topic, and illustrated with a hypothetical case study designed to point up the issues. The studies are made up precisely to agglomerate all the most difficult questions; there's no real "solution" for them, and they're not intended to represent actual histories or reports of litigated cases. The sections labeled *The Road to the Courthouse* deal with procedural issues: whom you can sue, for what ("cause of action"), where, when, and under what restrictions. The sections labeled *The Smoking Gun* deal with evidence: what you have to do to prove a case, and what evidence is acceptable (*admissible*).

ESSENTIALS OF PROCEDURE

The first stage of any civil suit involves the *pleadings*. The pleadings are fairly formal documents that lawyers exchange to let one another and the judge know what issues are involved in the case. (Whether the parties in the case know the issues is a function of the amount their lawyers tell them or the extent to which they demand to be involved.) The first pleadings are the *summons* and the *complaint*. The summons tells the defendant (or, in practical terms, the defendant's lawyers) that the defendant is being sued and when to show up for the initial court appearance. The complaint explains the legal theories behind the suit and what the plaintiff is asking for. In federal court, suit begins formally when the complaint is filed with the court. Some state courts do it that way; in others, the first shot is fired by serving the summons on the defendant, and filing with the court comes later.

The defendant produces a *reply*, either denying the charges or admitting the obvious (that the defendant really is an Illinois corporation that sold birth-control pills in Texas in 1981) but denying liability. On the theory that the best defense is a good offense, sometimes the reply includes a *counterclaim*, explaining why the plaintiff actually owes the defendant something. If there is more than one defendant, they can make *cross-claims* against each other: Defendant A demands something from Defendant B. Defendants can also become semi-plaintiffs by *impleading* someone else: dragging in someone else who they feel is entirely or partially responsible for the mess they find themselves in.

With any luck at all, the defendant(s) will be so unwilling to go through with the suit that they will make a reasonable settlement offer, the plaintiff will take the offer, and that will be the end of it. Otherwise, the case moves into *pretrial discovery*. The theoretical, and laudable, objective of discovery is to make sure that there are no secrets, that each side knows whatever the other side knows that is relevant to the case. In practice, discovery can be a way to drag out litigation for years and make it even more expensive, as plaintiffs' lawyers sift through mountains of rubbish obligingly provided by the defendant. But every now and then it all becomes worthwhile: the crates of files or miles of computer tape yield the crucial evidence establishing the defendant's liability.

In the federal system (most state systems are fairly similar) there are several discovery devices. The most common are *depositions, interrogatories,* and *notices to produce*. As discovery goes on, the plaintiffs can also be conducting independent investigations.

A *deposition* is like a mini-trial without a judge. The person giving the testimony is sworn in, and the lawyer demanding the deposition questions the witness, subject to objections on the record and questions from the other lawyer. The answers are taken down by a court reporter and transcribed, at not-inconsiderable expense. Depositions can also be taken on written questions, which is more convenient for the party requesting the information but not for the deponent (person giving the testimony). The lawyer who wants the deposition writes down the questions she wants answered; the deponent appears before a notary, is sworn in, and answers the questions, which are read out by the notary. Again, the answers are taken down stenographically and transcribed. The law is reluctantly catching up with the twentieth century: some courts are experimenting with tape-recorded and videotaped depositions.

You can take the deposition of anyone who can fog a mirror, but you can only issue interrogatories to a party in the case (plaintiff or defendant). Interrogatories are written questions, answered in writing. The answers are given under oath, but there's no need for a stenotypist or transcript.

A litigant can also demand access to documents or other things (crashed cars, flamed-out machinery, products returned as defective) that another party controls. Documents can be copied, and objects can be subjected to tests by experts.

When the discovery material has been processed, and before trial, each side provides the court (and its opponents) with a *brief*, stating its legal theories, what it wants the court to do, and the legal justification for the requests. "Legal brief," of course, rivals "military intelligence" as a contradiction in terms.

Many cases are settled at some point during the discovery process, or after discovery and before the trial starts. The best result for the plaintiff comes when the defendant is so terrified by the disclosures that a generous settlement is forthcoming; the worst, when the plaintiff runs out of money or patience and takes a small settlement or bugs out. A case can be settled at any time—in some dramatic instances, just before the jury reaches a verdict. Some of these settlements are much smaller than the jury verdict would have been—and some are much larger; that's what makes horse racing.

A person or thing can be brought into court by *subpoena* (literally "under pain"). A regular subpoena orders someone to come into court and testify, under pain of penalties for contempt of court. A subpoena *duces tecum* (which is Latin for "bring it with you") requires the production of documents or other things.

Although dramatic revelations (or dramatic anything) are rare in trials, the basic pattern of trials is about what you've seen in a thousand courtroom dramas: picking a jury (which can take weeks), opening statements, witnesses' testimony, exhibits, objections to questions and to the admission of evidence, closing statements, and the judge's instructions to the jury.

There are several ways a case can end, short of a full trial and a verdict (or judge's decision, in a court trial). If the complaint is so badly drafted (from the legal point of view, not the literary) that the plaintiff couldn't possibly win, the case can be dismissed for failure to state a cause of action. If the defense doesn't *move* (make a motion; that is, ask the court for something) to have the complaint dismissed, or if the complaint stands up, the next hurdle comes if the defense can argue that there are no real factual issues that call for a trial: that is, even if the plaintiff is right about the facts, the law prevents her from winning her case. This motion asks for *summary judgment*. It's possible, though not likely, that a summary judgment motion will be granted after trial begins—the underlying objective of the motion is to head off useless trials at the pass. The many times in this book that I say something like "The plaintiff may be able to prove . . ." or "It isn't impossible to show . . ." are not caused by professional pussyfooting, but by the fact that I'm summarizing an opinion in a summary judgment case; all that was decided in those cases was whether the charge was too flimsy to stand up, not the actual facts of the case. (The *opinion* is the written statement of the judge's decision.) A case surviving a motion for summary judgment can still bomb out later if the defense moves for a *directed verdict* at the close of the plaintiff's case. That is, the judge directs the jury to return a verdict for the defendant, because it's obvious that no sane jury could find for the plaintiff, even before the defense has stated its side of the matter. By this time the poor battered plaintiff's case has struggled past as many obstacles as a salmon pushing its way upstream to spawn.

The standard-model jury has twelve members and must be unanimous to reach a verdict; if the jury is hopelessly deadlocked, the case is declared a mistrial and has to be done over. (A mistrial can also be declared if something goes seriously haywire: if there is severe prejudice or misconduct on someone's part, for example.) Some states, however, require or allow six- or nine-person juries, and some allow a case to be decided by a majority rather than a unanimous verdict.

If the jury finds for the plaintiff, the defendant gets a couple more bites of the apple. The defense can move for a j.n.o.v. (judgment *non obstante veredicto*—notwithstanding the verdict), which will be granted if the judge finds the verdict entirely bizarre from the legal point of view—not just because the judge would have decided something different him- or herself. If the judge feels that a jury award of damages to a plaintiff is grossly inadequate or excessive, s/he can order a new trial, even if the defense doesn't ask for one. The plaintiff can appeal the new-trial order, but the appeals court will back up the trial judge unless there was a gross abuse of discretion. The trial judge can also offer the plaintiff a choice between *remittitur* (lower damages) and a new trial; if, however, the judge feels the damages are grossly inadequate, s/he can't order higher damages, but must order a new trial.

Finally, if either side—or both sides—is displeased by the outcome, it may be possible to appeal; up to the Supreme Court, if necessary, and if the High Court cooperates. Like the man said, it ain't over till it's over.

THE LEGAL WORLD-VIEW

In any intellectual discipline, whether that of the research scientist or the private eye, what you find depends on where you look. When a lawyer is preparing a case for trial, she wants to find out the facts of her particular case, and the applicable law. Informal interviews and discovery provide the former; legal research unearths the latter. (For the insatiably curious, I've discussed legal research in an earlier book called *Fighting Back*.)

Legal research provides only a partial (in both senses of the term) world-view. Most legal research involves reading cases that not only went to trial but were appealed; and, as we've said, appellate cases concentrate on legal issues, not the facts. The plaintiff and defendant are critically interested in who wins and who loses, and the amount of money involved; people who read the reported cases are interested in the legal principles to be distilled from the opinion.

The medical concept, "The operation was successful, but the patient died" has a legal counterpart in the test case that breaks new legal ground—but which the plaintiff loses, in a civil case, or in which the defendant goes to jail, in a criminal case. Often, a test case will give legal guidelines in an entirely untested field of law (this is called a "case of first impression"). In effect, the judge says, "To win a case of this type, you must prove A,B,C,D, and E." This is most enlightening for the plaintiffs of the future (and defendants of the future, who want to know what they can get away with), but a slap in the face with a wet fish for the actual plaintiff, who has proved A,B,C, and D and ends up losing the case.

What I'm driving at is that this book is a *legal* history of certain kinds of cases—not a history of who did what to whom and what the end result was. Sometimes only one or a few of many hearings in a case will be reported (in legal terms, that means that a judge's opinion is printed in a *reporter*, or collection of opinions). Cases decided entirely by a jury do not yield judicial opinions and therefore are not reported. Settlements won't be reported at all, though the information will be available if journalists (whether for specialized legal publications or mass-market media) find it out and decide to publicize it. However, because of sheer ignorance, lack of information, or sensationalism, newspaper reports can tell less than the whole truth about a case.

All U.S. Supreme Court opinions are published; no matter how silly they may be, no one wants to ignore them. The government itself publishes "official" reports. A case in the official reports is cited like this: *Roe v. Wade*, 410 U.S. 113 (1973). Legal citations (the references—the "address" of the case) always start with the volume number (goodness knows why), so this is a case decided in 1973 whose opinion is printed in Volume 410 of the U.S. Reports, starting on page 113. There are also two sets of unofficial reports, printed by private publishers and available in most law libraries: the Supreme Court Reports (cited as ——— S.Ct. ———) and the Lawyers' Edition, Second Series (——— L.Ed.2d. ———). The advantage of the unofficial reporters is that they include the official texts and summaries and the unofficial summaries and research materials provided by the publishers' editorial staff. (It is a deplorable, but common, practice for legal researchers to read the summaries—the head-notes—rather than the cases. For shame!)

As a convenience for those with different libraries, or as a further sign of obsessiveness, lawyers often give *parallel cites:* that is, if the opinion in a particular case is printed in more than one reporter, the lawyer will give all the citations.

Sometimes you'll see a cite like this: *Roe v. Wade,* 410 U.S. 113, 117 (1973). That means that the writer has quoted, or is about to quote, a passage from the opinion appearing on page 117.

There are no official reporters for lower federal courts; West Publishing Co. prints the cases its editors think are worthy of note in the various volumes of F.2d (Federal Reporter, Second Series—Court of Appeals cases) and F.Supp. (Federal Supplement—District Court cases). Cases they do not think worthy of note may be published unofficially in a looseleaf service (see page 19) like Fair Employment Practices Cases.

Most states have at least one set of official reporters; 119 Ga. 605 would mean page 605 of Volume 119 of Georgia's official reports. Some states have several sets of official reporters to deal with several levels of courts. Some states have just thrown in the towel and stopped publishing official reporters, because the ubiquitous Westerners publish "regional reporters" containing selected cases from the courts of a group of states. The regional reporters are A.2d (Atlantic Reporter, Second Series), N.E.2d (Northeastern), N.W.2d (Northwestern), S.E.2d (Southeastern), S.W.2d (Southwestern), and P.2d (Pacific). No Central. (See the chart on pages 313–314 for the regional reporter printing cases from your state.)

All federal statutes are collected in the United States Code, or U.S.C.; the unofficial versions, U.S.C.S. (United States Code Service) and U.S.C.A. (United States Code Annotated) have the full text of the law, plus legislative history (prior versions of the law and amendments) and summaries of cases interpreting the statutes. Again, the volume number goes first: Title IX, the federal law forbidding sex discrimination in education, is 20 U.S.C. §1681—section 1681 of Title 20 of the United States Code (§ is the section sign.) The federal regulations interpreting the federal statutes are found in the C.F.R., or Code of Federal Regulations. For example, Regulation B, the regulations for the Equal Credit Opportunity Act, start at 12 C.F.R.

§201.1—section 201.1 of Part 12 of the Code of Federal Regulations. Sometimes large chunks of the C.F.R. are called "Parts": for example, all of Regulation B is sometimes called 12 C.F.R. Part 201.

Every state has a Code, or set of state statutes. Some of the state codes have a uniform numbering system throughout: for example, Minnesota §241.61. Maryland, New York, and Texas have individual titles for various parts of the code (New York Penal Law, Texas Family Code, for instance); each named code has a separate numbering system. Some state codes are divided up into unnamed Titles (Maine Title 13 §202, for example, abbreviated ME T13§202) or Chapters (Massachusetts Chapter 112 §12Q, abbreviated MA ch 112§12Q). To make the already interminable notes a little shorter, I've referred to state statutes simply by name of the state and the section number of the *first* section involved, without bothering to note that the Missouri statutes are called Vernon's Annotated Missouri Statutes or that Maine's are the Maine Revised Statutes Annotated. Sometimes I refer to *session laws:* recent laws that have been passed by the legislature and signed by the governor, but not yet plugged into the official statute book. Session laws are cited by state, year, and section or chapter number: Oregon Laws 1983 chapter 505, and so forth.

Because new law is produced so rapidly, and copiously, many lawbooks have *pocket parts* (paperback pamphlets stuck into the back cover) to supplement the printed text with later information. Lawyers also rely on *looseleaf services* and legal journals for new information, information not available elsewhere, and commentary and analysis. A looseleaf service is a binder, like the ones you used to carry in junior high school, filled with printed pages explaining a particular area of the law. Every month, the subscribers to the service get some new pages, to be either added or substituted for older, obsolete pages. *Law Week* is one of the most respected looseleaf services. It comes in two volumes: one for the Supreme Court, one for all other courts, federal and state. There's a weekly newsletter summarizing the most important developments, and texts and summaries of important cases. A reference to 52 LW 3809 means page 3809 of Volume 52 of *Law Week. Law Week* is published by the Bureau of National Affairs, or BNA; they also put out the *Family Law Reporter* (FLR) and *Fair Employment Practices Cases* (FEP Cases; an essential reference for job discrimination cases). The Commerce Clearing House—CCH— publishes something similar called EPD *(Employment Practices Decisions).* For reasons I've never fathomed, the EPD and its sister publication, PLR *(Products Liability Reporter)* are organized by paragraphs, not page numbers: 32 EPD ¶32,053, for example.

Law reviews are scholarly publications, usually produced quarterly (or allegedly produced quarterly—delays are common) by law schools. Some of the articles are contributed by law professors, judges, and prominent lawyers; others (called "Notes" or "Comments") by students at the school.

Students also do the editing, giving a 23-year-old kid the opportunity to tell an eminent scholar or jurist that he's a lousy writer—an opportunity available in few other professions. The purpose of a law review article is to unearth every obscure statute or case that might be relevant to the subject of the article, then to attempt to make some sense out of this farrago; so law review articles are useful for those interested in a particular topic, enamored of casuistry, or too lazy to dig up the cases and statutes themselves. Law review articles are cited by the name of the author, title of article, volume number, the name of the magazine (generally the something-or-other *Law Journal* or *Law Review*), the page number, and the date, e.g., Gail R. Reizenstein, "A Fresh Look at the Equal Credit Opportunity Act," 14 *Akron L. Rev.* 215 (Fall 1980). The legal encyclopedia called *American Jurisprudence,* Second Series *(Am.Jur.2d)* performs the same service, on a less technical level. *American Law Reports (A.L.R.)* and its federal counterpart, *A.L.R. Fed.*, are similar; *Am.Jur. Trials* concentrates on litigation, and *Am.Jur. POF2d (American Jurisprudence Proof of Facts, Second Series)* deals with questions of evidence. I also got a lot of help from two newspapers: the daily *New York Law Journal (N.Y.L.J.)* and the weekly *National Law Journal (Nat.L.J.).*

It will soon become clear to you that this book has a great number of notes. To keep the pages uncluttered, they have a separate but equal section at the end of the book. Instead of numbers, I use references to the text. Some statutes and cases are cited directly in the text, though they're not necessarily more important.

1

SEX DISCRIMINATION IN EMPLOYMENT: SUBSTANTIVE LAW

Barbara Haggerty had two years' accounting experience when she was hired by Crichton Industries. When she started work in June, she was ushered to a small windowless cubicle. She never had to worry about being lonely, because her cubicle was located right behind the supply closet, and all the members of the typing pool had to pass by to get paper and ribbons. This was useful to Haggerty, who occasionally caught a typist on the wing and got her typing done on time. This happened only occasionally, however, because Haggerty's work was accorded the lowest priority.

In October, Crichton hired a young man who had received his BBA in accounting in June and spent the intervening time job-hunting. He was given a small office, with a window, near Haggerty's cubicle. From her vantage point, she was able to hear that he spent much of the day on the telephone, arranging lunch dates and squash games and talking to his girlfriend. Haggerty's typical travel assignment involved hopping the 2 A.M. plane to a suburb of Birmingham to see what had gone wrong with a routine audit. His typical assignment was a three-day seminar in Palm Springs, accompanying Crichton's Vice President for Finance.

One day, Haggerty had an instructive conversation in the ladies' room with the secretary who worked for the young man. She found out that he earned $4,000 a year more than she did.

The cynic might think that the entire apparatus for the redress of sex discrimination was an elaborate sham, a way to make women think that their rights were being protected. If an individual woman lacks the persistence (or the money) to keep fighting through endless levels of administrative proceedings and litigation, either it proves that her rights weren't really violated, that she's somehow culpable, or that she did not have the right stuff, doesn't it? Fortunately we are not cynical and can take all the ringing statements of rights and objectives at face value.

The most important federal sex discrimination law is Title VII, so called because it's Title (part) VII of the Civil Rights Act of 1964. Title VII says that it's an unlawful employment practice for an employer:

> (1) To fail or refuse to hire or to discharge any individual, or otherwise to discriminate against any individual with respect to his compensation, terms, or privileges of employment because of such individual's race, color, religion, *sex,* or national origin; or
> (2) to limit, segregate, or classify his [that is, the employer's] employees or applicants for employment in any way which would deprive or tend to deprive any individual of employment opportunities or otherwise affect his status as an employee, because of such individual's race, color, religion, *sex,* or national origin. [Italics mine.]

Sex was added to the laundry list at the last minute, by an amendment proposed by Representative Howard Smith of Virginia. It has been said he did it as a joke, to show how preposterous it was to have civil rights legislation at all—an absurdity that would become obvious once time was devoted to enforcing women's rights. Note that Title VII covers only *employment.* (The ERA, if ever ratified, would cover all areas of civil life.) Title VII sets restraints only on the actions of employers—a point that will be important in the discussion of sexual harassment.

An "employer" is further defined as a business having an effect on interstate commerce (which gives the federal government jurisdiction over that business's affairs) and having at least fifteen employees on each working day in each of twenty or more weeks in the year a charge is filed, or in the preceding year. (Therefore, it may be impossible to charge some employers with sex discrimination, either because their business doesn't affect interstate commerce, or because they don't employ enough people.) However, an employer is subject to Title VII if it has more than fifteen employees—not necessarily fifteen *full-time* employees.

Title VII is also binding on employment agencies and labor unions, so a woman who suffers discrimination from either can complain to the Equal Employment Opportunity Commission (EEOC) in the same way as against an employer. Job applicants can use the EEOC procedure, but independent contractors (free-lances) are not necessarily treated as employees.

It's legal for an employer to hire only men, or only women, for a particular job, as long as sex is a bona fide occupational qualification (BFOQ). Very few things are bona fide occupational qualifications. A director can demand that an actor rather than an actress play a particular role, or vice versa (Sarah Bernhardt's Hamlet and Dustin Hoffman's Dorothy Michaels notwithstanding), and a job can be restricted to men or women if the privacy of customers or clients is involved (washroom attendant, brassiere fitter). An odd 1981 decision says that being female is a BFOQ for being an obstetric nurse. The court's rationale is that a male nurse would violate the patient's right to privacy, and it would be inefficient for the hospital to hire a female nurse to accompany him on his rounds to protect the hospital from charges of sexual abuse. The Arkansas court recognizes that nearly all obstetricians are male (so much for the right of privacy) but says that there aren't enough female obstetricians to go around, so the hospital has to recruit most or all of its obstetricians from the male sex.

In any situation that doesn't involve a bona fide occupational qualification, Title VII makes it illegal to assign women only to certain jobs identified as "female," while other jobs are identified as "male."

The EEOC's Guidelines say that the following don't constitute BFOQs:

- An assumption that the turnover rate is higher for female than for male employees. ("If we give them the job, they'll just quit to have babies.")
- A belief that women are less capable than men of hard-hitting salesmanship.
- Customer preferences, unless authenticity or privacy is involved.

In other words, an airline can't refuse to hire male stewards (because men can serve dinner and demonstrate lifejackets efficiently), and restaurants can't refuse to hire waitresses for lucrative dinner shifts. However, Playboy Club patrons don't have to live in fear of being greeted, "Hi! I'm Tom, your Drag Bunny!" The right of privacy will be respected in most conventional situations. However, it isn't usually considered a violation of privacy for a female nurse to give a bedpan or bed bath to a male hospital patient (probably because the conventional wisdom is that (a) such tasks are done by nurses, and (b) nurses are female).

Some cases deal with an employer's contention that "sexiness" is a BFOQ. It's been held that an airline is in the business of transporting passengers from one place to another, not feeding their sexual fantasies— so an airline could not restrict the jobs of flight attendant and ticket agent to women, even though the airline's ad campaign claimed that the airline's advantage over its competitors was the greater attractiveness of its personnel. A restaurant was ordered to reinstate a waiter who was fired because the restaurant thought waitresses in scanty outfits would increase business. However, a television station *was* allowed to set different grooming standards for male and female newscasters, and to fire a woman newscaster for "below-average aptitude in matters of clothing and makeup."

The EEOC's Guidelines also require help-wanted ads to be sex-neutral, unless a BFOQ is involved. If there is no BFOQ, listing a job in a column labeled "Help wanted—male" or "female" will be considered sex discrimination.

There's a clear violation of Title VII when women and men receive "disparate treatment" (that is, are treated differently). An example would be an employer's policy of hiring men who scored over 60 on an employment test, or promoting men with "satisfactory" job evaluations, while requiring women to score over 90 or be rated "outstanding" for promotion. "Disparate impact" cases are harder to prove. In a disparate impact case, a "facially neutral" requirement (one that seems fair on its face) has a negative effect on women. For example, a minimum height requirement, or a requirement that a job applicant be able to lift heavy weights, has a disparate impact on women. One way the employer can avoid liability is by proving that the requirement, although it excludes more female than male applicants, is really necessary for efficient performance of the job (the "business necessity" defense) and isn't "pretextual" (made up to justify sex discrimination). Another way is for the employer to interview only female applicants for a certain number of jobs—say, to interview women only for five jobs, then to exclude all women under 5 feet 6 inches from consideration. In this case, the height requirement isn't considered discriminatory because the female job applicants are competing against other women, not against men. (If you're curious, designating certain jobs as jobs for women wasn't considered sex discrimination, because it was affirmative action designed to correct the past exclusion of women.) Similar reasoning was used in the unfortunately named case of *Malarkey v. Texaco, Inc.*: the court found that Title VII would not be violated even if, as the plaintiff claimed, promotion decisions favored young, pretty women over older, plainer women. After all, the promotions didn't go to men of any degree of youth or attractiveness.

Title VII covers both "sex" and "sex plus" discrimination. "Sex plus" isn't a new laundry product, but the term for discrimination based on sex and also on another factor. In other words, Malarkey's claim of sex plus discrimination was rejected by the court. An early "sex plus" case is *Phillips v. Martin Marietta Corp.* Martin Marietta had no objection to hiring women but wouldn't hire the mothers of pre-school children. Without much discussion, the U.S. Supreme Court held that an employer can't assert a business necessity defense for refusing to hire the mothers of small children if it agreed to employ the fathers of small children. If an individual woman missed work too often because of child care needs, it would be legitimate to fire her for poor attendance or lateness—but it isn't legitimate to refuse employment to all mothers of young children because of stereotypes about motherhood.

To violate Title VII, an action doesn't have to be entirely irrational, or entirely inspired by discrimination. An action that has several motives is illegal if any of the motivations are discriminatory.

The EEOC guidelines say that it's illegal (again, assuming a BFOQ isn't involved) to classify jobs as "male" or "female" or to set up separate lines of seniority or promotion ladders based on such qualifications. (It isn't illegal to *hire* only women, or mostly women for some jobs—secretary or office cleaner—as long as the jobs aren't classified as women's jobs, and as long as there is no discrimination against any males who apply for the job.)

The Guidelines also forbid seniority or promotion systems that favor "heavy" (i.e., male) jobs over "light" jobs (you-know-whose) if the system disguises sex discrimination or "creates unreasonable obstacles to the advancement by members of either sex into jobs which members of that sex would reasonably be expected to perform."

As I mentioned in the Introduction, whatever meager privileges women received through chivalry or protectionism tend to be withdrawn at the first demand for sexual equality—and well before equality becomes real. As a case in point, the EEOC Guidelines supersede state laws that set maximum hours for women or require a stated recovery period after childbirth. "The Commission has found that such laws and regulations don't take into account the capacities, preferences, and abilities of individual females and, therefore, discriminate on the basis of sex." If state law requires payment of a minimum wage or provision of rest periods, meal periods, or related facilities for women (e.g., a lunchroom), the Guidelines say that employers are not allowed to refuse to hire women because of the need to provide these benefits. However, the point is moot because the employer must provide equal benefits to men. If business necessity makes it impossible to provide the benefits to both sexes, employers can withhold the benefits from both sexes.

Professional firms (with law firms as a prominent example) are often organized as partnerships. Professionals start out as employees, and some of them are invited to become partners in the firm. Many of these firms have an "up or out" policy: those who don't "make partner" after a certain number of years get fired. Attorney Elizabeth Hishon left Atlanta's King & Spaulding when she was passed over for partnership. She sued under Title VII, claiming that she was promised fair and equal consideration for partnership when she was hired and that sex discrimination was the reason why she wasn't made a partner. (Everyone agreed that she was an excellent lawyer; the quality of her work wasn't at issue.) The District Court and the Eleventh Circuit tossed out her case, saying that partners weren't *employees*, so Title VII could not cover the decision to offer or deny partnership. The Supreme Court held that Title VII's legislative history doesn't show any intent to exclude partnership. The case was sent back to the Eleventh Circuit to give Ms. Hishon a chance to prove that she was promised a fair chance for partnership; if she had been, it would certainly be a "term or condition of employment." Before the case got there, it was settled, on terms that neither side would disclose. It isn't difficult to believe King & Spaulding guilty of sexism: in the summer of

1983, when the case was pending, the firm held a bathing-suit competition for female associates at the annual picnic. This was considered a step up from the traditional wet T-shirt competition.

EEOC Guidelines are not considered "administrative regulations" promulgated by Congress. Therefore, courts are not obliged to follow the Guidelines (though presumably they pay *some* attention). The Guidelines are generally more pro-employee than the relevant statutes or court cases, so they're good for making threatening noises at employers and for quoting as authority for a charge that a particular practice is discriminatory.

The EEOC, of course, tries to enforce its own Guidelines during the conciliation procedure and in any lawsuits it brings. (See pages 45–55 for an exhaustive discussion of the exhausting EEOC procedure.)

AFFIRMATIVE ACTION

As a result of Executive Order 11246, all companies that have contracts with the federal government worth over $10,000 (which equals about $1\frac{1}{3}$ coffeemakers) must have an affirmative action program for women and minorities. The contractor must take affirmative action in hiring, promotion, training, and all other aspects of its operations and must describe itself as an Equal Opportunity Employer in help-wanted ads.

A women who believes that she is a victim of sex discrimination should find out if her employer is a federal contractor (many, many companies, including some surprising ones, are) and, if so, should contact the Office of Federal Contract Compliance Programs (OFCCP). The main OFCCP office is located at 200 Constitution Avenue, N.W., Washington, D.C. 20210, and there are local branch offices. Complaints must be made within 180 days of the violation, unless there's a good reason why the complainant should be granted an extension (if the employer lied or concealed information, for example). The complaint should give the complainant's name, address, and telephone number, the federal contractor's name and address, a description of the discriminatory acts, and any other relevant information.

The OFCCP can send the file to the EEOC or hold its own investigation, and can either negotiate a compliance agreement or hold administrative proceedings. The proceedings may result in an injunction against further violations of Executive Order 11246 and, of more interest to the complainants, can also lead to an award of back pay for themselves. In an instance of flagrant abuse, the OFCCP can refer the case to the Department of Justice, which can prevent the offending company from getting any more federal contracts. *That* is generally enough to make them sit up and take notice; federal contractors are likely to do whatever is necessary to keep the corporate snout in the public trough.

Federal contractors *must* have affirmative action plans; other employers can, if they wish, have affirmative action programs. "Affirmative action" is another one of those mystical legal concepts (like "due process" or "speedy trial"). According to 29 C.F.R. 1608, it's reasonable action, taken on reasonable bases after reasonable self-scrutiny leading to a business's belief that it has practiced discrimination in the past, or has chosen its employees from a labor pool that was limited by racism or sexism. The EEOC dilates on this in 44 Federal Register 4422, saying that affirmative action is a policy chosen to overcome the effects of past or present barriers to equal employment opportunity. Affirmative action can include soliciting applicants from a minority organization (for example, contacting a women's bar association when a new general counsel is needed), setting goals for hiring or promoting a certain number of women or members of minority groups, sensitivity training for supervisors and co-workers, or choosing the female or minority candidate from among several equally qualified applicants.

A recent Illinois case approves a university affirmative action program that raises the salary of woman professors throughout the university even if, as a result of salary imbalance among departments, they end up better-paid than male colleagues with equivalent qualifications—provided that the program is reasonable and substantially serves its purpose of correcting proven salary discrimination.

Usually, though, women are paid less than similarly situated men. A 1983 article in that subversive feminist rag *The Wall Street Journal*, quoting a Census Bureau survey, notes that in a lifetime of work women earn less than half of what men with similar education earn, and opines, "Some of the difference reflects the absence of many women from the work force during their childbearing years. But the size of the gap suggests that wage discrimination may be a factor." What a surprise! The Equal Pay Act is designed to provide redress. However, as owners of recalled cars know, design isn't everything.

THE EQUAL PAY ACT

Title VII is the most significant but not the first federal law dealing with sex discrimination in employment. That distinction goes to the Equal Pay Act of 1963 (29 U.S.C.S. §206(d)), which says:

> No employer having employees subject to any provisions of this section [the Fair Labor Standards Act, the basic federal wages-and-hours law] shall discriminate, within any establishment in which such employees are employed, between employees on the basis of sex by paying wages to employees in such establishment at a rate less than the rate at which he pays wages to the employees of the opposite sex in such establishment for *equal work* on jobs the performance of which requires *equal*

> *skill, effort, responsibility, and which are performed under similar*
> *working conditions.* [Italics mine.]

If there is a wage differential based on gender, the employer has to raise the lower wage (let's face it, the woman's wage) to meet the higher wage, rather than depressing the male wage to female levels.

There are four exceptions to the requirement of equal pay for equal work. (Remember these; they will reappear shortly.)

> [. . .] except where such payment is made pursuant to (i) a seniority system; (ii) a merit system; (iii) a system which measures earnings by quantity or quality of production; or (iv) a differential based on any factor other than sex.

In other words, more senior employees can be paid more for doing the same job; employees can get piecework wages or merit pay; and pay differentiations based on anything other than sex may or may not be legal, but won't violate the Equal Pay Act.

For purposes of the Equal Pay Act, "wages" includes commissions, bonuses, disability insurance, health insurance, leaves of absence, profit-sharing plans, retirement plans, and death benefits, not just hourly wages and annual salaries. So in one sense, the Equal Pay Act has wide coverage, because all forms of compensation are affected. In another sense, the Equal Pay Act is narrow, because it deals only with sex-based inequalities in pay in the same establishment (business location)—not with any other discriminatory act.

The Equal Pay Act (EPA) doesn't cover working conditions, so a woman college professor's claim that she was assigned a heavier workload than her male colleagues didn't state an Equal Pay Act claim, or so the Fifth Circuit held. However, she was allowed to pursue a claim that the extra workload reduced her potential income because she, unlike her male colleagues, had no time for lucrative private tutoring. A year earlier, a Florida District Court also said that assigning extra work to women only doesn't violate the EPA. However, when different amounts of money are involved, the EPA springs to the rescue. For instance, a Detroit health club violated the EPA by paying a lower commission per membership sold by woman managers to women than per membership sold by male managers to men, even though both groups of managers earned about the same amount because more women bought memberships.

If jobs are genuinely different, it's legitimate to pay those who do them differently. However, a bank can't devise an unstructured "executive training program" for its male tellers and use it as an excuse for paying them more than female tellers. If a male proof operator and a female proof operator are doing the same job, the employer had better have a good explanation why the man's greater experience or non-job-related education entitle him to a higher salary.

Similarly, a violation of the EPA was found when a hospital paid orderlies more than nurses' aides for substantially the same work, despite the employer's contention that the orderlies earned higher pay because they did heavy lifting and provided security for the aides working the night shift. The court looked at the substantially identical nature of the jobs and held that the employer's rationales were pretexts.

The case of *DiSalvo v. Chamber of Commerce* makes two interesting points: first, that the EPA looks to the job rather than the title; second, that a woman can make an EPA case by comparing her salary to her male successor's, not just by comparing her salary to a male co-worker's. But if a woman has a unique job, she can't win an EPA suit by claiming a man would have been paid more for doing the same job *(Rinkel v. Associated Pipeline Contractors)*.

Originally, the Department of Labor's Wage and Hour Division enforced the Equal Pay Act. The Carter administration transferred enforcement responsibility to the EEOC. In 1983, a court decision held the transfer illegal, for subtle Constitutional reasons having to do with the balance of power among the branches of government. However, the EEOC hung onto EPA cases. Various federal courts disagreed about which agency was the right one to enforce the statute, and the Supreme Court several times refused to touch the issue with a ten-foot pole. The whole thing might have lingered forever as a perpetual Con Law exam question, but Congress settled it via H.R. 6225, signed into law October 19, 1984. This bill says that it's perfectly all right for the EEOC to enforce the EPA (and the Age Discrimination in Employment Act, which was involved in the same controversy).

BRIDGE OVER TROUBLED WATER: THE BENNETT AMENDMENT

Although Title VII is broader than the EPA, there's an area of overlap: unequal pay for equal work violates both. The Bennett Amendment, 42 U.S.C.S. §2000e–2(b), is intended as a bridge between the two laws; but this bridge, like so many others in the United States, has infrastructure problems and can be quite dangerous to navigate. The text of the amendment is:

> It shall not be an unlawful employment practice under this sub-Chapter [Title VII] for any employer to differentiate upon the basis of sex in determining the amount of wages or compensation paid or to be paid to employees of such employer if such differentiation is authorized by provisions of §206(d) of Title 29 [the four exceptions to the Equal Pay Act—see page 28 if you've forgotten].

There was a lot of confusion about what this means, but it's now fairly well settled that the effect of the Bennett Amendment is to "plug in" the EPA exemptions to Title VII. Title VII is broader, and claims can be brought under Title VII that would be barred under the EPA. However, employers have a defense to Title VII claims if the wage differential was based on seniority, merit, piecework, or factors other than sex.

Good try but no cigar: the employer in *Corning Glass Works v. Brennan* claimed that the pay difference was based on a factor other than sex—"market differentiation." Market differentiation was a posh way of saying that women would work for less than men would. The Supreme Court, without much discussion, pointed out that it would be hard to find a factor that more clearly *was* one of sex. But the Corning Glass rationale, like Corningware itself, proved sturdy and almost unbreakable in a variety of temperatures. Variations on the theme of "market differentiation" have been played throughout the seventies and eighties.

It's clear that the EPA covers only equal pay for equal work (well, functionally identical work—an EPA case can be made if there are minor differences in job duties). Therefore, the EPA can't be used to bring a "comparable-worth" claim: that is, a suit based on a claim that the women who do one job are paid less than men who do a *different* job that is of identical or inferior value. Can Title VII be used as a vehicle to bring comparable-worth suits? In 1981, the Supreme Court ended years of uncertainty by pronouncing a resounding "maybe."

COMPARABLE WORTH

Most women who work for pay (and all full-time housewives) have "pink-collar" jobs: sex-segregated jobs held mostly or entirely by women. Pink-collar jobs vary in educational background required and in job duties; some pink-collar workers assemble small objects in factories, others sling hash, carry bedpans, or teach little kids. Most pink-collar jobs have a lot in common, though. They call for stereotypically feminine qualities (deference, lack of initiative, tolerance for boredom). There's little day-to-day variety or opportunity for promotion in many of these jobs, and whatever supervisory jobs exist tend to be held by men. Coincidentally, pink-collar jobs tend to be wretchedly paid and provide few employee benefits such as pensions or health insurance.

Although it's simple justice for woman engineers or corporate lawyers to be paid as much as their male counterparts having equal qualifications and responsibility, there aren't a great number of woman engineers and corporate lawyers. For women in "women's" jobs, it matters a lot more whether "women's" jobs are paid at least as well as "men's" jobs of equivalent skill and responsibility. As we all know, they aren't; and there's no clear legal mandate for changing the situation.

The irony (well, one of them) is that many "comparable-worth" claims cite as evidence job-rating surveys prepared by the employer. The rating systems assign point values to various jobs (e.g., senior secretary, 120 points, junior secretary, 100 points, handyman, 90 points). The theoretical purpose of the rating system is to set pay scales. Many a time and oft, however, women find they are paid less than men doing different jobs with the same point value or even a lower point value; or the women's job is rated lower than the men's job, but the salary gap is larger than the difference in the ratings.

The 1977 *Christensen* case involved clerical workers (female) and physical plant workers (male). The two jobs were rated at the same point value. However, the proposed salary was less than the janitors earned on the open market, so their salary—but not the clerical workers'—was adjusted upward. The court said, "We do not interpret Title VII as requiring an employer to ignore the market in setting wage rates for genuinely different work classifications." In other words, the Eighth Circuit didn't feel it was bound by the *Corning Glass v. Brennan* case, because the male and female workers in that case were doing the same jobs; here, the jobs were different.

Three years later, the Tenth Circuit would say much the same thing in the case of *Lemons v. City & County of Denver*. The city's compensation plan was based on the salary "key classes" of employees earned on the open market in the community. The plaintiffs, licensed practical nurses, pointed out that they didn't *want* the lousy pay LPNs earned on the open market; they wanted to earn as much as workers whose worth to the city was equivalent. To the Tenth Circuit, Title VII wasn't intended to upset certain traditions—such as the tradition of paying practical nurses poorly.

Several other interesting cases were decided in 1980. *Futran v. Ring Radio Co.* was similar to *Corning Glass*, but involved unique professional jobs rather than large numbers of factory jobs. *Futran* makes it clear that a radio station isn't justified in paying a male talk show host more than a female talk show host simply because she was willing to work for less.

The landmark case of *IUE v. Westinghouse* made two important points. First, the Third Circuit found that the Bennett Amendment should be interpreted to mean that Title VII is broader than the EPA. Therefore, the EPA requires equal work, but Title VII doesn't. However, because of the Bennett Amendment, any of the four EPA defenses (see page 28) is also a Title VII defense for the employer.

The second point this case makes is that if a plaintiff can prove her employer deliberately set wage rates lower for "women's" job classifications than for "men's" job classifications, she has a Title VII case. Although this is a step forward, it's always hard to prove that anyone *deliberately* did anything.

A year later, the Supreme Court reached similar conclusions in *County of Washington v. Gunther.* The case involved a county job evaluation system that set the value of female prison guard's job at 95 percent of the value of male guard's job—but the women were paid only 70 percent as much. The Supreme Court's rather cautious opinion says that a Title VII claim can be brought even if there is no male employee holding an equivalent but better-paid job, as long as none of the four EPA defenses is available. *Gunther* certainly doesn't make every comparable-worth case an instant win; it merely says that it isn't entirely impossible to make a sustainable comparable-worth case.

As a case in point, Christine Plemer was, of all things, an Equal Employment Opportunity Representative for a corporation. The EEO Representative was supposed to report to the EEO Officer, but that job was vacant for eight months. Plemer applied for the promotion, but the employer hired a man for the job—at an annual salary almost $9,000 higher than Plemer's. At this insult, Plemer quit her job. The last straw came when a man was hired to replace her—at a starting salary 6.8 percent higher than her final salary. The Fifth Circuit delivered the final kick in the teeth. Plemer's legal theory was that the EEO Officer's job was worth more than her former job as EEO Representative—but not $8700 a year more. The court was underwhelmed by this contention, because Plemer didn't introduce evidence of an employer-generated job rating system.

> Plemer asks too much. She would have the courts make an essentially subjective assessment of the value of the differing responsibilities of the positions of Plemer and Willis [the EEO Officer] and then determine whether Plemer was paid less than the value of her position because she was female. If she had shown that the employer had placed those values on her and Willis' respective duties and was paying Willis the full value while paying her less than her evaluated worth, her claim could be considered. However, it is not the province of the courts to value the relative worth of Plemer's and Willis' differing jobs, given the absence of either evidence of a kind similar to that delineated in *Wilkins* [another Fifth Circuit case—see page 62] or any direct or otherwise clear evidence as to how the company valued the positions.

This is pure banana oil. Courts make such specific, essentially subjective judgments every day in setting damages—deciding how much money a person would have earned if s/he hadn't been paralyzed by the defendant's negligence, or how much the plaintiff should be compensated and the defendant punished, for libel or copyright infringement. (In many cases, courts can transfer the responsibility for a while, because the jury, if there is one, sets damages; but in a non-jury trial, or appellate review of a jury case, the court has the problem all over again.) Anyway, in a case like Plemer's the court can't go far wrong. As Plemer conceded that Willis's job was more valuable than her own, the range of discretion was between $0 and $8700 a year—considerably less than infinity.

In December 1983 the case of *AFSCME v. State of Washington,* 33 FEP Cases 808 (W.D. Wash. 1983) was decided. Judge Tanner found a Title VII violation because Washington State's civil service employees in female-dominated job classifications earned about 20 percent less than employees in male-dominated classifications that had received equivalent ratings. Earlier in 1983, the Washington state legislature passed two comparable-worth bills, one providing money for a 1984 salary increase for employees in the underpaid classifications, the other providing for pay equality by 1993.

The judge found this too little, too late, and required immediate pay equality, not equality in a decade. He imposed an injunction against further pay discrimination, ordered back pay (both salary and benefits unjustly withheld) and appointed a Special Master to monitor compliance with his order.

The state complained that forking over the money would devastate an already weak economy. The judge's riposte was that, as 1978's *Manhart* case (453 U.S. 702) makes clear, Title VII doesn't allow employers to defend against a sex discrimination charge by whining about the expense of remedying the discrimination. He didn't make the common-sense rejoinder that convicted criminals are not reprieved merely because it would be inconvenient to spend the next ten years in stir.

Judge Tanner's opinion was greeted with (excessively optimistic) hosannas from the feminist community and (histrionic) weeping and gnashing of teeth from the business community; certainly his decision, unless reversed on appeal, will cost the State of Washington many bucks (perhaps a billion).

The *AFSCME* case is very significant for Washington's treasury (if the state responds by increasing income and/or sales taxes, the underpaid state workers will have the privilege of paying for their own raises), and many similar lawsuits have already been filed against the civil services of other states. Judge Tanner's ruling should also be useful against large employers who have carried out job-rating surveys, though it will be harder to apply against smaller or less systematic employers.

Nursing is traditionally a woman's profession, and nursing school professors at the University of Washington are traditionally paid less than professors in other departments of the University, or nursing professors elsewhere. The Western District of Washington said that this was regrettable but not illegal, because market factors determined the academic pay scale, and because teaching nursing wasn't comparable to teaching other disciplines. The Ninth Circuit disageed with both these conclusions but affirmed the District Court anyway, holding that the plaintiff's statistics did not account adequately for the rank, academic degrees, and prior experience of the professors used as a sample.

Summing up: comparable-worth claims are hard to prove, but not entirely impossible, and the *AFSCME* case will be a valuable precedent. If the employer has set up an allegedly objective set of pay classifications, and if the plaintiff can prove discriminatory intent in underpaying women for their classification, the plaintiff can win her case. But if the employer is minimally bright enough to avoid writing down the classifications, the plaintiff could be out of luck. (However, the case of *Taylor v. Charley Bros.*, 25 FEP Cases 602 (W.D. Pa. 1981), uses the employer's *failure* to do a job-evaluation study as evidence of a pattern of discrimination— something for other plaintiffs to keep in mind.)

If the employer does have a series of classifications and a collective management IQ over 75, it can also avoid liability by paying women whatever wretched fraction of male salaries it claims their jobs are worth. I'm not aware of any case in which a woman has successfully challenged a rating system, showing, for example, that a job rated as 70 percent as valuable as a predominantly male job was really 80 percent or 105 percent as valuable.

A cheering fact, in a gallows-humor sort of way, is that a bad economy tends to force men into previously all-female jobs. Although working women then face more competition for the same unglamorous jobs, those positions are sometimes upgraded in title, pay, and esteem because they are no longer pink-collar jobs.

STATE LAWS ON EMPLOYMENT DISCRIMINATION

Almost all of the states have laws that are similar to Title VII. There are six hold-outs—Alabama, Arkansas, Georgia, Mississippi, Texas, and Virginia. (The fact that these states don't have Fair Employment Practice laws is significant because complainants in these states can get an immediate EEOC investigation, without going through a state investigation first.) These state laws typically forbid sexual, racial, religious, or national origin discrimination in employment. Usually, they set up a Human Rights Commission or other state agency to enforce the law.

Forty-two states have Equal Pay Acts calling for equal pay for equal work. Iowa, Louisiana, North Carolina, and Vermont have laws forbidding employment discrimination but no law requiring pay equity. Arkansas and Virginia, on the other hand, have equal pay laws but no general statute forbidding employment discrimination.

Six states have tackled the comparable-worth problem by passing laws on the subject: Kentucky, Minnesota, Oregon, South Dakota, Tennessee, and West Virginia. (The Minnesota law covers only state employees.) In general, the laws require equal pay for work comparable in character and skill level. The Minnesota law is the only one to mention male and female jobs; the South Dakota law refers to jobs differing only in physical strength (so that employers there won't be able to get away with requiring male employees to do an occasional bit of well-paid heavy lifting); the Tennessee law requires equal pay for work comparable in skill, effort, and responsibility performed under substantially similar working conditions.

PENSIONS AND BENEFITS

The cost of employing a person hovers around 133 percent of the employee's salary, once the employer pays Social Security and other payroll taxes and makes the necessary payments for the pension plan, health insurance, and other employee benefits. The total can go much higher.

For highly paid executives, tax-free employee benefits and perks are more appealing than straight salary, which the IRS can chomp on. For rank-and-file employees, health insurance is essential because illness can be financially as well as physically crippling. At either end of the scale, then, so-called fringe benefits are central to the economic well-being of working women.

Federal pension and benefit law runs to many millions of obscure words, but nowhere does it say that an employer must provide *any* pensions or *any* employee benefits. If the employer does offer pensions or benefits, certain quite complex and technical rules must be followed. One purpose of the rules is to see that the IRS gets its pound of flesh; another is to see that the top executives don't take all the goodies, leaving nothing for the rank and file. (The legal and accounting specialty of "executive compensation" or "pay planning" consists of finding legal ways to blunt the effect of these rules.)

Working women can lose out in three ways. First of all, many women don't have employer-paid pensions, either because they have ill-paid pink-collar jobs where pensions are unavailable, or because they're self-employed businesswomen or professionals. Second, many women interrupt their paid work lives one or more times for childbirth and child care. These interruptions make it harder for women to stay at a job long enough to "vest" (have an indisputable legal right to receive the money the employers paid into their pension accounts). (See page 38 on the ameliorating effects of recent legislation.) Third, women have traditionally had smaller amounts deposited into their pension accounts, or received smaller pension checks than men receiving the same puny salaries. The rationale, apart from sheer bigotry backed up with enforcement power, is that the life-span of the average woman is longer than that of the average man.

I say that the mini-payments are traditional, because the Supreme Court has found both of these practices illegal. The *Manhart* case says that it's a violation of Title VII for an employer whose pension plan requires contributions from the employees to charge women more for the same pension coverage than men paid. The Court reached this result despite the employer's argument that actuarial considerations demanded the higher contributions. The Court's rationale was that Title VII protects, and demands fair treatment for, individuals—not groups.

Five years later, the *Norris* case looked at the problem from the other end: if a female and a male retiree have pension accounts of the same size, is the employer justified in paying smaller monthly checks to the female retiree? *Norris* says no: once again, individual rather than group equity is required.

Those two basic questions are settled, but it will take years of hassle to catch up with frank violations and to hear the many, many cases raising questions that are variations on a theme.

The problem of sex-based actuarial tables comes up in other contexts: the issue of unisex insurance (see pages 100–102) and gift taxation (see page 102), for example. Perhaps the question is becoming moot. As women drink and smoke more, drive more miles so that they can pile up more cars, and spend more time in workplaces that expose them to toxic chemicals and induce stress, the "gender gap" in life expectancy may narrow or vanish.

In the meantime, it has been pointed out ad nauseam that white people have a higher life expectancy than blacks or Hispanics, but employers have never felt a compulsion to pay larger pensions to black retirees. Things are complicated by the fact that it's hard to assess a person's racial background, but generally fairly easy to tell if an employee is male or female. Again, employees who are nonsmoking, marathon-running teetotalers tend to outlive their colleagues who wash down the post-prandial Twinkie with a six-pack, but it costs too much to monitor the health habits of every participant in a pension or benefit plan, adjusting payments accordingly.

An interesting letter to the *Wall Street Journal*, published in June of 1983, suggests that inequities tend to come out in the wash anyway. Pension plans allow retirees to choose a "joint and survivor" option: that is, pension payments will be made to the retiree and, after the retiree's death, to his or her surviving spouse. Because men tend to marry women who are younger than they are, and women have a longer life expectancy, the employer can anticipate several years of payments to a male retiree's widow. Whether the payments are made to a female retiree or a male retiree's widow, the longer female expectancy is a factor in the employer's pension payments. In fact, a male employee choosing joint and survivor payments will probably obligate the employer to make payments for more years than in the case of a female retiree. Assume that a male and female worker both retire on the same day, which happens to be their joint sixty-fifth birthday. Both choose joint-and-survivor pension payments. Her husband is sixty-eight; his wife is sixty-two. Her husband dies at seventy-three, on the same day as the male retiree. The female retiree continues to receive her pension checks; the widow of the male retiree starts to collect survivor's benefits at the age of sixty-seven. Both women die at the age of seventy-five. On the face of it, it seems that the employer suffered because the female retiree lived—and collected benefits—for twice as many post-retirement years as her ex-colleague. But the man collected benefits for five years (ages sixty-five to seventy) and his wife collected survivor's benefits for eight years (her ages sixty-seven to seventy-five), a total of thirteen years versus the female retiree's ten (*her* ages sixty-five to seventy-five).

As might be expected, the EEOC's Guidelines on fringe benefits are very pro-employee:

- Sex discrimination in fringe benefits is forbidden.
- Making benefits (e.g., health insurance) available to the dependents of employees only if the employee is a head of household (earns more than 50 percent of the family income) is forbidden. Although the head-of-household requirement is facially neutral, it discriminates against women, because of the common assumption that men are "bread-winners" and working women's income is supplementary.
- It is no defense for the employer to prove that providing fringe benefits to one sex is more expensive; benefits, rather than dollars expended, must be equal.
- Pension and retirement plans are not permitted to set different retirement ages for men and women, and can't differentiate in benefits because of sex.
- Any benefits available to the husbands of employed women must be available to the wives of employed men, and vice versa. "An example of such an unlawful employment practice is a situation in which wives of male employees receive maternity benefits while female employees receive no such benefits."

In 1983, the U.S. Supreme Court considered the converse of the last statement: can an employer provide maternity benefits for its own female employees while denying them to wives of male employees? The Supreme Court said no: male employees, in effect, got less coverage than female employees, so Title VII was violated.

There is a feminist issue involved here, of course, but in a quixotic way. The Supreme Court's decision made more health benefits available to the pregnant, all of whom, given the current state of technology, are female. On the other hand, the direct beneficiaries are employed men, because the out-of-pocket cost of their wives' pregnancies will decrease. It's another case of bedfellows making strange politics.

Another of the EEOC Guidelines on the subject has fared less well in court. In mid-1983, the Ninth Circuit upheld a plan that limited medical insurance coverage to employees and the dependents of "breadwinners" (who earned more than half the family income); dependents of those who worked for what the employer considered "pin money" did not get medical insurance coverage. The court recognized the disparate impact on woman workers, but accepted the employer's business necessity defense. The employer claimed that it had a finite amount to spend on employee benefits, and the "breadwinner" rule made it possible to provide the greatest overall benefits for all the employees at a tolerable cost. However, another case rules that the employer isn't allowed to decide that men and only men can be "breadwinners" or "heads of household." The test must be at least facially neutral (e.g., the over-fifty-percent-of-family-income test).

The Retirement Equity Act of 1984 (P.L. 98-397, 98 Stat. 1426), signed into law on August 23, 1984, goes a long way to correct the inequities between women's and men's pensions. Employers must allow all employees over twenty-one (it used to be twenty-five) to participate in any pension plan the employer maintains. Employees must be given credit toward vesting (the inalienable right to receive part or all of the money in one's pension account) for work for the employer starting at age eighteen (formerly age twenty-two). An employer can give an employee on maternity or paternity leave up to 501 hours' credit to prevent a "break in service" (period of time when the employee isn't working for the employer; a break in service can sometimes mean forfeiture of pension credit for work done before the break). An employee who is covered by the plan and has less than five years' service can take a break of up to five years without losing vesting credit for the work done before the break.

To protect the spouses of covered workers who die before they reach retirement age, all vested plan participants have to be offered a choice of pension pay-out plans, including one that pays either the worker or his or her surviving spouse for a stated number of years, and one that pays the surviving spouse if the employee died before reaching retirement age. Either of these options means smaller pension checks than a "single life" annuity payout that stops when the worker dies. Again to protect spouses, employees must get their spouses' signatures before waiving the right to get joint and survivor (payable to worker and/or spouse) and pre-retirement survivor payment plans.

The Retirement Equity Act applies to "plan years" beginning after December 31, 1984 (a pension plan year can start on a day other than January 1), except for pension plans established under union contracts. For those plans, the effective date of the changes is either January 1, 1987, or the date the contract expires, whichever is earlier.

NEPOTISM RULES (NO-SPOUSE RULES)

Coverage for the dependents of employees is less of an issue if the employee's spouse works at the next desk or farther down the assembly line, because in that case the spouse has his or her own medical benefits. However, it's fairly common for employers to maintain a policy forbidding the employment of a married couple, or of a couple one of whom is in a position to supervise the other.

The EEOC has not taken a clear stand against these nepotism rules. The Commission does say that rules forbidding or restricting the employment of married *women* but not of married *men* violate Title VII. (This would be an example of "sex-plus" discrimination—see page 24.) The Guideline goes on to say that a BFOQ *may* be present to justify limitations on employment of married women:

> We express no opinion on this question at this time except to point out that sex as a bona fide occupational qualification must be justified in terms of the peculiar requirements of the particular job and not on the basis of general principle such as the desirability of spreading work. [That is, when jobs are scarce, an employer can't rationalize sexism by rationing jobs, one to a family.]

For example, unless a BFOQ can be proved, it's illegal sex discrimination to allow spouses of full-time employees to work part-time but not full-time. At least two courts have reached opposite conclusions about "no-marriage" rules for working women. Both cases involved stewardesses. I assume the no-marriage rule was inspired by the airlines' advertised image of stewardesses as airborne Penthouse Pets, and a belief that male travelers would be unable to enjoy ogling and leering at a married woman. Surprisingly, the earlier case (*Sprogis v. United Air Lines*) struck down the no-marriage rule and the later case (*Stroud v. Delta Air Lines Inc.*) upheld it. The *Sprogis* court (the Seventh Circuit) found that being unmarried wasn't a BFOQ for the job of stewardess and also found that the rule constituted sex discrimination. At that time, United Air Lines had a few stewards, but they worked exclusively on flights to Hawaii and military flights; women worked as cabin attendants on commercial flights in the continental United States. Six years later, on much the same facts (an airline employing only stewardesses would not employ married women), the Fifth Circuit upheld the no-marriage rule. The Fifth Circuit said that the rule wasn't sexually discriminatory, because only women were affected by it: there were no stewards, and therefore no stewards who were permitted to retain their jobs after marriage.

On the ground, the more common rule followed by companies isn't to hire spouses or the spouse of a current employee, and to require that if co-workers marry, one must quit.

Several cases, using varying and potentially confusing lines of reasoning, uphold the validity of these no-spouse rules:

• *Harper v. TWA*, 11 FEP Cases 1074 (8th Cir. 1975) did not find a violation of Title VII in the no-spouse rule. The plaintiff presented statistical evidence of discrimination, but the court found the evidence unpersuasive, because the small sample involved wasn't statistically significant. The plaintiff also asserted that the no-spouse rule had a disparate impact on women: since the wife is usually the lower-paid spouse, she is more likely to lose her job as a result of the policy, because it's economically rational for the wife to quit and her husband to keep his job. As we'll see, this argument works sometimes, but the Eighth Circuit was unconvinced, saying the plaintiff had not proved this assertion.

• In 1976, a New Jersey District Court approved an insurance company's policy forbidding one spouse to supervise another (*Smith v. Mutual Benefit Life Insurance Co.*, 13 FEP Cases 252). The West Virginia District Court reached a similar conclusion in *Southwestern Community Action Council, Inc. v. Community Services Administration*, 462 F.Supp. 289 (D. W.Va. 1978).

• The Seventh Circuit agreed with a plaintiff's contention that a no-spouse rule was discriminatory; as the plaintiff showed, seventy-one of the seventy-four people unemployed by the rule were women. However, the court accepted the employer's business necessity defense (that the no-spouse rule promoted an efficient working environment) even though the employer didn't provide statistical proof of its contention. The court's rationale was that marriage creates intense emotion that carries over to work; married employees would tend to take the same side on issues and, if necessary, cover up for each other. In any case, one spouse might have to supervise the other, leading to marital disharmony. (*Yuhas v. Libbey-Owens-Ford Co.*, 562 F.2d 496 (7th Cir. 1977).) Similarly, a company can maintain a policy of refusing to allow two spouses to serve as district agents, because a married couple filing a joint return would have enhanced opportunities to manipulate the accounts: *Klanseck v. Prudential Insurance Co.*, 509 F.Supp. 13 (D. Mich. 1980).

• An employer can also maintain a policy that requires employees to choose between continued employment and marriage to an employee of a competitor of the employer: *Emory v. Georgia Hospital Service Association*, 4 FEP Cases 921 (1971). This creates a particular dilemma for ambitious woman executives; after graduating from college or professional school (where they dated or married men in the same line of work, who then go on to work for the same employer or one of its rivals) they tend to spend all their time either at work (meeting fellow-employees) or at industry-related events (where they meet the competition).

• You don't even have to be married to fall afoul of a no-spouse rule. The plaintiff in *Espinoza v. Thoma*, 17 FEP Cases 1362 (8th Cir. 1978), lost her job as a result of a no-spouse rule invoked because she was living with a fellow employee. The court found that the policy wasn't unconstitutional, not impermissibly vague, not indefinite, and could lawfully be applied to cohabitants as well as spouses.

In general, a company can maintain a no-spouse policy provided that the decision about who gets the axe is left to the couple, or dismissals are nominally based on seniority rather than sex discrimination. The Fifth Circuit, though, struck down an anti-nepotism policy that was valid on its face but applied in a discriminatory manner. A married couple refused to decide which one should become jobless, so the employer fired the wife. The court found this to be an impermissible use of stereotyped assumptions.

Several cases find for the employee because the employer applied its no-spouse rule inconsistently:

• EEOC Decision No. 75-239 (1976), which is printed as CCH EEOC Decisions ¶6492, found for the employee on two grounds. First of all, the EEOC accepted statistical evidence showing that, because almost all the employees were male, refusal to hire the spouses of employees had a disparate impact on women. The second ground was the inconsistency with which the policy was applied. Several husband-wife pairs, hired before the policy was devised, worked together efficiently, showing that the policy wasn't necessary to the employer's efficiency or profitability.

• The plaintiff in *Linebaugh v. Auto Leasing Co.* made a prima facie case of sex discrimination by proving two things: that she was as qualified as some of the men hired, and that some of the men hired were married to company employees, so the only reason for refusing to hire her was sex discrimination.

• In 1976, New York State's highest court struck down New York University's comprehensive no-spouse policy. The plaintiff proved adverse impact on women, and the court didn't buy the university's business necessity defense based on an assertion that the no-spouse rule promoted efficiency. The plaintiff had been married to an NYU employee and working for the university for several years in a part-time job on a non-tenure track. The university didn't invoke the rule until she applied for a job carrying the possibility of tenure. New Yorkers have to watch out for a 1980 case *allowing* application of a no-spouse rule even though the employee had held the job and been married to a fellow-employee for four years. The Court of Appeals found that the no-spouse rule was rational and therefore upheld it.

• A less-drastic restriction (that a secretary transfer to another department so that she wouldn't have access to files and records about her husband) was disapproved in EEOC Dec. No. 79-59 (1979). The EEOC sensibly pointed out that men, who were much more likely to have free access to the company files, weren't required to transfer.

Just as there is a category of illegal "sex-plus" discrimination, there is "marriage-plus" discrimination:

• An employment agency violated Title VII by refusing to refer a woman for jobs because she was married and therefore not a "head of household"—EEOC Dec. No. 79-46 (1979).

• Refusing to hire an applicant for a job as a traveling saleswoman because she might need time off to care for her sick husband was an instance of sex discrimination. The company, which was willing to hire men with sick wives, was using stereotypes about the woman's role in family life rather than rational business judgment—EEOC Dec. No. 71-2613, 4 FEP Cases 22 (1971).

• Shooting for the foot department: telling a black woman employee that she didn't need a job anyway because she had a white husband is sex discrimination as well as racial discrimination.

• Union women may be able to use the grievance procedures of the union to challenge a no-spouse provision as an unfair labor practice.

• Eighteen states have laws forbidding discrimination on the basis of marital status. (The states are Alaska, California, Connecticut, Florida, Hawaii, Illinois, Maine, Maryland, Michigan, Minnesota, Montana, Nebraska, New Hampshire, New Jersey, New York, Oregon, Washington, and Wisconsin.) However, these laws seem to be interpreted to mean that it's illegal to refuse to employ or promote married people (or single people, or divorced people) merely for that reason. The one case I've seen on the point, *Campbell Plastics, Inc. v. N.Y. State Human Rights Appeal Board,* 440 N.Y.S.2d 73, 81 A.D.2d 991 (1981), says that enforcement of a reasonable no-spouse policy *is* legal and doesn't constitute discrimination on the basis of marital status.

MÄDCHEN IN UNIFORM?

There wouldn't be an industry advising people how to dress for success, and providing them with appropriately drab costumes, if clothing didn't make a powerful impression on its beholders.

Although the politics and semiotics of men's clothing are important, they exist over a much narrower range than women's clothes. A male blue-collar worker wears overalls or other work clothes. A white-collar man wears a suit, shirt, and tie, or (perhaps) pants, shirt, tie, and sport jacket or sweater. Certainly many people find men sexually attractive, but it isn't regularly assumed that the sight of a man in a well-cut suit turns anyone into slavering, snarling maniacs.

A woman can appear for work in anything from a full-length nun's habit to a g-string and pasties, depending on the nature of the job, the employer's requirements, and her own taste. In white-collar and professional jobs, one school of thought has it that women should wear feminized versions of male business suits so that they will appear authoritative. Another school says that women must dress in a more feminine fashion, because quasi-male garments (especially neckties) are perceived as threatening. You pays your money and you takes your choice.

A uniform is an ambiguous signal. A gold-braided officer's uniform, dripping with medals, signals prestige. (And, interestingly, women who enter prestigious uniform jobs—military, police, fire department and the like—often find that they are required to wear uniforms that won't fit a female body—the Army, for example, has had persistent trouble with women's boots.) However, most uniforms signal low status. Nurses and nurses' aides wear uniforms; interns wear whites or hospital greens; residents wear white coats or jackets—and attending physicians wear their own clothing.

As a case in point, a Michigan hospital required its female lab technicians to wear nurses' uniforms—white dresses or pantsuits conforming to certain standards, white shoes, and certain colors of underclothes (unspecified in the opinion—I assume white or flesh-colored). Male lab technicians wore a white lab coat over their street clothes—in other words, they dressed like doctors. A woman lab technician refused to comply with the rule and was fired; the court found that the rule was a clear instance of sex discrimination based on stereotypes, and ordered her reinstatement.

Ever since the eighteenth century, European visitors to our shores have noted with surprise that it's difficult to hire American servants, and impossible to induce them to wear livery, which is viewed as an insult to free Americans. The cases dealing with uniforms and dress codes for working women are interesting because they show something about attitudes to woman workers as economic producers, as low-status people, and as sex objects.

An Illinois bank allowed its male employees to wear whatever "appropriate business clothing" they chose. Female employees were required to wear "career ensembles" (that is, uniforms). The bank selected appropriate skirt, pants, vest, jacket, and top, and the women were given discretion to combine these elements. Women could wear their own clothing on a couple of "glamour days" a month, when the uniforms were being cleaned. The Seventh Circuit had no trouble in declaring the policy to be sexually discriminatory. The bank functioned quite well despite the absence of uniforms for the men, and quite well on "glamour days."

However, presumably it would be legal for a business to require *all* employees, or all employees holding certain jobs, to wear uniforms, or to require all employees to wear "appropriate business attire," as defined by the employer.

At least one case upholds an employer's dress code forbidding woman employees to wear pantsuits. According to a Missouri district court, a plaintiff who was fired for wearing pants to work didn't make her prima facie case of sex discrimination, so the employer didn't have to prove a business necessity for the policy.

Some uniforms are designed to express efficiency while suppressing the sexual attractiveness of the wearer. Others are designed to have precisely the opposite effect, by compressing the wearer's person and exposing her legs and chest. For example, a woman who worked as a lobby attendant in an office building was ordered to celebrate the Bicentennial in an abbreviated costume that exposed her not merely to the weather but to repeated instances of sexual harassment. Male lobby attendants weren't required to demonstrate Bicentennial spirit by appearing for work in loincloths, war paint, and feathers; they were permitted to work in normal clothing. The EEOC found that requiring working women to wear sexually provocative costumes is "sex-plus" discrimination. The Southern District of New York agreed, holding that Title VII requires elimination of all disparate treatment of the sexes that limits employment opportunities for women. Forcing women to wear a revealing and provocative uniform limits women's employment opportunities in two ways. First of all, only conventionally attractive women will be selected for the job; second, women will be required to submit to sexual harassment as a consequence of the required uniforms.

A Michigan District Court said that a requirement that cocktail waitresses wear sexually provocative clothing, which led to repeated sexual harassment of the waitresses, *could* be a violation of Title VII. However, the suit was dismissed as moot: there was nothing the court felt it could do. An injunction was no longer required (the employer's policy had changed); the plaintiffs did not ask for back pay, and they were not entitled to damages from the employer, so the court could not order the employer to pay any money.

2

SEX DISCRIMINATION IN EMPLOYMENT: PROCEDURAL LAW

Lhe preceding chapter gives a summary of the substantive law that determines whether an employee's legal rights have been violated. But once she knows that she has a triable case, her troubles are only beginning, and there is an infinitude of rules to be followed; failure to comply can mean anything from the need for tedious amendments to the deep-sixing of an otherwise meritorious case. So it's important for civil rights lawyers to memorize the rules, and for their clients and potential clients to have some sensitivity to the procedural issues. The most important point I can make is that, if you think you have or might have a case under a state fair employment law, Title VII, or the Equal Pay Act, make a preliminary appointment with a lawyer as soon as possible to see if you *do* have a case, and what to do next. It's better to invest a small legal fee to find out that you don't have a sustainable case than to lose a good case because it was brought too late, or in the wrong form, or because the wrong kind of evidence was presented.

THE ROAD TO THE COURTHOUSE

• Most of the states (all except Alabama, Arkansas, Georgia, Mississippi, Tennessee, and Texas) have Fair Employment Practices laws, and human or civil rights agencies that are supposed to enforce these laws. This fact is crucial to the would-be plaintiff in a sex discrimination case. Either to relieve the EEOC of administrative burdens that can better be carried by the states or to jerk the complainant around, or both, the EEOC "defers" to state civil rights agencies for sixty days. That is, the complainant has a choice of either making a complaint with the state agency and filing with the EEOC sixty days later or after the agency has finished its investigation, or filing directly with the EEOC. If the complainant goes to the EEOC first, the EEOC will send the complaint to the appropriate state agency. The state agencies are also called "deferral agencies" or "706 agencies" because the deferral procedure is outlined in §706 of the bill that became Title VII. The EEOC keeps the charge in "suspended animation" during the sixty-day period. The complainant doesn't have to file with the EEOC again. By the way, there is a special name for a Title VII complainant (just as "prosecutrix" is a special term used only for a rape victim): she's called the "charging party." I love that name; it makes a simple CPA or administrative assistant sound like an enraged rhinoceros.

To be more specific, there are two kinds of 706 agencies: "deferral" agencies, whose investigation takes priority over the EEOC investigation, and "notice" agencies (the EEOC does the original investigation and notifies the agency of the result). The names and addresses of all the 706 agencies are given in 29 C.F.R. §1601.74, but the list isn't divided into notice and deferral sub-lists, so you'll have to call the agency or ask your lawyer.

I say "ask your lawyer" because, although it isn't legally required that a charging party be represented by counsel, I earnestly recommend it. The timing requirements are tedious for some steps, quite short for others (see page 58). The best way to cope with the "hurry up and wait" routine is to have a lawyer who understands the facts, knows whom to interview, and has a litigation plan ready to go if private litigation is called for.

If you go to the EEOC before you get a lawyer, 29 C.F.R. §1601.28(b)(1) and (d)(1) make the Regional Attorney in every EEOC District Office responsible for helping charging parties find lawyers. Each District Office has a list of attorneys with Title VII experience who are willing to take such cases. Most of the lawyers on the list are willing to gamble on an award of counsel fees (see pages 67–69), but some of them want the money up front—an important point to discuss during your initial contact with the attorney.

To a certain extent, the decision about where to file first is a strategic one. According to an influential legal encyclopedia, the state procedure is like saying "May I" when playing Giant Steps. It doesn't really do anything for you, but they throw you out of the game if you don't do it. Remember that if you go to the EEOC first, they'll automatically send the charge to the 706 agency. If you start with the state agency, you can't depend on their passing the file to the EEOC when they complete their investigation or when the sixty days are up. You'll either have to nag the 706 agency or file with the EEOC yourself; it's probably easier to start at the EEOC. If a charging party's case involves some claims that are covered by state law and some that aren't (e.g., failure to promote due to sex discrimination, plus sexual harassment, in a state that has no anti-harassment law), the EEOC defers only the charges covered by state law.

In a case like this, it pays to file with the EEOC first so the EEOC can get moving on the harassment claim.

Some states, taking a leaf from the EEOC's book, have "waived deferral." In other words, they don't require the EEOC to wait for a state investigation. In those states (e.g., Pennsylvania), the charging party can file the complaint with the EEOC, and the EEOC can start investigating immediately, without waiting for sixty days.

The good news is that sometimes the state agency will actually *resolve* the problem by negotiating a settlement that is acceptable to the charging party. This is more likely if there is only one charging party, not a group of them. One District Court adds that if the state agency acts like a court and makes a decision based on the facts of the case, the decision is final—a Title VII claim can't be based on those same facts.

It also helps if the employer is cooperative. If the employer is determined to stonewall, few states have an effective enforcement mechanism. In fact, according to *Am.Jur. Trials*, some 706 agencies have a policy of closing their files immediately if they find out that the charging party has a lawyer and the lawyer is interested in bringing suit in federal court. Paradoxically, the agency is doing the charging party a favor by closing its file. Once the state agency has finished its proceedings, the EEOC can start its own investigation, even if the sixty days have not elapsed. The EEOC doesn't treat the closing of the state file as evidence that the charge is unfounded.

THE EEOC COMPLAINT

Whether the charging party goes to the 706 agency or the EEOC first, she will eventually sign a verified (sworn) EEOC complaint. It isn't particularly formal. The complaint (a.k.a. the charge) must contain:

- The charging party's name and address (she must also notify the EEOC of any change of address while the charge is pending so the EEOC can keep her informed about the progress of the investigation).
- The employer's full name and address (the employer is technically referred to as the respondent).
- The approximate number of employees the respondent has (so the EEOC can find out if there are fifteen or more—the minimum number required for Title VII to apply).
- Whether the charge has been filed with the 706 agency; if so, the date of filing.
- A statement of what the discriminatory practices are, when they started, and if they continue until the present time.

A lawyer can be helpful in "framing the charge" (setting it up and deciding what should be included). The charge should include everything under the heading of sex discrimination or sexual harassment that can reasonably be claimed. Not to worry, though: the charge can be amended later to add new allegations. If new allegations *are* added later, they are considered made on the date of the original filing with the EEOC (a point of some importance where time limitations are involved). And, fortunately, the new charges don't require an additional sixty-day deferral period.

The charge can be mailed in, either on an official form or in an informal letter. The EEOC rewrites it to conform to official specifications after an interview with the charging party. If the charging party can't come to the EEOC's main office in Washington, or to a local branch office, the whole thing can be done by mail. The charge must be signed and verified. The verification is, "I swear or affirm that I have read the above charge and that it is true to the best of my knowledge, information, and belief."

The charge *is* sworn, so charging parties must be truthful, but they don't have to be tactful or pull their punches. The EEOC, for this purpose, is considered equivalent to a court, so no one can be sued for slander, defamation, or libel for statements made to the EEOC.

Once a charge has been filed, the charging party needs the consent of the EEOC to drop it. (This is similar to no-drop policies in domestic violence cases—see pages 122–123—and presumably has the same motivation: to protect complainants against retaliation by putting the onus for the complaint on the prosecuting agency.)

The EEOC notifies the respondent of the charge within ten days of the filing. Usually this is done by serving a copy of the charge on the respondent, unless "providing a copy of the charge would impede the law enforcement functions of the commission." Since the charge includes the charging party's name and address, it may be worthwhile to ask that the charge *not* be served. Title VII makes it illegal to retaliate against a person seeking to enforce her or his rights, but the better part of valor is discretion. On the other hand, even if a copy isn't served, the respondent gets a notice containing the charging party's name. This is no big deal if the charging party has already quit or been fired but can be a live issue if she still works there. One way around this is to have an organization (i.e., the local NOW chapter) file the charge on behalf of the charging party; then the notice will carry the name of the organization and the employee will remain anonymous for a while longer. Another way around it, if there is a group of employees and they plan an eventual class action, is to have only one of them "bell the cat" by filing an individual charge that later serves as the basis of the class action. If the charging party doesn't believe that the anti-retaliation provisions will protect her, it's unlikely but possible that the case can be handled as a "commissioner charge"—one with the EEOC itself as the formal complainant. The EEOC won't do this unless it thinks the discrimination involved is serious enough, and is legally provable, so that it's worth the Commission's time and trouble. The EEOC can also initiate its own commissioner charges in "pattern or practice" cases—that is, cases in which there has been a policy of discriminating.

THE EEOC INVESTIGATION

Title VII directs the EEOC to determine whether a charge of discrimination is legally well founded "so far as practicable, not later than 120 days after filing." You should live and be well so long. The EEOC may then make a "no-cause" determination (that is, that the charge doesn't add up to a provable case of illegal discrimination). If a no-cause determination is made, the charging party can demand a "right-to-sue" letter from the EEOC; once she has this letter, she can proceed directly to federal District Court and sue the employer. The EEOC's no-cause determination isn't binding on the District Court (which is why a charging party isn't allowed to go to court against the EEOC to appeal a no-cause determination). In fact, many private lawsuits have been won by charging parties who got no-cause determinations.

The other thing the EEOC can do is make a "reasonable cause" determination: "that the claim has sufficient merit to warrant litigation if the matter is not thereafter conciliated by the Commission or the charging party." After a reasonable cause determination, the EEOC is required to try to settle the matter through conciliation (out-of-court negotiation). If conciliation fails, the EEOC can sue the malefactor. If the EEOC continues delaying 180 days after the charge was filed, the charging party can get a right-to-sue letter on request. She can also get the letter earlier if the appropriate EEOC official certifies that the EEOC can't handle the charge in 180 days. If the charging party is eager to get to court, it's worth asking for this certification; the worst that can happen is that she will have to wait for the 180 days to pass before she can bring her own suit.

The trade-off involved in choosing between EEOC remedies and private suit is that the plaintiff(s) in a private suit have a strong incentive to push the case because it's the only case they have. The EEOC has lots and lots of cases, and in any event wasn't personally aggrieved. But the individual plaintiffs are paying for the case; if they let the EEOC do it, they pay only to the same extent as any other taxpayer (including the perpetrators of discrimination).

The EEOC has five methods of processing charges: the Rapid Charge Processing System, Backlog Charge Processing System, Extended Charge Processing System, the Early Litigation Identification (ELI) Program, and the Systemic Program.

Most disparate treatment cases (claims that the plaintiff, or all woman employees, were subjected to an openly discriminatory policy) are handled under the Rapid Charge Processing System. The point is to get a fast resolution at the conference with the respondent or soon afterwards. The EEOC tries to get the charging party to focus on the discrimination she herself suffered. If her allegations also apply to other employees, she'll have to be very insistent to get the EEOC to deal with the other claims.

The Backlog Charge Processing System covers charges that the EEOC didn't select for the Extended Charge Processing System or the Systemic Program. A disposal plan is made for each charge, based on what the charging party wants to do and on the EEOC's enforcement priorities. As of late 1983, EEOC Chairman Thomas said there *was* no backlog, so this program was more or less a dead letter. (As a former civil servant, I find it hard to believe that an agency exists without a backlog.)

Cases go to the Extended Charge Processing System if the EEOC can't arrange a fact-finding conference with all parties, if the fact-finding conference was inconclusive, or if a charging party who needs to remain anonymous makes an additional charge of further discrimination (e.g., after being demoted, a victim of sex discrimination is fired outright). The Extended Charge Processing System is also used for "disparate impact" cases (a seemingly benign requirement—such as a height requirement or a veteran's preference—has a negative effect on women or another protected group) and other cases that might lead to a lawsuit with the EEOC as plaintiff.

The ELI program is used to identify cases that the EEOC might wish to pursue as plaintiff. ELI cases usually begin with an individual complaint and are earmarked because the complaint has wider ramifications. If conciliation fails in an ELI case, the EEOC will probably sue, although the scope of the lawsuit will probably be narrower than a systemic case.

The Systemic Program is used (insofar as it's used at all) for cases of the utmost impact involving patterns of job discrimination. Cases in the Systemic Program tend to be commissioner charges, but an individual charge can be transferred to the Systemic Program if:

- The charging party presents a strong case that the employer had a policy or practice of discriminating against women.
- The respondent's percentage of woman employees is significantly smaller than the percentage of woman employees in comparable businesses.
- The employed women are concentrated in low-rank, low-paid jobs.
- The employer doesn't have a valid business necessity defense for the practice or policy.
- The employer is influential enough to be worth making an example of.

By the way, the Compliance Manual states that EEOC offices should be on the lookout for retaliation cases (cases in which employers penalize employees for asserting their rights under Title VII) and should expedite these cases. Therefore, if a credible charge of retaliation can be made out, it should be included in the original charge. If retaliation occurs after the charge is filed, the charge should be amended to include the new allegation.

In October 1983, Chairman Thomas told the Labor subcommittee of the House of Representatives that he did not think the Rapid Charge Processing System "is the system that will be in place for the future, nor is it the right system." The EEOC plans to involve its staff lawyers more in preliminary investigations and to de-emphasize settlement in favor of litigation. Thomas said that the EEOC would bring more pattern-or-practice cases. (They could hardly bring fewer: between 1972, when they gained the power to bring suits, and 1983, they brought the magnificent total of nine suits. It's nice to know that there were only nine instances of unredressed systematic discrimination in eleven flaming years, isn't it?)

Whichever program is selected, the usual investigation procedure starts by asking the charging party for a statement of:

• Each specific harm suffered, and the date on which it occurred (e.g., denying the charging party access to a training program).

• For each harm, the act, policy, or practice alleged to be unlawful (e.g., restriction of training to men).

• A statement of facts supporting the charge (e.g., statement by a supervisor made on 11/8/85 that "Oh, no, dear, you couldn't take that course. It trains sales managers, so of course a girl can't do it"; evidence that in the twelve years of the training program's existence, 142 men and no women took the course; statements from fifteen employees and ex-employees that they wanted to take the course but were denied admission or were discouraged from applying; evidence that eleven of those fifteen had qualifications at least as good as those of the men accepted for training).

Once again, it isn't a formal requirement that the charging party be represented by a lawyer, but a good lawyer can help marshal the facts that induce the EEOC to treat the case as (a) serious and (b) legally provable, rather than as a crank complaint.

Before the EEOC makes its "cause" or "no-cause" determination, it can require the respondent and charging party to meet at a fact-finding conference. The purpose of the conference is to define the issues, find out which facts are undisputed (e.g., does the company claim the charging party was fired for incompetence, or does it admit that married women were laid off first "because they don't need to work"?) Another purpose of the fact-finding conference is to gauge the possibility of a settlement without litigation.

This is called a "negotiated settlement" or "predetermination settlement" and is basically a private contract between the charging party and respondent. The EEOC does sign the settlement agreement, but only to state that it has not decided whether or not the charge is well founded and won't take any further action on the charge. If other, similar charges are pending (e.g., a commissioner charge against the same respondent, or similar allegations made by other employees), they won't be affected by the negotiated settlement.

The EEOC has the power to issue subpoenas requiring people to testify or to produce records and other documents for the EEOC to inspect and/ or copy. One compensation for the long wait is that the EEOC is acting as a truffle-hound, digging up the precious nuggets that the charging party can later use in a private suit. However, the EEOC won't give the investigation results to the charging party until she has a right-to-sue letter or until 180 days have passed. She then has to promise not to reveal the information except in the course of litigation; the EEOC's Form 167 is an Agreement of Nondisclosure. People who testify before the EEOC (a classification which includes the charging party, of course) can get a copy of the entire transcript, including the testimony of the other witnesses. However, for "good cause" (if the EEOC doesn't think access is a good idea) a witness can be denied access to the record apart from her or his own testimony. If the charging party is still an employee of the respondent, it may be a good idea to ask that the respondent's witnesses be restricted to seeing and copying their own testimony.

If there is no predetermination settlement, the EEOC must determine whether or not there is reasonable cause to believe Title VII was violated. If the EEOC makes a no-cause determination, it will close its file.

The EEOC will also close its file if:

- The charge wasn't filed in time (see pages 57–59).
- The charging party doesn't have the right to bring the claim, or the respondent isn't covered by Title VII.
- The EEOC loses touch with the charging party in the course of its investigation, or the charging party won't cooperate. In any of these cases, the EEOC sends the charging party a notice saying that the charge will be dismissed unless the charging party contacts the EEOC within thirty days.

Once the EEOC file is closed, the charging party can request a right-to-sue letter and bring a private suit.

On the other hand, if the EEOC does make a cause determination, its next step is an informal process of conferences and conciliation between the charging party and the respondent. The EEOC tries to persuade them to sign a contract settling the matter. If they do sign an agreement, the

EEOC is responsible for monitoring compliance by analyzing reports and documents and visiting the respondents for on-site review. At least that's the theory; I wonder how much of it can be done given current funding and priorities.

After the cause determination is made, the EEOC sends conciliation invitations to the charging party and respondent. (If an employer is the subject of several charges, and the EEOC has picked the case for its Systemic Program, all the charges are consolidated and sent to conciliation together.) The charging party can respond to the invitation by returning Form 153 (the EEOC equivalent of an RSVP card) by telephone, letter, or personal contact with the appropriate EEOC official. As always, the best strategy is to make a written record and keep a copy.

Before the conciliation conference, the EEOC sets up a preconciliation conference with the charging party. If she has a lawyer, the lawyer, not the charging party, goes to the conference. The preconciliation meeting is supposed to elicit the charging party's objectives, what she'll accept as a reasonable settlement, and any change in the facts since the charge was filed (a promotion or demotion for the charging party, a change in her salary or job title, changes in the employer's hiring pattern).

According to the Compliance Manual, the desired outcome of the conciliation conference is a written agreement that provides approximately the same benefits as the charging party would get if she won her case (or if the EEOC sued the respondent and prevailed).

The charging party doesn't have the right to bypass the conciliation process. On the other hand, the EEOC has to be given the opportunity to conciliate. If the EEOC doesn't bother, or botches up the conciliation process (by losing papers, failing to show up or even schedule meetings, or mortally offending someone), the charging party can't sue the EEOC in federal court, and isn't even entitled to make a charge against the EEOC under the Administrative Procedures Act.

If a settlement *is* reached at conciliation, it's *not* considered an admission of wrongdoing by the respondent, and every conciliation agreement includes a provision to this effect. If the charging party signs the agreement, she agrees that she won't sue the respondent for any act of discrimination covered by the agreement.

If the EEOC gets a settlement offer that it believes "affords full relief for the harm alleged by the person claiming to be aggrieved" (that is, that compensates the charging party fully for the discrimination she has suffered), the EEOC will dismiss the charge if the charging party won't accept the settlement. So she loses the possibility of further EEOC handling of the charge, but she gains the right to sue.

The trade-offs involved: the conciliation process is (relatively) quick and doesn't cost the charging party anything except time and annoyance (unless she has hired a lawyer at this early stage). But the settlement offer may be much less than the damages the charging party could obtain in court.

The EEOC, ever anxious to clear its files, is likely to put a fair degree of pressure on the charging party to settle; and the nature of settlements is that each side gives up something. The charging party may very well feel that she's suffered enough and is no mood to compromise, especially since the conciliation agreement isn't an admission of wrongdoing. Perhaps if every conciliation agreement required a top corporate official of the respondent to stand in the public pillory and be pelted with mud by aggrieved employees, this option would be more attractive.

However, if the charging party *does* reject the agreement and sue the respondent, she will certainly face a protracted litigation process, extending over several years. Unless her lawyer is willing to gamble on—and wait for—court-ordered legal fees (see pages 67–69), the charging party will have to pay lots of money for the privilege of being a plaintiff. There's no guarantee that the District Court will find for the plaintiff. Even if it does, she may not be satisfied with the remedies that the court orders. Finally, even if she's delighted with the outcome, the respondent may very well appeal the case, yielding more uncertainty and more litigation delay. The advantage of litigation is that, if the plaintiff wins, she can get a wide variety of remedies—but we'll be getting to that soon.

The EEOC can sign the conciliation agreement even if the charging party doesn't. That gets the respondent off the hook with the EEOC; the charging party can't benefit by the conciliation agreement, but can still bring a private suit.

A conciliation agreement is a contract between charging party, respondent, and EEOC. A consent decree is similar, but requires court approval and can be enforced by that court. What if the respondent, the EEOC, and *some* charging parties are willing to agree to a consent decree? Are the holdouts allowed to bring private suits against the respondent? The Fourth Circuit says yes, the Eighth Circuit and Eastern District of Missouri say no. Even the Fourth Circuit won't let the charging party sue if she took any money under the consent decree.

Not every attempt to conciliate works: either the respondent stonewalls or the best offer is pathetically unacceptable. In such a case, the EEOC has to decide whether it wants to sue the respondent—either on the individual charge or based on the EEOC's own identification of discriminatory patterns or practices of the employer. If the EEOC *does* sue, it must wait at least thirty days from the date the charge was filed.

If conciliation fails but the EEOC doesn't want to sue, or if 180 days have passed since the original filing and the complainant doesn't want to wait any more, she is entitled to a right-to-sue letter. Once she gets the letter, the EEOC will suspend the charge (but any commissioner charge against the same respondent stays in force).

TITLE VII LITIGATION

Whether the EEOC or the charging party is the plaintiff, the trial takes place in federal District Court. The trial is *de novo*—that is, it's a new trial, starting from the beginning, and not relying on the testimony before the EEOC or on the EEOC's conclusion.

If the case involves only Title VII claims, it will be heard by a judge alone, without a jury. But if the plaintiff has both Title VII and Equal Pay Act claims, the trial will be bifurcated (divided in two). A jury will hear and decide on the EPA claim, and the judge will decide the Title VII case.

If the plaintiff asks, and if the District Court thinks it is advisable, the court can appoint a lawyer for the plaintiff and/or let her bring her case without paying court costs, court fees, or posting a security bond for these costs and fees. Whether the court will do this depends on:

- Whether the plaintiff can prove she made reasonable efforts to hire a lawyer but could not do so (e.g., the only lawyer who was willing to take the case demanded $10,000 up-front money, and the plaintiff lacks a spare ten bills; or she has the money, but local lawyers are afraid to offend a powerful employer).
- Whether the plaintiff's claim seems to have merit rather than being frivolous. Some courts tend to see an EEOC no-cause determination as a sign that the case isn't strong enough to merit the appointment of a lawyer or waiver of costs; a reasonable cause finding makes a strong case for appointment.
- Whether the employee is doing well on her own ("pro se"). A lawyer will probably not be appointed if she is handling her own case competently.

If the EEOC is the plaintiff, it can go to court for "preliminary relief"— for example, asking for a temporary restraining order or preliminary injunction to prevent an employer from firing certain employees until their sex-discrimination case has been disposed of. What happens if a charging party wants to go to court for the same kind of relief, but it's too early to get a right-to-sue letter? At least eleven courts have grappled with this issue. Four Circuits and two District Courts say she *can* get preliminary relief (in appropriate cases, of course) without a right-to-sue letter; five District Courts say no.

A Title VII case is a fairly routine federal civil case. That is, it starts when the plaintiff serves the defendant with a copy of her complaint and files the complaint with the court. The complaint explains what the plaintiff requests from the court and explains what the plaintiff expects to prove about the defendant's wrongdoing. (After proceedings at a 706 agency, perhaps a fact-finding conference, and a conciliation conference, the charges can hardly come as a surprise.) The defendant sends the plaintiff, and the court, a copy of its answer.

One of the fundamental tenets of American civil trial practice is that each side is entitled to know, before the trial, the evidence the other side will present at trial—and any underlying facts, in possession of the adversary, that *won't* be presented at trial because they are unfavorable. The name of the process is *discovery,* and it's an exceedingly complex and expensive part of litigation. At one time, it was standard defense strategy to stonewall, forcing the plaintiff to go to court to collect every miserable bit of information. Now employers tend to be more subtle. This is the era of "back-up-the-truck" discovery. That is to say, the defendant obligingly provides millions of pages of documents or thousands of reels of computer tape or floppy disks, and it then becomes the plaintiff's problem to winnow this rubbish for the few nuggets of useful information. (Sometimes the plaintiff's patience is rewarded, because one of the documents is something like a memo saying, "Get rid of Collins before she finds out the female sales reps get $5000 a year less than the men.")

Whatever methods of discovery are used, the plaintiff's lawyer should be sure to get a statistical breakdown showing the number of people and the number of women in each department, job classification, and line of progression for promotion. Sometimes the statistics, by themselves, will be enough to make the first part of the plaintiff's case; even if that isn't true, at least the statistics can show that a business necessity defense is pretextual.

The Federal Rules of Evidence provide for three major "discovery devices" (or methods to get information): interrogatories, demands to produce, and depositions.

Interrogatories are sets of written questions sent to the defendant to be answered in writing (e.g., "How many people were hired under the job title Engineering Trainee during the period 1981 to 1983? How many of these trainees were female? List the name, educational credentials, prior job experience, and starting salary for each trainee.") The plaintiff's lawyer can include interrogatories with the complaint or can serve them later. If the plaintiff's lawyer realizes that some important questions have been left unasked, additional sets of interrogatories can be served—within reason. If the interrogatories are really frightening, the defendant may be willing to offer favorable terms for an out-of-court settlement. The more likely outcome is that the defendant will simply send two trucks instead of one.

It is important to phrase interrogatories very specifically, first of all so that the information received will be useful, and secondly so that the defendant won't be able to refuse to answer on the grounds that the questions are too vague. Every item and sub-item should be numbered individually, in case the defendant refuses to answer some or all of the questions and the plaintiff's lawyer has to go to court with a motion to demand answers. (A motion is a legal device under which one party—the movant—moves, that is, asks the court to do something; in this case, to order the defendant to answer the questions.)

The plaintiff's lawyer can also demand that the defendant produce certain documents (e.g., personnel records, payroll data) so that the plaintiff's lawyer can inspect and/or copy them. This demand can be combined with the interrogatories or issued separately.

Employers have to file various forms with the EEOC, containing various fascinating statistics about their employment practices; companies that do business with the federal government have to file even more documents with even more fascinating statistics. If the employer is shy about providing this information, it may be available directly from the EEOC or the Office of Federal Contract Compliance Programs.

It is also worth asking for raw data on punch cards or computer tapes (if the defense can get access to the appropriate equipment, of course) because the defendant is likely to turn over the whole mess without printing it out to check for embarrassing bits.

Interrogatories and demands to produce deal with papers and therefore are (relatively) cheap to issue and process. A deposition is the process of arranging for a live witness to appear and, under penalty of perjury, answer questions posed by the opposing attorney. Depositions are hellishly expensive, because each side has one or more lawyers sitting there (and getting paid), a court reporter takes the whole thing down (and gets paid), and then the court reporter's notes have to be transcribed and copied (by people who get paid). Of course, the defendant's lawyers are in no mood to speed the process or make it any easier. Depositions have another pitfall: they "train" the defendant's witnesses by showing them the plaintiff's strategy and the answers the plaintiff wants to hear.

After discovery is completed, and if the two sides haven't worked out a mutually acceptable pre-trial settlement, the case goes to trial. How long that may be after discovery depends on the state of the court calendar; it can be anything from a couple of months to several years.

HURRY UP AND WAIT: TIMING REQUIREMENTS

In addition to all the other hurdles that must be surmounted by the would-be Title VII plaintiff, she must conform to all the timing requirements. Some of the requirements specify the earliest date on which something can be done, others specify the last permissible date. The requirements are non-negotiable and unforgiving. Unless the charging party/plaintiff conforms to one of the rules or one of the established exceptions, she *can't* bring her claim, no matter how much justice is on her side.

- In a state with no Fair Employment Practices laws (Alabama, Arkansas, Georgia, Mississippi, Tennessee, Texas), or a state whose state law has less coverage than Title VII, she must file her charge directly with the EEOC and must file within 180 days of the unlawful employment practice.

- If she lives in one of the other states, she must file with the EEOC within three hundred days of the practice. If she goes to the 706 agency first, and it has dismissed the case (either because of a no-cause determination or to speed up the process), she must also get to the EEOC within thirty days of the state dismissal.

Okay, listen closely now. At first blush, plaintiffs in states without FEP laws, or with laws less inclusive than Title VII, get 180 days to file, plaintiffs in other states get 300 days. But what seems like 300 days is really 240 days.

- In *Mohasco Corp. v. Silver*, 447 U.S. 807 (1980), the Supreme Court said that a charge is filed when the EEOC gets it back from the 706 agency, not when the charging party strolled into the EEOC and filed a charge indicating that the state agency had not considered the case. However, most of the state deferral agencies have made agreements with the EEOC to let the EEOC take cases immediately, without deferral, if a case is filed more than 240 days but less than 300 days after the discriminatory act, and would therefore be too late under the *Mohasco* rule.

- Next problem: what if the charge *is* filed within the 300 days, but isn't timely under state rules? Say, for example, that state law calls for filing within 180 days, and the charging party files 211 days after the act of illegal discrimination. This gives the EEOC plenty of time to defer, yet still have a "filing" within 300 days. Many cases have dealt with this situation. About half the cases say that the charging party is fine, because she got the charge into, out of, and back to the EEOC in time. The EEOC's own regulations take this position (29 C.F.R. §1601.13(a) (3)). After all, Title VII is supposed to supplant less-liberal state laws—why not less-liberal timing requirements? The other courts take the tough but not unreasonable position that the deferral process has *some* meaning and isn't a mere rubber stamp. Under this theory, the EEOC should not handle claims if deferral would be unproductive because the claim is too late for the state agency to resolve it.

- If the EEOC decides to sue a respondent, it can do so at any time after thirty days post-filing if it has tried to negotiate a conciliation agreement and can't do it.

- If the EEOC continues dithering 180 days post-filing, if the EEOC makes a no-cause determination, or if the charging party refuses to accept a predetermination settlement or conciliation agreement, the charging party can get a right-to-sue letter; armed with this letter, she can institute a suit in federal court.

• The charging party *must* get the complaint into the District Court within ninety days of her receipt of the right-to-sue letter. The one exception is that asking the District Court to appoint counsel (see page 55) suspends the running of this ninety-day period. That is, the time the District Court takes to consider the request isn't counted as part of the ninety days. Most of the other timing requirements are *delays* (the EEOC must wait sixty days for the 706 agency, and thirty days to bring a suit); this one penalizes delay. It's a good reason to hire a lawyer as soon as possible. It's tough to interview several lawyers, hire one, and make sure that the lawyer understands the case and does enough preliminary investigation to file a well-drafted complaint—all in three months.

• The major exception to the timing rules is that, if there is a "continuing violation," filing a charge is timely if it's within 300 (or 180, in a state with no or limited employment discrimination laws) days of *any* part of the continuing violation. In other words, if the unlawful employment discrimination consists of firing the charging party on February 8, 1986, the timing requirement runs from that date. But if the practice in question is the underpayment of the charging party because she is a woman, any of her anemic paychecks can be used as the basis of the charge. Therefore, anything that can arguably be described as a continuing violation should be included in the original charge; it can be a lifesaver if the charge might be dismissed as time-barred. (That's lawyerese for "too late.")

• Another exception: the charging party's time to file charges runs from the time a reasonably prudent person would have been aware of the facts supporting the charge. So if facts were concealed by the employer (e.g., the employer told the charging party that no raises would be given that year, as an economy measure, while giving all male employees a raise and all female employees a song and dance), the charging party may be able to file based on the time she knew (or should have known) of the deception, rather than the date the salary directive took effect.

THE SMOKING GUN

Trial of a sex discrimination case is a three-step process. First, the plaintiff proves her basic (prima facie) case. Then the defendant has a chance to poke holes in the prima facie case by demonstrating that the plaintiff misrepresents the facts, or that being male is a BFOQ for the job in question (disparate treatment case), or that the practice complained of was a business necessity for the defendant (disparate impact). If the defense is persuasive, the plaintiff has a last chance to win by showing that the defense is only a pretext for discrimination, or by showing that the defendant would not have treated a man the way the plaintiff was treated.

The case of *McDonnell-Douglas Corp. v. Green*, 411 U.S. 792 (1973), outlines the prima facie case when an individual plaintiff claims disparate treatment (openly different standards for women and men):

• Plaintiff must state that she belongs to a class protected by Title VII— that is, that she is a woman. (If racial, religious, or national-origin discrimination is also involved, she should state that she belongs to that protected group as well.) If she alleges that she is a woman, it will be taken on faith; she doesn't have to introduce a chromosomal assay into evidence.

• She *does* have to prove that she applied for, or would have applied for if discriminatory policies had not discouraged her, a job opening that really existed and for which she at least appeared to be qualified; or she must prove that she performed satisfactorily at a job that wasn't slated to be eliminated for business reasons.

• She must also prove that the adverse job action (being rejected, disciplined, laid off, or fired) was taken in spite of satisfactory qualifications or performance, not because of poor ones.

The case of *Dothard v. Rawlinson*, 433 U.S. 321 (1977), is a good illustration of the three-step. This was a disparate impact case (based on a facially neutral requirement: that prison guards be of a minimum height and weight—standards that eliminated some men and most women). The plaintiffs made their prima facie case by demonstrating the difference in exclusions, using statistics. The Supreme Court agreed that height/weight statistics for the entire United States, not just the pool of job applicants, were relevant. The employer did not rebut the plaintiff's prima facie case; in fact, it didn't present *any* evidence showing that a particular height or weight was required for effective job performance. However, the Supreme Court *did* accept the BFOQ defense. The Supreme Court agreed that, if women want dangerous jobs, they're entitled to take that risk. However, the Court accepted the employer's argument that male prisoners wouldn't respect and/or fear woman guards, so *all* women would be unable to perform the job effectively. The plaintiffs could not rebut this defense to the satisfaction of the Supreme Court.

Sex discrimination isn't a "strict liability" offense; the plaintiff has to show the defendant's conduct was deliberate. But in a disparate treatment case, the plaintiff has to show that the defendant had a discriminatory *motive* for the policy. If the plaintiff claims disparate impact, all she has to show is that the policy wasn't adopted accidentally; she doesn't have to show that the employer intended to discriminate against women. So, at first blush, it seems easier to make out a case of disparate impact. However, it's much easier to show that the policy carrying the disparate impact was necessary or was shaped by business necessity. In order to rebut the plaintiff's prima facie case of discrimination, the employer doesn't have to convince the court that it acted on a legitimate, nondiscriminatory motive. All the employer has to do is show that the plaintiff failed to prove her case; the defendant-employer just has to show that some legitimate, nondiscriminatory reason for its conduct can be advanced (whether or not this was the employer's true motivation), so that the court has a genuine dispute about facts to be resolved.

If the defendant claims that being male is a BFOQ for the job, it must be able to claim that it has a factual basis for believing that *all* women, or *substantially* all women, are incapable of doing the job safely and efficiently. The plaintiff can rebut this contention by showing that women are *already* doing the job perfectly well, or by introducing expert testimony that a substantial percentage of women can do the job.

Courts differ on how much the plaintiff has to show to make her prima facie case. *McDonnell-Douglas* says she has to show that she had the minimum qualifications necessary for the job or the promotion involved. But *Canty v. Olivarez* requires the plaintiff to show that her qualifications were at least as good as those of the person who eventually got the job or the promotion; *Anderson v. City of Bessemer City* says her qualifications must be *better. East v. Romine Inc.* adds the further refinement that the plaintiff must prove that the employer continued to accept applications, refused to hire or promote the plaintiff, and then hired or promoted someone else after her application was rejected. But *Kennedy v. Godwin* says the plaintiff doesn't have to prove that she was the *most* qualified applicant, only that her application wasn't given objective consideration because of sex discrimination.

Equal Pay Act cases involve special problems of evidence. The Act refers to differences in pay in a "single establishment"—not in different industries, businesses, or even companies in an industry. This requirement has been interpreted very restrictively. For example, the Ninth Circuit has ruled that the various language schools owned by Berlitz are not a single establishment, so woman directors could not sue under the EPA based on the undisputed fact that woman directors of Berlitz schools were paid less than male directors. (They could still use Title VII.)

• The plaintiff has to prove that her job was equal to that of a better-paid male—it isn't up to the defense to prove that the jobs were different. (Maybe a *woman's* salary can be used as evidence: in a Title VII case, the Seventh Circuit found for one plaintiff who proved that her salary was lower than that of another woman, whose salary had been raised to spare the employer from sex discrimination charges. The Seventh Circuit held that the lower-paid woman was paid less than a man holding the same job would be paid, so she won her case.)

• A 1984 Ninth Circuit case holds that an EPA plaintiff proved her prima facie case by introducing a letter from her bosses saying that she did the same work in her job as a "student loan clerk" as better-paid men did as "financial assistants."

• As we've seen (on pages 30–34) comparable-worth cases are notoriously tough. However, it may be possible to use the fact that women are paid less than men with the same job point rating as evidence of the employer's *intent* to discriminate, even if a comparable-worth claim by itself wouldn't succeed.

• Remember the *Plemer* case (page 32)? Well, the *Plemer* court cited the case of *Wilkins v. University of Houston* approvingly as an example of adequate direct evidence in an EPA case. In the *Wilkins* case, the university established a salary range for each position, giving a minimum and maximum salary for each job. Twenty-one employees were paid less than the "minimum" salary for their jobs; eighteen of them were women. (Small world, isn't it?) Obviously not every discovery process will yield such evident illegality, but it gives you something to look forward to.

When the plaintiff charges that she was denied a promotion (rather than being denied a job), there are a few little twists. She may have to allege (in her complaint) and prove (at the trial) that she was in the "line of progression" for the promotion (or was discriminatorily denied access to the line of progression), if the employer has a formal linear structure. The employer's usual defense is that they gave it the old college try but couldn't find any qualified women, so the plaintiff, during the discovery phase, should get the employer to reveal the factors used in the promotion decision. Then the plaintiff can show, at trial, that the claimed business defenses are pretexts. These are considered signs of discrimination:

- Lack of a standard system of evaluation for raises and promotions
- Vague and subjective promotion standards
- Lack of job posting
- Failure to disclose the descriptions and qualifications required for the good jobs
- Promotion decisions left entirely in the hands of one supervisor (i.e., a possible bigot)
- Lack of an internal review procedure that can be used by an employee claiming discrimination
- Evidence that men consistently earn higher salaries than women
- Evidence that men were promoted ahead of women with more seniority and/or a better record of job performance.

Small companies are less likely to have formal systems of evaluation, so the plaintiff may fare somewhat better there than if she worked for a huge corporation with a complex of rules embodied in a series of procedure manuals. That's lucky because, as we'll see in a moment, the aggrieved employee of a small business is out of luck when it comes to statistical proof—the major source of evidence in Title VII cases.

STATISTICS

It is very useful, but not essential, for a sex discrimination plaintiff to be able to prove specific discriminatory acts aimed against her. It certainly makes a lawyer's afternoon, after sifting through reams of boring documents, to find a notation, "Get this broad out of here—we don't want Women's Libbers in our department," in the margin of the plaintiff's personnel file. But not every case involves such an epiphany, and in a class action (see pages 69–72), it's particularly difficult to find evidence of individual discrimination against every class member.

Therefore, most Title VII cases are proved statistically; the plaintiff makes her prima facie case by using statistics to show that the defendant-employer's policies treat women differently from men in hiring, job duties, pay, layoffs, or dismissal.

The statistics must come from the relevant labor market. If the plaintiff's skills are fairly modest or are skills that many workers share (e.g., typing, ability to drive a cab), the labor market to be studied is probably the labor market in the local area. The more professional and specialized the job (e.g., expertise in a particular branch of polymer chemistry), the wider the geographic area that should be studied. The court probably won't find discrimination just based on raw numbers (for example, the Mammoth Corp. has only one woman Ph.D. chemist) unless the plaintiff shows the gender breakdown of the relevant labor market, the people who actually applied for the job, and the people in the area who had at least the minimal qualifications for the job. However, if the case involves promotions, and the employer makes all its promotions from within (instead of hiring outsiders for the job), a fairly good argument can be made that the statistics to be examined relate to the employer's existing work force. An employer can use statistics to bolster its defense: if the percentage of woman employees at a particular level has increased significantly, this can show an attempt to correct past discrimination, even if the number or percentage of woman employees isn't very high. And, of course, all bets are off in a small company, because the limited size of the employee sample means that the figures introduced are not statistically significant.

The most common method of statistical analysis for Title VII is "multiple regression." If I understand it (and I'm not sure I do), multiple regression is done by adjusting the statistics to factor out certain things. If, let's say, the statistics are used in a pay discrimination case, the plaintiff's statistician shows that the lower pay of woman employees isn't based on experience (because women earn less than men with equal experience), skill (because women earn less than men with equal skill), productivity (you guessed it . . .) and other factors that might be raised as business necessity defenses. It's important to factor out the thing the statistician is trying to prove, for example, performance evaluations based on the supervisors' perceptions of appropriate behavior or ambitions for working women.

Naturally, once the plaintiff's statistician has spoken, the defendant's statistician will re-interpret the statistics from the defense point of view; District Judge Fred M. Winner, speaking in 1979, described Title VII class actions as "contests between college professor statisticians who revel in discoursing about advanced statistical theory."

REMEDIES

By the time a charging party has become a plaintiff, it's clear that she's not doing it for her health. It is not unlikely that she is an altruist who is interested in bettering the lot of working women; neither is it unlikely that, after all that trouble, she's going to expect something for herself. Therefore, the question of remedies—what she can get in an out-of-court settlement, or what a court can award—becomes important.

The usual elements of damages are:

- Hiring or reinstatement. *Garza v. Brownsville Independent School District*, 700 F.2d 253 (5th Cir. 1983), says that, because the objective of Title VII is to place the victim of discrimination in as favorable a position as she would have been in if there had been no discrimination, reinstatement or hiring preference should be given to almost all successful plaintiffs, and denied only in exceptional cases.
- Promotion
- Training
- Seniority
- Pay increases
- "Back pay"—not a posh part of Boston, but the wages, pension benefits, education benefits, pension accruals, and other compensation the plaintiff would have received if she had gotten the job or the promotion. Title VII (at 42 U.S.C.S. §2000e-5(g)) limits back pay to the two years before filing of the EEOC charge.
- Overtime the plaintiff would have received if she had gotten the job or the promotion.
- "Front pay"—sometimes the court decides that the plaintiff should be given a job at a particular level, but there are no openings. One way the situation can be handled is to award the plaintiff an immediate salary increase to the level of pay she will receive when the job opens up.

The other way, of course, is for the employer to "bump" whoever has the job and give it to the plaintiff. The bumpee, of course, has every right to be livid with fury and may have a triable reverse-discrimination claim; not very many cases approve bumping. District Courts in Arkansas and the District of Columbia have allowed it when the job is unique and *someone* has to be disadvantaged, but the Second, Fourth, Fifth, Sixth, and Eighth Circuits have turned thumbs down on the practice. (Bread and Circuitses?)

One of the basic principles of law is that injured parties have to "mitigate their damages"—that is, make the best of the situation: a plaintiff who is fired unjustly has to do her utmost to get another job. Once the plaintiff has proved her case, the defendant must prove mitigation of damages— that is, that the plaintiff's damages are not as high as she said, or that she took action to limit the damages. An example of the first might be proof that the plaintiff, fired in the sixth month of a pregnancy, had no intention of working after the baby's birth and therefore lost two months' wages, not two years' worth; an example of the second would be proof that the plaintiff in fact got a better job.

If the plaintiff can't or doesn't get another job after being fired, she will probably apply for unemployment compensation. Can she quit a job because of pay discrimination, claiming "constructive discharge" (i.e., that the discriminatory conduct was the equivalent of firing her)? It has been tried, and at least two courts (the Fifth and Ninth circuits) have said no: the cases are *Bourke v. Powell Elec. Mfg. Co.* and *Heagney v. U. of Washington,* respectively.

If she really *is* fired, and manages to collect unemployment benefits, should the amount of benefits be subtracted from the amount the employer has to pay? The Seventh Circuit, and District Courts in Connecticut and Florida, say yes; the Third, Fourth, Sixth, Ninth, and Eleventh Circuits say no.

Title VII doesn't spell relief "R-O-L-A-I-D-S"; what it has to say (at 42 U.S.C.S. §2000e-5(g)) is that the successful plaintiff is entitled to back pay plus "any other equitable relief as the court deems appropriate." Explaining this mandates a short detour to medieval England, and something of an oversimplification. Medieval England had two court systems. The church courts were allowed to respond to considerations of justice as well as the strict letter of the law (thus, the phrases "equity courts" and "equitable remedies"). The royal courts provided "legal remedies." By and large, the royal courts preferred to restrict themselves to ordering the losing party to pay money to the winner. The church courts could order one person to give property back to its rightful owner, or transfer property to someone else, and could order someone to do something or stop doing something (injunction). Ordering an employer to hire or promote someone, to remove derogatory remarks from an employee's records, or to publish newspaper ads informing former employees or job applicants that they may have a Title VII claim against the employer are all direct outgrowths of the church court's equitable remedies. The courts of the United States can provide both legal and equitable remedies, but traces of the earlier dual system remain in legal thinking.

The overall goal of equitable remedies is to do justice by putting the plaintiff in as good a position as s/he would have been in if the whole mess hadn't started in the first place. On the other hand, legal remedies quite often include what are called *punitive* or exemplary damages: the plaintiff gets lots and lots of money, and the defendant is punished with a pain in the pocketbook and made an example of. Then again, in many cases plaintiffs are awarded several different sums of money, each for a different reason: $X for medical bills plus $Y for lost wages plus $Z for pain and suffering, for example.

Not surprisingly, some Title VII plaintiffs have asked for punitive damages and/or compensatory damages (compensation for mental anguish, medical bills, employment agency fees, etc.). A few cases do allow compensatory and/or punitive damages, but most courts don't.

State cases have no such restrictions on damages; if it seems appropriate in the particular case, both compensatory and punitive damages can be awarded. Title VII preempts state anti-discrimination laws (that is, the federal court pays attention to the federal rather than the state statutes and case law), but there is a body of state law on many subjects the federal law doesn't cover. (More of this anon—see pages 85–86 for a discussion of remedies for sexual harassment.) Though it doesn't always seem that way, the court system is supposed to be efficient and to resolve as much as possible in a single proceeding. That's the rationale behind federal pendent jurisdiction.

"Pendent jurisdiction" is just what it sounds like: a plaintiff in federal court who also has a substantial state-law claim can "hang" the state-law claim from the federal claim and have the whole "necklace" appraised in federal court. This approach worked in the case of *Brown v. Blue Cross*. The federal claim was a Title VII claim. The state claim was for breach of contract; the plaintiff alleged that the employer violated the anti-discrimination policy stated in its own manual for employees.

In summary, Title VII litigation ain't been no crystal stair, but the persistent plaintiff can get largish sums of money and other remedies in addition to the satisfaction of knowing justice has been done. Sometimes a pretrial settlement is preferable, though. For one thing, the two-year limit on back pay doesn't apply to settlements, and the employer may be willing to open its coffers to get the obnoxious case over with before the lawyers own the company.

A 1983 settlement arranged by the EEOC was much heralded, for what seem to me to be the wrong reasons. The EEOC had been chasing after General Motors for ten years; in October, GM agreed to pony up at least $42.5 million dollars—the largest settlement in EEOC history. However, unlike a 1980 settlement with Ford Motor Company, which provided $13 million in back pay to 14,000 woman and minority workers, GM will spend most of the money (over a period of years—they don't have to fork over immediately) on education and training. In other words, colleges, universities, and in-house training programs get most of the money. A $4-million fund has been set aside for handling the seven hundred individual discrimination claims pending against GM; whatever isn't absorbed in administrative costs may be available as back pay for the victims. EEOC Chairman Clarence Thomas "feels really strongly" about this "new approach . . . a systematic answer to a systematic problem." (Surely he means a systemic problem, but what the hell.) "A lot of people would say that back pay was a necessity. I don't think so. We're looking at a systemwide issue and taking a different approach." As a labor lawyer told *The Wall Street Journal*, "It's obviously a good settlement for GM. Most of the money they were probably going to spend anyway." We have seen the future, and it's remarkably like the past.

Equal Pay Act cases, unlike Title VII cases, carry the possibility of double damages: 29 U.S.C. §216 says that an employer who violates the Equal Pay Act can be ordered to pay the successful plaintiff the amount she would have received if she had been paid fairly, plus the same amount again as "liquidated damages." The employer won't be liable for liquidated damages if it can prove it acted in good faith and had reason to believe it was in compliance with the Equal Pay Act. (The term "liquidated damages" means the damages are made "liquid"—in the sense of a liquid investment—by being expressed in exact monetary terms.) EPA plaintiffs are limited to two years' back pay—or three years if the violation was willful. The meaning of "willful" is a controversial legal issue, but for this purpose it generally means that the employer knew that the EPA applied to its operations and that the unequal pay wasn't an accident (e.g., a computer error). The employer doesn't have to have had evil intent or to have wanted to break the law. EPA plaintiffs are not entitled to compensatory damages for physical or mental suffering, and a plaintiff can't get both EPA and Title VII damages for the same offense.

ATTORNEYS' FEES

The "English rule" is that whoever loses a civil case has to pay his opponent's legal fees (take that, you swine!). The "American rule" is that, unless a statute says differently, both the winner and the loser are stuck with their own legal fees.

Luckily for Title VII plaintiffs, the statute *does* say differently: 42 U.S.C. §2000e-5(k) says that a court can award reasonable fees for the prevailing (winning) party's attorneys. If the plaintiff wins, she should be awarded attorneys' fees in all except "very unusual" or "special" circumstances. The plaintiff has "prevailed" if her claim isn't completely unsubstantial, her action has (at least arguably) advanced the purposes of Title VII, and the final outcome of the case favors the plaintiff's own personal interests. To "prevail" the plaintiff doesn't have to get everything she asks for—if she proves sex discrimination but doesn't get back pay, she still prevails. What if she loses the case—does she have to pay the defendant's legal fees (the hundred dollars or more an hour for the endless hours expended by the most prestigious—and expensive—firm in town)? Only if her case was frivolous, meritless, or groundless, or if she kept the employer in court long after it was obvious that she couldn't win.

The fees involved can include not only the attorneys' fees for the District Court trial, but representation of the charging party before the 706 agency and the EEOC.

Hourly fee awards can also be made for paralegals working on a successful Title VII case—even if the hourly fee, multiplied by the hours involved, is higher than the paralegals' salary. What if the plaintiff does some or all of the legal work herself—are legal fees available for this "pro se" (for herself) work? The consensus is that they are not, although the plaintiff may well be reimbursed for out-of-pocket expenses she has paid (phone calls, photocopies, transcripts, postage, travel to court or meetings in the lawyers' office, and the like.)

Even though it's pretty obvious that a prevailing plaintiff will get an award of counsel fees, the *amount* of the award is left to the discretion of the court. The general rule is that the normal rates that lawyers in the area charge are the starting point—even if the lawyer in question usually charges less. (This is a boon for Title VII plaintiffs, who tend to have struggling lawyers rather than old-line, "white shoe" firms.) The factors judges consider in setting fees include:

- The amount of time the lawyer spent on the case
- How hard the lawyer worked—some cases are notably harder to prepare than others, even if the same number of hours is involved
- The extent to which the lawyer broke new legal ground
- The amount of skill displayed by the lawyer
- The extent to which the case preoccupied the lawyer and kept him or her from doing other work (and earning other fees)
- Whether the lawyer's fee was fixed or contingent (a certain percentage of the recovery)—contingent fees can be higher, because the lawyer is taking a risk. (The agreed-on contingent fee is not necessarily a ceiling; a lawyer who gets unusually good results may merit a higher fee.)
- The lawyer's experience, reputation, and ability—the classiest firm in town is likely to get a higher fee than the sole practitioner with the ink still wet on a night-school diploma.
- The "undesirability" of the case—if the lawyer's name became mud

because of advocacy of this unpopular cause, compensation for this staunchness is in order.

We're talking about real money here. The lawyers for a chemistry professor whose sex discrimination class action against the University of Minnesota was settled after ten years got fees of $1,475,000. (The chemistry professor—who is now a lawyer, as it happens—got $100,000.) Originally the lawyers were awarded almost $2 million because the judge tripled the two law firms' normal hourly fees of $80 to $125. The judge said that adequate legal fees were required to deter potential discriminatory employers. (I'd say that whacking great awards to plaintiffs were necessary to deter potential discriminatory employers, but what do I know?) The university was going to appeal the fee award, so the university and the law firms agreed on a somewhat lower fee scale and immediate payment rather than payment over a number of years.

CLASS ACTIONS

All right, what's this class action business I keep mentioning? One way a case can be brought is "one on one": an individual plaintiff sues a single defendant. Sometimes one plaintiff has a grievance against several defendants, or several plaintiffs want to sue the same defendant for the same or related causes of action. The process of adding *parties* (plaintiffs or defendants) to a suit is called *joinder*.

At some point, joinder becomes impractical. If a drunk driver causes a six-car smashup in which thirteen people were hurt, and the property of eleven people damaged, it's reasonably easy to find them all and see if they want to sue or prefer to settle out of court (or forget the whole thing). But what about all the people who ever rode in a cab operated by a taxi company whose company policy was to rig the meters to produce overcharges? How do you find all of them, and does any court really want to handle 17,822 cases, all pretty much the same?

Theoretically, the answer is the class action: a single case that disposes of all the claims in a consistent fashion. (Otherwise some judges might make different rulings in factually identical cases governed by the same laws.) It's only theoretically the answer, because for various technical reasons involving civil procedure, not every group of plaintiffs that wants to maintain a class action is allowed to do so. A judge must "certify the class"—rule that it's an eligible class—before the case can be brought as a class action. Also for technical reasons, it's difficult or impossible to bring a consumer class action (except if a statute with special class-action provisions has been violated), but (relatively) easy to bring a civil-rights class action such as a Title VII case.

As you may or may not remember, the EEOC takes individual complaints, not class complaints (although its own pattern-or-practice investigations involve discrimination against a group rather than an individual). If several people make related charges at the same time, each signs an individual complaint. That way, if some withdraw their complaints, at least some complaints will remain in place for the EEOC to investigate. It isn't, mercifully, necessary for every class member to go through the EEOC conga line; only the representative party has to. A Title VII case can be based not only on the specific claims made in the individual plaintiff's EEOC charge but on other, related charges that do or could turn up in the course of a reasonable investigation. A class action can be based on an underlying EEOC charge that literally mentioned only discrimination against the individual charging party.

Federal class actions are governed by Rule 23 of the Federal Rules of Civil Procedure. (There is such an animal as a state class action, but we won't get into that here.) The would-be plaintiff has to meet all of these tests:

- The class must have so many members that joinder of all of them is impractical.
- All the members of the class must want the court to rule on the same legal or factual questions.
- The "representative party" or "named plaintiff" (the individual plaintiff whose name goes on the complaint) must be a fair representative of the class—the boss's daughter is unlikely to be the best representative of the rank-and-file.
- The representative party's claims and defenses must be typical of the claims and defenses of the other members of the class.

The class also has to meet *one* of these tests:

- The defendant acted or refused to act on grounds generally applicable to the whole class, so the court can order the same relief for the whole class. Courts are more sympathetic to a class action of this kind if most of the relief sought is equitable (i.e., ordering the defendant to do something—such as provide training—or stop doing something— such as placing married women's applications in the circular file) and the request for money damages is only incidental. This kind of case is called a (b) (2) class action, because it's described in Rule 23(b) (2).
- In a (b) (3) class action the number of legal and factual questions that apply to the whole class is greater than the number of questions that differ for individual members of the class, making a class action the best way to handle the whole assortment.

At first blush it would seem that every class action would be brought as a (b) (3) action, if only to demand more money from the defendant. (After all, it's tough for a lawyer to collect one-third of a training program as a contingent fee.) However, the representative party in a (b) (3) action has to notify all the members of the class at her own expense, to see if they want to "opt out" of (refuse to participate in) the class action. Members of the class in a (b) (2) class action don't have the right to opt out, and a court *can* order the representative party to notify all class members, but does not have to. There have to be lots of class members to bring a class action in the first place, so the task of notification is necessarily difficult and expensive. Add as well the fact that some class members will have to be tracked down.

In order to get the class certified, the plaintiffs' lawyer has to do more than quote Federal Rule 23 and gesture expansively; s/he has to present substantial evidence, statistics, answers to interrogatories, affidavits, and depositions, all to show that there is a grievance, and a class action is the best way to handle it. In other words, the plaintiffs' lawyer has to get a good solid head start on pretrial discovery (see pages 56–57) before it's at all certain that there can be a class-action case to bring to trial. In still other words, the original class members have to find a lawyer who'll waive his or her fee in the public interest, find a lawyer who'll take a big chance (and probably expect a big fee) by taking the case on a contingent basis, or pay a lot of legal fees without being sure permission will even be granted to try the case as a class action.

The cost factor is a powerful deterrent (unless the class happens to be made up of socially conscious millionaires). A deterrent for the lawyer, though not necessarily for the client, is that the contingent fee charged to a class is subject to review (and possible downward adjustment) by the District Court. A consideration (not necessarily a deterrent) is that any settlement or compromise of a class action also requires class approval (and all class members must be notified), so there's less flexibility than in an individual action. (The reason for this requirement is to prevent one or a few class members from making a quick deal with the defendant, taking their goodies, and forgetting the rest of the class members.)

Once certification is achieved, it's, according to *Am.Jur. Trials,* "unusual for the plaintiff to lose a Title VII class action." Of course, winning the case can provide only partial satisfaction. The employer may be enjoined against further discrimination and a vigorous affirmative action program created. That's very nice in the abstract, but buys no Hamburger Helper for the class members.

It is quite possible for individual claims to be joined to a class action. If that happens, the trial will be bifurcated (divided into two phases). The first phase involves proof of discrimination against the class and economic harm to the class. Proof is usually statistical—see page 63 concerning statistics in Title VII litigation. If, as is likely, the plaintiffs win at this stage, it's presumed that all the class members are entitled to back pay; it's up to the employer to show that some class members are entitled to less, or to nothing. In the second phase (usually proved by testimony or documents), individual claims are assessed: for example, some class members may be entitled to reinstatement, promotion, front pay, or the full two years' back pay, while other class members are entitled to less.

3
SEXUAL HARASSMENT: HEAVEN WON'T PROTECT THE WORKING GIRL

If the conventional wisdom is to be believed—and Claire Broudy isn't sure if it is—success in the corporate world requires a mentor. It took seven years of saving her secretarial salary and going to night school to finish college and get her MBA. Now she's clinging precariously to her position as a trainee in the foreign currency department of a major bank. All the other trainees are much younger, and seem much more comfortable on the fast track. One of the senior vice-presidents, Edward Rossmoor, has taken an interest in her progress (or perhaps only in her contours). Rossmoor has arranged that Broudy be appointed his personal assistant; her first assignment is to join him at a conference. She wonders how personal the assistance he requires will be, and what the consequences will be if she refuses (or misreads his intentions, and offers unsolicited sexual favors—perhaps undesired sexual favors). It was all much less complicated when she was a secretary, and one of her bosses told her she'd have to sleep with him to keep her job. She simply quit and found another job two days later. That option is no longer open to her.

Two of the oldest, wheeziest clichés are the villain demanding the heroine's virtue in lieu of the mortgage balance, and the villain demanding the heroine's virtue so that she can retain the menial job that is the sole bulwark between her numerous family and starvation. Once-fresh dramatic situations become clichés precisely because of their extreme credibility, which in turn promotes overuse.

Sexual harassment at work has not vanished from the earth; the forms it takes vary from an unabashed demand for sexual access in return for employment or continued employment to suggestions of promotion opportunities in exchange for being "nice," through allegedly affectionate poking, prodding, and squeezing. Verbal conduct ranges from unmistakable abuse to "cute," "friendly," "complimentary" remarks. The emotional climate in which sexual harassment takes place has changed since the days when "At last I have you in my power, me proud beauty" served the function now assumed by "Come here often?" The villainous mill-owner of melodrama assumed that his intended victim was a virgin and that he proposed to do her a substantial injury. Contemporary practitioners of sexual harassment are apt to assume, based on a victim's "provocative" appearance and conduct (e.g., showing up for the job outside the harem, in a garment other than a *chador*), that she is sexually experienced, if not wanton, and that they hold an irresistible fascination for her. Sometimes the harassing conduct is intentionally offensive. At other times, the perpetrator is genuinely surprised that the woman involved doesn't want to sample the sexual delights he promises, or isn't flattered by his slobbering over her new sweater.

Even legal commentators don't always take the problem seriously. Judges have referred to sexual harassment as "romantic adventures" and an otherwise excellent article refers to instances of harassment as "office romances" and is called "Love in the Office." "Bed-Wetting in the Office" or "Weenie-Wagging in the Office" would better express the level of dignity at which the perpetrators operate.

A working woman can be subjected to sexual harassment by her employer, by a supervisor, by co-workers, customers, or even subordinate employees. She can be fired outright or denied promotion because of her failure to acquiesce; or the working environment may be so intolerable that she quits her job. These distinctions are important, because they control the choice of remedies open to her, and the probability that she will succeed in getting any particular remedy.

Title VII doesn't specifically refer to sexual harassment (and Title VII was in effect for several years before the first courts allowed sexual harassment claims to be brought under Title VII), so the official legal definition of sexual harassment has developed through case law. NOW defines sexual harassment as "any repeated or unwarranted verbal or physical sexual advance, sexually explicit derogatory statement, or sexually discriminatory remark made by someone in the workplace which is offensive or objectionable to the recipient or which causes the recipient discomfort or humiliation or which interferes with the recipient's job performance." This is quite inclusive—too much so, in my opinion. There are remarks that are "sexually discriminatory" but don't really constitute sexual harassment. ("This world would be a better place if girls like you stayed home where you belong.") Remarks of this kind are really verbal employment discrimination and should be handled that way.

The EEOC's definition is both narrower and more sharply focused:

Harassment on the basis of sex is a violation of Section 703 of Title VII. Unwelcome sexual advances, requests for sexual favors, and other verbal or physical conduct of a sexual nature constitute sexual harassment when (1) submission to conduct is made either explicitly or implicitly a term or condition of an individual's employment, (2) submission to or rejection of such conduct by an individual is used as the basis for employment decisions affecting such individual, or (3) such conduct has the purpose or effect of unreasonably interfering wih an individual's work performance or creating an intimidating, hostile, or offensive working environment.

The District of Columbia takes an interesting approach. The Policy on Sexual Harassment, promulgated by Mayor's Order 79-89 (5/24/79), defines sexual harassment as exercise or attempted exercise of "the authority and power of his or her position to control, influence, or affect the career, salary, or job of another employee or prospective employee in exchange for sexual favors." The Policy lists six types of harassment as examples (but these are not the only actionable forms of harassment):

- Verbal harassment or abuse
- Subtle pressure for sexual activity
- Unnecessary patting or pinching
- Constant brushing against another employee's body
- Demands for sexual favors accompanied by overt threats concerning an individual's employment status
- Demands for sexual favors accompanied by implied or overt promise of preferential treatment with regard to an individual's employment status.

So far, the only way a federal sexual harassment case can be brought is under Title VII, which not only means that the whole process described on pages 45–59 must be gone through; it also means that the *employer* must be at fault (or must be legally responsible for the harasser's actions) and the harassment must be a "term or condition of employment."

In the early years of Title VII, that second part was the stumbling block; courts tended to rule that sexual harassment was a private matter between people, and wasn't job-related. Since 1977, there's been a growing awareness that sexual harassment *is*, among other things, sex discrimination. However, this is an area of the law in which it's especially crucial to be aware of the law in your own Circuit and District; quite often the same conduct will be condemned by one court and found not to violate Title VII by another court.

Barnes v. Costle, in 1977, was a breakthrough case. Earlier decisions shucked off sexual harassment as purely personal conduct by the harasser.

In *Barnes*, the D.C. Circuit said that if Barnes's job really was abolished because she wouldn't grant sexual access to her supervisor, that would constitute sex discrimination, even though not all women were solicited sexually. From this eminently sensible holding, the court took off on one of those bizarre flights of fantasy that so endears the legal profession to the public (the "pregnant man" case—see page 186—was another). The court went on to say that harassment by a bisexual supervisor would not be actionable because the harassment would not be restricted to members of one gender. This did not catch on to the extent of employers' advertising for managers "M/F, AC/DC" nor does it reflect the differential probability of knuckle sandwiches delivered by male and female victims of sexual harassment, whatever the supervisor's desires for his or her subordinates may be.

The *Barnes* court gave three reasons for making the employer liable: first, if conduct *could* be either discriminatory or innocent, the employer is in the best position to know the real motive (and eliminate discrimination); second, the employer, not the employees, has the power to enforce anti-harassment policies; and finally, a careful employer would, if necessary, err by being too strict in preventing violations.

In the same year, another landmark decision was handed down in the case of *Tomkins v. PSEG*, 568 F.2d 1044 (3d Cir.). *Tomkins* says that Title VII is violated when:

- The employer knows—or should know—that a supervisor has made sexual advances to, or demands on, an employee.
- The employee's performance evaluation, promotion, or continued employment depends on sexual compliance.
- The employer doesn't take prompt and appropriate remedial action once knowledge of the harassment is available.
- The plaintiff is treated differently than she would have been treated if she were a man—even if not all female employees are harassed.

However, a year later (in 1978) the D.C. Circuit took a giant step backward in the case of *Bundy v. Jackson*. Bundy was subjected to repeated sexual advances by her supervisors between 1972 and 1975. In 1974, "she informally complained by telephone to her supervisor, Swain. Swain, who was one of those making improper sexual advances to the plaintiff, did not appear to take the plaintiff's complaint seriously." (What a surprise!) "So lightly did Swain consider the matter that during the telephone conversation he said to the plaintiff '. . . any man in his right mind would want to rape you.' " (It's very significant that the D.C. District Court interpreted this remark as witty badinage, rather than the statement of a dangerous psychopath—or a man socialized in a very corrupt culture; notice that he didn't say "Any man in his right mind would want to go to bed with you" or "have an affair with you."

The court in the first *Bundy* case went on to say:

> Plaintiff's superiors appeared to consider the making of improper sexual advances to female employees as standard operating procedure, a fact of life, a normal condition of employment in the office. However, it also appears that the plaintiff's superiors did not consider the plaintiff's rejection of their improper sexual advances as a reason or justification for harassing the plaintiff or otherwise taking adverse action against her. It was a game played by the male superiors—you won some and you lost some. It was not a matter to be taken seriously. . . . There was no harassment of the plaintiff because of her prompt and continued rejection of the sexual advances of her male superiors, nor was she ever denied promotion for this reason.

Luckily, two years later, the D.C. Circuit reversed the District Court, finding that the lack of seriousness about the supervisors' conduct, far from absolving the employer, proved the plaintiff's prima facie case. As long as sexual harassment is standard operating procedure, the harassment is a term or condition of employment, and Title VII is violated.

By now, it's settled law that sexual harassment *is* illegal and actionable. The problem is to define what kinds of conduct constitute "terms or conditions of employment." Some courts insist on overt casting-couch routines, but others will find grounds for relief if the plaintiff's working conditions are hostile, offensive, or degrading, even if she was permitted to continue working among swine and boors.

In these cases, actionable harassment was *not* found:

• A supervisor's conduct (telling dirty jokes, putting his hands on the employee's shoulders) was judged to be merely personal acts, carried out without the employer's knowledge or approval; the plaintiff didn't have to submit to the advances to keep her job or enjoy the rights of employment (*Neeley v. American Fidelity Assurance Co.*).

• A fellow-employee's advances weren't sexual harassment: he wasn't a supervisor, didn't promise her anything (other than the dubious delights of his body), and she didn't have to sleep with him to keep her job or get a promotion (*Smith v. Rust Engineering Co.*).

• Although made by a supervisor, verbal passes "did not rise to such a level as to constitute a violation of Title VII," a 1979 case from the Southern District of Texas said; after all, the plaintiff wasn't fired for rejecting the advances.

• The plaintiff was fired after refusing her department chairman's "romantic advances" but had no case unless she could prove that the chairman was involved in the decision to fire her, or that the other defendants knew, or should have known, about the advances (*Fisher v. Flynn*).

• Sexual advances made by the company president weren't terms or conditions of employment, because the victim was neither threatened with losing her job if she refused nor promised anything for complying. Anyway, the victim never encountered the president after her orientation period— planes that pass in the night, so to speak (*Clark v. World Airways*).

• Use of coarse language that isn't specifically directed at the plaintiff isn't sexual harassment—especially if she uses it herself. (Fair enough: there's a difference between ". . . and then I told that fucking foreman that if he didn't get those fucking flanges I would shut down the whole fucking line," and "Hey, baby, wanna fuck?" the first is merely a social solecism, the second is personally threatening.) (*Halpert v. Wertheim.*)

• A supervisor's wandering hands and general boorishness (which he defined as "a show of support and encouragement") did not amount to sexual harassment because the plaintiff kept her job and continued to function efficiently in spite of the hassles (*Walter v. KFGO Radio*).

All of these cases, in keeping with reality, involve the harassment of women by men. I did unearth one case of a man charging harassment by a female supervisor. He lost, for one good and one bad reason. The good reason is that he bypassed Title VII in favor of another, but inapplicable, federal civil rights law (probaby this was done because the other law provides a wider range of possible damages). The bad reason is that the Seventh Circuit held that the supervisor discriminated against the plaintiff not as a man but as a former lover who had walked out on her, and, in the court's analysis, ex-lovers are not a protected group. If you ask me, this is as dumb as saying that sexual harassment isn't covered by Title VII because men only demand sexual acquiescence of women they find attractive, not of all women.

So much for the bad news. Now for the good news.

• Requiring a woman worker to wear a sexually provocative uniform that causes her to suffer harassment is illegal, "sex-plus" discrimination even though the harassment itself was carried out by members of the public; the employer was legally responsible because it forced the employee to wear the uniform.

• Flirtation (that is, sexually suggestive remarks that are not disagreeable to the recipient) isn't sexual harassment; neither is an isolated incident. However, repeated unwelcome advances cumulatively have the effect of a term or condition of employment and therefore violate Title VII (*Heelan v. Johns-Manville*).

• Sexually indecent remarks that are personally directed, not just "gutter language," can constitute sexual harassment ("Didja get any this weekend, Annie? I bet I can keep you happier than your old man") even if there is no direct demand for sexual access. A 1981 Tennessee case granted an injunction against further "friendly" badinage of this sort, even though some woman employees weren't offended by the remarks, or may have enjoyed them. It was enough for the court that the women who brought the suit were offended. This ruling is useful in the (not unlikely) event that a sexual harassment defendant claims that some of the "girls" were flattered by leers, ogles, lip-smacking, pawing, and related so-called attentions.

• A claim that the plaintiff's sexual relationship was motivated by her supervisor's statement that her job success depended on him and that he took reprisals against her after she ended the relationship was adequate to state a case under Title VII *(Koster v. Chase Manhattan Bank)*.

It has been an accepted principle for many years that a non-white employee who is forced to work in an environment heavily charged with discrimination has suffered an unlawful employment practice—constant use of racial epithets and Klan meetings in the middle of the shop floor, for example.

Brown v. City of Guthrie is a landmark case applying similar principles to sexual harassment cases. The plaintiff was a police dispatcher; the fun-loving cops kept skin magazines in the dispatcher's desk for leisure-time reading and asked her to rate herself against the centerfolds. The police lieutenant made lewd remarks and gestures and punished the plaintiff with extra make-work tasks when she protested. As the pièce de résistance, the jolly boys in blue videotaped the plaintiff while she was searching a prisoner and replayed the tape endlessly, with commentary. Certainly makes you feel safe, knowing you're protected by that caliber of man, doesn't it?

The Oklahoma District Court found that sexual harassment that permeates the workplace, creating an intimidating, hostile, or offensive working environment, *is* a term or condition of employment, so Title VII *has* been violated. This allows for many more cases to be brought—and won—than a narrower standard that sees a Title VII violation *only* when a supervisor demands sexual favors in return for hiring, promoting or refraining from firing a woman employee.

The case of *Henson v. City of Dundee* contains a definition of sexual harassment that can be very useful to other plaintiffs:

> Sexual harassment which creates a hostile or offensive environment for members of one sex is every bit the arbitrary barrier to sexual equality at the workplace that racial harassment is to racial equality. Surely, a requirement that a man or woman run a gauntlet of sexual abuse in return for the privilege of being allowed to work and make a living can be as demeaning and disconcerting as the harshest of racial epithets.

(I do mean "other" plaintiffs—this ringing declaration didn't do much good for Ms. Henson, who still lost her case.)

• *Robson v. Eva's Super Market Inc.* makes several very useful points. First of all, it says that Title VII covers constructive discharge (that is, conditions so intolerable that a worker *has* to quit) as well as hiring and outright firing. Second, it finds an acceptable Title VII cause of action in an assertion that a woman who worked as a supermarket counter clerk was assigned more onerous tasks because of her refusal to have sexual relations with a fellow-employee (a meatcutter—not the kind of job usually considered "supervisory").

• An employee's state of psychological well-being *is* a term, condition, or privilege of employment: *Phillips v. Smalley Management Services.*

• An air traffic controller suffered actionable harassment from both fellow employees and supervisors because the workplace was pervaded by sexual slur, insult and innuendo, and vulgar and offensive sexual epithets were used to and about the plaintiff; when she complained to her supervisor she was told that she could solve the problem by judicious promiscuity (*Katz v. Dole*). This is hardly the kind of appropriate supervisory action the courts have in mind.

• The test of actionable harassment, according to *Ferguson v. Du Pont*, is whether it's bad enough to have a serious effect on the employee's psychological well-being.

Employer Liability

But proving that harassment took place is only the first problem; the plaintiff also has to prove that the employer can legitimately be blamed for the harassment. (Remember, Title VII covers the actions of employers, unions, and employment agencies, not would-be Casanovas at the next desk.)

The EEOC's Guidelines say that an employer is responsible for sexual harassment committed by its employees if the employer knows or should have known about the harassment, unless the employer took immediate, appropriate corrective action. An employer can also be blamed for the acts of non-employees (such as airline patrons who take advantage of suggestive advertising to annoy the stewardesses) if the employer did not correct a situation it knew about, or should have known about. The Guidelines are entitled to deference from courts, but they don't have the force of law, so don't get your hopes up too high.

Different courts have reached different answers to the question of when the employer is on the hook. Although the differences in language are subtle, the differences in consequences are large. Fundamentally, the distinction is between making the employer responsible if it behaved badly (but not otherwise), and sticking it to the employer unless it behaved well. It is much easier for plaintiffs to win under the second standard.

These are some of the cases holding that the employer is liable only if it acts badly.

- *Ludington v. Sambo's Restaurants, Inc.*, 474 F.Supp. 480 (E.D. Wis. 1979), says the employer isn't responsible unless, in some active or silent way, it approved the acts of sexual harassment. In this case, the victims had complained to the management, which obviously was aware of the existence of alleged harassment, but they lost their case anyway.
- The employer is liable only if it knew about the sexual harassment and failed to take corrective action *(Martin v. Norbar, Inc.); Meyers v. ITT Diversified Credit Corporation* adds the requirement that the would-be plaintiff use the employer's internal grievance procedure before going to the 706 Agency or the EEOC.
- The *Ferguson* case mentioned above did not penalize the employer for the harassment, because the employer made a prompt investigation of the plaintiff's charges, took the charges seriously, and promptly took steps to remedy the harassment which did, in fact, stop.
- If the victim doesn't complain to the appropriate officials in the company, the employer won't even know about the situation, can't take steps to correct it, and can't be blamed for it *(Davis v. Western-Southern Life Ins. Co.)*.

However, plaintiffs do win a few (or there wouldn't be much point in writing this section):

- The employer has a legal duty to investigate complaints of sexual harassment. The employer's failure to investigate may lead to liability because the employer's willed ignorance gives tacit support to the acts of harassment *(Munford v. James T. Barnes & Co.)*.
- The employer is legally responsible for the discriminatory actions of supervisors (including sexual harassment) *unless* the supervisor violates the employer's stated policy, and the employer is unaware of the violation *(Barnes v. Costle)*.
- The employer will be blamed for a supervisor's sexual harassment if the employer had actual knowledge of the harassment at the time the victim was fired for noncompliance—even if the employer didn't know of the harassment at the time it occurred. And if the harassment is directly employment-related (e.g., an employee is told she has to accompany her supervisor to a motel in order to get her scheduled raise) and is carried out by a supervisor who has complete and sole power over employment decisions, the employer will be held responsible *(Craig v. Y & Y Snacks Inc.)*.
- *Miller v. Bank of America*, 600 F.2d 211 (9th Cir. 1979) makes the employer responsible for harassment by a supervisor who made or participated in employment decisions affecting the victim—even if the supervisor violated the employer's anti-harassment policy. After all, for a company to take an official stance against sexual harassment is hardly more

controversial than to be in favor of Mom's apple pie. As the Ninth Circuit phrased it:

> It would be shocking to most of us if a court should hold, for example, that a taxi company isn't liable for injuries to a pedestrian caused by the negligence of one of its drivers because the company has a safety training program and strictly forbids negligent driving.

In another formulation: talk is cheap.

• An employer was held liable (and its officers were held personally liable as individuals) when a woman employee was sexually harassed by the abusive language of her co-workers. The employer and officers were liable because they knew about the harassment but failed to take appropriate steps to end it. Telling the offenders to "knock it off" and holding occasional meetings to recite the rules about abusive language weren't enough. Appropriate corrective action might have been to give the culprits oral, then written warnings, then to suspend or fire them if their behavior failed to improve (*Zabkowicz v. West Bend Co.*).

THE ROAD TO THE COURTHOUSE

• If the victim is a union member, she may be able to use the union contract's arbitration mechanism and gain redress without going to court. However, arbitration more commonly comes into play when a woman's accusation of sexual harassment is believed, and the harasser is fined, suspended, or otherwise disciplined, and then protests the discipline by going to arbitration. Arbitrators usually agree that unwanted physical contact is an offense deserving discipline; the arbitration decisions are split about the proper punishment for verbal harassment. For example, the arbitration case of *Fisher Foods Inc.* upholds the suspension of a stockman for touching the breast of a sales representative; the arbitrators accepted her explanation that her complaint was delayed because she was worried about her new job. A housekeeping supervisor was fired, and his dismissal upheld, because he harassed at least three woman employees. He put his arm around one woman's waist, smacked his lips and commented on the attractiveness of another, and "undressed another with his eyes." The arbitrators upheld his dismissal because the harassment created stress and anxiety in the victims, affecting their mental health and impairing their job performance.

Arbitration could be the *only* method of redress available if the harassment is committed by a fellow-employee (not a supervisor), if the victim lives and works in a jurisdiction that will blame an employer only for sexual harassment committed by supervisors. If the victim is a union member and the harasser isn't (or if he belongs to a different union), she can probably count on her union's unhesitating support, but if both are union members, she may find that the union sides with the man.

• Courts are split as to whether a victim of sexual harassment has to go through arbitration first. A 1981 case from the Missouri District Court says yes, but a 1983 Georgia District Court case disagrees.

• Remember that sexual harassment comes under Title VII, so the entire Title VII song and dance is required. Note that, because Title VII defines the responsibilities of "employers," the victim has to sue the employer—*not* the supervisor or co-worker who harassed her.

• The court hearing a Title VII sexual harassment claim can exert "pendent jurisdiction" over state claims. (See page 66.)

• The state claims could include assault and battery, negligent infliction of emotional distress, intentional infliction of emotional distress, and intentional interference with the victim's employment relationship with her employer. Very few rank-and-file employees have formal employment contracts. They're "at-will" employees, which means that the employer has a basic right to fire them at will, for any reason or no reason. However, even an at-will employee can have a case if she's fired in bad faith, maliciously, or in retaliation for exercising her legal rights—for example, if she is fired for refusing to have sexual relations with her foreman.

• If the harassment includes physical touching instead of or in addition to verbal harassment and requests (or demands) for sexual favors, the employee can probably sue the perpetrator in state court for assault and/or battery. As Title VII and state fair employment laws don't cover assault and battery, the victim can go straight to court without engaging the machinery for sex-discrimination cases.

• Only five states (Connecticut, Illinois, Michigan, Minnesota, Wisconsin) have specific laws against sexual harassment, but the state fair employment practices laws that parallel Title VII have been used against sexual harassment in much the same way as Title VII has.

• If working conditions are so bad that the employee feels she can't continue working there, she may have a Title VII or a state fair employment practices law case based on constructive discharge. For example, sexual harassment by touching that is severe enough to constitute constructive discharge violates New York's Human Rights Law, even if the employee isn't threatened with being fired for non-compliance.

• What if an employee who claims constructive discharge applies for unemployment benefits—can her claim be turned down as a "voluntary quit"? *Caldwell v. Hodgeman* says no: the claims examiner must consider the "historical and continuing circumstances making up her work environment" and must determine whether the employee's perceptions about her job were reasonable or not. And, by the way, if a supervisor who commits harassment is fired for his conduct, he can't collect unemployment benefits.

• Harassment victims who work for state agencies have an extra weapon: they can sue, charging a conspiracy to deprive them of their civil rights under color of law (42 U.S.C.S. §1985(3)). This option isn't available to women employed by private employers. This statute is one of the Civil War Civil Rights Acts passed to punish official misconduct against freed slaves—but it can also be used for this limited purpose.

THE SMOKING GUN

Different cases have defined the prima facie case for sexual harassment differently; there are some elements that a sexual harassment plaintiff may *have* to prove so her case won't be dismissed, or *may* prove to strengthen her case:

• She belongs to a protected group (she's a woman).

• Compliance with unwelcome sexual advances was demanded so she could get a job or a raise, keep her job, get promoted, or otherwise benefit by employment.

• A man would not have been subjected to the same demands.

• She had at least the minimum qualifications for the job, promotion, or whatever.

• The working environment was "tainted" by sexual harassment so that it became hostile and/or unwholesome.

• The harassment had a negative effect on her job performance and/or physical, mental, or emotional health; it will probably be necessary to show that harassment was sustained, not an isolated incident or a few sporadic instances.

• A facially valid policy was applied in a discriminatory manner: for example, the rules forbid employees to punch time-cards for other employees who leave early—but the only employee to be disciplined had rejected a pass from her foreman a week earlier.

Or, if the employer cites some misconduct by the employee as a defense, claiming that the demotion, denial of promotion, or dismissal was the employee's fault, the employee can show that this is a pretext by proving that other employees weren't disciplined for the same conduct. The employer's personnel records can be subpoenaed to get this information.

• Courts find it hard to believe that a long-term employee with a good record could be fired for a minor infraction and tend to be receptive to an argument that retaliation was the real motive.

• Personnel records can be used to rebut a defense that the employee was disciplined for bad work, lateness, low productivity, etc.—does the record indicate anything like that? If it does, were the entries made after the fact to make the employer look good? Even if the entries are legitimate, why wasn't the employee warned and given a chance to improve her performance?

• It looks especially bad for the employer if the employee was promoted not too long before the retaliatory action, or if the personnel record shows favorable appraisals from supervisors who weren't involved in harassment.

• The shorter the time between the propositions and the firing (or other adverse action), the stronger the inference that one was a result of the other.

• An especially creative defense attorney sent interrogatories to a sexual harassment plaintiff calling for a listing of every sexual partner she had had in the preceding ten years. The District Court for the Northern District of California made it clear that employers have no right to ask questions like that. Rape shield statutes (see pages 133–134) exist so that rape victims don't have to suffer further from prurient (and irrelevant) inquiries into their sexual lives. And neither do sexual harassment victims.

REMEDIES

In a regular Title VII sexual harassment case, the usual Title VII remedies are available: e.g., injunctions against further harassment or back pay. *Kyriazi v. Western Electric Co.* says back pay should be computed based on the compensation of a comparable male worker, making allowances for his poor work record and for the promotion Kyriazi would probably have received if there had been no harassment. The New Jersey District Court also awarded her punitive damages of $1500 from each of the co-workers who harassed her and the supervisors who knew about the conduct but did nothing to help her. The court also forbade the Western Electric Company to reimburse the harassers for the damages; they had to pay out of their own pockets. This is satisfying, but unusual.

However, if an employee resigns because of sexual harassment, and a penitent employer offers her reinstatement at the same job level in another location, the employee refuses at her own peril. Turning down the employer's offer makes her ineligible for reinstatement or back pay for the time between the offer and the trial.

Pendent state claims are not limited to amounts available under Title VII, so the plaintiff may be able to collect some *real* money. If the state claim is basically a contract claim (e.g., that the employer broke its implied employment contract), a winning plaintiff is limited to compensatory damages. Compensatory damages might include job counseling costs, employment agency fees, therapy fees and other expenses the plaintiff encountered because of the defendant's wrongdoing. If the plaintiff wins

on a tort claim (a civil case for damages, such as battery, wrongful discharge, intentional infliction of mental distress) she may be able to get
punitive damages as well as compensatory damages. Punitive damages,
as the name suggests, are great sums of money designed to punish the
culprit by giving it a swift enough kick in the wallet to deter future wrongdoing. For example, the case of *Shaffer v. National Can Corp.*, 565 F.Supp.
909 (D. Pa. 1983), finds that a supervisor's attempts to extort sexual compliance from an employee, and retaliation against her when the attempts
failed, were outrageous enough to support a claim for intentional infliction
of emotional distress.

4

NON-EMPLOYMENT DISCRIMINATION

In the universe (well, to be more accurate, the solar system) of sex discrimination, discrimination in employment is the sun. Because the absence of a job, or the absence of a decent salary, has such a profound impact on a woman's or family's ability to survive, a great many employment discrimination cases have been litigated. The rules of law are complex, but some sort of sense can be made out of them because there is a central body of federal law (Title VII) and many related state laws.

The "planets" are other issues of sex discrimination. In line with the metaphor I'll be discussing nine areas: state Equal Rights Acts; the Equal Credit Opportunity Act and credit discrimination in education; sex discrimination in education; legal issues affecting lesbians; jury and grand jury service; sex-segregated insurance rates; surnames; clubs; and miscellaneous issues.

Sandra Lukacz married David Rubinek in 1972; they had two children, Rachel and Mark. The couple was divorced in 1979, and, under the name of Sandra Lukacz, she became fairly well known as a poet (as well known as poets get). She continued to use the Visa card she had gotten under the name of Sandra Rubinek, and in fact never mentioned her divorce; she continued making the payments as she always had, from her personal checking account. Now Lukacz and the man she lives with, Andrew Bailey, are considering marriage—but should she adopt his name? use a hyphenated surname? should they both use a hyphenated name? If he adopts Rachel and Mark Rubinek, should their names be changed? What if Sandra and Andrew have a child? Who, if anyone, should be notified of the marriage and whatever name she adopts?

AN ERA DETOUR

Okay, in law there are no quick fixes and no panaceas, but an Equal Rights Amendment at the federal level would make women's rights litigation easier, and legal analysis a whole lot easier. Women's rights litigation (and, more important, victory) can be achieved by using a patchwork of laws, and by making analyses of constitutional law that are more or less far-fetched. An ERA demonstrates a federal or state commitment to sexual equality and provides a basis for condemning sex discrimination that isn't reached by other laws.

The proposed federal Equal Rights Amendment, and most of enacted state ERAs, are quite mild when you consider their sulfurous reputation: they simply state that equality of rights under the law isn't to be denied on account of sex. (Seventeen states have ERAs; most include this language, some express the commitment to equality a little differently.) It should be of interest to Freudians to consider how much discussion of the ERA involves bathrooms. A federal ERA would desegregate public toilets only to the extent that any legislature or court would believe that anyone has a legal right to use the john of his or her choice. It is possible, though not very likely, that a federal ERA would legalize marriage between two women or two men. This has not been the case in any state with a state ERA, and gay rights activists have been citing women's rights precedents for years, with only moderate success. It's fairly clear that a ban on sex discrimination permits discrimination based on sexual *preference;* it would take either a comprehensive gay-rights amendment or amendments to state domestic relations laws to legalize homosexual marriages. (Fat chance.)

The other popular specter is conscription of women. First of all, nobody is being conscripted in the United States at the moment. Second, even if a hypothetical draft law is passed after a hypothetical federal ERA, it's by no means clear that the ERA has anything to do with combat service. Men might, not unreasonably, claim that *their* equal rights included the right to have a woman soldier at the front in their place. But this argument was raised before many courts by opponents of the former draft law; the courts were unanimously unimpressed. Women have served in the American military for many years in non-combat roles, and it would certainly be physically possible for women to serve as combat soldiers. Israeli, Arab, Irish, and German women have proved themselves as effective terrorists or soldiers in more formal combat; and a well-nourished American woman is physically more formidable than your average Laotian or Salvadoran male.

Some feminists say that it's unfair for women to be drafted, because we shouldn't be asked to risk our lives defending a country in which we're second-class citizens. That argument won't wash, since even in a conscript army members of the privileged class can usually finagle exemptions. In a volunteer army, most of those who sign up are so disadvantaged that military life (and possible military death) seems to be the best option open to them.

To sum up, Equal Rights Amendments smash neither sexism nor the

American Way of Life. They are an excellent riposte to those who are guilty of admittedly discriminatory practices and ask what the victim is going to do about it. Several of the sex-discrimination-in-education cases discussed on pages 92–97 were decided under state ERAs. Maybe the plaintiff would have been able to advance another argument that would have been convincing to the judges, but the state ERA made it easy for the judges to rule in their favor. State ERAs have also been used by men to challenge rape, child support, and prostitution statutes that are not gender-neutral: typical, just typical.

ECOA

One of the classics of discrimination—Sexism's Greatest Hits, so to speak— is credit discrimination: refusing outright to lend or grant a mortgage, charge account, or credit card to women, or to married women, or to widows or divorcees; or refusing to consider a married woman's income when a couple applies for credit. There were various justifications for the practice: that women were too flighty to pay bills in a world in which new hats were available, or that a married woman's salary was just pin money (an accurate expression of the amount, in many cases), or that she would just get pregnant and quit work, so her income wasn't reliable. The last gave loan officers a chance to ask total strangers about their sexual and contraceptive practices: a little fringe benefit in the otherwise gray and impersonal world of banking.

Life has been much less fun for credit grantors since the passage of the Equal Credit Opportunity Act, which makes it illegal for a grantor of credit to discriminate on the basis of sex or marital status in any aspect of a credit transaction. ECOA applies to mortgages, personal loans, cash advances, credit cards, sales of merchandise on credit, and consumer leases (e.g., automobile leases).

The implementing regulation, Regulation B, says that a creditor isn't allowed to take "adverse action" based on sex or marital-status discrimination. "Adverse action" means a refusal to grant credit in an amount and on terms reasonably close to those requested by the credit applicant; to terminate an account or change its terms unfavorably (unless, of course, the terms of *everyone's* accounts are changed unfavorably) or to refuse to add to a line of credit after a proper application has been made.

The focus of ECOA and Regulation B is to make sure that creditors examine an applicant's creditworthiness (that is, her ability to repay her debts, willingness to do so, and past history for repaying her debts or otherwise). Married women must be permitted to apply for credit without their husbands, and the woman's own income must be used to assess her creditworthiness. If a woman credit applicant works part-time, the creditor can't exclude that income from consideration or discount it, but can consider the amount of income and the probability that it will continue. All credit applicants must be told that they have the choice of reporting—or not reporting—alimony and child support as part of the income to be considered in granting or denying credit. If they do report this income, the creditor must treat the amounts as income "to the extent that they are likely to be consistently made"—in other words, fat chance. Creditors are not allowed to assume that women will or won't have children, or will or won't stop working if they do. Creditors *are* allowed to ask about the number and ages of an applicant's dependents (as long as *all* applicants, not just women or married women, are asked) but are *not* allowed to ask about an applicant's fertility, plans to have children, or birth-control practices. If a woman has or has had credit that she and her husband both used, or that she was legally responsible for, the creditor must consider these accounts in deciding whether the applicant is creditworthy. (This is tough luck for her if her husband is a consistent deadbeat.)

If a woman has a credit card or line of credit, and if there is no evidence that she is unwilling or unable to pay, the creditor isn't allowed to close the account, change its terms, or require a reapplication just because the woman's name or marital status has changed. However, if the account was granted because of her spouse's income at a time when her income by itself would not justify that amount of credit, the creditor can require her to apply again. But, as *Miller v. American Express* makes clear, the creditor can't maintain a policy of terminating credit automatically when a woman's marital status changes; after all, it's more than possible that the woman will have enough income to support an independent credit account. The plaintiff in this case was a recent widow who found that the American Express version of a condolence card was automatic termination (without notice) of her supplementary credit card because her husband, the primary cardholder, had died. The automatic termination violated ECOA, although American Express could have required a new application in order to see if her own income and assets were sufficient.

If the extension of credit involves collateral, or if a credit applicant cites the amount of property she owns to establish creditworthiness, a creditor isn't guilty of discrimination if it consults state property law or requires the signature of the applicant's husband (or any other person who has an interest in the property). Various states have varying laws about a creditor's rights to repossess or sell a married couple's joint property because of a debt only one spouse owes; creditors don't want to be left holding the bag in this situation. In a community-property state, the creditor can require the signature of the applicant's husband if the applicant doesn't have enough separate (non-community) property to entitle her to credit, or if her interest in the community property isn't great enough.

If a woman is applying for an individual account that isn't secured by collateral, the creditor can't even ask if she is married (unless she lives in a community-property state). Otherwise, the creditor can ask if she's "married," "unmarried" (a category including never-married women, divorcees, and widows) or "separated."

If the account or loan is a joint account, or can be used by both the applicant and her spouse, it's only reasonable that the creditor be allowed to ask questions about the husband, and to consider his creditworthiness as a factor in granting or denying the application. The creditor can also ask about the applicant's husband or ex-husband if the applicant chooses to include alimony or child support in the income considered, or if community property is a factor in the application.

It's very clear that individuals whose rights under the ECOA are violated can bring private suits against the malefactors. The statute provides for both actual damages (monetary harm suffered, plus, perhaps, embarrassment and harm to reputation for creditworthiness) and punitive damages (but probably only in really crass cases). In an individual suit, the maximum amount of punitive damages that can be awarded is $10,000; in a class action, the maximum is the smaller of $500,000 or 1 percent of the creditor's net worth. At least theoretically, plaintiffs who prevail can get punitive damages even if they have no actual damages and can get attorneys' fees (all prevailing plaintiffs can) even if all they get is a declaration that the practice was discriminatory and an injunction against continuation of the practice.

There have not been too many reported court cases on the ECOA (the FTC has had some success getting discriminatory creditors to agree to mend their ways); the trend seems to be to apply "disparate impact analysis" (see page 24); that is, a creditor can get in trouble if its practices have the effect of discriminating against woman credit applicants, even if the practices seem to be neutral on the face. For instance, the borrower in *Anderson v. United Finance Co.*, 666 F2d 1274 (9th Cir. 1982), met the creditors' standard of creditworthiness; the loan was based on her income and credit record, and her husband was disabled and on Welfare, but the finance company insisted on getting her husband's signature on the loan papers. (Sometimes one almost has to admire such ideology in the face of reality.) The Ninth Circuit pointed out that this was, indeed, discrimination as defined by the Equal Credit Opportunity Act, not the "technical violation" the lender said it was.

An engaged couple stated a claim under the ECOA in *Markham v. Colonial Mortgage Service Ass'n Inc.*: the mortgage company refused to consider both their incomes when they applied for a mortgage on the house they planned to live in after they were married. (Company policy called for consideration of both incomes in a two-earner married couple.) The D.C. Circuit said that this was marital status discrimination, and remanded the case to see if they were otherwise qualified for the mortgage.

TITLE IX AND DISCRIMINATION IN EDUCATION

Given the information that Title IX is the federal law forbidding sex discrimination in federally funded education programs, it would be logical
to conclude that it comes shortly after Title VII. It would be logical, but
wrong: Title VII is Title VII of the Civil Rights Act of 1964; Title IX is
Title IX of the Education Amendments of 1972.

The crucial part of Title IX (found at 20 U.S.C.S. §1681) says:

> No person in the United States shall, on the basis of sex, be excluded
> from participation in, be denied the benefits of, or be subjected to
> discrimination under any education program or activity receiving fed-
> eral financial assistance.

Title IX is all stick, no carrot: the federal government is supposed to cut
off funds to discriminatory programs, and all applications for federal funds
must be drafted to include assurances that the recipient won't indulge in
sex discrimination.

Of course there are regulations—it follows as the night the day—the
Regs are at 34 C.F.R. Part 106. They provide, among other things, that:

- "Federal financial assistance" includes federal grants or loans for construction purposes or for scholarships; student loans; grants or bargain-
  priced sales or federal property; and the services of federal personnel.
- Religious institutions are exempt, to the extent that religious tenets
  require sexual segregation; military institutions are also exempt (though,
  as a matter of policy, or perhaps PR, the service academies are co-
  ed), as are tax-exempt sororities and fraternities. (As we'll see below,
  private clubs get a real sweet deal.)
- Athletic programs must provide "equality of opportunity" for both
  sexes, though not necessarily equal funds for men's and women's
  athletics—much more of this below.
- "Any public institution of undergraduate higher education which traditionally and continually from its establishment has had a policy of
  admitting only students of one sex" is permitted to continue this
  policy. However, yet another reverse-bias suit, *Mississippi University
  for Women v. Hogan*, 102 S.Ct. 3331 (1982), found that excluding an
  otherwise qualified man from a state-funded nursing school (founded,
  as the name indicates, as a woman's college) violated the Fourteenth
  Amendment's guarantee of equal protection, and was therefore illegal;
  the court said that the Title IX exemption for single-sex colleges could
  not survive an Equal Protection challenge—which more or less says
  that Congress enacted a useless law, just for laughs.

At the high-school level, the situation may be different, at least for states with ERAs. Restricting admission to boys at an elite public high school was condemned, even though there was an allegedly separate-but-equal school for girls, because the boys' school had much better faculty and facilities.

As usual, these alleged explanations raise at least as many questions as they resolve. Perhaps the most important question got a tentative answer in February 1984 when the Supreme Court decided *Grove City College v. Bell*. The question is how specific Title IX is: that is, does the receipt of *any* federal aid require compliance with the anti-discrimination standards, or is Title IX "program-specific" (that is, applicable only to programs receiving federal funds)? The Supreme Court plumped for the latter position. I say that this is a tentative answer, because the decision was an extremely controversial one, greeted with much wailing and gnashing of teeth; and much legislation has been proposed to alter the result.

Although I hate to agree with arch-conservatives about anything (including the value of regular dental checkups) I think the decision was right, at least on the specific facts presented and the way Title IX is designed. (I'd prefer a comprehensive law against sex discrimination, but that's another question.) Grove City College did not want to be bound by Title IX and therefore did not apply for any federal financial assistance. (As they say in other contexts, if you can't do the time, don't do the crime.) However, some of the students got direct federal grants—Basic Educational Opportunity Grants, or BEOGs. The Supreme Court said that this federal financial aid triggered Title IX—but only as to the financial aid program. The financial aid program, in this interpretation, was required to be non-discriminatory; the rest of the school wasn't. If you ask me, it's a matter of supreme indifference to a school if its students pay their tuition by obtaining BEOGs, asking Daddy, clipping coupons, or knocking over gas stations. As Grove City College was willing to suffer the consequences of noncompliance—and in fact did everything in its power to avoid receiving federal money—I think it should be permitted to carry out its "conscientious objection" to Title IX.

Whether or not corrective legislation is passed, at least two circuits will probably find ways to distinguish *Grove City College*. This prediction is based on earlier cases they decided. The Third Circuit held that an intercollegiate athletic program was covered by Title IX because the university as a whole got federal money, even though the money wasn't earmarked for athletics. (Even those who agree with *Grove City College* might reach this conclusion; the endless athletic Regs show a strong government concern with athletic opportunity for women.) In 1983, the Fifth Circuit approved a cut-off of federal funds to all activities, not just student societies, because an all-male honor society's discriminatory activities "infect[ed] the entire academic mission of the university."

Whatever action is taken, it will probably have to be taken at the school level. Title IX punishes schools for discrimination by withdrawing their federal funds; it doesn't recompense *victims* of discrimination in education by providing damages for them. So a woman who is denied entrance to a school for discriminatory reasons doesn't have a right to sue the school for damages. But a school *employee* who suffers discrimination (for example, a woman athletic coach) can sue under Title IX; she also has a Title VII case if her pay is disproportionate to the pay of male coaches. But she can probably forget the Equal Pay Act, as coaching women's teams is considered different enough from coaching men's teams to rule out a claim for equal pay.

Clearly, a college can't restrict its *own* scholarship program to one sex or impose discriminatory criteria on scholarship applications. What about a private scholarship fund "for deserving young men"? Can a college or school district administer such a fund? The question came up twice in New York courts in 1983, and got two different answers. The Court of Appeals, New York's highest court, said that, although it would clearly be discriminatory (and illegal) state action for the school district to administer a single-sex scholarship fund, it would be all right for the school district to step aside and let private trustees administer it. A few months earlier, an intermediate appeals court handling the same case had ruled that the school district would violate the Equal Protection clause of the Fourteenth Amendment by acting as trustee of a scholarship fund restricted to young men. But instead of rewriting the will to provide a private trustee, they rewrote it to provide scholarships for deserving *students* (female as well as male).

The aspect of discrimination in education that has caused the most carrying-on must be athletics. The Title IX regulations say that interscholastic and intramural athletics must provide "equal athletic opportunity" for both sexes but hasten to add that "unequal aggregate expenditures for members of each sex or unequal expenditures for male and female teams" are not necessarily violations of Title IX. After all, if students—and especially alumni—were afraid that women's sports would get anything close to the support of Big Ten football or basketball, they'd tear down more than the goalposts; they'd tear down the whole school.

The factors in deciding whether the sexes have equal athletic opportunity include:

- Whether the available sports, teams, and competitive opportunities are suited to the interests and abilities of both sexes.
- The availability—and pay level—of coaches.
- Scheduling of, and facilities provided for, games and practice.

- Availability of housing, academic tutoring, and medical treatment for team members.
- Publicity for the teams.

An educational institution is allowed to maintain separate men's and women's teams if the sport is a contact sport, or if "making the team" is competitive rather than open to anyone who bothers who show up. If there's only one team, for one sex, and "athletic opportunities for members of the excluded sex have previously been limited" (in other words, if there's a men's but no women's team), women must be allowed to try out for the team—unless it's a contact sport. (Contact sports are defined as boxing, wrestling, rugby, ice hockey, football, basketball, and "other sports the purpose or major activity of which involves bodily contact.")

Whether conforming to ideology or reality, these guidelines allow schools to reserve almost all their athletic budgets for men's teams—as long as there are women's teams or co-ed teams for the (rather small) number of women who are willing to make a fuss about going out for a team, and as long as the women's or co-ed teams get some kind of budget, some equipment, and some coaching. Notice that equality of athletic scholarships isn't required: the millennium has not yet arrived. Neither is any particular balance between team and individual sports, or activities that are suited to a physical elite of young men in prime condition, rather than lifetime sports for the uncoordinated majority.

The issue of separate women's teams versus co-ed teams is a lot like the issue of sex-segregated versus unisex insurance: that is, whether to disadvantage the group for the sake of certain individuals, or disadvantage the individuals for the sake of the group. As sports are created and defined by male norms, most adolescent and adult males are better athletes than most adolescent and adult females (though it's certainly not true that *every* male is a better athlete than *every* female). So if it's necessary to try out for a team, most or all of the places on a co-ed team will go to males. Is the establishment of female teams ghettoization and denial of opportunity for superior female athletes who can make the team or an opportunity for female athletes with less talent, or less training, to achieve? Some courts, interpreting Title IX, the Equal Protection Clause, or the state ERAs, take one view; some take the other. (Since pre-pubertal girls tend to be larger and more mature than boys of the same age, they would be apt to snag all the places on co-ed Little League teams; to prevent this affront to the immature male ego—if this isn't a pleonasm—the argument raised is usually whether girls can play co-ed sports safely.)

- In 1982, an Illinois District Court permitted separate girls' and boys' basketball teams even though the plaintiff was a good enough basketball player to play on the boys' team. The court's rationale was that separate teams maximize athletic participation for average girls, who aren't good enough to be starters.

• But the next year, a Missouri District Court invalidated a rule of a high school athletic association that forbade mixed-sex teams and prevented a thirteen-year-old girl from trying out for a place on a football team for which she was, admittedly, qualified. The court found state action—and therefore a violation of Title IX—in the rules, and found that the violation would be excusable only on a showing that *all* boys, but *no* girls, could play football safely. Because there was no girls' football team, the court did not reach the question of whether an unusually talented girl could be restricted to the girls' team if the standard of play on the boys' team was higher.

• New York upheld a similar policy that excluded *boys* from girls' volleyball teams, on the theory that restricting girls' teams to girls was a way to redress earlier discrimination against female athletes.

Other types of legal analysis come into play (sorry):

• In Washington—an ERA state—it has been held that denying qualified girls the opportunity to play school football violates the ERA.

• A similar decision has been reached in Pennsylvania about a state interscholastic association bylaw that forbade girls to practice with, or play against, boys' teams.

• Another ERA state, Massachusetts, has struck down a proposed bill that would forbid co-ed football and wrestling teams, and a rule keeping boys from joining girls' athletic teams. In both cases, the standard was whether the ban served a compelling state interest, and no such interest was demonstrated.

• Equal-protection arguments were used in two recent cases: one found that separate girls' and boys' basketball leagues violated the Equal Protection clause even if the two leagues got the same facilities, funding, and coaching; and allowing two girls on each boys' team (and vice versa) wasn't good enough. The other case did not find an equal-protection violation in scheduling boys' tennis in the spring, girls' tennis in the fall (or vice versa) because the available facilities required "rationing," and one season was no better than the other.

Teachers and coaches sometimes bring Title IX or sex discrimination actions; and they can recover from a teachers' union that settles for grossly insufficient salaries for female coaches, as well as from the school district offering the unfair terms. But they're likely to lose the case if the female coaches' lower salary is based on the general inadequacy of the sports program for girls. If boys' teams get better facilities, more money, and more coaching, then male coaches of boys' teams are entitled to higher pay than female coaches of girls' teams, simply because they do more work. The situation is a lot like that of a workplace where all the workers who have seniority—and legitimate expectations based on seniority—are white males, because five or ten years ago only white males were hired. In that situation, too, past discrimination is reflected in the present state of affairs.

CLUBS WITH CLOUT

Part of the attraction that business and professional women find in exclusive clubs is simply that these clubs historically have barred women. As Tom Sawyer found out when he whitewashed the fence, people are apt to want to do whatever they're told they can't. Part of it's self-image: women believe that they're entitled to the rewards of success, including membership in prestigious clubs. Part of it's pragmatic: if corporate honchos promote their golf partners, and if multimillion-dollar deals are closed over martinis at the Plutocrats' Clubs, women want access to these opportunities. Women's networking groups take up some of the slack, but the powerless networking with the powerless is the baby-boom version of the blind leading the blind.

Private clubs get several kinds of favorable treatment from the legal system. First, clubs are usually organized as §501(c)(7) organizations (organized under §501(c)(7) of the Internal Revenue Code)—that is, they are considered non-commercial, non-profit organizations exempt from paying federal tax. Code §501(f) denies the tax exemption to clubs whose charters provide for racial discrimination, or most forms of religious discrimination—but sex discrimination, taken by itself, won't preclude tax-exempt status. It isn't uncommon for business to pay—and take as business deductions—their executives' dues at these clubs. If the club won't accept women as members, only male executives qualify for this little perk. This adds insult to injury for women executives, who not only lose out on a fringe benefit but can't make business contacts at the club.

Private clubs are also exempt from having to comply with Title VII in their hiring practices, so they can blithely restrict hiring, training, and promotion to any groups they wish to favor.

For tax purposes, the most important question is whether the purported club really is a not-for-profit association of like-minded individuals rather than a business operated to make a profit: businesses don't get a tax exemption. For civil rights purposes, the question is whether the club is a private club or a "place of public accommodation."

The Civil Rights Act of 1964 forbids segregation on the grounds of race, religion, or nationality in all places of public accommodation. This side of a federal ERA, it does *not* bar sex discrimination in public accommodations. On the other hand, thirty-two states have civil rights laws that forbid sex discrimination in "business establishments" or "places of public accommodation" (the language varies a bit); and in these states, the case law about racial segregation is useful in sorting out what is—or isn't—a private club. Groups trying to end racial segregation have had fair success in getting the tax exemptions of segregated clubs removed. The theory is that, to be a legitimate private club, an organization must exercise some degree of selectivity: it can't admit any Caucasian who applies but no blacks and still hope to hang on to its exempt status. Tax-exempt status also requires a real restriction of facilities: a country club can't be both racially segregated and tax-exempt if it offers its restaurants, bars, or other amenities to the public. (Because restaurants and bars are clearly public accommodations, it's illegal to segregate them; or, in those thirty-two states, to commit sex discrimination.)

We have yet another balancing test here: between the "right of association" that individuals have to choose their own preferred companions, and the right of individuals to carry out lawful activities in the place of their choice, whether other people carrying out their lawful activities approve of the first bunch or not. After all, the nominal reason for segregation laws is the discomfort caused to whites by the sight of non-whites in restaurants or the front of the bus. At least as viewed from the left, there *is* a distinction between the favored group's exclusion of the disfavored group, and the disfavored group's attempt to join and express solidarity (or laugh at the favored group). I think that it should be illegal for men to keep women out of business-related clubs, but not for a women's consciousness-raising group to exclude the inevitable man who wants to join the group to discuss the burdens machismo has placed on him, how mean his mother was to him, and how mean his ex-wife was to him.

New York ruled that a nonprofit organization whose objective was to promote safety and skill in boating could not restrict its membership to men: the organization was a public accommodation, not a private club. There were no selection standards: any man who passed a boating test could join. This lack of selectivity impelled the court to decide that membership should be open to *anyone* who passed the boating test and wanted to join.

The California civil-rights law is phrased differently, and forbids discrimination in "all business establishments of every kind whatsoever." California's highest court ruled that the Boy's Club isn't a business (whether or not it's a place of public accommodation) and therefore need not become the Boy's and Girl's Club if it doesn't want to.

A man belonging to a Connecticut club whose purpose, according to its corporate charter, was "to provide facilities for the serving of luncheon or other meals to members" sued the club, seeking declaratory and injunctive relief against the club's refusal to admit women as members or guests. The Superior Court held that the club had exceeded its legal authority as a corporation, because admitting women would not interfere with the corporate purpose. However, the court refused to order the club to admit a woman candidate proposed by the plaintiff—the particular woman wasn't a party to the action. You did not say "may I." You may not take two umbrella steps.

The Jaycees (new name of the Junior Chamber of Commerce) was a perfect test case, because it's so clearly a business-related organization. Its nominal objective was to provide business training and contacts for young *men*. The central organization firmly insisted that voting membership be restricted to men, although there were schismatic Jaycees chapters with woman members and woman officers. The central organization was sued in lower courts several times, with varying results. Massachusetts and Alaska state courts found that the Jaycees organization wasn't a place of public accommodation. A Minnesota District Court disagreed, holding that the Jaycees made its "goods and services" available to the public, and therefore was a place of public accommodation. The Eighth Circuit reversed, finding the members' right of association (or, in this case, right *not* to associate) superior to the state's interest in eliminating discrimination. The Supreme Court reversed again (*Roberts v. U.S. Jaycees*, 52 LW 5076 (1984)). The Court found the activities of the Jaycees organization were, in fact, matters of public accommodation. The chapters were neither small nor selective, and non-members participated in chapter activities without impairing the organization's effectiveness. The Supreme Court held that Minnesota acted properly, protecting its compelling state interest in ending discrimination by acting in the least restrictive manner.

As for the traditional, male-only "social" club, where some of the gentlemen filling the leather chairs are habitués and some are sons of habitués, there are several modes of attack:

• It is at least arguable that an employer violates Title VII and the Equal Pay Act by paying club dues for the male executives while not providing this benefit for their female counterparts.

• If the claim is that women's right to equal protection of the law under the Fourteenth Amendment has been violated, state action must be shown. There are three ways to do this: by showing that the "private club" performs a normal governmental function (e.g., taking care of a public park); showing that the government is significantly involved—by issuing licenses and providing a tax exemption, for instance; and by showing that state courts enforce discriminatory provisions such as restrictive covenants imposed by a homeowners' association.

• State action isn't necessarily involved because the club has a liquor license, but some courts will add up the instances of state action and make an overall finding of involvement.

• A liquor license, or license renewal, can be denied if granting it would be "contrary to the common good and public policy." Especially in an ERA state or a state with laws forbidding sex discrimination in public accommodations, feminists can appear at public hearings and argue against the club's application. Hearing dates can come from sympathetic clerks at the appropriate agencies, or by eagle-eyed scanning of those teensy-type Public Notices in newspapers.

• A state or locality can deny property tax exemptions to discriminatory clubs: Maryland did this to President Eisenhower's old haunt, the Burning Tree Club.

• One state, some cities, and many organizations and corporations have policies forbidding paying dues to, or holding functions at, discriminatory clubs.

In the end, it will probably be economic pressure that changes club policies, not the sudden descent of peace on earth and good will to persons. Clubs that were established at a time when millionaires were plentiful and income tax trivial now depend on employer-paid dues to stay afloat. If employers, prompted by feminist managers, stockholders, and customers, stop paying dues until the policy changes, there'll be some changes made.

UNISEX INSURANCE

Theoretically, the insurance industry is based on actuarial ratings of the likelihood of certain events. That is, the price of an insurance policy depends on the likelihood of the insured event. The "law of large numbers" makes it possible to predict, with a fair degree of accuracy, how many people in a given population will die in a given year; how many auto accidents will occur; how many houses will burn or be burglarized. The insurer can make a good estimate of the *number* of claims that will be filed, but not *who* will file the claims (short of sponsoring assassination to make the figures come out even).

As a general rule, women live longer than men, have fewer automobile accidents, and suffer more illness and disability. Not coincidentally, unless the law requires unisex pricing, women pay lower life insurance premiums (if they have any life insurance at all—men as either real or perceived breadwinners are much more likely to carry life insurance than women), lower automobile insurance premiums and higher health and disability insurance premiums. Until the Supreme Court clamped down, it was common for women to be required to pay more for pension coverage, get smaller pension checks, or both. Before these decisions were announced, there was much prediction, second-guessing, whining, and screaming to the effect that requiring an end to pension discrimination would murder the free-enterprise system or at least the insurance industry. Both seem to have survived (though I wouldn't bet my life on the extent of compliance with the decisions) and, although the same moans reverberate, I expect that both would survive unisex insurance.

As Jeanette Blevins pointed out in the *Women's Rights Law Reporter*, many group life insurance plans use unisex rate tables, and many group annuity plans use sex-based tables—so women pay more in both circumstances. Many, many people have pointed out that, although black people have a lesser life expectancy than white people, no insurer would have the gall to suggest that they pay more for life insurance. (You can be sure no one has suggested paying them larger pensions, on the grounds that they are off the insurer's hands in a shorter time.) Some insurers do offer lower rates for nonsmokers, but they are unlikely to calibrate rates based on the amount the insured drinks, the frequency with which she exercises, the quantity of toxic chemicals pumped into her body at work, or her tendency to indulge in Haagen-Dazs or other recreational drugs. All of these are relevant factors, but too difficult (and expensive) to monitor as they fluctuate. Except for a small number of transsexuals, everyone can readily (and permanently) be characterized as either male or female; and people are very unlikely to lie about the category to which they belong. Gender is certainly the most cost-effective criterion that insurers can use that retains any connection to reality.

The problem of unisex insurance is the same as that of affirmative action or the Title IX athletics rules: whether the needs of the individual or the group will prevail. Either way, somebody loses. Insurance companies make calculations based on average women, but make payments to individual women. The insurance industry claims that sex-typing is necessary to the economic rationality of the insurance system.

However, even with a couple of centuries of experience, they don't seem to have gotten it quite right yet. Figures from the American Council of Life Insurance, National Association of Insurance Commissioners, and the New York State Department of Insurance indicate that women's auto insurance premiums are 60 percent of men's premiums—but women account for only 50 percent of insurers' costs; for term life insurance, the women's premiums are 72 percent of men's, but women absorb 84 percent of the industry's costs; in annuities, women's premiums are higher—109 percent of men's—but their claim on the industry is disproportionately higher (114 percent of payouts to men). Women overpay for major medical insurance (148 percent of male premiums; 131 percent of costs) but underpay for disability policies (144 percent versus 166 percent). These figures don't show the real dollar impact, because the percentage of women insureds isn't equal to the percentage of women in the population, or even the working population. Many life, health, and disability policies are employer-paid group policies, and many women have low-paid jobs that don't provide such benefits. Many women don't bother—or can't afford—to buy individual policies.

If the much-vaunted actuarial method worked perfectly, women's premiums would match insurers' experience. Feminists say that unisex insurance would decrease the amount women pay for insurance; if coupled with an anti-discrimination provision, it would also make insurance more available. (Although most states at least nominally forbid sex discrimination in insurance, the laws refer to outright refusals to insure, not rates set high enough to scare away potential insureds.) The insurance industry, no the other hand, says that women will have to pay much more for insurance if unisex policies become mandatory. It is of course possible, though it seems hard to believe, that the insurance companies have been giving women a free ride all these years. Several bills mandating unisex insurance premiums have been kicking around Congress for several years; the main difference between them is the extent to which they would make the price changes retroactive. Perhaps I'm being cynical, but I rate the chance of passage somewhere between slim and none.

The first state to require unisex insurance overall is Montana. Four states (Hawaii, Massachusetts, Michigan, and North Carolina) have statutes requiring unisex auto-insurance policies. (Because unisex rates are higher than women's rates, it's interesting that this is the first area of discrimination to be attacked—once again, the frail males are protected against the onslaughts of the Amazons.)

Pennsylvania's Insurance Commissioner used the state's ERA to invalidate sex-based auto insurance rates and was upheld by a state court; the Department also entered into a consent decree under which an insurer agreed to unisex disability premiums. Michigan requires unisex rates for homeowner's insurance. The IRS now uses unisex tables to decide how valuable a gift of a life interest is (the right to use a property, or receive its income, during one's lifetime) and how much gift tax is due.

Overall, this is an issue that won't go away. The more women land jobs with significant salaries and with benefits worth mentioning, the more employers will have to pay for pensions and group insurance. Depending on the way the numbers work out, employers will either become the strongest advocates or the most passionate opponents of unisex insurance rates; after all, they'll be footing much of the bill. The insurance industry, by definition, will get all the premiums, and I doubt very much if they'll lose money on the deal. Their real problem is the cost of changeover: calculating new tables, printing new rate schedules. It has often been predicted that this will cripple the insurance industry. But after all, the tables have to be updated regularly in any event, and computers have replaced pencil-and-paper calculations. Anyway, the cost of getting caught should have been accepted as a risk of doing business (insurers certainly should know something about risk). It's not as bad as expecting freed slaves to feel bad about the financial loss to their former masters, but the difference is one of degree, not kind.

SURNAMES

Under English common law (the system of "unwritten law" that provides the background and general principles for English—and much of American—law) people could call themselves anything they pleased, as long as the name had not been selected with fraudulent intent. That is, a woman who felt more like a Rosamond DuCharme than a Gertie Buggins could use the more euphonious name; but she couldn't sign checks as the Duchess of York, however more welcome the Duchess's signature might have been than her own. This is still pretty much the American rule.

Social customs dictate (and dictated to a much greater extent in the past) that it's important for every woman to marry—to find a man who would "give her his name." If a woman marries, her children are legitimate and carry their father's (or, at any rate, her husband's) surname. Traditionally, an unmarried woman's children could be given their father's surname only under carefully specified circumstances: if he acknowledged his paternity or if a court had ruled that he was the father, for instance. At one time it was accepted custom for a woman to surrender not only her birth surname but her first name (the climax of the Judy Garland–James Mason version of *A Star is Born* is Vicki Lester's big speech beginning, "This is Mrs. Norman Maine"), which had the effect of rendering all of a particular man's wives identity-less and interchangeable.

Gradually, the idea that a woman—even a married woman—might have an independently cognizable identity has begun to sink in. Some women sign themselves after marriage with their own first names and their husbands' surnames; others use two surnames: Helen Wilfred might marry Don Simms and become Helen Wilfred Simms, for example. (I don't have a middle name because my mother intended to facilitate this practice. I've never been married, and I'm in a lot of trouble when asked to provide my middle name or a three-initial monogram.) Other women prefer to retain their "maiden" name—a practice that dates back at least as far as nineteenth-century feminist Lucy Stone—or to use hyphenated names. Sometimes their husbands adopt the same hyphenated names. (This isn't exclusively a twentieth-century or exclusively a feminist practice: sometimes elitism prevails over sexism, and English families may be known as Whoozit-Whatever, or Spanish families as de Tal y Cual, to preserve the prestigious name of a well-connected foremother.)

Some couples want to give their children a hyphenated or invented surname, or give the mother's surname to some or all of the kids. The last is a real defiance of convention, which decrees that children carry their mother's birth surname only if no father will accept responsibility for them.

Traditionally, widows retain the name Mrs. John Whatchmacallit until and unless they become Mrs. Michael Whatzisname. When divorce was impossible or unthinkable, it wasn't necessary to develop a convention for the names of divorced women. By the 1920s, though, Emily Post found it necessary to tell her readers that divorcees use both surnames. (In Mary McCarthy's *The Group,* when the horrible Norine Schmittlapp divorced Putnam Blake she took to calling herself "Mrs. Schmittlapp Blake.") But Mrs. Post warned that a divorcee who resumed her maiden surname would be broadcasting that she was the guilty party.

In those pre-no-fault days, there *were* guilty parties in divorces. Today, it's not uncommon for divorced people to remarry, or for a new husband to seek to adopt the ex-husband's children, or for the combined family to apply for a name-change for the children who have a different surname.

The simplest thing is for a woman to keep using her birth surname after she's married and to hang on to her Social Security cards, credit cards, and bank account in that name. If she *does* take her husband's name, she must remember to notify the many, many computers that have her name on file. Though it's of course illegal for creditors to cancel a woman's account merely because she marries, there's no point in exposing them to temptation.

If a woman adopts her husband's surname and changes her mind, either for ideological reasons or because he's no longer her husband, everyone has to be notified *again* (creating another opportunity to lose the file). It shouldn't be strictly necessary for her to go to court for a name change, but the court order may be reassuring to the various officious busybodies.

• A number of courts have ruled that a woman isn't obligated to assume her husband's surname on marriage.

• Requiring a married employee to sign a change-of-name form to her husband's name violates Title VII.

• Married women must be allowed to register to vote under their birth surnames or any other name under which they are known and which isn't adopted for fraudulent purposes.

• Regulation B (the Equal Credit Opportunity Act regulation) says that creditors must allow women to open accounts using their birth surname, spouse's surname, or a combined surname.

• The IRS will graciously accept tax returns from married taxpayers filing jointly who use different surnames. However, it confuses the computer to change the order of the names (e.g., from "Denise Lawson and Paul Garland" to "Paul Garland and Denise Lawson") or to contradict the sticker supplied by the IRS and file so that the first name given doesn't correspond to the first Social Security number on the sticker.

• If a woman uses her birth surname throughout her working life, there's at least a fighting chance that her earnings will be reported to the Social Security Administration properly. If she adopts her husband's surname, or adopts it and changes later, she must file Social Security's Form OAAN-

7003 ("Request for Change in Social Security Records") and get a new Social Security card for each change of name.

A woman who has reached retirement age can collect benefits either as a retired worker or as her husband's dependent wife or widow (but not both); the choice depends on which yields a higher benefit, which in turn depends on her husband's average earnings as compared to hers. (Because the Social Security tax is highly regressive, a two-earner married couple will probably pay close to twice as much tax as a one-earner couple, but will receive nowhere near twice the benefits; and women who work for pay subsidize women who don't.) Even if a woman claims dependent's benefits when she has never used her husband's surname, her marriage certificate (and, if necessary, his death certificate) will establish her entitlement to benefits.

• Several state laws requiring children born in wedlock to be registered under their fathers' names have been found unconstitutional, either because they restrict the parents' privacy or because no state interest for the policy has been shown. Other states have case law allowing parents to decide the kid's surname.

• Changing an existing kid's name can be more difficult (for example, in the wake of a divorce or remarriage); courts have discretion to turn down the name-change application if they don't think it's in the child's best interests. Furthermore, unless the child's father has abandoned or abused the child, courts are reluctant to eliminate the symbolic tie between father and child.

ISSUES AFFECTING LESBIANS

Just as black women face discrimination both as blacks and as women, lesbians face discrimination both as homosexuals and as women. However, civil rights laws are designed to protect against racial discrimination to a much greater degree than they are to protect against discrimination based on sexual preference. It's fairly well settled that Title VII doesn't apply to discrimination on the basis of sexual preference or sexual orientation. Unless the victim of discrimination happens to live in a city with a local ordinance forbidding sexual-preference discrimination in employment (e.g., San Francisco; Aspen; Anchorage; Ann Arbor; Detroit; Washington, D.C.; Portland, Oregon), her legal options for challenging discrimination are few. There are some interesting employment cases, though:

• An early (1973) California case, *Society for Individual Rights, Inc. v. Hampton,* finds a violation of the Fifth Amendment's guarantee of due process in a federal agency's refusal to hire or continue to employ lesbians unless the agency can prove a connection between lesbianism and decreased efficiency as a civil servant.

• A Maryland case of the same year, *Acanford v. Board of Education*, finds due process and equal protection violations in firing a teacher *only* because of homosexuality, with no proof of unfitness or improper actions on the job.

• According to California's *Gay Law Students Association v. Pacific Tel. & Tel.*, employment discrimination by sexual preference isn't a violation of California's Fair Employment Practices Act, but the state Constitution guarantees equal protection of the law to all people, and therefore forbids arbitrary discrimination in employment by public utilities (e.g., the phone company). Homosexuals as a class can't be excluded from employment opportunity unless a showing can be made that homosexuality renders a person unfit for that particular job.

• A high school teacher dismissed under a statute proscribing "immorality" sued under 42 U.S.C.S. §1983 (deprivation of civil rights under color of law) after she was fired because it became known that she was a lesbian. The statute was declared unconstitutional both because it was vague (no standard was provided for determining who is immoral) and because it did not require that any connection be shown between the "immoral" behavior and fitness to teach. In 1985, the Supreme Court was scheduled to decide a related case: whether teachers can, Constitutionally, be fired for "advocating" homosexuality as distinct from same-sex sexual acts.

• The military services can discharge servicewomen and -men for homosexual *conduct* while they are in the service, but a lesbian Army reservist succeeded in getting a writ of mandamus compelling the Army to reinstate her after she had been discharged for "homosexual tendencies." The Eastern District of Wisconsin ruled that her right of privacy was invaded by a discharge for homosexual tendencies, desire, or interest with no proof of overt homosexual acts.

• The case of *Valdes v. Lumbermen's Mutual Casualty Co.* presents an interesting twist. The plaintiff says she wasn't a lesbian but was fired because her supervisor *thought* she was, and that sexual preference was a criterion for woman employees but not for male employees. In other words, she presented a case of sex-plus discrimination. We'll never know what the outcome would have been (the case was settled) but the Southern District of Florida suggested that the employer would have won if it could prove that it discriminated against *all* homosexuals, but the plaintiff would have won if she could show that the anti-homosexual policy was enforced only against women.

• A woman graduate student was hired as an instructor for a college course and had an affair with one of her female students. She was rehired by the university the next year, at the same salary, but as a non-teaching research assistant. She sued but lost; the Middle District of Louisiana said that the university's action was based on her unprofessional conduct, not her sexual preference; and since she *was* rehired and her salary wasn't cut, she suffered no injury. While I can see the court's point, I doubt very much whether the university maintained the same policy for male instructors who became sexually involved with female students—or that those cases came to anyone's attention.

Outside of the employment area, there are fewer theories of law to pin a case on. It *has* been ruled that housing discrimination on the basis of sexual preference violates California's Unruh Civil Rights Act. New York law allows a court to terminate alimony in certain cases if a woman is living with a man not her husband and holding herself out as his wife. The New York Supreme Court said that this does mean another *man:* an alimony payor can't get off the hook because his wife cohabits with a female lover.

Probably the legal issue that belongs most distinctly to lesbians is the custody issue. At one time, discovery of a woman's lesbianism might very well mean not only that she lost custody of her children, but that she would not be permitted to see them. Today, there's a long string of cases stating that lesbianism, by itself, doesn't equal unfitness for custody. It's by no means automatic that a lesbian (or heterosexual) mother will get custody of her children on divorce, but the decision will be based on the best interests of the child, and except in the most flagrant cases of unfitness, the parent who doesn't have custody will have judicial authorization to visit the child(ren).

JURIES

Serving on a state or federal grand jury (which investigates or decides whether indictments should be handed down) or petit jury (which makes findings of fact in civil or criminal cases) is a civil right, but it's also a major nuisance. No one likes to be told that she isn't fit to serve on a jury; but on the other hand, most people, weaned on a steady diet of *Perry Mason,* are unprepared to be shuffled around from room to room, wait endlessly to be rejected or seated, and if chosen to listen to hours of assorted nitwits driveling about ullage holes or revocation of acceptance. Jury service is very disruptive of normal life—the pay jurors receive won't even pay a baby-sitter; and, although employers aren't allowed to fire anyone for jury service, they don't like having employees vanish for unpredictable periods of time. So an effort to make sure that women can serve on juries seems a bit quixotic. The issue is usually raised from the other side: that is, convicted defendants appeal their convictions, saying that their right to a fair trial was violated because the jury that indicted or convicted them excluded women, didn't have a fair proportion of women, or didn't permit women to serve as forepersons.

It's clear that it's illegal for a state or the federal court system to *forbid* women from serving on juries at all:

> The systematic and intentional exclusion of women, like the exclusion of a racial group [citation omitted] deprives the jury system of the broad base it was designed by Congress to have in our democratic society. It is a departure from the statutory scheme. . . . The injury is not limited to the defendant—there is injury to the jury system, to the law as an institution, to the community at large, and to the democratic ideal reflected in the processes of our courts.

> If it was ever the case that women were unqualified to sit on juries, or were so situated that none of them should be required to perform jury service, that time has long since passed.

It isn't permissible for a state to select jurors from a panel designed to have twice as many men as women, either.

Federal and some state laws outlaw discrimination in jury selection. That is, otherwise qualified citizens can't be excluded from jury duty if they ask, or if they have child-care responsibilities.

• *Taylor v. Louisiana*, cited above, says that a jury system which, in effect, drafts male jurors but accepts female jurors only if they volunteer, is invalid.

• It's no good either if, before the pool of potential jurors is made up, women can opt out by answering a question that is a prominent part of the questionnaire sent to potential jurors, and if they are given a second chance to withdraw before the prospective jurors appear for selection. The Supreme Court said that this procedure violated defendants' right to be tried by juries that represent a fair cross section of the community, without exclusion of any identifiable groups in the community. The Court acknowledged that some women have child-care responsibilities precluding jury service, but this could be handled by providing exemptions for women in this situation, rather than by screening out women at the beginning.

• A state procedure that lets any woman opt out of jury service just by sending a notice to the jury commissioner deprived the petitioner of her right to a trial by a jury representing a fair cross section of the community, and was therefore invalid. You think *you* have problems: the petitioner had been sentenced to "two consecutive death sentences."

• Virginia and Georgia have upheld an automatic exemption from jury service for women who are responsible for the care of small children, but Florida found the system unconstitutional because it exempted *mothers* only, not all custodial parents.

• The cases cited above involved challenges to the jury selection system by defendants. *Porter v. Freeman* is a class action brought by black women challenging the racial and sexual composition of the local petit jury. They won: even though the jury commissioners had taken steps to remedy the underrepresentation of blacks and women, they were ordered to make up a new jury list, using current population figures and wider sources of names and addresses.

• Many states excuse lawyers from jury panels; if lawyers are not excused, it's quite unlikely that any *other* lawyer will pick them to hear any case. But California attorney Carolyn Bobb was called for jury duty. During the *voir dire* (the examination of potential jurors to see if they are acceptable to both sides) the judge asked the women, but not the men, if they were married and their husbands' occupations. Ms. Bobb refused to answer the question, was held in contempt of court, and appealed the contempt citation. She won, 2–1, in the California Court of Appeals, which held that such discriminatory questioning was a "relic of a bygone age when women were presumed incapable of independent thought."

AND THE KITCHEN SINK

There are some interesting cases I'd like to discuss but can't fit into any other category:

• Article 120 of Louisiana's Civil Code, passed in 1804, which obligated a married woman to live with her husband and follow him when he changed his residence, was found unconstitutional in 1983 on the ground that it denies women equal protection of the law.

• A department store's practice of altering men's clothes without additional charge but charging for alterations to women's clothes wasn't a "deprivation of rights under color of law," and the state's failure to do anything to remedy the situation did not constitute state action.

• Wyoming's tradition of allowing consortium (tort damages compensating for the loss of a spouse's right to companionship and services—sexual and domestic) to men whose wives were injured, but not to women whose husbands were injured, was ended by the case of *Sheeler v. Trans Chem Inc.*, 520 F.Supp. 117 (D.Wyo. 1981). The rationale was that the custom was patently arbitrary and a clear denial of equal protection.

• A state law that forbade married men (but not married women) to transfer or mortgage the family homestead without the spouse's signature is unconstitutional. A statute that makes a distinction based on gender must have a substantial relation to the achievement of important government objectives—and this law didn't serve any valid state interest.

• Alabama's statute allowing widows but not widowers to elect against their spouse's wills (receive a statutory percentage, rather than the smaller percentage of the estate provided by the will) was held unconstitutional because it reflected outmoded, paternalistic assumptions about women. The law was therefore stricken from the books instead of being made gender-neutral.

• But an Arkansas law granting workers' compensation benefits to all widows of workers, but only to incapacitated, dependent widowers of workers, was rewritten to be gender-neutral; so was a Washington State limitation of Welfare benefits to the families of unemployed *fathers*.

• A Louisiana policy that permitted male prisoners, but not female prisoners, to become trustees, enter a work release program, or get a transfer to the prison farm was overturned because it violated the female prisoners' equal protection rights. But Kentucky was allowed to supply an attorney at the women's prison and not the men's prison, on the theory that women don't have a history of legal self-help and, until recently, had little access to legal resources. (I'm not sure I find this convincing.)

• A consent decree that sets standards for shelters for homeless men is equally applicable to shelters for homeless women; the women have an equal protection right to equal treatment, and there is no rational basis for refusing to grant women the protection of the same standards when their needs are as great.

• Woman runners and organizations of runners tried but failed to get a California District Court to order that women's 5,000 and 10,000 meter events be added to the 1984 Summer Olympics. The Ninth Circuit agreed with the District Court that neither equal protection violations nor violations of California civil rights laws were likely enough to be proved to justify the court order.

THE ROAD TO THE COURTHOUSE

• Private citizens who suffer credit discrimination in violation of the ECOA can sue either as individuals or as class members. If there's a pattern of discrimination, it's possible (though politically unlikely) that the FTC could go after the creditor.

• Except for faculty members, there doesn't seem to be a private right of action for damages for Title IX violations.

• Discriminatory private clubs can be attacked from several angles: a suit under the applicable public accommodations law; asking the IRS to investigate the validity of the club's tax exemption (either because the club is also racist or because it has too much outside income); trying to get its local property tax exemption revoked; and lobbying influential men and corporations into withdrawing memberships and dues until the policy is changed.

THE SMOKING GUN

• In an ERA state, a case can be proved just by showing that the plaintiff has been denied equality of opportunity because she is a woman.

• In a state forbidding discrimination in public accommodations or business, the plaintiff has to prove that the entity committing the discrimination *was* open to the public and/or a business, not a private club, religious institution, or other exempt category.

• Failing either of these, the plaintiff can assert her right to equal protection under the Fourteenth Amendment, or can claim violation of her civil rights under color of state law (42 U.S.C.S. §1981, 1983, or 1985, depending on circumstances). Either way, she has to show state action: an intimate involvement, not just a failure to stop the discriminatory practice. But it may be possible to show state involvement through a pattern of action and regulation: a club's zoning variance, liquor license *and* property tax exemption, for example.

5

SELF-DEFENSE AND DOMESTIC VIOLENCE

Jackie Keegan is a second-shift nurse at St. Andrew's Hospital. One of the interns usually gives her a ride home, but tonight she's holding the retractors for a complicated emergency operation. Keegan is uncomfortable about leaving the hospital after midnight, particularly because someone the newspapers call the "North Side Rapist" has committed at least six rapes in the past three months. Because cab drivers find the neighborhood of St. Andrew's—and the neighborhood where Keegan lives—too dangerous to venture into, Jackie Keegan takes the bus home. She's walking away from the bus stop when someone comes up behind her on the deserted sidewalk and wraps an arm around her neck. She reacts immediately, without thinking, by pulling out one of the hairpins that holds her nurse's cap and striking backwards for her assailant's eye.

Every year, many women are the victims of violent acts committed by muggers, rapists, burglars, husbands, and lovers; some women commit acts of violence as aggressors, in self-defense, or in retaliation; and nearly all women fear violence. Because of factors both mutable (conditioning, lack of training and experience in self-defense) and immutable (women are, usually, smaller and less muscular than men), women who are involved in violence are generally on the receiving end. Those women are usually victimized by men, not by other women; and women, quite rationally, are influenced in their choice of activities and places to live and work by their fear of violent crime. That's why the legal ramifications of the right to self-defense (when striking back will be considered justifiable—and therefore not a crime—rather than the crime of assault or homicide) are very important to a discussion of women's rights. However, legal concepts of self-defense (like so many other legal concepts) are male-oriented. The law of self-defense has not always come to grips with women's fear of, and possible responses to, street crime, rape, and family violence.

The idea that a man might have a *right* to go about his business unarmed and unmolested is a fairly recent one. Like the concept of a regular police force, it's probably a nineteenth-century idea. (The idea that a *woman* might have a right to go about her business, unarmed and unmolested, hasn't sunk in yet.) Medieval travelers couldn't depend on encountering roads, but they could predict encountering brigands; coach passengers stood and delivered to highwaymen, early train travelers contributed to the retirement funds of train bandits. The prevalence—indeed, universality—of what would now be called street crime influenced the development of the law of self-defense.

American law has also been influenced by the mystique of the Wild West. In a society with many guns and few other forms of entertainment, saloon shoot-outs will be common, and legal principles will probably adapt.

The general rule is that a person who is attacked—whether by a mugger, a burglar, the guy on the next barstool suffering from testosterone poisoning, or an abusive spouse—has a duty to prevent violence by retreating—getting out of the situation fast. (But see page 129; depending on the state, retreat may or may not be required at home, if the attacker lives in the same home.) If retreat is impossible, or would be useless because it would further provoke the aggressor; or if the victim *has* retreated and been pursued, the victim has a legal right to use violent means to protect herself. Most states further refine this by accepting a crime victim's home as her castle, so that there is no duty to retreat. Some states expand on *that* by saying that there is no duty to retreat if a person is attacked at his or her place of business or employment.

The degree of force used to protect oneself must be appropriate to the threat. If the victim reasonably fears that there is an imminent danger that s/he will be attacked, that another person will be attacked, or that a crime (e.g., larceny) will be committed, the victim is entitled to use physical force to protect people or property. Deadly physical force is physical force that, under the circumstances under which it's used, could readily cause death or other serious physical injury. Using a gun or knife is deadly physical force; so is karate or other martial art (literally) in the hands of an expert. Several state statutes mention the threat of imminent rape as justifying deadly physical force, while other statutes say that the use of deadly force is justified to prevent a felony (serious crime) or violent felony.

The legal right of self-defense depends on the immediacy of the threat; an action taken at gunpoint or while the actor is in a stranglehold is more likely to be considered justified than action taken in response to a spoken threat (with no weapon in sight or mentioned) or a threat of future retaliation.

Justification also depends on the state of mind of the person who responds to violence with violence. S/he must have a reasonable belief that his or her safety is threatened, and that s/he isn't overreacting by using deadly force in a situation in which it isn't justified. But it's permissible for a person under attack to use reasonable judgment in a stress situation, even if it later turns out that s/he was wrong. For example, if a mugger says, "Hand over your wallet—I have a gun" and the victim is an aikido blackbelt or carrying a gun, it's immaterial for legal purposes whether the mugger really did have a gun or whether he was insincere as well as larcenous.

If a person responds to an attack by using an illegal weapon (for example, an unlicensed gun or a can of MACE in a jurisdiction in which it's unlawful), it won't affect the claim of self-defense. However, the self-defender may face a separate weapons charge. That's possible, but not likely; it's not a popular kind of case to prosecute. New York newspapers devoted a lot of ink in the summer of 1983 to a sixty-three-year-old grandmother who scared off a remarkably pusillanimous gang of eight muggers by an unlicensed (and, it turned out, unloaded) gun. She was arrested on a gun charge but wasn't prosecuted. Some people feel it's better to react decisively to a perceived threat and sort it all out later. The folk saying is, "I'd rather be tried by twelve than carried by six"—you can tell it's an old saying because there are a lot of six-person juries these days.

These principles apply equally to women and men faced with violent situations. I'm not aware of many cases that focus on the difference between men's and women's different experience of crime. For one thing, women are more likely to be perceived as easy marks. For another, poverty is in large part an affliction of women and children, and poor people are more likely to be crime victims than the more affluent. (Stealing from the poor isn't an invention of the Reagan administration.) Most rape victims are women (and all but an infinitesimal fraction of rapists are men). Burglary or robbery victims may say they feel violated, but that grossly overestimates the horror of a property crime compared to a crime against the person. Most courts and statutes treat women and men with complete equality when they defend themselves against attack—once again, equality at its least convenient.

THE ROAD TO THE COURTHOUSE

• Very few self-defense cases involving crime victims reach the courts; it's usually fairly clear-cut that the victim had a right to protect her- or himself.

• The exception might be a clear case of overreaction (pumping a purse-snatcher full of lead) or a revenge or vigilante action that occurred after the crime and therefore could not protect anyone or anything against that criminal attack.

• People who defend themselves against property crimes tend to be exonerated, if not commended, by the legal system and by juries (if it gets that far). Women who defend themselves against rape may face more difficulties. Judges, who no doubt thought they were being adorable, have been quoted calling rape "assault with a friendly weapon" and "assault with failure to please" (Har-har). It is usually accepted that burglars and muggers pose a real threat, and have not dropped over to get subway directions, but sometimes women are treated as if they solicited, desired, or enjoyed the attentions of rapists and would-be rapists. (See pages 131–146 for more discussion on this subject.)

• As I say, the rules of self-defense evolved to deal with highwaymen and barroom brawls; it's hard to use the rules in connection with domestic assaults. (More of this on pages 126–130.)

THE SMOKING GUN

• Illinois' *People v. Shields* is interesting in this connection for two points it makes. First of all, it says that a law-abiding person, minding her (or his) own business, has no duty to retreat before using force when attacked. Second, it says that a person who is attacked by a much larger *unarmed* assailant doesn't have to wait to be beaten before s/he is justified in using deadly force to protect her- or himself. The implications for women are obvious.

• The implications are spelled out in the crucial case of *State v. Wanrow*. Washington's Associate Justice Utter devoted most of the opinion to questions of evidence involving the use of tape recordings of calls to the police emergency number. But he also discussed the proper jury instructions that should be given when a physically weak woman (the defendant in this case had a broken leg and used a crutch) uses deadly force to protect herself and others against a larger, stronger man. Utter found that the standard Washington jury charge violated Ms. Wanrow's Constitutional right to equal protection. The standard charge says that relative size and strength must be taken into account, but that a person can't use a weapon to repel an assault by an unarmed person unless *he* has reason to believe that *he* is in imminent danger of death or great bodily harm. The judge said, "In our society women suffer from a conspicuous lack of access to training in and skills necessary to effectively repel a male assailant without resorting to the use of deadly weapons." He makes it clear that the standard used to test self-defense must depend on the state of mind of the person fighting back—and not on what a hypothetical reasonable person, much less a reasonable *man,* would have done in the same circumstances. The judge said that Ms. Wanrow's action should have been judged by her own perceptions, including those perceptions formed by living in a sexist society. "The impression created [by the jury instruction]—that a 5'4" woman with a cast on her leg and using a crutch must, under the law, somehow repel an assault by a 6′2″ intoxicated man without employing weapons in her defense, unless the jury finds her determination of the degree of danger to be objectively reasonable—constitutes a separate and distinct misstatement of the law and, in the context of this case, a denial of equal protection of the law." Associate Justice Utter went on to say, "Until such time as the effects of that history [of sex discrimination] are eradicated care must be taken to assure that our self-defense instructions afford women the right to have their conduct judged in light of the individual physical handicaps which are the product of sex discrimination. To fail to do so is to deny the right of the individual woman involved to trial by the same rules which are applicable to male defendants."

The judge spoke in very general terms here. Although the *Wanrow* case is binding precedent only in the state of Washington, its language and concepts make it a good argument in any case in which a woman (a crime victim, a battered woman) is accused of making an inappropriate use of retaliatory force.

DOMESTIC VIOLENCE

Martha Willets has been married for seven years and has four children. The first time her husband hit her was when they were engaged and had a screaming row about the wedding reception. He was very apologetic, and she admitted that she had been wrong about the seating arrangements and the open bar. During the first year of their marriage, sometimes he would slap her or pull her hair. The beatings began during her first pregnancy. Since then, the frequency of beatings has gone up, from once or twice a year to once or twice a month. She's gone to the Emergency Room twice, once with a dislocated shoulder and once with a suspected miscarriage (the baby turned out fine), lost several teeth, and has stopped thinking of bruises and black eyes as noteworthy occurrences.

She doesn't want a divorce, but she doesn't want to be the victim of even one more assault. She can't leave her husband—she hasn't worked for money since a high-school stint behind Woolworth's candy counter, and three of her children are pre-schoolers. If she has a few drinks during the day, she feels less tense; so sometimes she has a few more drinks at night. She's afraid that unless the situation improves, someone will be leaving the house in a casket—maybe it'll be Martha, maybe it'll be her husband.

Spouse Abuse

A victim of burglary or mugging has a clear-cut legal problem. In the (somewhat unlikely) case that the malefactor is apprehended and the victim's property returned or crime-victim compensation paid, the victim's economic loss is reimbursed and his or her desire for vengeance is satisfied. For almost everyone, suffering a burglary or mugging is an infrequent experience. Again in most instances, the victim and the criminal agree that the criminal is doing something wrong. (The exception might be something like the Brinks robbery, in which the perpetrators are of the minority opinion that they are carrying out a legitimate act of war.) The victim may feel some degree of responsibility or may be criticized for imprudent pedestrian behavior or failure to live in a maximum-security facility, but the criminal gets most of the blame. The victim's emotions to the criminal are usually wholly negative.

A woman who is a victim of domestic violence is in a completely different position, and her legal problem is far from clear-cut. There's no doubt about the identity of her assailant, and he can generally be located if the victim wants him arrested and if the police are willing to arrest him. But domestic violence usually continues and often accelerates; a beating is usually one of a series, not an isolated instance. Often, the man who commits acts of domestic violence, the woman who suffers them, or both, think that his behavior is appropriate (she was "asking for it") or at least a morally neutral if inconvenient fact, like bad weather ("everyone does it"). If the victim thinks that battering a spouse or cohabitant is appropriate behavior, she is likely to feel that the beating is her fault, because she must have done something to deserve it. If she doesn't feel the behavior is appropriate or normal, she may blame herself for choosing an unstable husband or lover.

Most crime victims view those who victimized them with uncomplicated loathing; but most victims of domestic violence love, or at least loved, their assailants, and often feel remorseful or rueful about a deteriorated relationship. Even if there's nothing they'd like better than for someone to lock up the rat and throw away the key, someone has to support the family. If a battered woman leaves her abusive husband or lover, or if he leaves or is ordered out of the house, the incomes that probably fell short of the needs of one household will have to support two. I'm sure that somewhere or other, by diligent search, one could find a battered woman who derives masochistic gratification from the atmosphere of fear and violence in which she lives. Her less fortunate counterparts stay with physically violent mates because they have nowhere else to go. Some men are abused by their wives and lovers, and I don't mean to imply that the women are behaving appropriately. But most men are physically stronger than most women, and few men are economically dependent on women. So battered men have more alternatives (and almost as many champions) as battered women.

The law of domestic violence has evolved from pristine distillations of misogyny to well-intentioned attempts to do the impossible.

Eighteenth- and nineteenth-century English judges assumed, with no
particular legal authority, that husbands had a right to beat their wives,
at least if they showed the proper degree of Anglo-Saxon restraint. (One
suggested etymology for the term "rule of thumb" is the often-quoted
principle that a man could use a stick no thicker than his thumb to beat
his wife without incurring tiresome reproaches from the law.) In the United
States, some people believe that domestic violence is trivial, or funny, or
that women like to be beaten or provoke or deserve beatings. Some of
the people holding these attitudes end up in police uniforms or judicial
robes. The legal problems of family violence are problems of practice and
enforcement, not definition. In many states, the crime of rape is defined
to exclude marital rape from the criminal justice system (see page 142).
That's not the problem in family violence cases. It's illegal to assault
anyone, not just total strangers. So the legal structure for arresting (or
issuing Orders of Protection against) men who assault wives or live-in
lovers already exists. (As attorney and authority on domestic violence Lisa
Lerman points out, there are no special statutes or procedures to deal
with the serious problem of assault in relationships that don't involve
marriage or cohabitation.) There are several reasons why the legal structure
isn't used in every case in which it's appropriate:

• The police hate domestic violence calls, especially if an arrest is involved. They tend to believe (not without reason) that domestic violence
intervention is dangerous to the police. A high percentage of incidents in
which police officers are injured or killed arise in family violence situations—and sometimes it's the victim of the intrafamily assault who assaults
the police officer.

• The battered woman may want the police to stop the assault but not
arrest her assailant—because she cares about him, because she feels
responsible for the incident, because the family needs his earnings, because she doesn't want to hassle with repeated interviews and court ap-
pearances, because she's afraid of scandal or ashamed that her family is
involved in anything so sordid, or for a complex of reasons. Even if a
particular battered woman has none of these feelings, they may be ascribed
to her by police, social service workers, or court personnel.

• Prosecutors hate domestic violence cases. The stated reasons are that
public policy is to preserve families, not break them up, or that there's
no point in starting a prosecution because the victim won't go through
with it. I think both reasons are invalid. If a family exists on the basic
premise that one member can terrorize and brutalize the other members,
the family ought to be disrupted. When I was a prosecutor in Family
Court, we were delighted when *any* case was dropped. Any case that
could be gotten into the dead files with no one complaining was a blessing.
(At times, the sentiment approached "The only good case is a dead case.")
Our office didn't handle domestic violence cases, just juvenile delinquency

and some non-support cases. In New York City, a victim of domestic violence has the right to decide whether the case will be heard in Criminal Court as a misdemeanor case (in which event the D.A.'s office will either wash the case out or prosecute it) or in Family Court as a civil case (in which event the victim must either represent herself or hire her own lawyer).

• Some police, prosecutors, and judges see their role as one of conciliation, or else they feel that a man should not be driven out of "his" home. The latter proposition is hardly an acceptable form of reasoning. As for the former, I think that law enforcement officials and marriage counselors make valuable contributions to society, but that you would have to be pretty far out of contact with reality to confuse the two groups. Dr. Joyce Brothers doesn't have access to a SWAT team.

• However, the statutes of twenty-one states either provide for special training for police (so they can defuse a violent situation while remaining sensitive to the victim's rights) or require the officer at the scene to explain the victim's options to her and/or assist her by taking her to the court to file charges, to a hospital, or to a shelter. The Missouri statute specifies that family violence is to be treated as seriously as an assault by a stranger and instructs police to give priority to victims of repeated abuse. The Washington statute makes it clear that the primary duties of the police are to enforce the law and protect the complainant—not to close the file or give advice about factors leading to a happy marriage. It *is* possible for the legal system to combine sensitivity and vigorous enforcement of the law.

• The laws of most states call for funding of shelters for victims of family violence, or for grants to private organizations who operate shelters. This isn't to say that shelters don't exist in the other states, but they're not state-funded. Connoisseurs of gallows humor should note that about half the states collect funds for shelters by putting a surcharge on marriage licenses and/or divorce actions.

• Seven states (Arkansas, California, Indiana, Ohio, Rhode Island, Tennessee, and Texas) make special mention of intrafamily assaults in their criminal statutes. In the other states, domestic assaults are simply a subclass of assault.

In most states, domestic assault cases are usually handled via civil proceedings leading to an Order of Protection. Civil cases must be proved by a preponderance of the evidence; criminal cases (including assault) must be proved beyond a reasonable doubt. Forty-three states have laws of this type. The victim of domestic violence goes to the appropriate lower court (usually a district, county, or superior court, sometimes the court having jurisdiction over divorces). She signs and swears to a complaint or petition explaining the facts of the case. In about half the states, cohabitants as well as wives can apply for Orders of Protection. The statutes are tricky:

most of them say that an order of protection is available against abuse by "family or household members," but sometimes they go on to define "family or household members" for this purpose as legal spouses only. Usually there's a small fee (around $25) for filing the petition. In some states, the fee can be waived if the assault victim can't afford it, and in other states the filing is free. (It's not necessary to call the police, or have the batterer arrested, before filing a petition for an Order of Protection; on the other hand, if the police do come but are unwilling to make an arrest, or if the victim wants the police there to cool down the situation rather than make an arrest, the next step can be filing a petition rather than making a criminal charge of assault.)

After the petition is filed, the case is scheduled for a quick trial—most statutes specify within ten days. The petitioner is supposed to make sure that her assailant gets a copy of the petition and is informed of the hearing. For obvious reasons, the petitioner isn't allowed to serve the petition, but a friend or relative of hers (preferably one larger than the respondent— the respondent is the alleged assailant) or a paid process server can do it. Some statutes require the local police or marshal's office to serve the petition; ask the court clerk if this is true in your jurisdiction. (In the real world, though, they may refuse to serve the petition, or may put a low priority on the task.)

So that the petitioner can be protected between filing the petition and the hearing date, most states will allow a judge to issue a temporary Order of Protection or TRO (Temporary Restraining Order) on an *ex parte* basis. *Ex parte* means that only one side—in this case, the petitioner—is present to be heard. Luckily, since domestic violence doesn't keep bankers' hours, many states also allow judges or courts to issue emergency orders when the regular courts are closed. Generally, an emergency order lasts until the next regular court day; a temporary order lasts until the regularly scheduled hearing.

When the scheduled hearing is held (it may be postponed if the respondent hasn't been served with a copy of the petition, if he has been but doesn't show up, if he shows up and requests an adjournment to hire an attorney or try to get one appointed, if the lawyers want more time to prepare the case, if everyone is ready but the court is too busy to reach the case, or several of these successively), and if the victim proves her case by a preponderance of the evidence (her version of the events is more likely than not—a lower standard than the "beyond a reasonable doubt" standard used in criminal cases), the judge will issue a final Order of Protection. In most states, the judge decides how long the order should last, up to a specified maximum—somewhere between fifteen days and a year, depending on the state. Many of the statutes provide for renewals of the order if necessary; and if the victim is assaulted again, she can file another petition.

Orders of Protection vary, depending on the state, as to whether they are temporary or final, and on the facts of each particular case. The provisions of the order could include:

- The assailant is ordered not to subject the victim to any further acts of violence.
- He can be required to stay away from the place she works or goes to school, and to avoid harassing her.
- He can be ordered to move out of the family home.
- Alternatively, he can be ordered to pay for substitute housing for the victim and their children.
- He can be ordered to support the victim and children.
- A police officer or member of the sheriff's department can be present when the petitioner or the respondent moves out of the family home.
- Temporary custody of the children (with or without visitation by the batterer) can be granted to the victim.
- The petitioner and/or respondent can be ordered not to take the children out of the court's jurisdiction.
- The assailant can be ordered to pay the victim's medical bills, and compensate her for other direct damages (broken furniture, missed days at work).
- A "no-contact" order forbids the assailant to communicate, directly or indirectly, with the victim.
- The assailant, with or without the victim, can be ordered to get personal or family counseling.

Some of these provisions are truly giving away ice in the wintertime—after all, the respondent has no legal right to assault the petitioner in the first place—but some of them are substantial—such as ordering a man to leave the family home or cease all contact with the petitioner. The more substantial a change a provision will make, the harder it is to get it written into the order. Even if the court does order the respondent to move out of the family home (or if the petitioner moves out to protect herself and her children), the Order of Protection won't have any effect on the ownership of the family home. That can be settled by a separation agreement, or by a court with jurisdiction over separation and divorce actions.

The reason for bothering at all is that an Order of Protection is a court order, violation of which is contempt of court, a misdemeanor for which the contemnor (person committing contempt) can be arrested, fined, and/or jailed. (The Alaska and Colorado statutes obligate the police to use "every reasonable means" to enforce Orders of Protection.) In many states, copies of all Orders of Protection are sent to the police, theoretically so that they can check the files and swing into action when they get a domestic abuse call. (If there is an Order of Protection on file, the person calling the police should mention it rather than assuming the police will look it up.) The police really do respond more quickly to situations involving violation of an order than to other domestic violence calls—as if beating one's wife were good clean fun, but disrespect to a piece of paper were serious business. But then former Cabinet members Butz and Watts exited hastily more for *saying* stupid things than for anything they did. People are strange.

THE ROAD TO THE COURTHOUSE

• The first step is the Order of Protection procedure described on pages 119–121.

• If there is a fee for filing the petition and the petitioner is short of funds, she should ask to have the fee waived. This is called filing the petition *in forma pauperis* ("in the form of a poor person"). It is unlikely, but possible, that a Legal Aid or volunteer lawyer will be available to help her with her case.

• Even if the state statute doesn't require the police to inform victims of their rights, or if it doesn't direct court clerks to help abuse victims file petitions, they should be able to inform petitioners of available shelters and victim assistance programs. These programs can sometimes provide carfare or a ride to the courthouse, child care, and information about the likely outcome of the proceeding and alternatives to prosecution.

• In some areas the local prosecutor's office, rather than the victim, signs the petition. The theory behind this is that it demonstrates society's interest in preventing family violence: the state, not the victim, files the charge. Also in theory, the victim is only a witness, not an accuser, so further abuse in retaliation is less likely.

• For various reasons (apologies from the abuser, fear of retaliation, unwillingness to schlepp to court for repeated hearings, inability to get child care or time off from work to pursue the case) abuse victims may want to drop the case before the hearing. However, some areas (e.g., Seattle, Los Angeles, Santa Barbara, Westchester County) have a "no-drop" policy for civil or criminal domestic abuse cases: once the charges are filed, they won't be dropped, even at the request of the complainant. (The case can continue without the victim: in Seattle, in 1979–80, the prosecutors got convictions in one-third of the criminal cases in which the abuse victim did not appear or testify. The prosecutors used medical records, eyewitness testimony, and the testimony of police officers on the scene.) In Utah, an abuse complaint can't be withdrawn without the consent of the court. Kentucky takes the opposite tack: the matter will be dropped unless the victim signs the complaint within twelve hours of an arrest for assault.

In fact, Anchorage takes its no-drop policy to the extent that one complainant spent a day in jail for contempt because she refused to testify; Assistant Municipal Prosecutor Mike Marsh was quoted as saying that he regretted the result, but "Our only alternative was to drop the case and thereby show defense attorneys and defendants we won't stick to our guns." Therefore, before filing a petition or signing a criminal complaint charging assault, a victim of domestic violence should find out whether local prosecutors will be involved in the case, and whether they have a no-drop policy and how they enforce it. This could be a factor in the decision whether to pursue the case or not.

Lisa Lerman stresses that a no-drop policy, although sometimes harsh in effect, is intended to help the victims of abuse, and is often effective. Batterers frequently threaten victims with further abuse unless they drop the case. If the victim can show that it isn't in her power to withdraw the complaint, and that the state, not the victim, is handling the case, the batterer may not blame the victim or may feel that continued assaults are not in *his* best interests.

• Lerman also warns victims to be cautious about choosing mediation or other forms of "alternative dispute resolution" over the court system. The court system, for all its flaws, provides orders that can be enforced, decisions that can be reviewed by higher authorities, and official records that can be consulted. The stated purpose of mediation is to get both sides to reach an agreement. Sometimes mediators, motivated by sexism or tact, don't ask about violence; even if they do ask, victims may be unwilling to discuss abuse when the batterer is present. Even if violence is discussed, what if the batterer "agrees" to stop assaulting his wife if she "agrees" to improve her housekeeping and serve dinner on time? Does he then have a right to beat her if dinner is late? What if his hamburgers aren't rare enough, or he doesn't like the proffered brand of ketchup? Anyway, how can either party enforce a mediation agreement? There's no transcript or judge's order. It could perhaps be taken to a civil court as a breach of contract case, but then the victim has to prove that she was battered in violation of the agreement—no easier a task in a contract case than in an Order of Protection or criminal case.

• If the Order of Protection procedure is unavailable or undesirable, it may be possible to have the abuser arrested for assault. An assault case is a criminal case. Although steps are taken to protect the rights of the accused, it's still the State or the People against the defendant. An Order of Protection proceeding is a civil case, and often the emphasis is placed on compromise and conciliation. The victim of one or several beatings may be disinclined to meet her assailant halfway. Lerman warns that prosecutors may try to discourage inconvenient cases by frightening the victim, telling her that pressing her complaint will mean a mandatory jail sentence for her abuser. This is by no means true; jail sentences are rare, probation (often on condition of counseling—perhaps what the victim sought all along) much more common. On the other hand, if domestic assault cases are assigned to the same courtroom, and defendants waiting for their cases to be called hear a flagrant violator sentenced to six months in jail—well, consciousness can be raised abruptly.

• Police officers may claim that they lack the power to arrest a batterer unless they have seen the violent incident. But many states have amended their laws to allow an arrest without a warrant if the officer has probable cause to believe that domestic violence did occur. (The states are Alaska, Arizona, Connecticut, Georgia, Hawaii, Idaho, Kentucky, Louisiana, Nevada, New Hampshire—if the incident occurred within six hours before the police were called, New Jersey, New Mexico, North Carolina, North Dakota—within four hours of the incident, Ohio, Rhode Island—within twenty-four hours of the incident, Virginia and Washington.) Several statutes (e.g., Iowa, Massachusetts, Maine, Oregon) allow warrantless arrest for violation of an Order of Protection.

• Feminist and law-reform groups interested in improving the local response to domestic violence might adopt a New York strategy. A class action suit was filed against the New York Police Department and the Family Court, alleging that the existing system failed totally as a response to family violence. The case was settled by a consent decree, under which the police agreed that they would not refrain from arresting violent men because the victim had not gotten Orders of Protection, because the victim had or might choose to pursue the case in Family Court rather than Criminal Court or vice versa, or because the police officer believed conciliation was a better solution than arrest.

• The Oregon law says that the police "shall" arrest the violator of an Order of Protection; if they fail to do so, at least one case says that a victim of abuse can sue the police officers who fail to enforce a court order—and can also sue the city employing them. Her suit is a tort suit for negligent infliction of emotional distress, based on police failure to carry out their duty to enforce the order.

THE SMOKING GUN

• Sometimes the victim or someone else will call the police during a battering incident. The police officer may not believe there is enough cause to arrest the batterer; or he may make an arrest, but the prosecutor declines to press charges for lack of evidence, because the victim is unwilling to prosecute, because the existing case-load is too heavy, or because the prosecutor believes an Order of Protection will resolve the matter equitably. But whether there is a civil or criminal trial, a police officer can be a valuable and impartial witness to the condition of the victim, the condition of the premises, and the lack of injury to the batterer. (Even if the officer can't remember the incident s/he will have a notebook used to make official records at the scene of the incident.) However, if a police officer is subpoenaed as a witness, the proceeding may have to be adjourned one or several times until a date can be found that fits into the officer's duty schedule.

• There may be eyewitnesses to the beating, or witnesses who can testify to the victim's cuts, bruises, and other evidence of assault.

• Hospital and medical records of treatment can be admissible evidence; so can photographs taken by a friend, showing the victim's condition after the assault. (The person who took the photographs will have to come to court and testify that these *are* the photographs that s/he took, explain the circumstances under which they were taken, and state that the photographs are an accurate picture of the victim's condition at that time.)

• It's possible that the batterer will deny that the incident occurred at all; this can be rebutted by the testimony of eyewitnesses, those who heard screams and objects being thrown, emergency-room personnel, etc.

• The batterer may also claim that the incident was a fistfight rather than a physical attack on a weaker adversary. This is harder to rebut unless there are witnesses; but the judge's sexism can be turned to advantage here—perhaps the judge will believe that women are incapable of violence, and therefore the complainant must have been the victim of an assault.

• Many assailants, and some law enforcement officials, believe that a woman deserves to be beaten as a punishment for certain forms of behavior ("She asked for it"). The 1976 New Jersey case of *State v. Brown* is interesting in this context. The assault victim in this case *literally* asked for it: she told her husband he should beat her if she fell off the wagon. She did, he did, and he was arrested and convicted of assault. The court pointed out that the state is the prosecutor in an assault case, and it's the state's position that assaults are to be prevented if possible and punished if prevention isn't possible.

Many states provide some degree of "intrafamily immunity" from tort suits: that is, family members face limits on suits against other family members for negligence or other torts. However, a recent Seventh Circuit case allows one family member to sue another for assault.

BATTERED-WIFE HOMICIDES

Ed Surrey has promised to take his family on a Fourth of July picnic. When he wakes up (awakened by a crying baby) he finds that there are no clean shirts; his wife Ann didn't get around to doing the laundry. He puts on yesterday's shirt and goes to the dresser drawer, where he keeps his spare cash, to get money for gas. There's no money there. He goes down to the kitchen and asks Ann what the hell she did with the money; she says that she paid the electric bill. What about the money he gave her for the electric bill? New shoes for the kids. Why isn't there any clean laundry? She stopped off at Kearney's Tavern for a couple of beers. He grabs her shoulders and shakes her—the usual prelude to a beating. But this time she's holding the knife she was using to slice leftover baked ham for sandwiches. She stabs him four times.

Sometimes domestic violence ends spontaneously: the batterer's emotional health improves, his drug or alcohol problem abates. Sometimes family therapy or pastoral counseling improves the situation. Sometimes the couple divorces, or one party or the other walks out. Sometimes the abuse continues. Sometimes it continues until one of the spouses dies—of natural causes, or by strangulation, by poison, at the point of a gun or knife.

Men commit the vast majority of violent crimes, but only about half the spouse murders. Sometimes women kill husbands or lovers in self-defense; sometimes with premeditation, motivated by greed or jealousy; sometimes without thinking, because a weapon is available in a moment of anger.

There are various levels of the crime of homicide (killing a human being under circumstances that are considered punishable), and terminology and sentences vary from state to state. The level of the crime depends on the presence or absence of two things: *actus reus* ("evil" or criminal act) and *mens rea* ("evil mind"—the state of mind necessary for an illegal action to constitute a crime. In late 1983, a member of the Senate Foreign Relations Committee delivered an interesting Freudian slip when he said our Latin American allies had the same mens rea as the United States). The most serious crime is deliberate, premeditated killing; killing in pure self-defense under the permitted circumstances isn't a crime at all. For the cases in between, the level of the crime depends on the motive and state of mind of the killer.

If it's uncontested that a woman killed her husband, cohabitant, or lover, and if she states that the killing was related to abuse she suffered at his hands, there are three major defense tactics. The three approaches are philosophically very different, and each raises very different legal issues and requires different kinds of evidence.

• If she killed under circumstances that her home state accepts as complete self-defense, she isn't guilty of any crime. However, if this defense strategy doesn't work, she will certainly be convicted of some degree of homicide—possibly murder, if the judge or jury doesn't believe her or concludes that the action was premeditated.

• If it's conceded that she killed under circumstances that don't constitute self-defense, but wihout premeditation, defense strategy is to try for an acquittal or for a verdict of guilty of a lesser degree of homicide. Depending on the state, it could be homicide committed during extreme emotional disturbance, in the heat of passion, or even temporary insanity. However, the defense strategy is to focus on the circumstances of the killing, arguing that the circumstances were special. Even if the plea is temporary insanity, there is no contention that the defendant's mental condition is in any way impaired outside of that situation.

• Defense strategy in some cases focuses on the defendant as a special kind of person. These cases posit the existence of a battered-woman syndrome. Victims of this syndrome are said to have low self-esteem and a psychologically symbiotic relationship with their assailants. Those suffering from the battered-woman syndrome learn helplessness, both through their socialization and through the violent relationship. The combination of factors leads them to believe that they can't escape from the violent relationship. Under this theory, a sufferer from the syndrome comes to believe that the only way out of her situation is death—hers or that of the man who victimizes her. The battered-woman syndrome prevents her from finding any other alternative. This theory has not influenced any state's legislation, and courts are divided as to its acceptance. The danger of basing defense strategy on the syndrome is that the defendant may be found to have a permanently impaired mental condition and may be committed to a mental institution for an indefinite length of time. If she had been found guilty of some degree of homicide, she would probably have been eligible for parole after several years in prison.

THE ROAD TO THE COURTHOUSE

• If a battered woman kills her husband or lover, the fact of the killing and the identity of the killer are seldom in dispute; in fact the killer is often the one who calls the police to report the crime. So there are few or no factual issues—the legal issues involve the characterization of the incident (whether it's justifiable or criminal; if criminal, the degree of the crime).

• Plea-bargaining is a real possibility if the defense of justification isn't raised, and if the prosecution is willing to accept a plea to a lesser degree of homicide. In other situations, there will have to be a full trial. If the defense believes there is any meaningful possibility of acquittal (either because a strong legal case can be made or out of sympathy for the victim of flagrant abuse), the defense will want a full trial and won't accept a plea bargain involving a long prison term. Political reality dictates that prosecutors can afford to lose a notorious case (and battered-woman homicide cases tend to be tried in the newspapers) far better than they can afford to accept a plea to a minor charge in a homicide case.

THE SMOKING GUN

• If the defense theory is self-defense, in some states it's the responsibility of the defense to prove this. (The legal term for something that must be proved this way is "affirmative defense." The alibi is a typical example: if the defendant claims that s/he could not have committed the crime because s/he was somewhere else at the time, s/he must prove it.) In other states, if the defense offers *any* evidence at all that the killing occurred in self-defense, the prosecution must prove this wasn't the case. Naturally, the burden on the defense is less if it has to introduce *some* evidence of self-defense than if it has to prove that point.

• The next issue in a self-defense case is whether the killing was legally justified as a spontaneous reaction to danger or whether it was premeditated. This depends both on the circumstances and on the killer's state of mind at the time of the killing.

• In order to constitute self-defense, the killing must have been motivated by a reasonable good-faith belief that killing was necessary to avert a threat of death or great bodily harm.

• A finding of justifiable homicide is possible even if the killer used a weapon to defend herself against an assailant who was beating her with his fists. (Of course, the provenance of the weapon matters: did she use something that came to hand, or did she use a gun that she had bought several weeks before?) The case of *Kiess v. State* is interesting because it says that the use of deadly force can be justified if great bodily harm is inflicted (or even threatened) by someone much larger and heavier than the one who kills in self-defense—and even if the killer is armed and the assailant uses his fists. The Illinois case of *People v. Reeves* also makes it clear that beatings as well as attacks with weapons count as great bodily harm. The defendant in *Reeves* had been beaten many times in the past, and knew that her husband was capable of inflicting great bodily harm; the decision makes it clear that she was entitled to use deadly force to protect herself. (Reeves shot her husband during a struggle in which several witnesses saw her husband choking and beating her.) The California case of *People v. Bush* says that the defendant, who had been threatened with death during two earlier beatings, was entitled to a jury instruction saying that a person whose life has been threatened is entitled to quicker and more drastic methods of self-defense than a person who has not been threatened. However, an earlier California case, *People v. Lucas,* points out that threats that are not accompanied by actions creating a reasonable fear of imminent bodily harm won't constitute justification.

• The courts are split on whether a claim of self-defense can be made if the killing takes place after, rather than during, an incident of abuse. Maine, for example, says yes; Indiana and Ohio say no.

• The defense may be able to introduce evidence of prior violent acts by the deceased, to show the killer's fear of further abuse. However, the violent acts by the deceased must be reasonably contemporary with the killing.

• According to a 1981 law review article, a "psychological autopsy" of the deceased can be a successful defense strategy, leading to at least one acquittal and two verdicts of voluntary manslaughter (a much less serious charge) in murder cases. The "psychological autopsy" focuses on the character of the deceased, the nature of the relationship, and the continuing violence that led up to his death.

• As discussed on page 113, some states require a person to retreat before using deadly force, even in his or her own home. In an intrafamily homicide case, there's the further question of whether a person has a duty to retreat when attacked by someone else who lives there. Michigan, Pennsylvania, and South Carolina say there is no duty to retreat when a person is attacked at home by a spouse or cohabitant. New Jersey has ruled both ways; Connecticut imposes a duty to retreat if the attacker shares the home. The Florida rule is that there is at least a limited duty to retreat, as far as another room, to avoid the conflict. Carolyn Wilkes Kaas, in a 1982 article in the *Connecticut Law Review*, suggests another line of argument: that a woman who has a reasonable belief that the legal system can't protect her (for example, one who has suffered repeated abuse even though she went through the whole Order of Protection procedure) has no duty to retreat, because even retreat can't ensure her safety.

• Just as the cases discussed on pages 139–140 show that consent to one sexual act isn't legally equivalent to consent to other sexual acts, the 1981 Pennsylvania case of *Commonwealth v. Watson*, 431 A.2d 949, makes it clear that staying with an abusive husband isn't legally equivalent to consent to further abuse.

• If the defense strategy is to show that the killer suffers from the battered-woman syndrome, the defense will probably want to introduce expert testimony (e.g., from a psychologist or psychiatrist) about the battered-woman syndome and its relevance to the case. The general rule of evidence is that most witnesses are allowed to testify only to what they did, saw, and heard; not their opinions or the conclusions they drew. An expert witness, qualified by special training and skill, *is* allowed to give opinion evidence (for example, a ballistics expert can testify that, in his or her opinion, a bullet was fired from a particular gun). But experts can give opinions only on matters that are outside a layperson's knowledge. Some courts will allow expert testimony on the battered-woman syndrome (e.g., District of Columbia, Georgia, New Jersey, Washington) while others rule it out, on the grounds that the syndrome isn't scientifically established, or that the jury can make up their own minds; the issue isn't one that demands special expertise (Ohio, Wyoming).

6
RAPE

Rape is an unusual crime, especially devastating to its victims because it associates sex with violence rather than with love or the sharing of pleasure. If the rapist is a stranger, the victim can begin to see all men as potential attackers; if the rapist is a former friend or a husband, the basic premises of the victim's emotional life are challenged.

The law of rape has evolved in a way that suggests that rape is an atypical crime, in that men have to be protected against vengeful women, women who can't distinguish between fantasies and reality, women who provoke men and then refuse to provide them with the sexual release they are entitled to. State statutes and cases have moved much closer to the victim's view, but the transition isn't yet complete. To understand the present status of rape law, it's necessary to understand the weird, and often contradictory, attitudes that formed the traditional law of rape:

- Being raped is exciting, romantic, and glamorous; women want to be raped, and are hypocrites if they don't admit it.
- A woman who isn't sexually responsive (especially if she is not sexually responsive to her husband) deserves to be raped; afterwards, she will be grateful for having had her womanhood awakened.
- A woman who acts in a way that she perceives as seductive, or that a man perceives as seductive, is offering sexual favors to all men. If she rejects any one of them, he is justified in raping her—she asked for it.
- A woman who isn't conventionally attractive (especially an older woman) should be grateful if she is raped, on the grounds that other sexual opportunities are not available to her.
- A woman who hitchhikes, goes into bars alone, or permits men to buy her food or drinks either offers herself indiscriminately as a sexual partner or "asks for it" if she is raped.
- A decent woman would rather die than be raped; a woman who survives rape without being physically mangled must, therefore, have either cooperated in the crime or wasn't really a decent woman. The phrase "death before dishonor" implies that being raped is somehow

more dishonorable than contracting cancer of the liver, seeing your child killed by a hit-and-run driver, or any other horrible thing that could happen.

- Women are either "good" (virgin until marriage, monogamous after marriage) or "bad"; "bad" women are likely to be lying when they charge a man with rape.
- A woman who has agreed to have sex with more than one man will agree to have sex with any man, at any time.
- A woman who is angry at a man is likely to fabricate a charge of rape against him.
- If a woman consents to have sex with a man at one time it means that that man has a right to have sex with the woman at any time he chooses—especially if he is her husband.

These attitudes, and others equally Neanderthal, have influenced the development of the law of rape; the law has changed over time, but legislators, judges, and juries often retain some of these attitudes. That's why a rape victim is technically referred to as the "prosecutrix," a term that isn't used for the victim of any other crime, and one that suggests that the whole thing is her idea. Traditionally, rape was sexual intercourse with a woman accomplished by force overcoming her "uttermost resist-ance" or "earnest resistance," and there are hundreds of cases discussing what constituted adequate resistance for the purpose. In this view, sex is a kind of entitlement program: if a man is attracted to a woman, he is *entitled* to have sex with her unless she demonstrates her lack of consent by physical combat. State statutes have been modified over time, so that now the usual requirement is that the prosecution prove that the rape victim was subjected to physical force or to a believable threat of serious physical injury. In some states, the threat can be either to the victim or to another person (for example, to the victim's child); in others, the threat can be either of present violence or future retaliation. However, the pros-ecution must be able to prove, beyond a reasonable doubt, that the rape was accomplished by some form of violence or an adequately terrifying threat, though it's no longer necessary for the rape victim to prove physical resistance if she was too frightened to fight physically, or if physical re-sistance would have been useless. But the victim may still face skepticism from the police, prosecutors, judge, or jury, that nonconsensual inter-course was "really" rape if no physical struggle took place, or that undesired sexual intercourse is itself an assault.

Rape, unlike other crimes, traditionally required corroboration (support of the victim's testimony). The prudent criminal (of any kind) will normally avoid committing a crime where there are witnesses, and will try to be careful about scattering evidence around. The law has always recognized this, and many convictions have been based on the uncorroborated testimony of the crime victim, with his or her word against that of the defendant. But nineteenth-century statutes called for corroboration of rape charges (sometimes of every element of the crime: that the victim had sexual intercourse, that it was against her will, that she struggled, and that the defendant is the person who committed the rape). Corroboration requirements made it difficult to bring rape cases, and almost impossible to get a conviction. Therefore, the statutes have been amended, and judges have decided that corroboration isn't necessary, or at least that credible (believable) testimony doesn't have to be corroborated, though testimony that strains belief may have to be. Whatever the law of a particular state is, it naturally strengthens the prosecution's case if one or more elements of the victim's testimony can be corroborated—if a witness saw the rapist fleeing the scene, for example, or if there is medical testimony showing recent intercourse, injury to the victim's sexual organs, cuts and bruises, or any other point that the prosecution is trying to prove.

The next problem is demonstrating that the victim did not consent. Obviously this is a problem if the rapist was the victim's husband or lover; but, surprisingly, the consent issue is also raised in rapes by strangers: "The accused had allegedly raped the complainant after breaking into her home, tying her hands, threatening to kill her, and covering her head with a pillow. The defendant argued that there was insufficient evidence of force to establish beyond a reasonable doubt that the woman was raped against her will." Victims can expect to be asked if they consented to the actions of armed strangers who accosted them, dragged them into cars, threatened or beat them.

Corroboration has been traditionally demanded because rape victims have been seen as inherently less credible than victims of other crimes; women who weren't considered sexually virtuous were also considered less credible than men, or than virtuous women. There has also been a pervasive but unstated belief that women who are willing to consent to *any* form of nonmarital intercourse will consent to *all* forms of nonmarital intercourse. Therefore, it was traditionally considered probative for men other than the defendant to testify (whether truthfully or perjuriously) that they had had sex with the rape victim. Quite often, this had the effect of convincing the jury that the victim either had not been raped or wasn't deserving of the protection of the law. Even if the defendant *was* convicted, at least the victim had been publicly humiliated. If rapists can be said to have fellow-feeling for other rapists, they made life easier for future rapists, because future rape victims, aware of the ordeal they would undergo, would be much less likely to press charges. Fortunately, most of the states recognized that it's inappropriate to place the victim on trial by requiring her to disclose, and be cross-examined on, her entire sexual history. Therefore, forty-five states have some kind of "rape shield" law: laws that restrict the amount of evidence about the rape victim's sexual history that can be introduced at a public trial. (Alabama, Illinois, Kansas, Oregon, and South Dakota don't have rape shield laws; Arizona, Connecticut, Maine, and Utah don't have rape shield statutes, but arrive at similar results through case law.)

The typical rape shield law says that the defense must notify the judge and the prosecutor, a certain number of days before the trial, that it intends to introduce evidence dealing with the victim's sexual history at the trial. Before the trial, a closed hearing is held—the jury isn't present, and neither are the press nor the public—to determine whether the information is so useful to the determination of the truth that it should be admitted as evidence. If the probative value is greater than the prejudice to the victim, the judge agrees that the evidence can be used at the trial; otherwise, it can't be revealed to the jury or the public. The technical details of the various statutes vary. In some states, *any* evidence about the victim's sexual history can be used at trial if the judge allows it after the pre-trial hearing. However, in most states only three kinds of evidence can be introduced even after the pre-trial hearing:

- Evidence of sexual contact between the victim and the defendant.
- Evidence to show that semen, venereal disease, or pregnancy that the victim says come from the defendant really have another source (for example, the victim says that she was impregnated by the rapist; the defendant claims that the victim was impregnated by someone else; or the defendant claims that the semen found when the victim was examined in the hospital emergency room was present because the victim had had intercourse with someone other than the defendant).
- Evidence that rebuts (contradicts) evidence of *good* sexual character introduced by the prosecution.

The final hurdle is the jury charge. If the victim has survived the rape, decided to press charges, been able to convince the police that a rape really did occur; if the police can locate and arrest the rapist, if the prosecutor decides the case warrants prosecution, if the Grand Jury indicts; if the case goes to trial (no one has decided to drop the charges, and the defendant hasn't made a plea bargain); and if the entire case has been heard, the victim may hear the judge tell the jury that "rape is a charge that is easily made, but difficult to disprove," and warn the jury not to place too much credence in the victim's testimony. This is called a "Hale charge," after Sir Matthew Hale, a seventeenth-century judge and legal scholar, who pointed out that unfounded rape charges are a common weapon of vengeful women. Hale will pop up again, like King Charles's head, in the discussion of marital rape. Hale also presided over witch trials (literal witch trials, not political kangaroo courts); it's interesting to note that his fantasies about female sexuality are still quoted approvingly, but his fantasies about female magical powers are not. At one time, several states required the Hale charge. Now it's required in Nevada, but only if there is evidence that the complainant has maliciously fabricated the charge. The Hale charge has been allowed in New Mexico, South Dakota, Wisconsin, and Wyoming, but cases from Arizona, Alaska, Florida, Georgia, Indiana, Iowa, Louisiana, Maryland, Utah, Virginia, and Washington say that it's improper. Judges in Arkansas, Colorado, Hawaii, Idaho, Massachusetts, and Minnesota can either give the charge or refuse to give it, as they see fit; and if California, Delaware, Kansas, Maine, Nebraska, or Oklahoma judges refuse to give the instruction, the defendant can't get his conviction reversed for that reason. Therefore, the prosecution should always ask the judge not to use the Hale charge. Because the charge is a serious one, the judge will certainly instruct the jury to deliberate carefully and accept only evidence that they find credible; that should give enough protection to the defendant.

There are three main types of forcible rape: stranger rape, "date rape," and marital rape. Each one presents different problems of evidence and trial strategy.

STRANGER RAPE

Lily Blair didn't notice that a man had followed her into the building where she lived, or that he went up the stairs with her. When she unlocked the door to her apartment, he pushed her into the apartment and locked the door behind them. "Don't scream," he said. "I have a gun. If you do what I tell you, you won't get hurt." He raped her, took her handbag, and asked if she had any other money in the house. She told him that she had $75 in a coffee can in the cupboard; he took that too, and left. A few minutes later, Lily looked out the door to see if he had left and ran down the stairs to the apartment of a friend of hers who lived on the second floor. She pounded on her friend's door and screamed. Her friend opened the door, heard what had happened, and took Ms. Blair to the nearest hospital emergency room. She then called the police from the emergency room.

THE ROAD TO THE COURTHOUSE

• The major problem in a stranger rape is getting an arrest, because of the difficulties of identification. According to the Uniform Crime Reports for 1974, the arrest rate for reported rapes was about 50 percent. Many rapes—perhaps most rapes—are not reported, because the victims are too terrified and humiliated to report the crime, because they don't think the rapist will be caught and convicted, or both. Only 60 percent of those arrested were charged with rape—the police can "unfound" a case they don't think is sustainable, and prosecutors have discretion to pursue or drop a case. Forty-nine percent of those charged were either acquitted or had their cases dismissed. Thirty-five percent of those charged were convicted of rape, and 16 percent were convicted of lesser offenses (for example, simple assault). So, in 1974, the odds were about 15 percent that a man who had committed a reported rape would be convicted of *something* (51 percent of 60 percent of 50 percent) and less than 10 percent that he would be convicted of rape. As so many rapes are not reported, rapists can be reassured by the odds against their apprehension and conviction.

Assistant Attorney General Lois H. Herrington, speaking about a Justice Department study of rapes that occurred between 1972 and 1982, said, "Sexual assault victims would be more likely to report the crime if they did not fear becoming entangled in the morass of an insensitive criminal justice system." (The report was discussed in *The New York Times*, March 25, 1985, page A17.) According to this long-term study, only about half of the 1.5 million women who suffered rape or attempted rape used the criminal justice system. Either they were ashamed or frustrated, believing that their attackers either would not be caught or would not receive any substantial punishment.

• If the police believe the charge is well founded, they will investigate and try to make an arrest. The victim will be questioned one or more times and may be asked to look at photographs and/or assist a police artist in compiling a sketch of the rapist. If an arrest is made, the victim will be asked to identify the rapist. The normal procedure, to protect the rights of both the accused and the victim, is for the victim (and any other witnesses) to sit behind a one-way mirror and pick the rapist out of a number of other men in the lineup.

• Local procedure varies. After the arrest there will be one or several hearings so that the arrestee can be charged with the crime, so that the strength of the case against him can be assessed, and so he can be given an opportunity to get a lawyer. If the victim is unwilling to prosecute, if there is little or no evidence apart from her testimony, or if she is a poor witness, the case is likely to "wash out" before trial. Prosecutors have large caseloads and must divide their energies among many cases. The amount of attention a particular case gets depends on official policy (a stress on sex crime prosecutions, for example) and on individual reactions about rape and about the particular victim.

• If the Grand Jury has indicted and/or other preliminary hearings have sustained the case against the defendant, the case will be set down for a full trial. At this stage, the defense lawyer can ask for separate hearings on questions of evidence: whether the police violated any rights of the arrestee, for example. If the defense wants to introduce evidence about the victim's sexual history, the "rape shield" hearing will be held at this stage.

• If, after all that, the case is still being maintained and the defendant hasn't copped a plea, the case will be tried. The defendant gets to choose whether the case will be heard by a judge alone or by a judge and jury. It's usually good strategy for a rape defendant to demand a jury trial. The prospect of testifying about being raped in front of a jury will discourage many rape victims, and juries are likely to be swayed by appeals to their own sexual attitudes about appropriate feminine conduct even when the legal case against the defendant is quite strong. (For example, one of the jurors who convicted Inez Garcia for killing a man who had raped her told a journalist that the rapist was "just showing her a good time" rather than inflicting bodily harm on her.)

THE SMOKING GUN

• Because there may be a long time between the rape and the time the case finally comes to trial (if it does at all), the victim may have difficulty remembering some details of the incident. Therefore, she should take detailed notes, as soon as she can tolerate the process, of everything she can remember. The rules of evidence of most states will allow her to take these notes with her on the witness stand, so she can refresh her memory (the technical term is "present recollection revived"). If she can't remember some details, even with the notes, the notes she took can probably be admitted into evidence separately (as "past recollection recorded").

• Although the defendant in a stranger rape isn't unlikely to claim consent (for example, the man who raped Lily Blair might claim that she invited him to her apartment for the purpose of having sex with him), the real issues will be identification (whether the defendant is the man who committed the rape) and the presence or absence of force. If Lily Blair didn't see the gun, she may face problems convincing the jurors that she did not have to resist the rapist. However, there are many cases indicating that, for legal purposes, force can be implied. The 1975 Indiana case of *Beard v. State* says that physical resistance isn't required where it's prevented or averted by threats or the victim's fear; in the same year, the Illinois case of *People v. Wilcox* said that resistance isn't required where it would be futile and endanger the victim's life, the victim was overcome by superior strength or was paralyzed by fear. Again in 1975, the Missouri court said in *State v. Gallup* that a rapist who dragged the victim out of her date's parked car, blindfolded her, and pushed her into a station wagon, telling her, "Don't fight me and you'll be all right," had indeed threatened her, and it wasn't necessary for her to prove that she had resisted. The

1970 case of *Johnson v. U.S.*, from the District of Columbia, says that consent isn't shown when resistance is overcome by threats putting the victim in fear of death or of great bodily harm. If she *had* seen the gun, it would strengthen her case, but it isn't unreasonable to believe that a rapist who claims to be armed is telling the truth, and it's not unreasonable to fear death or great bodily harm from an armed assailant.

• The prosecution must be careful to avoid introducing testimony that could be interpreted as evidence of the victim's good reputation or previous chastity; this evidence could be used as the basis of the introduction of rebuttal evidence.

• Kansas will allow a rape crisis counselor or other expert witness to testify about the rape-trauma syndrome (common psychological responses to rape). For example, if the rape wasn't reported immediately, the defendant may claim that the charge of rape is fabricated; the expert witness rebuts this by showing that the traumatized victim needed time to be able to deal with the incident. However, testimony of this type must be handled very carefully—there's a risk that a rape counselor who testifies about rape trauma might also have to testify about feelings of guilt and responsibility expressed by the victim.

California, Minnesota, and Missouri have refused to allow expert testimony on the rape-trauma syndrome, holding that there's not enough scientific evidence that there really *is* a rape-trauma syndrome as distinct from individual reactions of victims.

DATE RAPE

Patty Woodhall and Michael Loewe worked in the same office. They had dated several times, and their rapport was beginning to grow. On the night of the incident, they dined in a romantic little restaurant, danced to soft violins, then went to Loewe's apartment. Woodhall was aroused and anticipating lovemaking with pleasure. They sipped brandy until midnight, when Loewe stood up, stretched, yawned, and said, "Got an early day tomorrow. I'll get you a cab." Woodhall knocked him down, broke his jaw, removed his clothes, and repeatedly jammed a bottle into his anus. When he called the police, he was treated with barely disguised contempt, asked why he had let a woman into his apartment if he didn't intend to have sex with her, asked if he enjoyed the assault, and warned that if he were foolish enough to pursue the case he would be subjected to prolonged and humiliating questioning about his social and sexual habits.

Just kidding, folks! This scenario is implausible for several reasons (not least the unlikeliness that a woman would derive any gratification from the attack), but if it did happen, the perpetrator would be guilty of rape, sexual assault, or sexual battery in one of the thirty-five states in which the rape statute is written in gender-neutral terms. In the real world, women are much more likely to be attacked by men who date them, work with them, offer them lifts, or buy them drinks, than men are by women who stand in those relations to them. Just as the major issue in a stranger rape is identification, the major issue in a date-rape case is consent. Especially if the rape victim wasn't severely beaten, the trial can turn into a "swearing contest" in which the rape victim describes the rape and the defendant describes a delightful romantic evening, attributing the charge to the complainant's need to rationalize pregnancy or venereal disease, to excuse infidelity, or to seek vengeance for some real or imagined slight.

In five states (Delaware, Hawaii, Maine, North Dakota, West Virginia) it's a mitigating circumstance (lowers the degree of the crime) if the victim was the rapist's "voluntary social companion" on the occasion of the crime. In Delaware, this provision applies only if the victim earlier consented to sexual contact. In Hawaii, it applies if the victim had consented to sexual contact of the same type some time in the preceding month; in Maine, if she allowed some kind of sexual contact on that occasion; in North Dakota, it's a mitigating factor if the victim ever allowed "sexual liberties" (a revealing phrase; the tone of disapproval comes through, implying that once a woman enters the demi-monde she forfeits the protection of respectable society).

THE ROAD TO THE COURTHOUSE

- A date-rape case follows the same pattern as a stranger-rape case.

THE SMOKING GUN

- The focus in a date-rape case is directly on the victim, and on the credibility of her account of the events leading up to the rape. Because many rape-shield laws make an exception for testimony about prior sexual activity between the victim and the rapist, the victim must be prepared for admission of testimony of this type and for questions about her past relationship with the rapist.
- However, at least some courts understand that consent to sexual activity isn't a lifetime carte blanche: "The previous consent to sexual intercourse and the fair implication that the witness would have been willing even on this occasion to engage in the acts previously consented, doesn't give the defendant a license to forcefully require other sexual acts which the complaining witness testified were against her will." (*People v. Wilcox.*) The 1980 Utah case of *State v. Myers* says

The view so expressed [by the trial judge at the sentencing hearing] seems to suggest that if a woman is "friendly" in accepting the proffered hospitality of a man for food and drink, and engages in "necking," that is, kissing and hugging, and that this persists over a period of time, she loses her right to protest against further advances the man may desire to force upon her; and thereby subjects herself to such advances and should be deemed to consent to intercourse if he, but not she, so desires. Neither this Court nor the law will justify any such conclusion.

The victim in *People v. Edmond*, a 1979 Illinois case, had accepted rides home from the rapist, a colleague of hers, on two prior occasions. On the day of the rape, she waited several hours at their workplace so that he could give her a ride home (there had been a severe snowstorm, but public transportation was still running); it took several hours for the drive, which was interrupted first by a detour she suggested so she could get her shoes fixed, next by a breakdown of the defendant's van, and finally by the rape. She was examined at a hospital, where contusions, swelling, and lacerations of her face, and a chipped tooth, were observed. When the defendant was arrested, his hand was bitten where she said she had bitten him during the struggle. The court summed up the situation this way: "Based on these facts, defendant argues that complainant consented to a day of adventure which included sexual intercourse with the defendant. We disagree. Although complainant may have consented to a ride home and to the defendant's company during the ride, neither the facts nor the law warrant an inference that she also consented to sexual intercourse." Similarly, another Utah case, *State v. Herzog*, says, "The fact that the prosecutrix accepted a ride from the defendant, accompanied him to a store where she bought beer for the two of them, and even agreed to ride into the canyon with him, is not legally determinative of the question of consent. One does not surrender the right to refuse sexual intimacy by the act of accepting another's company, or even by encouraging and accepting romantic overtures."

• Even imprudent behavior doesn't remove a woman from the protection of the law. The victim in *Commonwealth v. Gouveia*, a 1976 Massachusetts case, climbed out of her boyfriend's car after a party (she and her boyfriend may or may not have been making love in the car; it's not clear from the decision). She was drunk, and she discovered that her wallet and car keys were missing. She encountered the defendant, who suggested that she lie down in his van; she did, and this is where the rape took place. The judge said, "We need hardly add that the defendant had no right to appeal to the jury on the basis that by her conduct the victim had forfeited any claim to protection from rape." Of course, it's quite necessary to add that.

- The rape-shield laws of some states do permit evidence of the victim's sexual conduct with men other than the defendant; in these states, if the rapist is convicted, he may appeal on the basis that this evidence should have been admitted. If that happens, the prosecutor handling the appeal can cite cases like Michigan's *People v. Thompson*:

> The problem is, however, that there is no fundamental right to ask questions that are irrelevant . . . The fact that a victim has consented to sexual intimacy with a third party does not indicate consent to intimacy with the defendant . . . the state clearly has a legitimate interest in encouraging the rape victim to report the crime and to prosecute and present testimony against the offender. These interests are served by discouraging the usually pointless and sometimes cruel treatment of rape victims in the criminal justice system. Moreover, there is the possibility that in its deliberations the jury will consider the "bad character" or "provocative behavior" of the rape victim whose life history has been paraded before it in the most intimate detail.

Or, as the Wisconsin court said, reasonably enough, in *Milenkovic v. State*, (1978),

> There is no authoritative or convincing evidence in the record or cited by the defendant which suggests that consent to sexual intercourse on one or many occasions produces an invariable propensity to consent or the likelihood to consent to the defendant. Even if promiscuity suggests the likelihood of consent to any person, it in no way suggests that the woman will then claim rape.

MARITAL RAPE

In the early years of their marriage, Dora Wills's husband would occasionally become abusive and beat her severely. Although she did not enjoy the beatings, she did enjoy the aftermath, when Bob would become tender and loving. The beatings are more frequent now, and are usually followed by a rape; Bob seldom initiates intercourse except in connection with abuse, perhaps because the stimulus of violence has become necessary to him. Dora envies her friend Ellen Lewis. Ellen's husband occasionally demands his "marital rights," but he doesn't beat his wife—unless Ellen is too ashamed to mention it.

The very earliest traditions analyze rape as a property crime. The rape victim's father found himself saddled with a defiled, and hence unmarriageable, daughter; or perhaps she could be married off, but to a less desirable marital prospect. That's why it was sometimes possible for a rapist to escape punishment by marrying the victim. He made up for the father's loss that way. The victim's feelings can be imagined, but then no one asked her. Once a woman was married, her husband had a property right in her fidelity, because it was necessary to have legitimate heirs for his assets. Under this analysis, marital rape was a non-crime; a trial for rape in marriage would be as senseless as a prosecution for stealing one's own property. (Michael Freeman points this out in an article in the Winter 1981 issue of the *Family Law Quarterly*.)

The ineffable Matthew Hale is still being quoted to the effect that once a woman marries, her consent to marriage equals a surrender of any right to refuse sexual intercourse.

In most states, the rape laws are written to define the crime as sexual compulsion directed against a person who isn't married to the perpetrator. The law is written this way in Alabama, Alaska, Arizona, Colorado, Delaware (but if a wife suffers serious physical injury in the course of the rape, her husband can be convicted), Idaho, Illinois, Indiana, Iowa, Kansas, Kentucky, Louisiana, Maine, Maryland, Michigan, Minnesota, Missouri, Montana, Nevada, New Mexico, New York, North Carolina, North Dakota, Ohio, Oklahoma, Rhode Island, South Carolina, South Dakota, Tennessee, Texas, Utah, Vermont, Washington, and West Virginia. In some states, cohabitants are treated like married couples—that is, rape may be bad manners, but it isn't a cognizable crime: this is true in Alabama, Kentucky, Maine, Minnesota, Montana, and West Virginia.

Some states have what is called a "common-law marital exception": that is, they don't have statutes answering the question, but it's presumed that they follow the tradition that makes it impossible to prosecute a husband for raping his wife. The states that are considered to fall into this category are Arkansas, Florida, Georgia, Hawaii, Mississippi, Nebraska, Oregon, and Virginia.

However, in August 1984, a Florida jury convicted William Rider of kidnapping and sexual battery committed against his wife during an ongoing marriage. The defendant claimed that his wife "had asked [him] to rip off her clothes as part of a sexual game." No comment.

After all, as California State Senator Bob Wilson was stupid enough to remark where a journalist could hear him, "If you can't rape your own wife, who can you rape?"

Occasionally the legal system is asked to explain the rationale behind these rules. Either Matthew Hale is trotted out again or the apologist says that intact homes must not be disrupted by criminal proceedings. (It has often been pointed out that rape is fairly disruptive.) This rationale doesn't work at all once the couple have been divorced, or once they have separated. Therefore, many states do treat the rape of a woman by her estranged husband as a crime. The technical details vary: sometimes it's a defense that the victim has not instituted an action for separation or divorce; sometimes the law defines the action as criminal if the two are just living apart, sometimes they must be living apart under a judicial decree, or either a decree or a written agreement. (The states involved are Alaska, Colorado, Idaho, Indiana, Iowa, Kentucky, Louisiana, Maine, Maryland, Michigan, Minnesota, Montana, Nevada, New Mexico, New York, North Carolina, Ohio, Rhode Island, South Carolina, Tennessee, and Utah.) The common denominator is that, to be protected against rape, a woman who is estranged from her husband must go through a certain amount of rigamarole, and probably incur a certain amount of expense; she must also have decided that the marriage is over and taken legal steps to bury it. (Thomas Burrows makes this point in his article in the *University of Illinois Law Review*.) In most states, a woman has no recourse in the criminal law system if her husband rapes her during a continuing marriage, while they are still living together.

Sometimes even separation won't give a woman legal protection, as in the Virginia case of *Kizer v. Commonwealth*, 11 *F.L.R.* 1011 (10/12/84). A man's conviction for raping his wife was set aside by the state Supreme Court, on the theory that she had not made it clear to her husband that the marriage was over. They were separated, and she had not voluntarily had sexual intercourse with him in six months, but Ms. Kizer had cancelled a planned visit to a divorce lawyer before the attack. That she might want—and deserve—to think about the future of her marriage while remaining free from sexual violence doesn't seem to have occurred to the court.

There are exceptions to the rule that rape during a going marriage won't be treated as a crime. California's Penal Code includes a separate section dealing with rape of a spouse but requires the victim to report the crime within 30 days or lose her remedy. In Connecticut, sexual assault in a marriage or cohabitation relationship is a B felony—the same level of seriousness as a first-degree sexual assault. Massachusetts statutes didn't settle the question, but the case of *State v. Chretien* did: the court allowed a man to be convicted for the rape of his estranged wife, on the grounds that the state's Domestic Violence Act defined "abuse" to include forced sex. This showed that the legislature viewed marital rape as a problem; they wanted the procedures of the Domestic Violence Act to be one of the remedies (but not the only remedy) available to wives victimized by forced sex. The New Hampshire statute makes it clear that a husband *can* be guilty of the rape of his wife; the New Jersey law says that the perpetrator of a sexual assault is "not presumed incapable" of the crime because he (or she) is married to the victim. The Wisconsin and Wyoming laws are similar.

New York's statutes still maintain the spousal exemption, but the rule has been changed by case law. *People v. Liberta*, 11 *Family Law Reporter* (*F.L.R.*) 1119 (Ct. of Appeals 12/20/84), holds that husbands can be charged with the rape of their wives, even in a continuing marriage.

Effective February 19, 1985, Pennsylvania's H.B. 281 makes it illegal to rape one's spouse or cohabitant by use of force or threats "that would prevent resistance by a person of reasonable resolution." However, it's only a second-degree felony; a stranger rape is a first-degree felony.

Many years ago I read one of those family-chronicle sort of novels; I don't remember the title or author, but I do remember the situation. One of the characters was the wife of a senior military officer. She was gang-raped and severely beaten. When her husband came to visit her in the hospital, his first words to her were, "But if that's what you wanted, why didn't you come to me?"

In her 1979 study, Lenore Walker found that nearly all battered women had been raped by their husbands. Laura X, an activist for battered women, says, "There is nothing more domestic and nothing more violent than marital rape"; the subject forms a bridge between the law of domestic violence and the law of rape.

THE ROAD TO THE COURTHOUSE

• In many jurisdictions, a man can't be prosecuted for the rape of his legal spouse (and, in some jurisdictions, of a woman living with him); in others, the two may have to be legally separated, or in the process of obtaining a divorce or legal separation. If a woman doesn't conform to her state's categories, she will have to look for other avenues of redress—maybe the remedies available to battered women (see Chapter V) or a prosecution for simple assault for the other injuries she received during the incident.

• Victims of marital rape have a problem that doesn't face victims of stranger rape or date rape—they are often economically dependent on the rapist. Therefore they may hesitate or find it impossible to take action that could result in the arrest or jailing of their husbands.

THE SMOKING GUN

• If a woman is raped by her ex-husband after divorce, she may be able to introduce evidence of earlier rapes during their marriage and separation during the trial for the post-divorce rape: see the Wyoming case of *Vasquez v. State*.

• The pre-*Liberta* New York case of *People v. De Stefano* is interesting. It modified New York statute law by saying that a husband who is living apart from, but not legally separated from, his wife can be guilty of her rape. The court's rationale is that a woman's right to privacy gives her a right to have an abortion without her husband's consent, so she must also have a right to refuse the act that could lead to a pregnancy that she could terminate unilaterally. Anyway, the marriage itself isn't irrevocable, so her consent to the marriage should not be treated as indefinite consent to sexual intercourse.

• The *De Stefano* case also makes it clear that, if a woman has an Order of Protection against further violence (see pages 119–122), rape is certainly a violation of this order.

CIVIL SUITS

A crime is an act that is considered to be an offense against the state; the state prosecutes crimes. A tort is an act that is considered to be an offense against another person; the person who feels injured has the right to sue the alleged tortfeasor (person who, it's claimed, committed the tort(s)). It's perfectly possible for the same action to be both a tort and a crime. Criminal cases have to be proved beyond a reasonable doubt, using evidence obtained without violating the Constitutional rights of the accused. Insofar as the victim is represented at all, the prosecutor speaks for the victim. At least the victim isn't expected to pay for the privilege. Civil suits for tort are instituted by private parties, who pay for their own lawyers (though, if they win, they may be reimbursed by the losers). To win a civil suit, it's only necessary to show that your contention is more likely than not, a standard that's easier to meet than proof beyond a reasonable doubt; and there are fewer restrictions on collecting evidence in civil cases. The conviction and sentencing of a criminal may give the victim moral satisfaction and a feeling of safety; winning a tort judgment gives her the right to collect money.

Rape falls into the category of being both tort and crime, but that's of academic interest, as few rapists have any assets to speak of.

For a civil suit by a rape victim to be worthwhile, she must find a defendant who not only violated a legal duty but who has enough assets or enough insurance to be worth suing.

• The owner or manager of the building in which the rape occurred may be liable, if he/she/it was aware of poor security, the possibility (or actual occurrence) of crimes on the premises, and if no action was taken to correct the condition; see the 1970s District of Columbia case, *Kline v. 1500 Massachusetts Avenue Apartment Corporation*.

• If the rapist is regularly employed, and his job gives him access to rape victims (for example, if he has a passkey), his employer may be liable if no inquiry was made into the employee's past history: *Ponticas v. KMS Investment*, a 1983 Minnesota case.

• It's at least a jury question whether a hotel keeper should be held responsible for a sexual attack made on a hotel guest in a public area of the hotel: (Missouri, 1983: *Virginia D. v. Madesco Investment Corp.*). The case of *Garzilli v. Howard Johnson's Motor Lodges*, a 1976 federal case, assumes without discussing it that the motel *should* bè held responsible for the victim's rape by an intruder who entered through glass doors that appeared to be secure but weren't. The only issue the court raised was whether the victim (whose professional name is Connie Francis) was entitled to the very extensive damages she was awarded for the loss of her career. The Eastern District of New York court found that the damages weren't excessive. If security devices are installed in a motel *after* a guest is raped, the victim may be able to use this fact as proof that security was inadequate when she was attacked. (Eighth Circuit: *Anderson v. Malloy.*)

• A long shot: in 1976, a California court found that a therapist who treats a patient s/he believes to be dangerous has a duty to warn the patient's potential victims and can be held liable by the eventual victims for failure to warn.

7
WOMEN'S HEALTH ISSUES

In 1954, Jane Bodmer was a confused, angry, and resentful teenage bride, grateful at least that she wasn't a teenage unwed mother. She couldn't afford a private doctor. Maybe the hospital clinic told her she was getting a new drug as part of an experiment. She doesn't remember; she kept her appointments and swallowed whatever she was told to swallow. The marriage dissolved shortly after her daughter Angela was born. Jane always felt guilty—about getting pregnant out of wedlock, about raising a daughter without a father, and certainly about the cancer that ravaged Angela's body and has left her weak, scarred, and unable to bear children of her own. Sometimes Jane wonders if God is punishing her—but why do it by giving a hideous disease to Angela?

As a result of both biological (only women get pregnant) and social factors (in general, women are more concerned with their attractiveness to men than men are with their attractiveness to women), women use certain drugs and devices to prevent unwanted pregnancies, maintain wanted pregnancies, cope with menstruation and morning sickness, and attain more socially acceptable breast sizes. No medical intervention is entirely without risks; and the risks of these particular procedures give rise to legal issues of such hellish complexity that only a bar examiner could love them.

PRODUCTS LIABILITY

If American law had been created at one time, by one or more omniscient theoreticians, it might make some sense. But it grew like a fungus. From time to time, scholars and legislators have tried to organize the law into watertight compartments, each with its own rules, procedures, evidentiary requirements, and statute of limitations.

At first, there was a subcompartment of the law of contracts called breach of warranty. If a manufacturer promised that goods had certain qualities (or if a promise of passable quality could be implied), and if the promise was violated, the manufacturer could be sued for breach of warranty.

The compartment marked "torts," in turn, had a subcompartment labeled "negligence." If the manufacturer exercised less care than a prudent manufacturer would have exercised, and therefore produced a defective product, the victim of that defect could sue for negligence. There were certain problems with this scheme. First of all, in the not unlikely case that a carelessly manufactured object breached its warranties, it was inconvenient to encounter different rules for each end of the case. Second, a system that was (barely) workable when informed buyers bought products they understood directly from the manufacturer developed gaping rents when consumers bought more complicated and more dangerous products from the last in a series of middlemen. A farmer could inspect a set of horse harness before he bought it, and could recognize any defects and either reject the harness or get the harnessmaker to fix it. But the average befuddled consumer discovered the defect in his Hupmobile or her bottle of Moxie only when it blew up.

Eventually a new compartment was constructed and identified as "products liability," combining negligence and breach of warranty and throwing in a few grace notes of its own. Products liability goes beyond negligence. Because many modern products are quite dangerous, or can turn out to be dangerous many years after manufacture, sometimes manufacturers can be held liable even if they weren't negligent. This is called "strict liability," or "liability without fault" (which is rather difficult to imagine). Under this rubric, a manufacturer can get in trouble for defective manufacture (the product doesn't match up to the manufacturer's specifications, as in the hypothetical case that the pill is 75 percent DES and 25 percent rat poison) or defective design (the design of the product, not manufacturing problems, makes it dangerous).

When courts are faced with a strict liability issue, they usually quote §402A of the Restatement (Second) of Torts. A Restatement is produced by a group of legal scholars who try to make some sense out of a particular area of the law. Restatements have no official status whatever, but are accorded much respect by judges.

Section 402A makes anyone who sells a product "in a defective condition unreasonably dangerous" liable for personal injury and property damage caused to users of the product. The seller is liable if it's in the business of selling products of that type, and if the product is supposed to (and does) reach the consumer substantially in the form in which it was sold. In other words, this provision doesn't apply to amateur or casual sales, or to products that have been monkeyed with after they leave the prospective defendant's hands. But strict liability *does* apply even if the "seller has exercised all possible care in the preparation and sale of his product." The manufacturer or dealer is on the hook, provided the plaintiff can prove the product was indeed "in a defective condition unreasonably dangerous."

That theory works well enough for chain saws that could have been designed with better guards, or for automobiles that could have been designed so that they don't double as flame-throwers. But what about dangers that can't be anticipated, because they are identifiable only by later scientific advances? What about products whose risks *are* known, but whose benefits are deemed to outweigh the risks?

That's where the famous "Comment k," "Unavoidably unsafe products," comes in. (It's a comment to §402A.) As the Restatement says, some products (especially drugs) "in the present state of human knowledge are quite incapable of being made safe for their intended and ordinary use." The example they give is the Pasteur rabies vaccine. The vaccine is in fact dangerous, but it's two weeks in the country compared to untreated rabies, which nearly always causes an unusually horrible death.

> The same is true of many other drugs, vaccines, and the like, many of which for this very reason can't legally be sold except to physicians, or under the prescription of a physician. It is also true in particular of many new or experimental drugs as to which, because of lack of time and opportunity for sufficient medical experience, there can be no assurance of safety, or perhaps even of purity of ingredients, but such experience as there is justifies the marketing and use of the drug notwithstanding a medically recognizable risk.

The manufacturer of such "unavoidably unsafe products" isn't subject to strict liability "for unfortunate consequences attending their use, merely because he has undertaken to supply the public with an apparently useful and desirable product, attended with a known but apparently reasonable risk." If the product is "properly prepared and accompanied by proper directions and warnings," it isn't considered defective at all; nor is it unreasonably dangerous. Therefore, strict liability doesn't apply; and since the manufacturer wasn't negligent and didn't warrant that the drug was free of side effects, the injured consumer is out of luck.

The bottom line is that, in a case involving a drug or medical device, the manufacturer will try to get it classified as an unavoidably unsafe product (and is fairly likely to succeed). In that case, the plaintiff has to prove that the drug or device was sold without adequate warnings. So much for the general problems of products liability for drugs. Each of the products I'm going to discuss has its own theoretical problems, and its own technical litigation problems to bedevil plaintiffs and plaintiffs' lawyers.

DES

In 1937, British researchers developed a method of making a particular female hormone synthetically. The discovery was of major importance for endocrinology. Instead of a tiny amount of hormone being available to the medical profession at a huge price, a huge amount was available at a tiny price.

The British group didn't patent its work, so the new technology was immediately and completely available to American drug manufacturers. Depending on how cynically you see things, either the manufacturers then explored ways in which this new drug could help humanity or, having a cure without a disease, they went looking for ways to make a buck. At any rate, there was some evidence that the synthetic hormone DES prevented miscarriage, and that women who took DES during pregnancy had larger, healthier babies. (There are several related artificial hormones; the most commonly prescribed was diethylstilbestrol. I'll use "DES" to refer to all the hormones.)

In 1947, based on data submitted by several drug companies (a fact that will become important later) the Food and Drug Administration approved DES for use in pregnancy to prevent miscarriage. In 1962, the FDA decided DES was no longer a "new drug," so manufacturers were allowed to enter the DES market without submitting research data to the FDA.

The late forties and fifties were the baby boom years, and anything that was believed to promote fetal health was eagerly prescribed. Some doctors prescribed DES for patients with a history of miscarriages; others for patients whose current pregnancy was risky; still others prescribed it for *all* their pregnant patients. Some of the women were told it was a new drug, "DES" or "stilbestrol"; some were told it was a "hold-the-baby-in" pill, and some were told nothing at all. For some doctors, DES prescriptions were too routine to be noted in the records. It's impossible to tell how many pregnant women took DES; estimates range from half a million to three million.

It is also impossible to tell how many companies manufactured DES; again, estimates range from one hundred to three hundred. Since DES was a generic drug, pharmacists filled DES prescriptions with whatever brand of the drug they happened to stock. Generally, neither the prescription nor the pharmacist's records indicated the brand of drug supplied.

However, in the early fifties, clinical tests at the University of Chicago and Tulane University showed that ingestion of DES during pregnancy caused *more* miscarriage and sicker babies; the research results were published in prestigious medical journals in 1952 and 1953. (The FDA didn't require drug manufacturers to supply proof of the efficacy of drugs until 1962; before that time, the entire licensing process was concerned with safety.)

Late in the sixties, there were several reports of teenage girls with a very rare genital cancer called adenocarcinoma, a disease that was previously believed to be almost entirely restricted to older women. As more and more cases were reported, a connection was discovered: these young women's mothers had taken DES during pregnancy. The evidence piled up, and in 1971 the use of DES as a miscarriage preventive was banned. The drug was still permitted to be used for other medical applications—including, of all things, an abortifacient (the "morning-after pill" used to prevent implantation of a fertilized ovum).

"DES daughters," women whose mothers took DES during pregnancy, suffer a variety of health problems. A small percentage of them have developed or will develop adenocarcinoma, and may have to undergo radiation therapy, chemotherapy, and/or removal of ovaries, uterus, or vagina. Some of them die of adenocarcinoma; others recover. Some DES daughters are born with an abnormally shaped cervix, or develop a condition called adenosis (abnormal cells in the vagina and cervix). Adenosis isn't cancer but is sometimes considered pre-cancerous. Women with adenosis or cervical dysplasia (abnormal anatomy) have a high miscarriage rate as well as a (well-founded) fear of developing cancer. Some DES sons are born with abnormal testicles and are at increased risk for testicular cancer.

It isn't known what percentage of DES daughters will develop adenosis (estimates range from 30 to 90 percent) or how many women with adenosis will develop cancer. If it's true that 90 percent do develop adenosis, and that three million pregnant women took DES, there are about 1,350,000 potential plaintiffs in the DES case; even if the real figures are 30 percent and half a million, that's 75,000 potential plaintiffs—a heavy burden for the courts.

In some ways, DES cases are simple. The DES daughters are certainly not contributorily negligent; they weren't even born when their mothers took the drug. Reasonably speaking, the mothers can't be blamed for taking prescription drugs on the advice of their physicians. It's well accepted that there's a direct connection between DES, adenocarcinoma, adenosis, and genital abnormalities. So what's the problem?

DES cases are in fact a nightmare for plaintiffs' attorneys because despite all these plus factors, there are two very serious problems: identification and statute of limitations.

Remember, DES was sold as a generic drug. If it had been a patented drug, there would have been only one manufacturer during the patent period. If it had been marketed under strong trademarks, it would be possible to trace at least some sales to particular manufacturers using these trademarks. But the stuff was doled out like crackers from the old cracker barrel. Even if the pharmacy or doctor kept records going back fifteen, twenty, or twenty-five years, the records would probably indicate only that DES was prescribed and supplied, not who the manufacturer was.

The purpose of a statute of limitations is to keep potential defendants and courts from being bothered by stale claims. Potential plaintiffs have to put up or shut up—file suit within a certain number of years, or lose all possibility of legal redress. This works perfectly well in the average fender-bender automobile case or exploding-soda-bottle or self-starting-chain-saw case. It's quite clear when the injury occurs and when the suit can and must be filed. But some cases have a "long tail": either it takes a long time for the injury to develop (e.g., years of breathing asbestos fibers) or a long time for the plaintiff to recognize that an injury has occurred. Pain or disability suffered by women—especially if the genitals or sexual function is involved—is sometimes diagnosed by male doctors as a psychiatric problem (the woman uses her symptoms to gain attention or defer unwanted sex) or a political one (she hasn't adjusted to her female role—that is, she doesn't know her place). By the time a DES daughter is injured, or knows she is injured, the statute of limitations may already have run, so no suit is possible.

Although there are generic drugs, there is no such thing as a generic lawsuit. The plaintiff must sue at least one identifiable defendant, and if the plaintiff can't prove that one or more of the named defendants is liable, she will lose her case—even if it's obvious that *someone* is liable.

In short, somebody is going to lose out: either the plaintiff or the drug company, which marketed a product conforming to what was then the standard of medical knowledge, and which may or may not have manufactured the actual pills consumed by the plaintiff's mother. It's very much like a firing squad: somebody gets a blank cartridge so that each member of the firing squad can feel guiltless of the shooting because he *might* have had the blank. Of course, whatever the subjective feelings of the firing squad, the guy facing the other way is still dead.

Similarly, the DES victim is absolutely innocent, and there's a lot of feeling that she should recover even if recovery is impossible under traditional legal theories. Four major, and some minor, theories have been developed by courts trying to find a remedy for the plaintiffs.

Liability Theories

The four major theories are:

• Alternative liability: this theory is based on a classic tort case in which three men went hunting and two of them fired at once; one bullet struck the third man. Clearly, then, one of the hunters shot him; the other was just as negligent but did not in fact shoot him. The court allowed the plaintiff to sue both the hunters; it was up to them to prove that the other guy did it. In the DES context, the plaintiff seeking to establish manufacturers' liability has to sue *all* the manufacturers, then let them point at each other. The problem is that there were at least a hundred manufacturers making DES during most of the time it was prescribed; some of the marginal manufacturers are no longer in business; and much time can be consumed in discovery and at trial sorting out which manufacturers were in the DES business when the plaintiff's mother was pregnant. The leading alternative liability case is Michigan's *Abel v. Eli Lilly and Co.*, and this theory has also worked in Pennsylvania *(Erlich v. Abbott Laboratories)*. The plaintiff in the latter case sued the manufacturers of 90 percent of the DES available at the time of ingestion; the court allowed the application of alternative liability even though not all the possible defendants were sued.

By and large, though, alternative liability serves as a tool of analysis for law review articles and as a straw man to be knocked down by courts refusing to apply this theory, as in the 1981 New Jersey case of *Namm v. Frosst*, for example, or Florida's 1982 *Morton v. Abbott*. The *Namm* case makes the sensible point that the manufacturers don't have much chance of identifying the guilty party either.

• Enterprise liability is another straw man. Enterprise liability requires suing all of the manufacturers in a particular market. *All* of the manufacturers are considered liable under this theory, if they make virtually identical products to the same specifications. Enterprise liability was applied in a classic case in which a boy was injured by a blasting cap; all six manufacturers of blasting caps (a generic product) were held liable. But these six manufacturers controlled the entire blasting cap industry; judges refusing to apply enterprise liability generally point out that the DES manufacturers sued controlled less than all the market. Anyway, when all the manufacturers are sued, the manufacturer of the dangerous device is necessarily included; if they're not all sued, it's possible that the real manufacturer will be passed by (like the wicked fairy in Sleeping Beauty) when subpoenas are handed out. But in this case, it's those who are invited, not those who are passed over, who are angry.

• Concerted action: under this theory, everyone who manufactured DES is jointly and severally liable to everyone hurt by the product. The essence of joint and several liability is that the plaintiff is allowed to sue only one of the possible defendants, all of them, or anywhere in between, and can collect her full damages against any defendant. If the defendant doesn't like this, it has to haul others causing the same harm into court and make the court order them to pay up (the technical term for this is "contribution"). The leading case under this theory is New York's 1982 *Bichler v. Lilly.*

As a refreshing change, this theory is based on moldy old antitrust cases instead of moldy old tort cases. A conspiracy to fix prices can be established by showing "conscious parallelism": that is, that the conspirators raised and lowered prices (more of the former, of course) at about the same time. In other words, legal action (changing prices) can be part of a conspiracy to commit illegal price-fixing. But the analogy with DES is less than perfect: the drug companies, in providing information to the FDA, did something legal for a *legal* purpose (getting approval for a drug which, as far as they or anyone else knew, was safe). The *Bichler* court found that the four manufacturers the plaintiff sued had engaged in conscious parallel conduct by selling DES without testing it on pregnant animals or monitoring its effect on human pregnancy. But it took a number of tragedies like those of thalidomide and DES itself to create scientific sensitivity to the dangers of drug use during pregnancy; I'm not sure that Lilly and the other eleven companies didn't follow what was, for that time, normal scientific procedure. Anyway, only twelve companies provided the information used by the FDA in approving DES for use in pregnancy. The remaining horde of manufacturers relied on the FDA's approval. It seems to me that the FDA is at least partly to blame; it could have demanded better studies, and documentation of the effect of DES on pregnant animals, before approving the drug for use in pregnancy. At least two plaintiffs have taken this tack and sued the FDA. They lost: private individuals are not allowed to sue the FDA for botching the job of drug regulation. Government officials, in general, are given wide discretion and are immune from suits based on good-faith though ham-fisted actions.

• Market-share liability is used when the plaintiff can't identify the manufacturer of the DES her mother took. (If she can make the identification, she must sue that manufacturer and that manufacturer only.) The plaintiff who uses a market-share liability theory has to sue enough manufacturers to ensure that there's a good statistical likelihood that the actual manufacturer is a defendant. Then it's up to the defendants to prove that they couldn't have manufactured the drug taken by the plaintiff's mother (e.g., they never sold DES in that state, never manufactured a pill of that size, shape, or dosage). Defendants can cross-complain (bring other manufacturers in as defendants). The defendants who can't exculpate themselves must pay damages corresponding to their "market share": that is, if Lilly had 50 percent of the market, it must pay 50 percent of the damages. The leading case for this theory is *Sindell v. Abbott Laboratories*, 26 Cal.3d. 588, 607 P.2d 924, 163 Cal.Rptr. 132 (1980), *cert.den.*, 449 U.S. 912.

An often-quoted New Jersey case, *Ferrigno v. Lilly*, also favors market-share liability; but two later New Jersey cases say that New Jersey plaintiffs have no case unless they can identify the manufacturer of the particular pills ingested by their mothers.

Florida, Massachusetts, Missouri, South Carolina, and Texas also require identification of the manufacturer as an absolute prerequisite to bringing suit. As it's usually impossible to remember the brand of drug taken fifteen or twenty years earlier, and equally impossible to get the answer from inadequate or nonexistent records, these are noticeably unhealthy states for DES suits.

On the other hand, South Dakota and Wisconsin have been much more accommodating to DES plaintiffs. The 1983 South Dakota case of *McElhaney v. Lilly* allows the plaintiff to recover without identifying the specific manufacturer and without suing all the possible defendants. The South Dakota District Court said that, under the state's strict liability law, the plaintiff has to prove only three things:

- She was hurt by a product.
- She (or, in this case, her mother) was a foreseeable consumer of the product.
- The product was unreasonably dangerous when it left the seller's control.

Once the plaintiff has proved this, it's up to the defendants to exculpate themselves. As they probably have no better idea than anyone else who manufactured the drug taken by the plaintiff's mother, the plaintiff isn't unlikely to win.

The Wisconsin decision, *Collins v. Lilly,* is both detailed and controversial. (It uses negligence, not strict liability, theories.) The Wisconsin Supreme Court said that the lower court should not have dismissed the plaintiff's case just because she couldn't identify the manufacturer. The Supreme Court's position was that, because identification is so difficult and the defendant is in a better position than the plaintiff to absorb the damages, the plaintiff can win her case by proving:

- Her mother took DES during pregnancy.
- The defendant(s) produced or marketed the dosage and kind of DES the plaintiff's mother took.
- The defendant(s) owed a duty of care to the plaintiff, and breached this duty (e.g., the defendant(s) should have conducted more comprehensive, or more sophisticated, tests before marketing the drug).

If the plaintiff sues only one defendant and can prove that the defendant could have manufactured the drug involved, *Collins* lets her collect all her damages from that one defendant. If she sues several defendants, the jury must allocate her damages among the defendants who couldn't clear themselves. The allocation is supposed to penalize the manufacturers who were most negligent the most heavily. The factors to be considered include:

- Whether the defendant tested DES for safety and efficacy.
- The role the particular defendant played in getting DES approved as a miscarriage preventive.
- The manufacturer's market share.
- Whether it provided adequate warnings.

- Whether it sold DES when it knew or should have known of the dangers.
- Whether it took steps to reduce the risk.

However, even the *Collins* court would not impose punitive damages, holding that the plaintiff did not prove that the defendant acted wantonly, willfully, or with reckless disregard for or indifference to the drug user's safety.

The *Collins* theory is very favorable to plaintiffs, because they can recover if they sue even one defendant who could have made the offending pills. But I don't think other courts will rush to follow. For one thing, it's hard to decide whether manufacturers who prepared the FDA application were more or less negligent than the "me-too" manufacturers who made DES after the FDA gave its approval. It's possible to argue that Corvairs are less safe than other automobiles or that Dalkon Shields are less safe than other IUDs and therefore that their manufacturers are negligent; but how can one manufacturer of a uniform product be more negligent than the other manufacturers?

Washington State came up with a new twist in *Martin v. Abbott Laboratories,* 53 *LW* 2216 (Sup.Ct. 10/4/84). A plaintiff doesn't have to identify the defendant precisely, and doesn't have to join manufacturers with a substantial share of the market. All the manufacturers who are potentially liable are assumed to have had equal market shares until they prove otherwise. This approach is similar to the "market-share" rule of the *Sindell* case, but the manufacturer has two chances: to free itself from liability entirely by showing it didn't sell DES in the relevant market at the relevant time, or to reduce its liability by showing that its market share was smaller than the presumption of equality would suggest.

Statute of Limitations

Plaintiffs are expected to be reasonably prompt in pursuing their claims; it's hard for anyone to find evidence by searching a cold trail; and, sooner or later, the legal system concedes that bygones should be bygones. Therefore, all civil cases have a statute of limitations: a time period within which the case must be brought. A "stale" case will be dismissed at the outset. The length of the statute of limitations varies by state and also by the type of case. Depending on the state and the theory on which the plaintiff sues, the statute of limitations can be as short as two years or as long as twelve. But DES-related cancers are generally found when their victims are adolescents. Even if the harm complained of is an abnormal cervix (which the potential plaintiff was born with), it probably won't be discovered until her first pelvic exam—probably when she's a teenager. It is universally agreed that it's tough luck for the plaintiff if she finds out that she's been injured at a time when it's too late to sue. Some states (e.g., Tennessee, New York) express sympathy for the victim but still close her out of the courthouse: the statute of limitations starts to run when the plaintiff's mother took her last DES pill, and ends however many years later. But Tennessee law—like the law of most states—has a loophole that can help many DES plaintiffs. A personal injury suit for harm to a minor can be brought by that minor within one year of reaching her majority (18 or 21, depending on the state), even if the action would be too late under other applicable rules. A Florida court simply refused to apply that state's twelve-year statute of limitations in a DES case, holding that the time limitation violated the Florida Constitution's guarantee of access to the state's courts.

In some states, plaintiffs get the benefit of the application of common sense. In those states, the statute of limitations runs from the discovery of the injury, so the plaintiff isn't expected to sue before she is aware that there's something to sue about.

In Michigan, for example, the statute of limitations doesn't start to run until the plaintiff discovers her injury. If the plaintiff can, by investigation, discover the manufacturer of the DES pills her mother took, the statute of limitations doesn't start to run until she identifies the manufacturer.

> This Court does not think the drug companies can reasonably expect to be immune from suit before their customers or, in this case, their children have a fair opportunity to discover the company's tortious conduct. In drug cases, most of the evidence necessary to prove or defend against liability is likely to be documentary in nature, not the kind that is lost [or] becomes unreliable as time passes. Companies maintain records of the testing of their drugs, and hospitals maintain records. The passage of time in drug cases also increases the amount of scientific knowledge concerning the drug and its alleged harmful effects. In fact, the passage of time here undoubtedly will aid the eventual fact-finder in finding the truth in this case.

That reads well, and I'm glad they found for the plaintiff, but it works better as rhetoric than as logic. For one thing, records get lost, or are destroyed simply to make room for newer records. Especially in the DES context, some information that later proves to be necessary is never recorded. For another thing, a manufacturer's acts in 1947 can't be judged by the standards of 1983 medical science.

In Illinois and Ohio the statute of limitation starts to run when the plaintiff knows (or could have known, with reasonable care) that she has a physical problem and that someone else might be responsible for it. The Pennsylvania rule is a little different: the statute starts to run not when the plaintiff actually finds out about her injury, but at the time when the knowledge was available (which is probably earlier than the time when a reasonable plaintiff would have found it out). This worked out very badly for the plaintiff in *O'Brien v. Lilly,* who sued more than three years after she read an article about the medical problems of DES daughters. The products liability statute of limitations was two years, so her case was too late using that criterion. The breach of warranty statute of limitations was four years—but four years from the ingestion of the substance, not four years from discovery of the injury. But the plaintiff's doctors, obeying her parents' request, told her she did not have cancer, and her mother repeatedly denied taking DES during pregnancy. The dissenting judge made some good points:

> Patients have always been told to "go to your doctor" for advice, but the majority has now imposed a different standard, which is "disregard your mother and disregard your doctor but go to *Newsweek* to learn the etiology of your condition." . . . There is a cruel irony in the majority's ruling. The very *Newsweek* article which they rely on as compelling a teenager to conduct an investigation would never be admitted into evidence if one were attempting to prove that DES causes cancer.

So the very articles that infuriated drug companies when they appeared may end up shielding them from liability.

Usually the plaintiff can choose between suing in her own state's state courts and suing in the nearest federal court. If the defendant(s) don't like the particular court in which the case was originally filed, they may be able to get it moved to another court by claiming "forum non conveniens"—an inconvenient place of trial. The plaintiff's original choice depends on where she thinks she can get the best deal: the most liberal theories of recovery, the longest statute of limitations, the highest recoveries in comparable cases, the smallest backlog so her case can be heard fast. Federal judges are usually considered more sophisticated than state judges; this may or may not be an advantage in a particular case. The process of choosing a court is sometimes called "forum shopping": although there are no Columbus Day sales, it's possible to get a better deal in some courts than in others. But once the case is brought (or transferred from one court to another), the court that eventually hears the case has to decide which state's law to apply.

Choice of Law

DES (and other prescription-drug cases) can lead to a game of Ping-Pong in which the court must decide the state whose law is to be applied. In a typical case, the plaintiff's mother could have taken DES in State A and given birth in State B; the plaintiff, who lives in State C, sues several drug companies that are incorporated in States D, E, and F but are doing business throughout the United States.

There is an arcane legal discipline called "choice of law"; its basic principles are that a state court usually applies the law of the state in which the harm occurred, unless the legal philosophies of the two states are irreconcilable (this principle is called "lex loci delicti," the "law of the place of the wrong," though losing litigants may feel the law of the wrong place was applied). Federal courts generally apply the law of the state in which they are located (unless a federal point of substance or procedure preempts state law), and this includes that state's choice of law principles.

The South Carolina case of *Mizell v. Lilly* is a fairly straightforward illustration of these rules. The plaintiff's mother lived in California when she took the DES, so the plaintiff's cause of action arose in California. She sued six manufacturers in the South Carolina District Court. She couldn't identify the manufacturer, but sued all the corporations that manufactured and distributed DES in California at the time her mother took the drug. She would have had smooth sailing if the court had applied California's "market share" rule derived from the *Sindell* case (see page 154). Unfortunately, the plaintiff encountered the "public policy" exception to the "lex loci delicti" rule: the federal court refused to apply the California market-share theory because it violated the public policy of South Carolina.

If you've got that one under your belt, consider *Trahan v. Squibb*. The plaintiff's mother took DES in South Carolina. The plaintiff was a Tennessee resident, and her DES-related problems were diagnosed in Tennessee. She sued in the Middle District of Tennessee on a strict liability theory; but South Carolina doesn't recognize strict liability and Tennessee does. So if the federal court applied South Carolina law, the plaintiff would lose. The federal court followed Tennessee choice of law principles (lex loci delicti). But where was the place of the wrong—South Carolina, where the drug was ingested, or Tennessee where (as far as anyone knows) the harm was manifested? The *Trahan* court ruled for the plaintiff on two grounds: first, that Tennessee was the place of the wrong because that was where the "last event necessary" to make the defendant liable took place, and second, that the public policy of Tennessee required the application of strict liability.

State Laws

In New York, doctors and nurse-midwives providing prenatal care must notify mothers-to-be of all drugs to be used during pregnancy and delivery. This is obviously aimed at preventing further DES or thalidomide tragedies. If women are given this information (either by law, volunteered by the doctor, or as a result of persistent nagging), it's important for them to record the name of the drug(s), the manufacturers, the dosage, when it was taken, and what the drug looked like (yellow capsule, white pill scored down the middle, etc.). Then this information has to be kept someplace accessible and retrievable, in case it's (regrettably) necessary to treat side effects or bring a product liability suit.

If it were left up to health insurers, the policies of DES victims and their families would be rewritten to exclude DES-related health problems from coverage. Several states (e.g., California, Maine, New York) nip this tactic in the bud by making it illegal.

Maine, New Jersey, and New York have state-funded programs to inform the public about the dangers of DES, to provide screening for DES-exposed persons, and to collect scientific data. The screening can either reassure DES daughters (and their mothers) or let them know in time to start treatment; the statistical information gathered by the registries can be useful in a suit.

THE ROAD TO THE COURTHOUSE

• If at all possible, the plaintiff should find out who made the actual DES her mother took, then bring suit against that manufacturer. Depending on state law, the facts of the case, and the plaintiff's lawyer's preferred strategy, the suit can be based on negligence (failure to test DES properly before marketing it), strict product liability, breach of warranty, and/or improper marketing.

• If the manufacturer can't be identified, the plaintiff must use one of the liability theories discussed on pages 152–156; even if the theory isn't recognized in her state, she may be able to bring a test case that changes the law.

• Because a prescription drug has to be sold with proper warnings (see page 149 for more discussion), it might be possible to win by showing that the defendants' advertising and promotion practices were overenthusiastic and negated the warnings, causing doctors to overprescribe the drug.

• Most of the suits are against drug companies, not against doctors for malpractice. This is probably because of the likelihood that a doctor will be retired (or dead) fifteen or twenty years after treating the plaintiff's mother. Anyway, drug companies tend to have resources far in excess of the average malpractice policy.

My belief is that it should be possible to divide DES cases into two groups: those arising out of DES prescriptions between 1947 and 1952 or 1953, and those from 1953 to 1971. The earliest prescriptions were made when, as far as the medical profession knew, the drug was effective against miscarriage. But once the studies casting doubt on the drug's effectiveness became available, doctors and drug companies should have known that the drug should be prescribed with great care or not at all. I think the cases should also be analyzed in terms of the real danger of miscarriage.

Prescribing DES in 1949 for a woman who was desperate to carry a pregnancy to term after repeated miscarriages was a rational medical judgment, and its dangers a regrettable risk of even the best medical care. But prescribing DES in the sixties when there was no reason to fear miscarriage in a particular case shows contempt for patients (and for women) highly unbecoming to an ob/gyn. The Massachusetts court in the third *Payton* case (437 N.E.2d 171, 1982) said that DES daughters had no right of action against drug manufacturers because they wouldn't have been born in the first place if it weren't for DES, and life with an increased risk of cancer is legally preferable to not being alive in the first place. It seems to me that it's up to the individual to decide this; and also that DES wasn't particularly effective to begin with; furthermore, a number of high-risk pregnancies result in normal births even without drug treatment.

• No one asked me this either, but I think the fairest way to deal with the DES dilemma is to set up a "super-fund." DES victims would present their evidence to a special master; if the master found that a DES-related injury was present, s/he would set damages, and the drug companies would share the damages based not on their market share but on their *profit* share in the DES market for the year of ingestion. That way, liability would be equalized between large and small manufacturers, and between manufacturers who invested heavily in research to get the drug approved and those who rode on the coattails of the earlier manufacturers.

• DES daughters can sue for actual physical injuries or abnormalities they have suffered, but not for their increased risk of developing genital cancers. DES mothers can't sue for their own increased risk of cancer or for guilt and mental anguish caused by fearing that a daughter will develop cancer, or watching her suffer or die. Cases of this type are sometimes called "cancerphobia" cases, but a phobia is an irrational fear, and the fear that DES daughters may develop a rare but terrible disease is both rational and well founded.

• On the other hand, women who were given DES without their informed consent have succeeded in suits for battery and breach of duty to warn against both the university conducting the experiments and the manufacturer.

• What if the drugstore where the plaintiff's mother bought DES, or the drug manufacturing company, has changed ownership in the intervening decades? A 1979 California case holds the successor manufacturer strictly liable for DES made by its predecessor, if the plaintiff can't sue the predecessor directly (for example, if it has gone out of business), if the successor had enough information to gauge the risks of liability before buying the predecessor's business, and if it could spread the risk among its current customers (a posh way of saying that it could raise drug prices to compensate).

On the other hand, a 1980 Michigan case refused to hold a drugstore liable, because it had no connection with the plaintiff's mother or with a sale of DES sixteen years before the present owner bought the drugstore. I think that's fair: a drug company can research a potential acquisition a lot more thoroughly than a pharmacist can investigate every prescription ever filled by a drugstore. California says DES mothers can't sue the pharmacies at all.

THE SMOKING GUN

- If the plaintiff's theory is that the manufacturer should be held strictly liable because the drug was marketed improperly, the plaintiff will probably have to prove that the manufacturer submitted fraudulent information to the FDA, or withheld important information that would have kept the drug from being approved.

- Remember, the drug manufacturer isn't liable if the drug was "unavoidably dangerous" if its benefits outweighed the risks that were known or reasonably foreseeable at the time of use. The *Ferrigno* case says that strict liability can be applied in only two situations: if the drug could not reasonably have seemed useful and desirable at the time it was manufactured, or if the risks recognized by the medical profession outweighed the usefulness of the drug. The factors in balancing risk and usefulness are: the benefits the drug provides; how common the adverse reactions are; how serious they are; the availability of a safer alternative product; the manufacturer's ability to reduce product risks without reducing effectiveness; and the cost of making such improvements. But the *Needham* appeals court said that the lower court should not have admitted evidence of the drug's lack of effectiveness in preventing miscarriage. That case was tried as a failure to warn case, and the manufacturer's defense was that it had no way of knowing there was anything to warn against; the question of usefulness didn't arise. Two years later, a Louisiana court ruled that cancer risk is a factor in deciding whether a drug was unreasonably dangerous, but the evidence must be limited to the period of time ending with the plaintiff's conception.

- Proving the issues in a DES case is made easier by a procedural device called collateral estoppel. If an issue is exactly the same in two cases, the parties in one case may be able to use the determination in the other case instead of having to present all the evidence at trial. It saves time (and money) to be able to quote another court's conclusions rather than dragging in expert witnesses. DES cases are especially favorable for collateral estoppel, because the fact situation is so straightforward: the plaintiff certainly wasn't negligent, her mother wasn't negligent in taking the drugs prescribed for her, and there are no intervening causes. (In contrast, if two families sue a car company because a relative died in an allegedly unsafe car, the manufacturer can claim that the deaths may have been caused by or contributed to by lousy driving, incompetent auto mechanics, or dangerous road conditions.)

Collateral estoppel may be available (depending on the particular court's theories of civil procedure) if the issue involved is the same as the issue in the earlier case; if the issue was actually litigated in the earlier case (not conceded by one side or the other, or shuffled off by a court that found it unnecessary to reach the issue); and if the issue was necessary and essential to the earlier decision. As an example, the New York case of *Kaufman v. Lilly* prevented Lilly from re-litigating the *Bichler* decision's "concerted-action" theory. The plaintiff in *Kaufman* could have a shorter and simpler trial by relying on the *Bichler* case.

If attorneys know that several similar cases are pending, or if their efforts are coordinated, collateral estoppel affects trial strategy. If it's at all possible, the strongest case for the plaintiffs should be tried first. That way, the other plaintiffs can use collateral estoppel. But if the first case is a loser, the defendant gets the benefit of collateral estoppel—it's already been decided that the defendant is *not* liable.

BIRTH CONTROL PILLS

Between the time of the discovery of the connection between sex and pregnancy and the twentieth century, women were inspired to chastity by fear as well as moral feeling. The disgrace (and practical problems) of bearing an illegitimate child restrained many women who otherwise would have yielded to some combination of their own desires, love, wish to please, and emotional blackmail. This was essential for the maintenance of patriarchy (which depends on women's premarital virginity and marital monogamy), but the inconvenience to individual men was obvious.

Over the years, various contraceptive methods, ranging from wishful thinking to moderately scientific arrangements, had been tried with various degrees of success. Coitus interruptus and condoms interfere with male sexual pleasure, and since men never get pregnant no matter how reckless they are sexually, they may get a little careless from time to time.

The diaphragm, developed in the 1920s, has the advantage of being an effective, woman-controlled contraceptive, and the disadvantages of inconvenience and the need to keep buying expensive, vile-tasting spermicides. Some people dislike the premeditated air that diaphragms give to sex: a woman either has to plan to be swept off her feet and insert the diaphragm in advance, or request to be put back on her feet so she can get her diaphragm.

Birth control pills dramatically changed the balance of power between men and women (though in complicated ways that can't be claimed as a clear-cut victory for either side). By taking one pill a day, an action entirely removed from sex, a woman could virtually guarantee that she would not become pregnant, no matter how often she had sex or with how many partners. In short, a woman who took birth control pills had the same sexual freedom as a man. Like a man, she could suffer consequences of sexual freedom, whether in the form of a broken heart, a messy divorce, or a social disease; but if she took the pills on schedule, she could be close to certain that the consequences would not include pregnancy.

In the nineteen sixties, various other social changes (from the role of youth to the quantity and design of female underwear) were conducive to an undeclared war known as the "Sexual Revolution." The Vietnam War wasn't declared either, but it, too, had long-lasting effects. The distinction between "nice girls" and "bad girls" was more or less erased. The advantage to women was that they could seek sexual gratification openly. The disadvantage was that some men began to treat sexual access to particular women as a public utility. (It is less crushing to the average ego to be told, "No, I'm saving myself for marriage," than, "I wouldn't sleep with you if you were the last primate on Earth.")

As public debate about the "New Morality" and "sexual freedom" continued to swirl, and as women pondered the real advantages and disadvantages of the changes in mores, scientific evidence about the dangers of oral contraceptives began to accumulate. Pill users had a higher rate of embolism, and a much higher rate of strokes, than non-Pill users of the same age. On the other hand, they had somewhat less breast and uterine cancer, and it was theorized that there was some protective effect. One idea was that the health of Pill users should be compared with that of other healthy women; another idea was that it should be compared with other *fertile* women, because the Pill, by virtually eliminating the risk of pregnancy, also eliminated the risk of pregnancy complications. Later, more sophisticated statistical studies showed other patterns: that early formulas with a high dose of hormones were more dangerous than low-dose pills developed later; and that the health risks were much greater for smokers than for non-smokers. Birth control pills were associated with, of all things, decreased sexual desire—like alcohol, they increased the opportunities for lechery and took away the performance. Pill risks also increased dramatically with age.

The litigation issues are different for Pill cases than for DES cases but are no less thorny. Birth control pills are brand-name drugs; even if doctor's or pharmacy records are defective, the plaintiff is likely to remember the catchy name and distinctive packaging of the drugs she took. Injury is more likely to manifest itself before the statute of limitations runs, so there's less need for procedural devices to escape the harshness of statute of limitations rules. The major issues in Pill cases tend to be the adequacy of warnings and overpromotion by drug companies. Many cases are brought strictly as malpractice actions, or both the prescribing doctor and the manufacturer are sued.

Warnings and the PPI

The general rule is that an unavoidably unsafe drug isn't unreasonably dangerous (and therefore its manufacturer isn't liable) *if* the drug is sold with the proper warnings. But when a prescription drug is sold, usually the drug company is obliged to warn the *doctor*, not the potential users of the drug. The theory is that the doctor is the "learned intermediary": the manufacturer warns the doctor, who then decides whether the drug should be prescribed and interprets the warnings to the patient. That's why the average drug ad in a medical journal consists of a large photograph, a block of copy explaining that the drug not merely cures all human ills but gets patients out of the office before they have a chance to annoy the doctor, and a page of small print disclosing the side effects, contraindications, and the drug manufacturer's lack of surprise if the patient drops dead simply because she's handed the package containing the prescription. It is in the manufacturer's best interests to provide a good strong warning (but not so strong that doctors won't prescribe the drug); and manufacturers are required to keep up with medical knowledge and to amend the warnings accordingly. There's something a little disingenuous about all these warnings: something like the compressed grapes that were sold during Prohibition with a warning that they must not be dampened and left around, or they would ferment. Not, let me hasten to add, that I think doctors or drug companies *want* women to be injured; but the earnest recitation of symptoms and contraindications is hard to square with selling the stuff in the first place.

That's where the plaintiff's theory of "overpromotion" comes in. If the warning is inadequate or barely adequate, huge splashy ads or battalions of detail men bearing golf balls may induce a doctor to prescribe the drug in inappropriate cases. It is important to remember that ordinary medical education includes little information about drugs and that there is no generally accepted, objective source of drug information for doctors. The publication doctors usually consult, the *PDR* (*Physician's Desk Reference*) is a collection of drug *ads;* all the information comes from the drug companies, and the publishers make no attempt to verify the scientific correctness of any claims.

However, the doctor in the case of *Chambers v. G. D. Searle & Co.* was also a pharmacology professor, so the plaintiff couldn't raise the overpromotion issue; it was presumed that the particular intermediary was learned enough to make up his own mind about the merits of the drug. The plaintiff in *Spinden v. Johnson & Johnson* was equally unsuccessful.

The New Jersey court said that the drug company's two ads in medical journals, plus a policy of giving free samples, did not add up to actionable overpromotion. It's a fine philosophical point whether a warning can be inadequate when the doctor doesn't bother to read it in the first place— it's like the proverbial tree falling in the deserted forest. But a 1983 Michigan case says it's up to the jury to decide whether the doctor's failure to read the *PDR* or the warnings in the package should relieve the manufacturer of liability. Two years earlier, the First Circuit said firmly that the physician's carelessness would not get the manufacturer off the hook if the inadequacy of the warning might have contributed to the carelessness.

Since 1975, birth control pill manufacturers have been required to warn patients directly. Every birth control pill user must be given a brief summary of Pill risks and side effects, and a leaflet known as the Patient Package Insert (PPI) giving a more detailed explanation of contraindications and side effects that should be reported to a doctor. Not only are these inserts informative (if the patient reads them in the first place) but they have legal significance. In some states (e.g., Michigan, Wisconsin) if the manufacturer neglects to provide these legally mandated warnings, it's automatically considered negligent, and the plaintiff doesn't have to prove specific acts of negligence.

THE ROAD TO THE COURTHOUSE

• The injured plaintiff can sue the prescribing doctor, the Pill manufacturer, or both. But if the plaintiff sues the manufacturer in its home state or federal district, that may not be a possible forum for suing the doctor.

• The suit against the doctor is based on a malpractice theory. For example, *Hamilton v. Hardy* found malpractice because the plaintiff's doctor did not terminate her birth control pill prescription when her headaches worsened; eventually she had a stroke. The plaintiff in *Klink v. Searle* also suffered a stroke; the appeals court upheld a malpractice verdict against the doctor who prescribed birth control pills to find out why the plaintiff wasn't menstruating. The doctor claimed the plaintiff had not made out a prima facie case because medical authorities disagreed about the dangers of the Pill. The appeals court said that the plaintiff *had* presented credible medical evidence.

• Various theories have been tried against manufacturers: failure to warn, overpromotion, fraud (knowingly false statements of significant facts, made to induce people to rely on the false statements), breach of warranty, negligent testing of the drug before offering it for sale, strict liability. Unfortunately, these theories don't always work.

• For cases in which the plaintiff was more successful, we have *Ortho Pharmaceutical Corp. v. Chapman*, 388 N.E.2d 541 (Ind.App. 1979), and *Wooderson v. Ortho Pharmaceutical Corp.*, 235 Kan. 387, 681 P.2d 1038 (1984). Ms. Chapman sued on theories of negligence, breach of warranty, and strict liability, and won at the lower court level. The manufacturer appealed. The appeals court said that the plaintiff gave at least enough evidence for the jury to find that the warning was inadequate; and there was a jury question as to whether the inadequate warnings were a proximate (direct) cause of the plaintiff's injuries. A jury awarded Ms. Wooderson $2 million in compensatory and $2.75 million in punitive damages for the destruction of her kidneys by Pill-induced disease; the award was upheld on appeal. The Kansas Supreme Court found that the birth control pills the plaintiff took were the only reasonable explanation of her illness; that the manufacturer knew of the danger of kidney disease; and that it should be punished for its flagrant failure to warn of a known danger.

• Furthermore, 1985 seemed to signal a trend toward holding manufacturers liable for failure to warn the Pill user directly, even if the manufacturer complied with the FDA labeling requirements. The case of *Stephens v. Searle*, 12 P.S.L.R. [BNA] 160 (E.D. Mich. 2/14/85) holds that the manufacturer has a duty to warn of potential Pill dangers; the FDA's jurisdiction over prescription drug labeling doesn't preclude the Pill user from suing the manufacturer. The Massachusetts case of *MacDonald v. Ortho Pharmaceutical Corp.*, 53 LW 2462 (Sup.Jud.Ct. 2/28/85), similarly imposed a duty on the manufacturer to warn of the danger of strokes (not just the danger of blood clotting, as required by the FDA). To the Supreme Judicial Court, contraceptive pills are unlike other drugs—the user is basically healthy, has little opportunity to consult with her doctor about the medication, and may get a whole year's supply at one time, so she is unlikely to remember the physician's warnings. Therefore, the court argued, the usual practice of warning the "learned intermediary"—the doctor—isn't good enough in this context. The Pill user must be warned directly.

• A product is "unavoidably dangerous" (and its manufacturer isn't liable) if the product's benefits outweigh the risks and the warnings are proper. The *Chapman* case says that the Pill could be described as unavoidably dangerous (as long as the right warnings are given) because the "public benefits" outweigh the known risks.

• But only pills with low hormone levels are unavoidably dangerous: more dangerous higher-dose pills don't qualify. At least in New Hampshire, the manufacturer of the high-dose pills can be held liable for defective design (i.e., excessive hormone content) and for failure to warn doctors of the additional risk of the high-dose pills.

• In Illinois, the statute of limitations against a birth control pill manufacturer starts to run when the plaintiff knows or should know that she was injured by a drug, and runs for five years. So a plaintiff crippled by blood clots in her legs was time-barred in a suit brought against a manufacturer more than five years after she discussed Pill risks with her mother and some friends, even though her doctor "laughed and said she should not worry, that the pills did not cause blood clots and that they would not harm her in any way." However, the doctors, who got her into the mess in the first place, weren't allowed to assert the statute of limitations in her malpractice suit. In this case, like *O'Brien v. Lilly* (page 158), the plaintiff's information from non-scientific sources was used to foreclose her litigation options. This seems to me essentially unfair, since magazine articles or lay opinions can't be used to *prove* the plaintiff's case.

THE SMOKING GUN

• The manufacturer can get off the hook by proving that the plaintiff was unusually susceptible to stroke (e.g., had high blood pressure before she began to use oral contraceptives). On the other hand, a circumstance like this strengthens the malpractice case; after all, the doctor is supposed to be aware of the patient's physical condition and is supposed to use this information in prescribing the appropriate method of birth control.

• If the patient withholds information (e.g., doesn't mention toxemia in an earlier pregnancy), this, too, can benefit the manufacturer: it makes it impossible for the adequacy of the warnings to be assessed, because the prescribing doctor was unaware of the plaintiff's real physical condition.

• What if the plaintiff makes the risks of Pill use worse by smoking cigarettes? In a suit against a doctor and a birth control pill manufacturer, the jury found that the manufacturer was 35 percent at fault and the doctor 65 percent at fault. The defendants appealed, and the appeals court ruled that the jury had enough evidence to define the cause of the plaintiff's stroke as smoking plus the Pill. Even if the warnings were adequate in general, they were inadequate about smoking. But the plaintiff could not overturn the jury verdict to make the drug manufacturer solely liable.

• Plaintiffs can use the doctrine of *res ipsa loquitur* in actions based on contraceptive-pill-related strokes. *Res ipsa* is a tort doctrine; the phrase is Latin for "the thing speaks for itself." The classic case was brought by a disgruntled tobacco-chewer who found a human toe in a package of tobacco. Though he couldn't quite explain how it got there, he contended, and the court agreed, that severed toes don't wander into tobacco pouches and someone in a responsible position must have been at fault. Similarly, young women don't get strokes unless something is drastically wrong; and it can be inferred that young Pill users who have strokes suffer as a result of the medicine.

INTRAUTERINE DEVICES (IUDs)

The IUD, like the birth control pill, is an attempt to separate contraception from sex. Theoretically, the IUD is even more foolproof than the Pill, as it simply has to be inserted and later removed whenever the user wants to restore her fertility. It's a one-time decision, but Pill users must remember to take the drug each day or twenty-one days a month.

Again like the birth control pill, things didn't work out that way. Claims against IUD manufacturers are long-tail claims in two ways: first of all, it may take years for the user to suffer consequences (or find out the cause of her injury). Second, the "long tail" attached to the IUD, intended to make it easier to check if the IUD is in place, may act as a wick to draw harmful bacteria into the uterus. No one's quite sure; no one knows how IUDs work either (it's theorized that a foreign object in the uterus keeps fertilized eggs from implanting and developing into fetuses). Some IUDs are reasonably well behaved, others end up on the user's pillow (inconvenient but not dangerous) or punch holes in her uterus and end up nestled on her bladder or floating in the abdominal cavity. There are stories of babies being born with an IUD clutched in a chubby fist, but it's more likely that a pregnancy with an IUD in place will result in an ectopic pregnancy (outside the uterus), a septic abortion (a miscarriage accompanied by an infection) or an induced abortion to prevent these dangers, than in a normal birth. These "serious" side effects are in addition to "normal" side effects of pain on insertion and heavier menstrual bleeding and more severe menstrual cramps for IUD users.

IUD manufacturers are required to provide proper warnings for their product; and once again, the rule is that the warning is supposed to be given to the "learned intermediary," the doctor, who decides what to tell the patient (but who has a duty to give her enough information to provide her informed consent). But certain IUDs (ones using heavy metals, drugs, or "active substances" in addition to the basic structure of the device) are considered "new drugs" by the FDA. Manufacturers of these devices must provide uniform labeling and instructions for doctors and information for the patient (a description of the IUD, its effectiveness rate, contraindications, side effects, and directions for use).

IUDs were promoted and described in the press as one-time contraceptives, and were likely to appeal to women who couldn't afford or who disliked seeing doctors. Paternalistic doctors and social workers were also likely to recommend (or apply pressure for) IUDs for clients they felt were unfit mothers and too stupid or careless to use other forms of birth control. Women whose routine medical care is poor or nonexistent can suffer injuries caused by IUDs for many years before the cause of the injury is diagnosed (or properly diagnosed).

That is to say, the now-familiar statute of limitations problem pops up again. But in some states, plaintiffs get a break. For implanted medical devices such as IUDs, some states use a "discovery rule": the statute of limitations starts to run either when the plaintiff discovers she has been injured, or when a reasonably diligent plaintiff in the same situation would have discovered her injury. In Wisconsin, the statute starts to run on the earlier of these two dates.

In New York, if the suit is based on negligence or strict liability, the plaintiff has three years from the date of the injury (e.g., perforation, development of pelvic inflammatory disease); if her theory is breach of warranty, she has four years from the date of *insertion* to sue. So, unless the IUD causes injury in the first year, there can't be a lot of successful breach of warranty cases brought under New York law.

The California rule is even more generous to plaintiffs: the statute of limitations is one year after discovery, not just of the injury (assuming the plaintiff is "blamelessly ignorant" of the cause) but of her doctor's malpractice. The jury has to decide whether the plaintiff acted reasonably and with appropriate diligence.

The plaintiff in *Martinez v. Rosenzweig* seems to have been at least as diligent in inquiry as her doctor and doesn't seem to have known much less about gynecology. Her IUD was inserted in 1973; in that year, she became pregnant with the IUD in place. "She asked him [Dr. Rosenzweig] what had happened to the IUD and he replied that he wasn't sure, it had probably dropped out or would come out when the baby was born." The baby never was born: the plaintiff miscarried in 1973. She continued to be treated by Dr. Rosenzweig for abdominal pain until 1975. Then she gave it up as a bad job and went to another doctor, who found the IUD in her abdomen and removed it. "It would appear reasonable that Mrs. Martinez did not know or have reason to know the nature of her problem when a gynecologist, who is a specialist in those matters, did not discover it." But it was still a question for the jury when she should have known something was wrong: perhaps she should have decided, at some point, that Dr. Rosenzweig didn't have much of a grasp on the problem and gone to another doctor without letting two years elapse.

Compare the Ninth Circuit case of *Philpott v. Robins* (decided under Oregon law, a state with an eight-year statute of limitations). The case went against the plaintiff. Her IUD was put in place in 1971 and she suffered a hysterectomy in 1973. The eight years had run by the time she filed her suit, even though she didn't discover the connection between the two facts until 1981. A Michigan plaintiff ran into a different problem: her suit was filed with the court on time, but she didn't meet the six-month deadline for serving process on the defendant after instituting her suit.

Both Arizona and Indiana have two-year statutes of limitations and both had recent similar Dalkon Shield cases turning out badly for the plaintiff. In the Arizona case, *Mack v. Robins*, 573 F.Supp. 179 (1983), the plaintiff's IUD was inserted in 1971. She suffered severe abdominal pain in 1979. Pelvic inflammatory disease (a severe, widespread infection) was diagnosed and she had an emergency hysterectomy a few days later. Her doctors told her that the Dalkon Shield had caused the infection. But it wasn't until 1981, when she read newspaper articles about the dangers of the Dalkon Shield, that she knew that the injury could have been caused by a *design defect* in the shield (in other words, that there was a possible legal case, not just an ordinary misfortune). She filed suit within two years of reading the articles, but more than two years after her hysterectomy. The Arizona District Court ruled that her suit was time-barred, because her cause of action accrued when she was told the *fact* that her IUD had caused the infection, not when she learned the legal significance of the fact. (It seems excessively hard that plaintiffs be expected to be legal as well as medical experts; but as Jeremy Bentham said, lawyers are the only persons in whom ignorance of the law isn't punished.)

The Indiana plaintiff (*Neuhauser v. Robins*, CCH PLR ¶9940, S.D. Indiana 1983) fared even worse. She got an IUD in 1972 and became pregnant with the IUD in place in 1974. After a miscarriage in June 1974, the IUD was removed. She developed uterine cancer in 1975 and had a hysterectomy in that year. In April 1981 she saw a television discussion of Dalkon Shield risks, and filed suit in October 1981. She certainly acted promptly after seeing the show, but not promptly enough for the court, which ruled that her cause of action accrued in 1974, when she miscarried. Even if she was under continuing medical care (so that the statute of limitations wouldn't start running as long as she was under treatment) the medical treatment ended with her last cancer operation in 1978—so, under all the arguments considered by the court, her suit was time-barred.

If the applicable statute of limitations has run, the plaintiff's last chance is to prove a factor that will toll (suspend) the statute of limitations. (Send not to know for whom the statute tolls; with any luck at all, it tolls for thee.) For example, nearly all the states let a person who is injured as a minor sue for a certain period of time after reaching majority—even if the injury occurred many years earlier. If a doctor or manufacturer fraudulently conceals important information, the plaintiff won't be harmed by the statute of limitations during the period of concealment. This theory was applied against the manufacturer in *Knaysi v. Robins*, 679 F.2d 1366 (11th Cir. 1982). The argument was that both the doctor and the patient justifiably relied on the manufacturer's statements that the Dalkon Shield was a safe and effective contraceptive. Although the manufacturer was aware of the significant risk of pregnancy followed by septic abortion (what happened to the plaintiff), Robins continued to sell and promote the device. But other, similar cases have not found fraudulent concealment. A group of California cases involving Robins's Dalkon Shield IUD was tried together, and the claims were ruled time-barred because the court believed that any fraud that took place occurred before the IUDs were installed.

The plaintiff in *Miller v. Mobile County Board of Health* also claimed fraudulent concealment by the manufacturer, and also lost her case. Her IUD was inserted in 1970. In 1972, when she was pregnant, she hemorrhaged and expelled the IUD; she had a miscarriage nine days later. At that time, she wasn't aware that IUDs could cause hemorrhage or miscarriage; she was alerted to the possibility by a magazine article she read in 1979. She filed suit within a year of reading the article. If she had been able to prove fraudulent concealment, her suit would have been timely, because Alabama plaintiffs have one year after the discovery of fraud to sue. But because she did not prove fraud, the statute of limitations wasn't tolled, and her case was time-barred. Once again, reading magazines proved hazardous to the plaintiff's legal health.

The Eleventh Circuit case of *Sellers v. Robins* reads like a law school exam question; it involves most of the major issues in IUD litigation. Like the *Miller* case, it was decided under Alabama law, so the statute of limitations was one year for tort claims and four years for breach of warranty claims. The plaintiff's Dalkon Shield IUD was inserted in April 1972; she became pregnant in 1973; and she had many severe gynecological problems from 1973 on. In 1974, Robins sent a letter to doctors warning them about the Dalkon Shield and suggesting that they stop inserting new Dalkon Shields in patients. However, the plaintiff's doctor neither told her about the letter nor removed her IUD. The plaintiff, once again, read a magazine article in December 1980 and filed suit in June 1981. She would have been in time if the court had accepted her argument that the time to sue ran from the time she read the article, or that Robins had fraudulently concealed the dangers of the Dalkon Shield by warning doctors, but not IUD users, in 1974. But the court did not accept the fraudulent-concealment claim, and said, "At no point, however, did Carol ask her doctors what caused her medical problems. A person exercising due diligence would have been prompted to inquire about the cause of such grave ailments." (The court didn't refer to the doctor, or to any Robins executives, by their first names.) But isn't it due diligence to place oneself under medical care and let the doctors deal with the problem?

In contrast, the California case of *Tresemer v. Burke* agreed that the plaintiff had a failure-to-warn case against Robins because the manufacturer did not warn users about dangers the manufacturer discovered after the device was used in medical practice. In other words, there was a continuing duty to warn users about newly discovered information.

Damages

Although some Dalkon Shield litigants lose their cases, and some settle their cases for comparatively small sums (e.g., $15,000 in one Oregon case), Robins has been fighting hard because losing a case usually involves major dollars. So far, the largest award has been $6.8 million in Colorado— $600,000 compensatory damages, $6,200,000 in punitive damages. In late 1983, a Florida plaintiff was awarded $4.9 million. A Minnesota plaintiff was awarded the comparatively modest sum of $1,750,000: $250,000 in compensatory damages, the rest punitive.

The Wall Street Journal of November 5, 1984, reports a settlement of 198 Minnesota cases for a total of more than $35 million. That brought the total paid to all victims to about $245 million—not including litigation costs. At the end of 1984, Robins took dramatic action to end all Dalkon Shield–related litigation. In the preceding decade, over 10,000 suits had been filed; in December 1984 almost 3,800 were still pending. Robins applied to the federal District Court in Richmond, Virginia to have all punitive damage claims consolidated into a single class action, and to have an alternative dispute resolution system (e.g., arbitration) set up for compensatory damage claims. Plaintiffs' lawyers weren't too enthusiastic about the plan, believing that the company might get off too lightly if a judge viewed all the cases together and spared the corporate pocketbook by going easy on awards to individual plaintiffs. When there's only one plaintiff, or a small group of plaintiffs, the focus is on their individual suffering; when they're a faceless mass, there's a tendency to think tenderly of the stockholders and show a little mercy to the bottom line.

In April 1985, Robins made tort law (and accounting) history by setting up the largest reserve fund ($615 million) ever established for the eventual settlement of product liability claims arising from a medical device. The reserve fund sent Robins's books plummeting into the red; the company reported a gigantic loss for 1984, especially the fourth quarter. The reserve was intended to cover both the compensatory and punitive aspects of future claims and claims now pending—not the 8,300 claims that had already been fully litigated or settled by the end of 1984 for a total of almost $315 million.

The case of *Hilliard v. Robins* gives a good discussion of damage issues in IUD cases. First, the plaintiff has to prove that she is entitled to compensatory damages. Even if she can't present medical bills or testimony from doctors, the jury will be able to infer her pain and suffering if her testimony is convincing enough. In the *Hilliard* case, the appeals court said that a verdict of $600,000 compensatory damages wasn't excessive—the plaintiff had a hysterectomy after two abortions and six abdominal operations; in addition to her pain and disability, her earning capacity was impaired.

Once compensatory damages are proved, the plaintiff can show that she is entitled to punitive damages by showing the defendant's conscious disregard for the safety of others; its awareness of the probable dangerous consequences of its actions; and its willful and deliberate ignoring of these facts and consequences.

In February 1985, special masters in a Minnesota Dalkon Shield case, after studying documents that the plaintiffs wanted to see but that Robins claimed were privileged, found evidence that Robins's actions constituted "at least a prima facie case of a massive fraudulent scheme perpetuated on the public." The special masters stated that they would continue reviewing the documents, and would release documents related to or used as part of the fraud. Although federal judges don't have to accept the findings of special masters, they usually do accept them; if this is done, Robins won't only be stigmatized for concealing damaging facts about the Dalkon Shield, but will face the disclosure of harmful documents.

There was evidence of further wrongdoing in a Florida Dalkon Shield case. A new trial was granted in the 11th Circuit case of *Harre v. Robins*, CCH PLR ¶10,349 (1/21/85), because the Court of Appeals held that a doctor who testified for Robins gave false testimony, and that the IUD manufacturer must have known that the doctor's testimony contradicted testimony he had given in another Dalkon Shield case in San Francisco. Ms. Harre lost her case at the trial level because the jury believed the medical witness, Dr. Louis G. Keith, when he testified that studies "being done under his direction" ruled out the plaintiff's contention that the IUD string had served as a wick for harmful bacteria.

THE ROAD TO THE COURTHOUSE

• The plaintiff can sue the doctor, the hospital or clinic where the IUD was inserted, and/or the manufacturer. Although the Dalkon Shield has attracted the most attention, and its manufacturer, Robins, the most lawsuits, other models of IUD can cause actionable damage.

• Theories can include manufacturer's negligence (marketing the IUD without testing adequate to disclose its dangers), fraudulent concealment (nondisclosure of later-developing evidence of IUD risks), express warranty (that a particular model was a superior IUD), failure to warn, and overpromotion. Some of the IUD ads in medical journals are high—or low—points in medical misogyny, hinting that the IUD is a great way to shut up dumb broads who are too stupid to use other methods of contraception.

• If the IUD contains metal coatings or drugs and therefore falls under the FDA's PPI requirement (see page 169), failure to provide these warnings is considered negligence *per se* (by itself) in some states. If the manufacturer is guilty of negligence *per se*, the plaintiff can win just by showing the absence of the required warnings.

• The National Women's Health Network sued Robins, seeking a declaratory judgment (statement by the court) that the Dalkon Shield is defectively designed and seeking a worldwide recall of these IUDs. (Robins suggested in 1974 that doctors stop inserting them and in 1980 suggested that doctors remove Dalkon Shields then in use; but neither statement was compulsory, and both were directed at doctors, not IUD users whose contacts with doctors might be infrequent or nonexistent. It wasn't until 1984 that Robins made a public announcement telling users to have the Dalkon Shield removed and offering to pay the medical costs of having the device removed.) The Network lost the case; but, for one reason or another, in October 1984 Robins started the $4 million recall campaign, informing all Shield users that they should have the device removed, setting up a 24-hour information hot line, and offering to pay the cost of Shield removal.

• Courts that are willing to be innovative can streamline IUD litigation significantly. For example, in late 1983 there were dozens of Dalkon Shield cases pending in the Minnesota District Court (and dozens had been settled). Four of the eight Minnesota federal judges were assigned to seven of the cases, and, to speed the trials, each side was limited to six expert witnesses. Three of the cases were set for trial at the same time on the same floor of the courthouse, which made it easy for plaintiffs' lawyers to hold strategy conferences, exchange information, and share videotaped evidence. Unfortunately, the plaintiffs weren't allowed to use the *Strempke* case (see page 292) to assert collateral estoppel (pages 162–163), which would *really* have shortened the trial because the plaintiffs would only have had to prove their damages.

The seven pending cases were settled in February 1984, for a reported total of $4.6 million. One impetus for the settlement may have been Judge Miles W. Lord's order that Robins turn over tens of thousands of documents that the plaintiffs sought in discovery and that the manufacturer claimed were privileged. The documents have been turned over to special masters in Richmond, Virginia, who will determine whether the documents are privileged or can be subpoenaed by other plaintiffs.

Judge Lord criticized Robins for its failure to recall the IUDs in 1974, when the Dalkon Shield was taken off the market: "Under your direction, your company has in fact continued to allow women, tens of thousands of them, to wear this device—a deadly depth charge in their wombs, ready to explode at any time. The only conceivable reasons you have not recalled this product are that it would hurt your balance sheet and alert women who already have been harmed that you may be liable for their injuries." That sums it up, all right.

Robins brought Judge Lord up on charges of judicial misconduct for his expression of indignation. The offending remarks were erased from the record, and Judge Lord was reprimanded, but the misconduct charges were dismissed.

• Plaintiffs and potential plaintiffs can get information from the National Women's Health Network's Litigation Information Service. Plaintiffs' lawyers can get information about Dalkon Shield cases by joining the Dalkon Shield Groups coordinated by New York attorney Paul Rheingold. These groups (available only to plaintiffs' lawyers, not to plaintiffs themselves, or defense lawyers) provide background information, newsletters, and copies of depositions and Robins documents already obtained through discovery in other Dalkon Shield cases.

• Sybil Shainwald of the National Women's Health Network warns that defendants may try to put the plaintiff's sexual history into the case by claiming that her injuries were caused by sexual promiscuity rather than the IUD. This contention is probably wrong (but at least rational) if the injury is pelvic inflammatory disease (PID), which can result from untreated gonorrhea, but is completely bizarre if the IUD perforated the plaintiff's uterus or caused a septic abortion (conditions which are entirely unrelated to the plaintiff's sexual practices). So the plaintiff's complaint should make it clear which category her injury falls into. If she has developed PID, it may be necessary to go to court during the discovery stage for a protective order requiring the manufacturer to direct its inquiries elsewhere. If the court is unsympathetic, the plaintiff may want to settle the case rather than go to trial—but of course manufacturers offer smaller settlements when they have the plaintiff over a barrel than when the position is reversed.

• The Canons of Ethics obligate lawyers to inform the public about the law but also forbid us to improve our cardio-vascular conditioning by chasing ambulances. An Ohio lawyer took out newspaper ads with a picture of a Dalkon Shield, informing Shield users that they might be able to sue the manufacturer. He was brought up on charges of unethical conduct and rebuked—for recommending himself in an ad, for mentioning contingent fees without fully revealing his fee arrangements, for accepting clients to whom he had given unsolicited legal advice, and for including an illustration in his ad. The lawyer's appeal was one of the first cases argued before the Supreme Court in October 1984. The Court will have to decide whether the public's need for information about legal rights outweighs the legal profession's opinion of its own dignity and the risk of disseminating biased and inaccurate information.

THE SMOKING GUN

- A doctor's affidavit isn't required to prove that a plaintiff has filed suit within the time required by the statute of limitations: hospital records will serve to prove the point.
- It's up to the jury to decide whether the plaintiff is contributorily negligent (that is, can't recover because her negligence contributed to the injury—the rule in some states; in other states, the plaintiff's comparative negligence just reduces her recovery) if she sues a city agency for its negligence in inserting an IUD without removing the IUD already there—if the plaintiff doesn't mention the first IUD.
- Equally, it's a jury issue whether a doctor is negligent if he never bothers to read the X-rays he ordered to determine if the plaintiff's IUD had wandered into her abdomen. The court in *Killebrew v. Johnson*, 404 N.E.2d 1194 (Ind.App. 1980) said that the jury could certainly deduce that abdominal pain that stopped when the emigrant IUD was removed was in fact caused by the IUD. The defendant-doctor claimed that the plaintiff might not have wanted the IUD removed even if it *had* been found; if the jury went so far as to believe that, it would influence damages, not whether the plaintiff would win or lose her case. (Typically, the opinion here refers to the defendant as "Dr. Johnson" and the plaintiff as "Laura.")
- California's *Hilliard v. Robins* discusses the evidence that can be admitted in a Dalkon Shield case. The Court of Appeals ruled that the trial court should have admitted evidence that the Dalkon Shield could cause septic abortions and deaths (to prove that Robins was aware of the danger), evidence that Robins failed to test the device properly (showing conscious disregard for the safety of others) and evidence that the Dalkon Shield was taken off the market because of pressure from the FDA, not as an internal decision made to protect IUD users (showing a deliberate failure to avoid harmful consequences). The usual rule of evidence is that anything occurring after the plaintiff's last use of the product is inadmissible—but the *Hilliard* court said that such evidence should have been admitted on the issues of malice and punitive damages.
- The Colorado case of *Palmer v. Robins* holds that reports of other women's bad reactions to the Dalkon Shield were admissible evidence in the plaintiff's case as long as they were used only to show the manufacturer's knowledge of the dangers and failure to warn doctors of known dangers. The manufacturer's own record of septic abortions reported by Dalkon Shield users was also admitted into evidence: hoist with their own petard.
- Similarly, the Eleventh Circuit case of *Worsham v. Robins* (CCH PLR ¶10,101 (1984)) allows the admission into evidence of adverse reaction

reports to prove that the manufacturer knew of the dangers, and of other lawsuits, to prove the dangers of the IUD and the manufacturers' knowledge of the risks. There was a real "smoking gun" in this case: a document containing a statement by Robins's house counsel that taking the IUD off the market would be a confession of liability. It, too, was admitted into evidence, and doubtless had some impact on the $1.45 million ($950,000 compensatory, $500,000 punitive damages) verdict for the plaintiff.

DEPO-PROVERA

Reliable contraception that isn't related to particular acts of intercourse is a great idea, even if some variations (birth control pills, IUDs) proved to have too high a proportion of sour notes. How about an inexpensive shot that provides three months of protection against pregnancy? No IUD to migrate or perforate; no need to remember to take a pill each day. Once again it seems too good to be true, and it is.

The chemical name of the injectable contraceptive is medroxyprogesterone acetate; the trade name is Depo-provera. It's manufactured by Upjohn. Upjohn began studying Depo-provera as a contraceptive in 1963 and applied for FDA approval for this use in 1967. The application was denied, renewed, and denied again. In 1972, a study linked Depo-provera to breast cancer in beagles; depending on whom you ask, this either is or isn't relevant to women. Identified dangers to women include menstrual irregularities, thrombophlebitis, worsening of liver disease, worsening of breast cancer, and permanent infertility. These contraindications are listed by the FDA, not some radical feminist group. Depo-provera is considered a "new drug," so women who get contraceptive shots must be given a booklet explaining the risks of the drug. (It would be a Patient Package Insert if there were a package to insert it in.)

You may perhaps be wondering why, if Depo-provera has not been approved for use as a contraceptive, there are *any* users to be given information booklets. The answer is that medroxyprogesterone acetate has been approved by the FDA for other uses (e.g., cancer treatment—ironic if it really is a carcinogen) and it's perfectly legal for a doctor to prescribe an approved drug for anything s/he thinks it will be useful for—whether or not the drug has been approved for that use.

The National Women's Health Network has filed a class action suit against Upjohn, seeking relief for particular victims of Depo-provera (e.g., several women who have had mastectomies); a judgment that Upjohn is responsible for selling a deceptively marketed, defective product, knowing that it would be used for contraception; an injunction against further sales; and a requirement that Upjohn locate all past and present Depo-provera users and pay their medical costs resulting from the use of the drug. In addition, according to the November-December 1984 issue of *Network*

News, the NWHN's bimonthly publication, on October 26, 1984, a special
board of inquiry assembled by the FDA recommended that the FDA refuse
to approve Depo-provera for contraceptive use. Their recommendation
may be conclusive.

The political issue is who decides what kind of contraceptive a woman
should use: the woman herself, or an overworked clinic doctor who is apt
to feel that a diaphragm is too much trouble—for the doctor—and that
the patient is too irresponsible to use a barrier contraceptive anyway.
Younger women and poorer women are more likely to be put in this
position. (They are also the women most susceptible to sterilization abuse—
see pages 219–222.)

The medical issue is the safety of artificial female hormones—hormones
used in birth control pills and Depo-provera. Similar hormones are given
to older and more affluent women as ERT (estrogen replacement therapy)
after menopause. Originally ERT was promoted as a way to stay "feminine
forever," sparing men the sight of a woman who looked her age. The
current rationale is that ERT helps prevent osteoporosis and prevent age-
related changes in the genitals that impair older women's sexual expression. Medical opinion is divided as to the magnitude of risks of ERT (some
say that it increases the risk of breast and cervical cancer) and whether
the risks outweigh the benefits.

TAMPON LITIGATION

In 1971, epidemiology showed that a very rare disease (adenocarcinoma)
was becoming much more prevalent, and established a link between adenocarcinoma and maternal use of DES during pregnancy. Similarly, in
1980, epidemiology showed an increase in cases of a rare disease called
toxic shock syndrome (TSS) among women of menstrual age and established a link between tampon use and TSS. The evidence was especially
striking as to a connection between TSS and the super-absorbent Rely
tampons manufactured by Procter & Gamble. (Rely tampons were taken
off the market in 1980.) But Procter & Gamble isn't the only manufacturer
whose products are linked with TSS: a jury verdict of $500,000 in com-
pensatory and $10,000,000 in punitive damages was assessed against an-
other company, Johnson & Johnson, manufacturers of o.b. tampons. In
April 1985, Beatrice Co., manufacturers of Playtex tampons, and Tambrands, Inc., manufacturers of Tampax tampons, announced a recall of
super-absorbent tampons containing polyacrylate. These tampons would
no longer be manufactured; would be removed from store shelves; and
purchasers could return the front panel of a box of super-absorbent tampons to receive a coupon for a box of tampons made of traditional, and
presumably safer, fibers. Beatrice Co. responded to the suggestion made
by Kansas District Judge Patrick F. Kelly, who said he might reduce or

eliminate the $10 million punitive damage component of an award against Playtex if the super-absorbent tampons were taken off the market. Tambrands evidently could see which way the wind was blowing without a weatherman.

The leading decision (rather than settlement) in a tampon case is *Kehm v. Procter & Gamble,* a 1983 Eighth Circuit case. An award of $300,000 to the widower of a Rely user was upheld, on the grounds that the tampons were defective and unreasonably dangerous because they encouraged the growth of deadly bacteria, and the manufacturer had breached its duty to warn:

> In failure-to-warn cases, as in strict liability cases generally, liability does not turn on whether the risk of harm runs to a substantial number of persons. Rather, in determining whether a manufacturer has a duty to warn, courts inquire whether the manufacturer knew that there were even a relatively few persons who could not use its product without serious injury, and whether a proper warning would have helped prevent harm to them.

So even if Ms. Kehm died because she was especially susceptible to toxic shock syndrome, her survivors are entitled to a judgment based on Procter & Gamble's failure to warn. However, the Eighth Circuit ruled that punitive damages were inappropriate: that P & G did not act wantonly or recklessly.

The Eighth Circuit agreed with the trial court that epidemiological evidence about TSS rates should have been allowed: after all, P & G's expert witnesses were allowed to testify. Complaints from Rely users and the fact that the product was taken off the market were also allowed into evidence. The Fourth Circuit has taken a similar position.

In 1980, the University of Wisconsin did studies that show a strong connection between tampons and TSS, and particularly implicate Rely tampons. Procter & Gamble tried to keep these studies out of the discovery process, saying that they were "work product"—internal documents that should be exempt from discovery. But the Kansas Supreme Court, like the Eighth Circuit in *Kehm,* has said that these documents are not privileged. The availability of this information makes plaintiffs' cases much stronger (not only establishing the connection between tampons and TSS but showing either failure to test—or the tampon manufacturers would have known the facts—or sale of a product known to be dangerous and concealment of the damaging facts). This may lead the manufacturers to be willing to reach more settlements: for example, a Missouri case based on the death of a fifteen-year-old Rely tampon user was settled for $625,000 in August 1983. Early in 1985, a federal jury in Kansas awarded over $1 million in compensatory, more than $10 million in punitive damages to the estate of a woman who died of Toxic Shock Syndrome at the age of 21, leaving two children. In this case, the tampon involved wasn't a Rely tampon, but a Playtex Super Deodorant Tampon. The Minnesota epidemiological studies were introduced in evidence, and probably were very influential. (This is the case in which the judge suggested that a product recall could lead to a reduction or elimination of punitive damages.) The case is *O'Gilvie v. International Playtex Inc.*, number 83–18848–K, discussed in David Ranii's article, "TSS Victim's Estate Awarded Over $11 Million," appearing on page 6 of the *National Law Journal* for March 11, 1985.

However, Procter & Gamble won a major TSS case in Missouri in 1984, probably because the jury did not believe that the plaintiff had proved the connection between tampons and the disease. This defeat may make plaintiffs more willing to accept modest settlements to avoid the uncertainties of trial, even if there is a small possibility of recovering a very large verdict.

The traditional happy ending for a supernatural horror story is to show the heroes triumphant over ghouls, witches, vampires, or cognate menaces. The traditional twist ending is to show the menaces sneaking back, perhaps in another form.

Sure enough, a modest news item in *The Wall Street Journal* of December 7, 1983, deals with an FDA investigation of a suspected connection between Today brand contraceptive sponges and TSS . . .

OTHER ISSUES

For obvious reasons, it's difficult or impossible to assess the effect a drug will have on a pregnant or laboring woman or on the fetus. There are severe ethical problems involved in experimenting on pregnant women or on the tissue of aborted fetuses; animal experiments are useful but can't provide all the information needed. The upshot is that sometimes medical procedures or drugs are found to be harmful after a certain number of women die or are injured; after a certain number of babies are stillborn or born with congenital abnormalities.

For example, Bendectin was sold as an anti-morning-sickness drug until June 1983, when its manufacturer, Dow Chemical Co., said it was no longer worth keeping it on the market: the cost of liability insurance made the newly unpopular drug too expensive. Dow kept raising the price of the drug, to a final price of $1 a tablet (one way of protecting the poor against drug-related injuries). A Dow spokesman said, "But we figured we can't raise the price of it anymore, and we don't want to raise prices on our other drugs." Sometimes the benevolence of manufacturers is amazing.

By the summer of 1983, over 300 suits had been filed, alleging that

Bendectin caused birth defects (limb malformations and intestinal abnormalities) but few cases had been tried.

In a case filed in 1977 and tried for the first time in 1981, the jury awarded $20,000 to the parents of a boy born with limb defects (but nothing to the boy himself). The trial judge threw out the award on the ground that it was a compromise verdict. (See page 294.) The case was retried amid allegations of misconduct by the plaintiffs' attorney. Not only did the plaintiffs lose the case on retrial, they were ordered to pay the defendant's legal costs.

Things looked better for the plaintiffs in 1983's *Oxendine* case. A trial restricted to the issue of negligence awarded $750,000 compensatory damages to the family of a girl whose deformed right arm was allegedly caused by her mother's use of Bendectin. But the award was set aside in September of 1983, after the judge reviewed the scientific evidence, and a third trial was scheduled. As of March 1985 the case was still up in the air.

The plaintiffs in *Koller v. Richardson-Merrell*, another 1983 Washington, D.C., case, won a battle (surviving a summary judgment motion) but lost the war (the District Court ruled that they didn't prove that Merrell tested the drug inadequately or fraudulently misrepresented the drug).

In short, Bendectin plaintiffs haven't been doing very well in court. One ray of hope for plaintiffs: in September 1983 the FDA sent a bulletin to doctors reporting three studies about Bendectin and birth defects of the intestine. Two studies showed a connection, the third exculpated the drug.

In March 1985, a jury hearing more than 1,100 consolidated Bendectin claims dismissed the entire case; they simply didn't believe that the causal connection between the drug and the birth defects had been established. It will be hard for other Bendectin plaintiffs to overcome the effect of this major case.

In 1983, the FDA issued a warning against using a particular childbirth local anesthetic (bupivocaine) at its highest concentration; sometimes it causes cardiac arrest, though the lower concentration is less risky but still provides pain relief. (It's an interesting question why the lower concentration isn't standard—but then, to the American psyche, more is usually better.) Drugs (oxytocins such as Pitocin) used to induce labor can also be dangerous to both mother and infant. It's one thing if the risk is undertaken because there's an urgent medical necessity for inducing labor, and something else entirely if "babies by appointment" are scheduled for the mother's or (especially) the doctor's convenience. The medicalization (or overmedicalization, depending on how you look at it) of childbirth is a political question: who will control the means of reproduction? As for the legal questions, they arise in the context of straightforward medical malpractice cases. Unfortunately for plaintiffs, the standard in malpractice cases is what a reasonable physician would do, following reasonable and accepted medical procedures. The courts don't provide a forum for challenging accepted medical procedures.

An interesting sidelight on the medical profession and women's health issues: one method of making women's breasts appear larger is to insert a plastic bag filled with silicone or sterile salt solution. Because the breast implant is an implanted device, not a drug, the statute of limitations starts to run when the implant ruptures or otherwise causes damage, not when it's installed (see page 170). A Texas doctor used a saline-filled breast implant with a notable lack of success: because the implant (which was taken off the market in 1979) was designed defectively, it tended to collapse and leak. Forty-eight of the eighty sets of implants that the doctor installed failed, and he lost a lot of income because he had to remove the deflated implants free. He sued the manufacturer and was willing to settle the case for $90,000. The manufacturer refused, and the jury brought in a verdict of $11.1 million dollars: $40,000 for attorneys' fees, $123,000 economic loss, $1 million for the doctor's mental anguish (the poor dear) and $10 million for punitive damages. *Patients* who had had malfunctioning breast implants filed a number of suits. Many of the suits were settled, generally for amounts around $10,000—which goes to show you that, if you have to choose whom you'll anger, pick a comparatively powerless group like woman patients: stay on the right side of doctors.

8

PREGNANCY, CHILDBIRTH, AND MOTHERHOOD

Rachel Sollenberg hates to be type-cast, but she's fallen into every demographic cliché about the baby boom. She's thirty-three and worried about the increased risk of birth defects for the children of older mothers. She was worried about the possibility of infertility, but now that she's pregnant, that concern has been ruled out. She's happily married, but not so blissful that no third party can be permitted to interfere with this folie-à-deux. She has a reasonably good job (though she *was* passed over for promotion recently). Her talented, ambitious assistant can certainly handle Rachel's workload while she's on maternity leave, but is unlikely to step aside graciously when she's ready to return to work. How long a leave should she request, anyway? What'll happen to her child if she rushes back to work as soon as she's recovered from the physical stress of childbirth? What'll happen to her career if she devotes three, or six, or ten years to unpaid full-time child-rearing? What'll happen to the Sollenberg bank account if her husband's income has to handle all the mortgage payments and supermarket bills, plus tricycles, orthodontia, summer camp, and college tuition?

For years, the male chauvinist mantra has been, "Give a woman a good job, and she just goes and gets pregnant." That was easy enough to laugh off in the days when career women were necessarily celibate (because marriage meant instant dismissal) or, when they chose to remain unmarried and/or childless, either by preference or because they were too terrified to do anything to jeopardize their hard-won freedoms.

However, for a variety of reasons (more women demanding male-dominated jobs—whether as electricians or neurosurgeons; inflation) many women who already have children are entering the labor force, and many women in the labor force become pregnant and intend to remain working through pregnancy and after the children are born. Single mothers don't even have the option of quitting and relying on a husband's income. Some accommodation has to be made, for practical as well as legal reasons. (Most women who work for pay have sex-segregated "women's" jobs, so they can't *all* be fired and replaced by men without raising the wage scale dramatically. As for women who've forced their way into jobs traditionally held by men, they tend to have special skills, be essential for demonstrating the employer's commitment to equality, or both.)

Elizabeth Janeway said, sensibly, "If we, as a society, want children, the question is how we, as a society, will take care of them," but this intelligent perspective has not trickled up to policy-making levels. Simplistic feminism and simplistic anti-feminism are both plausible on some issues, but both break down when pregnancy and childbirth are discussed. At one end of the spectrum, it's easy enough to say that a woman's (and particularly a mother's) place is in the home. But whatever health the economy has depends on frantic spending by consumers. If married women stop working, their families have to reduce spending drastically, there must be a strong increase in the wages of married men, welfare benefits must increase, and/or a "family" or "children's" allowance must be paid by the government. Most of these ideas are politically unpalatable—especially to conservatives.

One version of simplistic feminism says that women are entitled to equality, if not indeed superiority, because of their purity and their role as mothers of the race. The other version holds that women are entitled to equality because we're just like men. But so far, all the people who conceive and bear children, and most of the people who handle the day-to-day care of small children, are women. (Though I read articles about embryo transfer technology avidly, longing for the day when Jesse Helms can be kept barefoot, pregnant, and in the kitchen.) Even if working women emulate the heroine of *The Good Earth* and return to work in the rice paddies minutes after childbirth (passing the Buck, so to speak) *someone* has to take care of the kid.

Pregnancy, childbirth, and motherhood involve substantial economic questions. Who pays for the cost of the delivery—and should the payment be for a midwife's services performed at the woman's home, or the services of an obstetrician and anesthesiologist in an operating room equipped with tons of electronic equipment? Is paid or unpaid maternity leave available? Does it matter if the pregnancy is normal or involves complications? Must a mother lose her accumulated seniority and vacation time when she's on maternity leave?

Unfortunately for my thesis that no legal question has a straightforward answer, there are simple legal pronouncements on many of these issues. As a result of the Pregnancy Discrimination Amendment and the EEOC's Guidelines and Questions and Answers, employers are obliged to treat disability arising from pregnancy (either normal pregnancy and delivery or complications of pregnancy) in the same way as any other temporary disability that isn't occupationally related (a broken leg, or a heart attack); if some complication of pregnancy or delivery makes it impossible for a woman worker to return to work at all, her disability must be treated like any other nonoccupationally caused permanent disability. In other words, if an employer pays employees who are on sick leave, it must pay employees on maternity leave. If (as is much more common) sick leave is unpaid, employers are not compelled to pay workers on maternity leave. If the employer pays medical and hospital bills for temporarily disabled employees, it's legally irrelevant what *kind* of disability is involved. If employees with gallstones retain their accrued seniority and can use accumulated vacation time if they're unable to return to work when their sick leave expires, you guessed it. Pregnancy by itself isn't a disability as long as the employee is able to work. When she becomes unable to work— either because of complications or because of childbirth and recovery— she is temporarily disabled.

In a way, this is simple good sense; after all, an employee creates equal inconvenience for the employer no matter why she or he can't work. But from another point of view, it creates conceptual problems. Pregnancy is a natural (though not inevitable) function of the female body. It could be argued that some diseases are the *fault* of those who guzzle, smoke, or stuff themselves into illness, but it can't be argued that they *wanted* the disease. But most parents love their children, want children, and sometimes go through considerable inconvenience to be able to conceive, and certainly go through a good deal of inconvenience once the baby is born.

The birth of a baby is usually greeted with joy, anticipation, and pleasure. Victims of disease or injury just want to be finished with the whole miserable business. Even if a woman decides that having a baby was a horrible mistake, she can't send the kid back for a full refund; she has to see the thing through. The diseased appendix that is removed or the broken bone that is put in a cast doesn't have wants, needs, or opinions independent of the person whose body contains them. A baby, once born (or once conceived; it depends on whom you ask) is a human being who requires care. The analogy between pregnancy and disability isn't perfect, but it's the best we've got. To find out the source and development of the analogy, it's necessary to consider:

PREGNANT PERSONS AND THE PDA

Between the effective date of Title VII and 1976, a variety of courts decided a variety of pregnancy-related cases. We won some and we lost some. Nineteen seventy-six is the date of the notorious *Gilbert* case (*General Electric Co. v. Gilbert*, 429 U.S. 125). The issue was whether an employee benefit plan committed illegal discrimination by providing medical benefits for nonoccupational temporary disabilities but not for pregnancy. The Supreme Court thought it over and found no sex discrimination. The Court said that General Electric had simply divided its employees into two groups, pregnant persons and non-pregnant persons. Pregnant *men* didn't get a nickel more in benefits than pregnant women, so Title VII wasn't violated. Under Title VII, *women* were a protected group, but pregnant persons weren't.

Although the *Gilbert* case was overruled by Congress, traces of its rationale survive. A much later case, *Tranquilli v. Irshad,* 33 FEP Cases 131 (Ill. 1983), allows an employer who interviews only women for a particular job (and therefore, necessarily, hires a woman) to refuse to interview a pregnant job applicant. (As the receptionist—a woman—so charmingly put it, "I don't want a pregnant broad working for me.") The Illinois Appeals Court felt that it wasn't sex discrimination to favor non-pregnant women over pregnant women.

A major result of the hoopla over the *Gilbert* case was the passage of 1978's Pregnancy Discrimination Amendment (42 U.S.C.A. §2000e(k), which was plugged into Title VII. The first part of the PDA says:

> The terms "because of sex" or "on the basis of sex" include but are not limited to, because of or on the basis of pregnancy, childbirth, or related medical conditions; and women affected by pregnancy, child-birth, or related medical conditions shall be treated the same for all employment-related purposes, including receipt of benefits under fringe benefit programs, as other persons not so affected but similar in their ability or inability to work, and nothing in §2000e-2(h) of this title [the provisions about bona fide seniority systems] shall be interpreted to permit otherwise.

(The second part of the PDA deals with health benefits for abortion; I'll get to that on page 258.)

The PDA has two major effects. First, it requires that employees disabled by pregnancy receive equal treatment with other temporarily disabled employees. Second, it requires a consideration of the individual pregnant woman and her personal ability to work, to do her regular job minus certain tasks, or her inability to work at all. Employers are limited in their use of stereotyped assumptions about the ability of pregnant women to work. (More of this anon, on the subject of compulsory maternity leave.)

The PDA has been explicated, at length, in EEOC Guidelines, which are found in 29 C.F.R. §1604.10 and in the Appendix to the Guidelines. The Appendix, in the form of Questions and Answers, starts on page 138 of the CFR pamphlet containing §1604.10. So far, the Guidelines and Questions and Answers have held up pretty well in court, but remember that this EEOC-generated material doesn't have the force of law. Courts are supposed to listen to it but are not compelled to obey.

The PDA, the Guidelines, and the Questions and Answers don't require an employer to *start* a program of sick leave or health insurance benefits simply to cover pregnancy. But if the employer has a sick-leave policy or a benefits plan, the message is rather like that of the golden rule: Do unto the pregnancy-disabled as thou wouldst do unto the temporarily disabled.

By the way, it's a violation of Title VII for an employer to fire an employee for becoming pregnant out of wedlock (because no rational relationship was shown between marriage and the employee's ability or inability to work while pregnant) or to refuse to grant maternity leave to a prospective unwed mother. On the other hand, although restricting disability benefits to pregnant employees who are married violates Title VII, it isn't a violation of the Equal Pay Act, so the plaintiff can forget about double damages.

Several states have adopted the PDA, or the PDA without the abortion provisions (Connecticut, Hawaii, Kentucky, Maryland, Michigan, Minnesota, Ohio, Oregon, South Carolina). Some states (e.g., Iowa, Wisconsin) have case law similar to the PDA. Alaska forbids pregnancy discrimination that isn't motivated by a BFOQ (Bona Fide Occupational Qualification—see page 22); the Maine law requires an employer to base decisions on the pregnant employee's ability to work; Maryland defines pregnancy as a temporary disability.

California, Massachusetts, and Montana have especially wide-ranging laws about employment during pregnancy.

Section 12945 of California's Government Code forbids employers (unless there is a BFOQ) to use pregnancy, childbirth, or a related medical condition as a reason not to promote a woman employee; to fire her, discriminate against her, or remove her from a training program. If she can finish a training program at least three months before her maternity leave is scheduled, the employer can't deny access to the program. Of course, maternity leave must be treated like a leave for temporary disability with regard to accrued leave and accrued vacation time. The employer must allow reasonable maternity leave (but doesn't have to permit leaves longer than four months). If the employer has a policy, practice, or union contract calling for a transfer of temporarily disabled employees to less strenuous jobs, the employer must transfer a pregnant employee on request and on the advice of her doctor—if the transfer can be reasonably accommodated. But the employer isn't required to create new jobs, remove an employee to transfer the pregnant employee, or provide an undeserved promotion to a less strenuous job.

A pregnant worker in Massachusetts (under chapter 149 §105D) who has held a full-time job for three months (or completed the employer's probation period) is entitled to eight weeks' maternity leave if she gives two weeks' notice. (The employer decides whether the leave will be paid or unpaid; guess which is more common.) The employee doesn't accrue seniority while she is on maternity leave; but if temporarily disabled employees are entitled to health insurance while they're on leave, so are pregnant employees. Workers are entitled to reinstatement after maternity leave but can't "bump" other workers.

Montana's Code §49–2–310 and –311 make it illegal to fire an employee because she's pregnant; to refuse to grant reasonable maternity leave; or to impose an unreasonably long compulsory maternity leave. If the employee's doctor certifies that she is medically unable to work, the employer must provide disability coverage and let her use accrued leave. After maternity leave, the employee is entitled to reinstatement at her former job or a comparable job. However, a private employer (not a government agency) need not reinstate an employee if the employer's circumstances have changed so that it's impossible, or unreasonable, to do so.

FIRING, COMPULSORY LEAVE

Since the Pregnancy Discrimination Act, it's illegal to fire a woman simply because she's pregnant. An argument could be made that employees are fired not because they're pregnant, but because pregnancy makes it impossible for them to do their jobs. Section 1604.10(c) of 29 C.F.R. (the EEOC Guidelines) says that it's a violation of Title VII to fire a pregnant employee because the employer doesn't allow medical leave, or allows medical leave that is insufficient for childbirth and recovery—but only if the policy has a disparate impact on women (that is, if medical leave is equally unavailable to men, the employer is off the hook) and only if the policy isn't justified by business necessity. In a disparate treatment case, of course, the plaintiff must prove discriminatory motive, but the employer's only defense to a prima facie case is the narrow BFOQ. (In a disparate impact case, the plaintiff doesn't have to show discriminatory motive, the employer can defend itself by proving business necessity, and the plaintiff can win by showing that the purported business necessity is just a pretext.)

Perhaps because they tend to be both middle-class and unionized, teachers and stewardesses have been especially litigious, so most of the cases on maternity leave and termination of employment come from these two groups.

• For example, a 1979 case from the Fourth Circuit finds a prima facie violation of Title VII in a requirement that teachers report their pregnancy to the employer as soon as the pregnancy is confirmed, if pregnancy is used as the only reason for refusing to renew a teaching contract. There wasn't enough evidence in the record for the court to consider the business necessity issue.

• Two early EEOC decisions find a Title VII violation against an airline and a union because of the airline's policy of firing pregnant stewardesses rather than offering them a leave of absence. The EEOC said that firing the employee is only acceptable if the job can't be kept vacant or handled by a temporary replacement, and that the employer can't use compliance with a union contract as a defense to Title VII liability.

For both legal and practical reasons, then, pregnant employees usually have a certain amount of leave. Employers are not required to retain employees who (for whatever reasons) are physically unfit to do their jobs, and employees want at least enough leave time to prepare for delivery and recover physically from childbirth. (See pages 201–204 on the vexed question of "parenthood" leave—time after the delivery needed for child care, not physical recovery.) But what if the employer demands compulsory maternity leave for a period before or after delivery, when the employee is willing and feels able to work?

• An employer can't set a maternity leave policy that presumes that *all* pregnant women are unfit to work.

• A policy calling for compulsory maternity leave for teachers at four months or five months of pregnancy violates the Due Process Clause of the Constitution (Title VII wasn't considered in this pre-PDA case). The Supreme Court said that the rule was too sweeping. It isn't necessarily true that women at that stage of pregnancy are physically unfit to teach. The opinion continues with some highly quotable language about undue penalties for the childbearing decision, and women's due process right to be free of governmental intrusion into the private right to raise a family. However, the Supreme Court did uphold the employer's requirement that teachers notify the school board of their pregnancy; the Court found a business necessity justification for the requirement. (Another difference between pregnancy disability and other disability: it's possible to notify an employer of a present pregnancy and apply for leave at a future date, but one can hardly give notice of a pending heart attack.)

• Various stewardess cases reach different conclusions. Some cases allow mandatory—and unpaid—maternity leave for pregnant stewardesses as soon as the pregnancy is confirmed, on the grounds that non-pregnancy is a BFOQ for stewardesses. However, *Burwell v. Eastern Air Lines Inc.* holds that mandatory maternity leave in the first trimester of pregnancy violates Title VII; mandatory leave in the second trimester is justified by business necessity.

All these cases discuss the BFOQ and business necessity defenses in terms of the airline's duty to provide safe transportation for passengers, and whether pregnancy will interfere with a stewardess's performance of her duties. Possible harm to the fetus is *not* considered here. (More of this anon, in the discussion of fetal protection programs on pages 191–199.)

• The *National Airlines* case denies that non-pregnancy was a BFOQ for airline ground crew.

• An employer is allowed to require compulsory pregnancy leave late in pregnancy—say, in the eighth or ninth month. *De Laurier v. San Diego Unified School District* holds that even this minor a requirement of mandatory leave *is* prima facie sex discrimination but accepts the employer's business necessity defense.

• The purpose of Title VII is to eliminate disparate treatment of the sexes based on sexual stereotyping (e.g., that men can do heavy lifting, that mothers of young children are incapable of concentrating on their work), not to impose a new set of stereotypes unsuited to the needs of individual women. Therefore, an airline's maternity leave policy for its ground crew wasn't discriminatory, because there was no across-the-board policy of mandatory leave at a certain point in pregnancy: the employee, her doctor, and the airline's medical examiner made an individual decision based on the employee's desire and ability to keep working. Similarly, it was permissible for an insurance company to tell a pregnant employee to start maternity leave on the date recommended by her doctor and to return to work sixty days post-delivery if her doctor agreed that she was medically qualified to return to work.

• Maternity leave just has to be treated as leave for temporary disability, not better. For example, the *Conners* case involves an employee whose employer's policy was that *all* leave was discretionary. Conners' request for leave was denied because she was a mediocre employee and had used up all her vacation time and sick days. The employer did grant discretionary maternity leave to other, more valued, employees, so the policy wasn't (illegal) sex discrimination, but (permissible) favoring of more efficient employees.

FETAL PROTECTION PROGRAMS

By now, most employers have realized that so unsubtle a gesture as refusing to hire women, or married women, or mothers, is likely to have adverse consequences sooner or (probably) later. But what about a more sophisticated theory: refusing to employ women in situations that expose them to radiation or toxic chemicals, on the grounds that they *could* become pregnant, and the fetus could be damaged? In practical terms, an employer can't restrict the employment only of pregnant women, because by the time a pregnancy has been confirmed the embryo may have received enough dosage to cause serious damage.

Fetal protection is necessarily an emotional issue; after all, no one will take a strong stand in favor of miscarriage, deformity, or mutation. Some people who are opposed to funding benefits for children are staunch advocates of fetuses. Nonetheless, the idea that benevolent corporations defend vulnerable fetuses against the actions of their mothers, who fiendishly scheme to work for a living, is hard to credit.

The legal issues are necessarily complex. Several areas of law are involved: tort law (suits by parents—or former fetuses—for injuries sustained while a pregnant worker was exposed to toxic substances); administrative law (the powers, and responsibilities, of the EEOC and OSHA—the Occupational Safety and Health Administration); contract law (what a union contract says about a worker's right to be transferred to less hazardous work); evidence (was the baby born deformed because of the mother's exposure to vinyl chloride, the fact that the mother got pregnant at the age of thirty-nine, the father's exposure to lead, the toxic waste dump just upstream of the reservoir, or one or more other factors). Understandably, then, the legal situation is confused. Even if it could be argued that a woman who chooses to work in a dangerous environment has assumed the risk that she will be harmed, and should not be allowed to sue the employer, or even if she has signed a statement giving up her right to sue, she can't sign away the child's right to sue. And what about the rights of third parties; can another employee be fired, or transferred into the dangerous job, so that the pregnant employee can be spared the exposure?

A very early case, not specifically dealing with toxic substances, says that maleness isn't a BFOQ unless there is evidence that virtually all women are incapable of doing the job. Pregnant women can be excluded from jobs if heavy lifting is an essential part of the job; but *all* women, under this analysis, can't be excluded on the off-chance that they might be pregnant. *In re National Airlines* and *Zuniga v. Kleberg County Hospital* say that the BFOQ and business necessity defenses can only be raised if pregnancy interferes with safe and efficient operation of the employer's business. In the former case, that means providing safe transportation for airline passengers; in the latter, providing adequate patient care. Any possible damage to the fetus, in this analysis, is the mother's problem. It's up to her to evaluate the risks and decide whether to retain her job or leave. Any risk of suit is the employer's problem; it has to assess the risks and decide how to face them without discriminating against the employee.

In 1981, the EEOC, OSHA, and the Office of Federal Contract Compliance Programs got together and proposed guidelines for fetal protection programs. The proposed guidelines were open to comments from interested parties. The agencies, ventilated by heavy fire from all directions, dismissed the whole mess and withdrew the proposed guidelines:

> Upon reviewing the comments, the agencies have concluded that the most appropriate method of eliminating employment discrimination in the work place where there is potential exposure to reproductive hazards is through investigation and enforcement of the law on a case by case basis, rather than by the issuance of interpretive guidelines.

One can understand how the agencies feel—peacemakers must rely on blessings, because they can't expect earthly rewards—but it's pretty tough on woman workers, who have to be prepared for a protracted siege of litigation if they are exposed both to toxic substances and discrimination described as "fetal protection."

When the EEOC considers a fetal protection policy, the factors in its evaluation include:

- Does the employer have real evidence of danger to fetuses, or is it an assumption made without scientific backing? Is the research balanced? (Most of the studies cited to justify fetal protection programs assess the effect of toxic substances on *men*—not women, children, or the unborn. On the other hand, very few people are willing to play "you-bet-your-fetus" in the interest of scientific accuracy.)
- Are all reproductive hazards covered equally?
- Whether the policy is applied consistently (many toxic substances damage sperm—are fertile women, but not fertile men, excluded from jobs?).
- Has the employer assessed the possible damage to the families of male workers who carry home contamination by chemicals or radiation?
- Has the employer been the subject of other allegations of discrimination?
- Did the employer explore any alternatives to excluding potentially fertile women from the job: respirators or transfers for employees who expressed a concern about the hazards? If so, were the reasons for rejecting these alternatives valid?

It's interesting to note that fetal protection programs tend to be created in two situations: airlines (because pregnancy interferes with the "flying bunny" image of stewardesses) and factory jobs of a kind traditionally held by men. As far as I know, no effort has been made to keep men out of jobs that could damage sperm or cause infertility; and no effort has been made to keep women out of jobs as nurses or anesthetists, although certain anaesthetic gases can deform fetuses or cause genetic damage.

Radiation

When radiation, rather than toxic chemicals, is involved, the Nuclear Regulatory Commission's Guidelines say that woman workers must be notified of hazards from ionizing radiation at work, but they can choose to keep working. The Guidelines suggest that they avoid becoming pregnant until they can get a transfer or temporary assignment to a job with less radiation exposure; if this is impossible, they might "consider leaving their jobs." Certainly they consider it every morning when the alarm clock goes off; women don't often take dangerous factory or laboratory jobs because the jobs are exciting or glamorous, but because they're the best (or only) jobs available. The cases dealing with workers' radiation exposure during pregnancy are a little more realistic:

• EEOC Dec. number 75–055 disapproves an employer's conduct in offering a pregnant employee exposed to radiation a choice between unpaid leave and resignation because lay-off and transfer to a low-exposure job were reasonable alternatives. (The employer had transferred a male employee who was unable to do his former job because of disease.) The EEOC also held that it was sex discrimination to rehire the employee, after birth of her child, at a lower salary and without her accrued seniority.

• EEOC Dec. number 75–072 says it's unlawful sex discrimination to force a pregnant X-ray technician to resign her job. Certainly her job could be harmful to a fetus, but this did not justify the employer's failure to explore other alternatives (a lay-off, assignment to clerical work or other work with limited radiation exposure). The employer claimed that it would be impossible to find a qualified X-ray technician for a temporary assignment. The EEOC rejected this attempt at a business necessity defense, because there was no evidence that the employer had looked for a temporary replacement.

• In *Hayes v. Shelby Memorial Hospital*, the court rejected a BFOQ defense (because the employee could do her job efficiently) and a business necessity defense (because not getting sued is different from safe operation of a business) to sex discrimination charges brought when a pregnant X-ray technician was fired. The employee wasn't awarded back pay for the time between her discharge and the time she started work again with another employer. She was so fed up wtih the treatment she had received that she didn't look for another job, and therefore did not mitigate her damages. However, she did get an award for the difference in pay between what she would have earned at her old job and what she did earn at the new, lower-paid job.

• The question of temporary replacements comes up again in the *Zuniga* case. The Fifth Circuit said, "We fail to see how a hospital with a high X-ray technician turnover rate located 45 miles from the X-ray technician school that had supplied its most recently hired employee, could not have found a temporary replacement for that employee during her leave of absence." To make things worse for the employer, it had a policy of granting leaves for "advanced study, personal or family health," and protecting a fetus against damage promotes both personal and family health.

The OSHA Angle

OSHA has been assigned the modest task of protecting all of America's workers from occupational injury and disease. Given a tiny staff and budget, saddled with a nitpicking series of regulations covering everything from lead poisoning to the dimensions of urinals, it isn't surprising that OSHA has not managed to fulfill its mission.

The central statement of OSHA's philosophy is the General Duty Clause of the Occupational Safety and Health Act (29 U.S.C.S. §654(a)(l)), which requires every employer to provide every employee with a workplace "free of recognized hazards which cause or are likely to cause death or serious injury." The fetus, of course, isn't an employee; but it could be argued that OSHA is supposed to protect the employee's health and physical functioning, including the ability to have healthy children.

Many hours of drafting (and litigation) have gone into the OSHA standards for lead exposure. If workers *are* exposed to lead, the employer must provide a medical exam on request of any employee who "desires medical advice concerning the effects of current or past exposure to lead on the employee's ability to procreate a healthy child." If the employee asks, the examination must include a pregnancy test or laboratory evaluation of male fertility. The objective of the testing is to "identify and perhaps remove workers who may wish to plan pregnancies or who are pregnant." In other words, employers have to make medical advice available to lead-exposed workers, but don't have to transfer pregnant or potentially pregnant workers to safer jobs.

OSHA has rules for exposure to many other substances. For example, since exposure to DBCP (1,2 dibromo-3-chloropropane, a pesticide) can cause sterility, OSHA requires the employer to take complete medical and reproductive histories of workers exposed to this chemical and must have its doctors examine the genito-urinary systems of the workers affected.

The whole issue of occupational health is a political hot potato. Employers are reluctant to spend the enormous sums of money required to eliminate chemical and radiation hazards to adult workers; it would take incredible pressure to get them to protect employees against the much smaller doses that could harm a fetus but not an adult.

Sterilization

Probably the most notorious fetal protection policy was that maintained by American Cyanamid at its Willow River plant in West Virginia. Certain jobs were restricted to men, women past childbearing age, and women who could prove that they had been surgically sterilized. Five woman employees did undergo sterilization so they could keep their jobs.

OSHA's Review Commission (qualifying for the Pontius Pilate Award of 1981) found that American Cyanamid's fetal protection policy wasn't a violation of OSHA's general duty clause:

An employee's decision to undergo sterilization in order to gain or retain employment grows out of economic and social factors which operate primarily outside the workplace. The employer neither controls nor creates these factors as he creates or controls work processes and materials. For these reasons we conclude that the policy is not a hazard within the meaning of the general duty clause.

A Title VII challenge to the policy did better. The case, *Christman v. American Cyanamid,* was brought as a class action and settled in the fall of 1983. American Cyanamid agreed to pay $200,000 in damages to the women who underwent sterilization, agreed to discontinue the policy, and agreed to hire women for the jobs in the same proportion as their proportion of total applicants. Note that the settlement deals with employment opportunities for women—not cleaning the work environment to make it safe for the born or unborn. With luck, this is a tacit admission that the policy was a pretext for discrimination all along.

Under California law (Government Code §12945.5) it's illegal for an employer to require any employee to be sterilized as a condition of employment. Feminist and law-reform groups in other states may want to campaign for adoption of a similar law.

Other Labor Law Issues

Some employees whose work environment could be hazardous to a fetus want to continue working—if they can be transferred to a safer job. For example, Connecticut state law requires employers to make a reasonable effort to transfer a pregnant employee (who has given written notice of pregnancy) to a less hazardous temporary job if either the employer or the employee is concerned about fetal hazards. More to the point, the employer must inform the employees of this possibility. In general, Connecticut employers are not allowed to ask about employees' or job applicants' pregnancy, fertility, family responsibilities, or childbearing plans; but the employer can ask if a BFOQ is involved, or if the employer warns about fetal risks before requesting the information. After the warning is given, and on the employee's request, the employer must take reasonable measures to protect the employee's reproductive capacity and the health of the fetus. "Reasonable measures," for Connecticut purposes, are "those measures which are consistent with business necessity and are least disruptive of the terms and conditions of the employee's employment." In other words, it's more likely that the employer will have to provide a respirator or lead apron for the employee than that the employer will have to install a new filtering system.

• The Fifth Circuit found that an employee was constructively discharged after she told her employer of her pregnancy and was assigned to warehouse duties that she felt could lead to a miscarriage. Nor was the court swayed by the employer's proof of a legitimate business reason for the assignment, nor by the fact that she was replaced by another, non-pregnant, woman. The plaintiff's victory, however, was mostly symbolic. She didn't ask for (and didn't get) an injunction against further hazardous transfers of pregnant employees; and the court refused to award her back pay.

• If a union contract requires disability leave, with continuation of health insurance, when an employee presents medical proof of disability, is a pregnant employee "disabled" when she is able to do *some* jobs but three doctors told her to avoid heavy lifting and chemical exposure (both parts of her regular job)? The union said yes, the employer said she wasn't disabled (and thus entitled to leave) and that an assignment to lighter work was impracticable. The case went to arbitration. The arbitrator ruled that she *was* disabled from performing her regular job. She *could* have been reassigned to the warehouse—she had worked there before, and a job opening existed when she asked for a transfer. The arbitrator gave the company a choice: either agree that she was disabled and pay her the sickness and accident benefit, or give her her regular paycheck for the time involved.

• As the plaintiff in *Doerr v. B. F. Goodrich* learned, you can't neglect the formalities. The plaintiff was hired as a bagger (an entry level job) and was promoted to First Class Charge Operator. The employer's policy called for excluding women of childbearing age from contact with vinyl chloride. The plaintiff was demoted back to bagger, but continued receiving the higher salary. The day after the plaintiff filed with the EEOC, she applied for an injunction against enforcement of the policy. The District Court for the Northern District of Ohio turned her down. First, she hadn't shown a possibility of irreparable injury if the injunction were denied. She was receiving the higher salary based on her promotion, she had not proved that removal from the vinyl chloride area would hurt her career development, and the EEOC could provide whatever remedies were appropriate.

• At first glance the case of *Salazar v. Marathon Oil Co.* looks like bad news. The Texas District Court found that it wasn't a violation of the Equal Pay Act to pay a man more than a woman doing the same job—if the man was a senior employee who had been demoted from a better-paid job because he was physically unable to perform it. Presumably, then, if the only way a pregnant woman can be protected from toxic substances is to demote her, she should be paid her former salary while she works at the temporary job.

• The plaintiff in *Fancher v. Nimmo* worked for the Veterans' Administration; she was a technician in a nuclear medicine lab. General federal policy, and VA policy, call for modification of duties or temporary transfers for pregnant employees who might encounter fetal hazards at work. The plaintiff had gotten reassigned during her first three pregnancies. During her fourth pregnancy, the lab was reorganized so that all technicians were required to rotate through the "hot" areas of the lab. The plaintiff was allowed to avoid heavy lifting but required to rotate to the "hot" areas. She was given an ultimatum: either stay on full duty, take early maternity leave, or accept a permanent reassignment to the biology lab. Although the job in the biology lab was better paid, it constituted demotion and had fewer opportunities for promotion than the nuclear medicine job.

After the plaintiff's baby was born, she was offered reinstatement at the bio lab at the grade, salary, and step level she had before maternity leave. She refused, demanding reinstatement at the nuclear medicine lab. When this was denied, she quit her job and filed charges, claiming constructive discharge.

The District Court agreed that her employer should have listened to its own policy and allowed her to keep her old job, with appropriate modifications to limit her radiation exposure. The required transfer was an instance of disparate treatment. The District Court granted the plaintiff a declaratory judgment that the employer had discriminated against her, attorneys' fees, and a permanent injunction directing the VA to pay attention to its own personnel policies. So far, so good; but that's all the court gave her. It ruled that she had not been constructively discharged, and she wasn't granted reinstatement, back pay (remember, the bio lab paid better than the nuclear medicine lab) or front pay—a reminder of the equivocal nature of victory.

• Finally, to end this section on a (qualified) up note, *Wright v. Olin* is the leading case on fetal protection programs. Unfortunately, the Fourth Circuit refused to condemn fetal protection programs in general:

> By this, we necessarily reject any contention that under Title VII a woman's right to make her own choices respecting workplace hazards rather than submit to discriminatory restrictions is exactly paralleled by a right to make the same choices on behalf of her unborn children . . . On this basis we hold that under appropriate circumstances an employer may, as a matter of business necessity, impose otherwise impermissible restrictions on employment opportunity that are reasonably required to protect the health of unborn children of woman workers against hazards of the workplace.

But the *Wright* court also sets restrictions on fetal protection programs, ruling that such programs constitute prima facie sex discrimination. To justify such a policy, the employer must provide objective evidence (not just an honest belief) that a woman's exposure to a toxic work environment creates a significant risk to the unborn. The employer also has to show that only female, not male workers, need be barred to protect the unborn.

And even if the employer can prove all this (there isn't much solid, well-documented research done on fetal hazards) the employee can still win her case by showing that the employer could institute feasible policies that would protect both jobs and fetuses.

BENEFITS

All fringe benefit programs, according to 29 C.F.R. §1601.10(d), must treat "women affected by pregnancy, childbirth or related medical conditions the same as other persons not so affected but similar in their ability or inability to work." Restricting disability benefits for pregnant employees can also be a violation of state laws against unfair employment practices.

The EEOC's Questions and Answers on the Pregnancy Discrimination Amendment (Question 11) says that an employer has to apply the same policy to absences related to pregnancy as to all other absences. For example, if employees are allowed to use up their (paid) vacation time before being placed on unpaid sick leave status, pregnant employees must have the same option. Several court cases agree:

• Pregnant employees must be allowed to use their accrued paid sick days before unpaid maternity leave begins—*De Laurier v. San Diego Unified School District,* 588 F.2d 674 (9th Cir. 1978); *Castellano v. Linden Board of Education,* 79 N.J. 407, 400 A.2d 1182 (N.J. Sup. 1979); *Farley v. Ocean Township Board of Education,* 174 N.J. Super. 449, 416 A.2d 969 (1980).

• If non-pregnant, temporarily disabled employees can use up vacation days before going on unpaid disability leave, so can employees disabled by pregnancy. This is more important than it seems at first glance. In *Harriss v. Pan Am World Airways,* the airline's policy of requiring stewardesses to cash in their accumulated vacation leave (that is, be paid rather than be treated as on leave) before their mandatory maternity leave was found to be a violation of Title VII. Employees who were on vacation continued to accrue seniority; their company-paid life insurance continued in effect; and they could travel free or at reduced rates. None of these advantages was available to employees on sick leave. The California District Court ruled that pregnant stewardesses should be allowed to use up their vacation time, enjoying these advantages, before starting maternity leave.

• However, if an employer doesn't continue the salary of disabled employees, it's under no obligation to continue the salary of employees on maternity leave.

• What if the state law on occupational disability provides for shorter benefits for pregnancy (e.g., six weeks) than for other disabilities (say, twenty-six weeks)? Question 19 says that the employer can't rely on the state law as an excuse for providing lesser benefits for pregnant than for non-pregnant disabled employees. On the other hand, the employer can't be *blamed* for complying with the state law. *Barone v. Hackett* says that an employer doesn't violate Title VII by making its mandatory contributions to a state disability fund that provides unequal pregnancy benefits—especially since the employer in this case maintained its own disability plan that conformed to the EEOC guidelines.

• Employers don't have to provide *any* health benefits for employees, but if benefits are provided, they must be equal for both sexes. Similarly, the employer need not provide benefits for the families of employees; but if family benefits are provided, male and female employees must receive equally inclusive benefits for their families. Therefore, in *Newport News Shipbuilding Co. v. EEOC*, the Supreme Court ruled that health insurance plans must provide the same pregnancy coverage for the wives of male employees as for female employees.

SENIORITY

This is getting boring. According to 29 C.F.R. §1604.10(b), accrual of seniority during maternity leave must be treated the same way as accrual of seniority during disability leave. This is very important for those companies—and those jobs—where pay increases, training, and promotion are available in strict order of seniority.

Even before the Pregnancy Discrimination Act, the practice of requiring pregnant employees to give up accumulated seniority when they went on maternity leave was ruled illegal. If a court orders that an employee be reinstated after a discriminatory dismissal for pregnancy, her seniority must be computed from the date she was hired to her last day at work, plus the time period from her application for reinstatement to the date of the court decision. Given the amount of time it takes most cases to get into court, and the further time it takes for them to be decided, this can add up to quite a bit of seniority.

UNEMPLOYMENT COMPENSATION

The general rule is that those who are "voluntarily unemployed"—those who quit or have otherwise shown themselves unwilling to work—can't collect unemployment benefits. Otherwise, employers would have to foot the bill every time employees decided that a reduced income from unemployment benefits was better than five days a week of the crummy job. (Perhaps if the policy were changed it would motivate the employers to make jobs more tolerable. Hmm.) Therefore, before 1976, women who lost their jobs for becoming pregnant were often denied unemployment benefits as well, on the theory that they had chosen to become pregnant and therefore were voluntarily unemployed. The change came about when the Federal Unemployment Tax Act (FUTA) was amended to read, "no person shall be denied compensation under such state law [unemployment compensation act] solely on the basis of pregnancy or termination of pregnancy." However, this is true only if the employee is fired while she is still able and willing to work. An employee on maternity leave was legitimately denied unemployment benefits because she had left the employment market until the baby's birth, and there was no evidence that jobs were available for which she was qualified. It's also necessary for the employee to play the game before collecting unemployment benefits: she must apply for maternity leave (if her employer offers it) and must discuss the possibility of returning to her former job, or a comparable job, after childbirth. Otherwise she is considered voluntarily unemployed and therefore ineligible for benefits.

RETURN TO WORK POST-DELIVERY

Question 9 of the EEOC's Questions and Answers on the Pregnancy Discrimination Act says, "Unless the employee on leave has informed the employer that she does not intend to return to work, her job must be held open for her return on the same basis as jobs are held open for employees on sick or disability leave for other reasons." However, courts have placed some limits on this sweeping statement:

• If an employer's policy is to fire all employees who don't return to work after using up their sick leave, the employer can fire an employee for failing to return to work after using up her maternity leave.

• A business-necessity defense is available if the job no longer exists when the employee wants to return to work: for instance, if business has diminished so that the employer can't afford to return the employee to the payroll, or school enrollment has diminished, so that a teacher's position has been eliminated.

• The same defense is available if the employer must fill all vacant jobs immediately with permanent full-time employees. But even in this case, the EEOC says the new mother should be put on a preferred recall list for the next job for which she qualifies, rather than being fired outright.

Employees on maternity leave may face two problems with reinstatement, even if their old jobs are available. First, the employer may demand that they return to work before they are ready to do so, or be fired. The employer violates Title VII unless the time limit (say, sixty days after delivery) is the same as the time limit imposed for temporary disabilities.

The converse is that an employee may be physically recovered from childbirth and eager to return to work, but the employer refuses to re-employ her until a certain amount of time after delivery has passed. In this situation, as in the imposition of compulsory maternity leave, the employer is required to use the employee's ability to work (requiring a doctor's certificate is permissible) rather than a fixed schedule as a standard.

> A policy, therefore, that is founded on generalizations, such as most women after giving birth are fully recovered within six weeks, or that most women do not return to work after giving birth, is discriminatory because it makes no provision for considering individual capabilities.

If a woman applies for reinstatement but can't return to her former job, either because there are no jobs available (either her job has been eliminated, or immediate hiring of a permanent replacement was a business necessity) or because her employer insists on a certain period of time passing between delivery and return to work, she is entitled to collect unemployment benefits for the time she wanted to and could have been working.

One creative employer required employees to have a normal menstrual cycle before returning to work. The Fifth Circuit identified this as "sex-plus" discrimination, holding that the employer wasn't entitled to create a sub-class of women (i.e., new mothers whose menstrual cycle had not resumed) in order to discriminate against them. The employer did not introduce any evidence of business necessity for the practice. Although the court did not discuss it, the policy also had a negative impact on women who breast-fed, because lactation delays the return of menstruation. But then breast-feeding is a part of motherhood, and motherhood raises troublesome questions as well as floods of sentimentality.

MOTHERHOOD/PARENTHOOD

Once you have a baby, in the cogent words of Jean Kerr, thereafter you *have* it. Fathering a child can be a one-shot deal (in both the figurative and literal sense of the term), but motherhood involves more than the (considerable) effort of pregnancy and delivery. This is where the analogy between pregnancy disability and other temporary disability breaks down. Once a woman has recovered physically from childbirth, she is a mother, and someone (though not necessarily the mother or any blood relative) has to take care of the child's physical and emotional needs. Once a temporarily disabled employee recovers from sickness or injury, he or she goes back to work, period. No one feels guilty about neglecting the appendix that was removed two years ago; no one needs time off to go to a gallstone's piano recital or confer with a broken leg's fourth-grade teacher. Kids, as independent individuals, sometimes get sick or have school holidays; so do housekeepers, even paragons who work for $100 a week and no Social Security.

In one sense, the problem is that little or no provision is made for *parenthood,* for either biological or adoptive parents. But since in most families women assume or are given the lioness's share of child-care responsibilities, the most crucial problem is the lack of provision made for *motherhood.*

The concept of "sex-plus" discrimination comes from *Phillips v. Martin Marietta,* 400 U.S. 542 (1971), which finds sex discrimination in a company's willingness to hire fathers, but not mothers, of young children. The discrimination was "sex-plus" because only one group of women (mothers of young children) suffered. A 1978 Seventh Circuit case reaches a similar conclusion: that it's illegal for an airline to fire stewardesses who were mothers, or to force them to take ground-crew jobs, when no restrictions were placed on the employment of stewards who were fathers. The airlines did not produce evidence of excessive absenteeism or poor work performance of stewardess-mothers. They claimed that it would be too expensive to retrain stewardesses returning to work after maternity leave (reminiscent of the old joke that you can't give [pick your least-favorite ethnic group] more than a ten-minute coffee break, because after that you have to retrain them) but didn't prove that retraining would be more expensive than training a new stewardess to replace the one who was fired.

The Pregnancy Discrimination Act doesn't mention post-childbirth leave for breast-feeding or child care, but several decisions hold that Title VII requires employers to treat a request for additional leave in the same way they would treat a request for discretionary non-medical leave (e.g., education, a reservist's military obligation). If the employer *never* grants discretionary leave, it need not provide time off for mothers; if it grants leave liberally for other non-medical reasons, it had better be kind and disposing toward mothers.

Several cases deal with fatherhood leave:

• Insult to injury department: the policy of giving male teachers a day of paid leave to attend the birth or adoption of a child, while maternity leave was entirely unpaid, violated Title VII by giving male employees a benefit female employees couldn't have.

• Just because a union contract provides that teachers on maternity leave can contribute toward their pensions doesn't mean that male teachers on child-care leave can do the same—the New Jersey court said that the provisions of the contract referred specifically to pregnancy. (To stand up to Title VII scrutiny, the system would also have to deny mothers on child-care leave the option of paying for pension credit.)

• A 1975 opinion that never mentions Title VII says that an employer can refuse to let a male employee use some of his sick days to participate in the birth of his child. First of all, the employer has a rational basis for distinguishing between employee mothers and employee fathers. Second, sick leave is for the employee's own illness, not for anyone else's. This decision could have negative effects on women who want to use their sick days to care for sick children.

Understandably, some women get tired of attempting to be Superwomen in a society that locks them out of phone booths. Can a woman who quits a job because its schedule conflicts with her family responsibilities collect unemployment benefits? At least one case says yes: a laundry worker tried to get her work schedule changed so she could take care of her two children. When this was impossible, she quit because the hours and overtime required couldn't be reconciled with her child-care obligations. She was denied unemployment benefits on the ground that she had quit her job voluntarily; but the Supreme Judicial Court of Massachusetts ruled that family responsibilities can be a valid reason for turning down a work assignment. A work assignment that can't be reconciled with such personal responsibilities might equal constructive discharge.

CHILDBIRTH

At one time, standard procedure was for babies to be born at home, with the assistance of female relatives and the local midwife. Doctors would not deign to be involved in such a sordid—and female-dominated—process. This was lucky for mother and infant, since before the recognition of the germ theory of disease, doctors were more likely to infect the mother than to help her. The first hospitals were places where the poor and friendless went to die; no one would give birth in a hospital if there was any alternative at all.

In the nineteenth century, the situation began to change. Medicine had more to offer (and vastly greater pretensions): a scientific knowledge of anatomy, antisepsis, anaesthetics. Doctors had been using forceps in complicated deliveries for centuries (and keeping this knowledge from midwives). Anaesthesia in childbirth became fashionable (because several of Queen Victoria's numerous children were born with the assistance of chloroform) as well as a blessing for women in long, painful labor. Anaesthesia made surgical operations of all kinds less stressful for both patient and surgeon and made delivery by Caesarean section a (you should pardon the expression) viable option for both mother and infant.

Anaesthesia and operations are associated with sickness and with hospitals. Childbirth became medicalized. The medical profession, and eventually the laity, thought of childbirth less as a family function appropriately occurring at home, more as a medical function appropriately occurring in a hospital. As medicine evolved, it developed more and more techniques to facilitate difficult childbirth and save lives.

No one would quarrel with the use of these heroic measures in the appropriate cases. The problem is that sometimes the techniques that save lives in emergency cases are applied, routinely, to normal childbirth. Risks that would be justifiable by the possibility of saving life or health are too great when the potential rewards are smaller. A hospital is always less familiar and less comfortable than one's home. The hospital is figuratively sterile, though not necessarily literally so—the problem of hospital-borne infection is perpetual and serious.

The ideal patient for a hospital birth is compliant with hospital routine and unconscious during delivery. The language here is significant: the doctor delivers the baby (like a UPS parcel) rather than the mother giving birth. The medical term for childbirth is management of labor. The metaphor is uncannily apt—but the mothers aren't unionized.

The basic rule seems to be that, for hospital births (the vast majority) hospital rules will determine the way that labor and delivery will be managed. If the hospital routine calls for routine fetal monitoring, then monitoring will be used in all cases (whatever the mother, or her doctor, prefers); if the drill calls for routine medication, all mothers—including those who prefer unmedicated childbirth—will get the medication. Although several cases have been brought to challenge such policies, courts don't like to interfere with hospital policies as long as the policies have *some* connection to reality. The standard patients' consent form will probably be construed as a consent to the hospital's policies and to whatever decisions its medical staff makes. However, if the consent form is vague, it will probably be construed in the patient's, not the hospital's, favor.

But if what is involved isn't routine hospital procedure but a significant medical decision, the doctor must get the informed consent of the patient; that is, the doctor must explain the proposed action, its advantages and disadvantages, and get some indication of consent from the patient. *Williams v. Lallie Kemp Charity Hospital*, for example, upholds an award of $25,000 to a mother for failing to inform her of the dangers, and get her informed consent, before proceeding with a vaginal delivery when a Caesarean was medically appropriate. A 1983 New York case says that the doctor has an independent duty *to the fetus* to get the mother's informed consent before treatment. In other words, both the child and the mother can sue the doctor (and probably the hospital) for the negative consequences of the failure to obtain informed consent.

If mother and/or child are injured by medical or hospital negligence, their recourse is the common or garden malpractice suit. Or, in a statement of exceptional crassness cited by the professional group of the Lamaze method of natural childbirth, "Regardless of one's philosophy, the time has come when electronic fetal monitoring and entering the delivery suite with an IV in place are necessities to protect the doctor and the hospital from lawsuits." When kindly old Doc rode his buggy through the snowstorm to assist a woman in labor, it was understood that his function was to help the woman and wait for nature to take its course. If mother, baby, or both died, it was accepted as the will of God. No one would think of suing Doc—both because he was a respected member of the community and because of the comparative modesty of his role. Since the present relationship between doctors and patients approaches an adversary relationship, and since modern obstetrics involves many interventions with nature (some of them lifesaving or healthsaving; some less dramatic, but beneficial; some harmless, but detrimental to the experience of childbirth; some dramatically detrimental to health), both lawsuits and "defensive medicine" are common.

It's understandable that doctors and hospitals want to protect themselves against gargantuan jury verdicts. It's hard to run an efficient hospital when babies insist on getting born on their own schedule, with no consideration for shift changes or delivery room schedules. But it's also understandable that mothers, as paying customers, want more control over the birth process. For the hospital, childbirth is routine, something that happens every day. Normal births—and most births are normal—produce no papers in the *New England Journal of Medicine*. For the mothers and fathers, childbirth is a very significant experience, occurring once or several times in a lifetime.

If a woman wants more control over the process of childbirth, the first step is to find a sympathetic doctor. The next—and probably harder—step is to find a sympathetic hospital at which the doctor has admitting privileges. At least two cases hold that childbirth isn't an "emergency," so hospitals can refuse to admit women in labor who are not patients of doctors practicing at that hospital. (One woman gave birth in the parking lot; the other died in the ambulance shuttling her from hospital to hospital). On the other hand, hospitals do have a duty to provide adequate care for their duly-admitted patients: a hospital was held liable for failing to maintain facilities for Caesareans (showing a conscious indifference to the welfare of the patients) and failure to warn the patients of this lack, so they could make an informed decision about whether to choose that hospital.

If a hospital decides that fathers should be pacing the corridor or buying rounds at the local saloon rather than holding stopwatches in the labor room, the hospital's decision will prevail over challenges by parents, doctors, or natural childbirth advocacy groups. The hospital's right to regulate itself prevails over an asserted right of marital privacy (claimed to give a couple the right to decide how their children will be born) and doctors' asserted right to decide how they will practice medicine. Since many systems of natural childbirth rely on the husband as labor coach, and many couples prefer, for other reasons, for the father to be present at the birth, it's important for a pregnant woman to find out well before the birth what the hospital's policy is. It may be necessary to change obstetricians to find one with admitting privileges at a more *simpatico* hospital.

A 1983 Michigan case, *Whitman v. Mercy-Memorial Hospital*, holds that the hospital violated the state law against marital-status discrimination by excluding an unwed father from the delivery room. (The hospital claimed that he wasn't a member of the mother's immediate family.) The court, as usual, genuflected to the hospital's right to set policy; but it held that, since the hospital allowed one non-medical person in the delivery room as a labor coach, the hospital could not apply this policy in a discriminatory manner.

Freedom of religion is considered strong enough to overcome the hospital's right to make its own rules. A New York court ruled that Orthodox Jewish parents have a right to have their sons' *bris* (ritual circumcision) performed at the hospital by a *mohel* (ritual circumciser) even if the *mohel* doesn't have hospital privileges. But the hospital has the last word: the father, the *mohel*, and those attending the ceremony must scrub and wear surgical gowns.

Non-Hospital Births

Some families prefer home birth, pointing out that it's less medically dominated, more family-oriented, a whole lot cheaper, and doesn't expose mother or infant to overmedication, hospital infections, or overuse of medical technology. Opponents point out that home births are frequently short of skilled assistance and never have advanced medical technology available when it's needed. Complications can develop suddenly and unexpectedly and can kill before the laboring woman can be rushed to a hospital (if any hospital will accept her without an admitting physician and guarantee of payment).

The law can't mandate hospital birth until and unless it can guarantee medical care for everyone in need, *and* provide that babies will be born on schedule, and not in taxis, police cars, ambulances, and other out-of-the-way places. But if anything goes wrong in a home birth, all participants face everything from recriminations to litigation to arrest. Doctors and licensed midwives tend to be leery of home births, because the standard of care in malpractice is accepted medical practice, and accepted medical practice calls for hospital birth. Unlicensed midwives can face criminal charges ranging from unauthorized practice of medicine to criminally negligent homicide. Home birth, then, has something of an underground aura. Although home birth has its partisans, organizations, and publications, it figures in few court cases or statutes. Probably the "we're-all-in-this-together" spirit (or a belief that the parents are legally chargeable with as much negligence as the doctor or midwife) prevents malpractice suits. After all, most home births result in a healthy mother and infant— babies have been getting themselves born long before hospitals, Blue Cross, or Medicaid existed.

The birth (or birthing) center is an attempt to combine family control of birth and a homelike atmosphere with the availability of medical technology and specialized assistance if—but only if—they are necessary. As of February 1984 seventeen states licensed birth centers (Alaska, Arizona, California, Georgia, Indiana, Kansas, Kentucky, Massachusetts, North Carolina, New Hampshire, New Mexico, New York, Utah, and Washington) and sixteen more states had bills pending or proposed regulations under consideration (Connecticut, Delaware, Florida, Hawaii, Maryland, Mississippi, New Jersey, Ohio, Oklahoma, Oregon, Pennsylvania, Texas, Vermont, Virginia, West Virginia, Wyoming).

Parents-to-be and holistic health practitioners aren't the only ones interested in birth centers. Insurers are also showing an interest. A birth center is less expensive to set up than a hospital because it has less hardware. Its patients are healthier to begin with (because cases are selected with an expectation of normal birth) and, because there is less medical intervention, there is less recovery time. Malpractice insurance premiums for obstetricians are high even by medical standards; malpractice premiums for midwives are much, much lower. Employers are likely to look with favor on anything that simultaneously reduces health insurance premiums and meets an employee demand. In the other corner is the medical establishment, motivated both by profit and a sincere belief that a highly medicalized birth is best for both mother and baby. It should be interesting to see who wins.

Who Pays?

Usually, of course, some kind of insurance plan (either private, like Blue Cross, or socially provided for the medically indigent, like Medicaid) pays the bill. If people paid all of their own medical bills directly, there'd be even more heart attacks than there are already. Reasonably speaking, most people pay their bills (and everyone else's) indirectly. Employers provide health insurance not as a pure act of benevolence but in response to employee demand and because, after taxes, it's cheaper than giving the employees more money.

The Questions and Answers on the PDA say, "Any health insurance provided must cover expenses for pregnancy-related conditions on the same basis as expenses for other medical conditions." Questions 25, 26, and 27 deal with reimbursement, dollar amounts, and deductibles for pregnancy and childbirth expenses. The Answers say that if the health insurance plan provides a flat rate benefit for other medical bills, it must provide the same flat rate for pregnancy and delivery costs; if it reimburses a certain percentage of the reasonable and customary charge, it must do the same for pregnancy and delivery. If a plan covers hospitalization only, it can limit reimbursement to the actual hospitalization to give birth. If visits to doctors' offices are covered for illness and injury, they must be covered for pre- and post-natal care. Any deductible imposed before the employer reimburses pregnancy- and delivery-related costs must be the same as the deductible in other situations, and the insurance plan must pay the same percentage of pregnancy and delivery costs as other employee health costs.

Blue Cross is trying to insulate itself from the (considerable) cost of maternity hospitalization: some Blue Cross/Blue Shield plans are offering cash and/or home nursing to new mothers who agree to leave the hospital in one or two days after birth, rather than the normal three days after an uncomplicated delivery.

A 1984 New York case shows exactly how expensive it can be to have a child without also having insurance coverage. The case ended happily for the parents because the hospital's ambiguous fee agreement was construed against the hospital. I suspect the judge was infuriated by the hospital's conduct; in effect, it tried to repossess the baby during the fee dispute.

But to start at the beginning . . . One of the defendants was pregnant with her second child. The first had been delivered by Caesarean section; the delivery involved a thirteen-day hospital stay and cost about $2,000, which had been paid by health insurance.

The mother-to-be called New York Hospital's clinic. She was told that, for mothers without health insurance, the clinic required a prepayment of $1,900, "which represented the usual charge for similar patients" (quote from the opinion). At that time, both defendants had jobs, but neither had health insurance. The clinic told her to apply for Medicaid; she did, but was turned down because the family income was too high.

The defendants raised the $1,900 and paid it at the mother-to-be's first visit to the clinic. They believed it was the full payment for delivery of the baby. No one mentioned that this amount was a down payment, that the bill was likely to be much higher (because Caesareans call for a long hospital stay) or that people ordinarily ineligible for Medicaid could get some Medicaid reimbursement for extraordinarily high medical expenses.

A healthy baby was born by Caesarean section. Usually the mother requires a ten-day hospital stay to recover (rather than one to four days in the hospital after a vaginal delivery). However, the defendant developed a respiratory infection and had to spend thirteen days in the hospital. Because she was breast-feeding, the baby, who was perfectly healthy, also stayed in the hospital. No one mentioned the extra costs, so the final bill— $5,617.15 for the mother, $1,825.56 for the baby—came as quite a surprise. The hospital cashier told the father that he would not be allowed to take the baby home unless he signed a guarantee of the $5,542.65 debt. He did sign, but the court refused to enforce the guarantee because it was signed under duress—the hospital virtually held the baby for ransom.

As the judge said, "As in all other aspects of its relationship with this patient, the Hospital's error was a condescending usurpation of the patient's decision-making role until it was too late for her to pursue an alternative. The [defendants] should have been able to decide on the nature and extent of medical services with a reasonable understanding of the fiscal consequences of their decision." It would be great if this case impelled hospitals to be less condescending and more informative to patients, but it will probably simply result in a rash of new admission forms, with an inch-high warning that any money handed over is just a down payment, and the hospital reserves the right to extract further, indefinite sums of money.

Midwives

In most states, the legal question isn't *whether* midwives are recognized and licensed (though it may be difficult for a pregnant woman to find a qualified midwife nearby). Instead, the legal questions involve who is entitled to be licensed as a midwife; who sits on the licensing board (do midwives regulate their own profession, or is the board partially staffed or controlled by doctors?); whether midwives must work under the supervision of doctors or are permitted to practice independently; whether midwives are restricted to normal deliveries or can handle complicated deliveries, prenatal care, birth control, and "well-woman" services; and whether health insurers will reimburse midwives for their services (so they can maintain independent practices) or channel the money through obstetricians.

Ten states (Idaho, Iowa, Kansas, Louisiana, Maine, Mississippi, Nevada, New Mexico, Vermont, Wyoming) don't mention midwives in their statutes. Nebraska, North Dakota, and Oregon statutes acknowledge them indirectly by requiring midwives to file birth certificates and/or use eyedrops to prevent gonorrhea-caused blindness of the newborn; Tennessee says that "unlicensed practice of medicine" doesn't refer to midwives. Evidently, then, the existence of midwives is recognized in these states, but the statutes don't say anything else about the licensing or qualification of midwives. Out of the remaining thirty-six states, sixteen will grant licenses to lay midwives and twenty restrict licenses to certified nurse-midwives. "Lay midwife" in this context is something of a misnomer. A lay midwife isn't someone who wanders in off the street to the licensing board because having babies is, like you know, so groovy, but a person who isn't a registered nurse but who is a graduate of an approved school of midwifery. A certified nurse-midwife is a registered nurse who has additional training in midwifery. Advocates of lay midwifery say that nurses are trained to be subservient to doctors and to care for sick people in hospitals; pregnant women aren't sick and don't necessarily give birth in hospitals. Advocates of certified nurse-midwifery say that nurses are trained to preserve health, that they are becoming less subservient as they realize the dignity of their own profession, and nursing training is important for recognizing potential complications that should be referred to a doctor. (Sometimes the term "lay midwife" is used to refer to an unlicensed person; but in this book, I use it to mean a licensed midwife who isn't a registered nurse.)

Different states allow different degrees of power to licensed midwives. California midwives are not allowed to use forceps or other instruments, drugs other than antiseptics, or to turn a baby who is presenting unfavorably; but North Carolina midwives can give anaesthetics, and South Dakota midwives can prescribe medication. Washington midwives can administer local anaesthetics and administer drugs prescribed by a doctor. In several states (e.g., Alabama, Florida, Maryland, North Carolina, Oklahoma, Utah, Wisconsin) midwives can provide prenatal care; but in Connecticut, midwives are not allowed to see a pregnant patient until she is at least in her seventh month. In Maryland, North Carolina, Oklahoma, and Wisconsin, midwives can provide routine "well-woman" gynecology care. The midwifery laws of several states (e.g., Massachusetts, North Carolina, Pennsylvania, Washington) mention birth centers or other out-of-hospital settings. Florida midwives have the responsibility for seeing that "the setting in which the infant is to be delivered is a safe and hygienic one," which seems to me to be a clear authorization of midwife-assisted home birth. The Utah midwifery act goes even further: "This act shall in no way or at any time abridge, limit, or change in any way the right of a mother and/or father to deliver their baby where, when, how and with whom they choose regardless of certification." That seems to include not only home birth but relieves the parent of liability for choosing an unlicensed midwife. However, licensed nurse-midwives in Utah can practice only in health care agencies, doctors' offices, and public health agencies. Nurse-midwives must have a practice agreement with a doctor, must participate in a delivery only if the midwife and physician agree that the delivery is likely to be normal, and nurse-midwives aren't allowed to exceed the responsibilities the practice agreement gives them.

This brings up the question of autonomy: should midwives be independent health practitioners or assistants to doctors? Most of the midwifery statutes don't take up the question explicitly. The ones that do vary widely in their definition of the midwife's role. In Alabama, Colorado, North Carolina, South Dakota, and West Virginia (unless the midwife is a staffer at a maternity or family planning service), the midwife must be under the direct supervision of a doctor. Wisconsin midwives must practice in a health-care facility that has an agreement with a supervising doctor (the doctor supervises the facility, not the midwife), and the midwife must refer any complications of pregnancy or delivery to a doctor. Washington also requires midwives to consult physicians about abnormal developments. Georgia law requires midwives to call in a doctor if the baby has not been born spontaneously in a reasonable time after the onset of labor. Oklahoma midwives must practice "within a health care system which provides for medical consultation, management, or referral." Massachusetts requires the midwife to be part of a health care team that includes a doctor. In Florida, the focus is on getting the informed consent of the mother-to-be; and the midwife must have a written treatme.it plan providing for emergency medical care. That implies that a midwife can legally conduct a normal delivery herself with no medical supervision. (If you are thinking that these distinctions are another load of legalistic garbage, there may be something in that; but there is a real difference between assisting a doctor, being part of a team that includes a doctor, and serving as an independent professional who consults a doctor in difficult cases—much as a family practitioner might consult a specialist.)

Even a favorable legislative climate won't guarantee smooth sailing for midwives or doctors associated with midwives. Hospitals are not legally compelled to give all qualified doctors, or all qualified midwives, admitting privileges; doctors can do a good deal to make other doctors uncomfortable. Some malpractice insurance companies are controlled by doctors, and cancelling a doctor's malpractice insurance will certainly cause him to sit up and take notice.

In 1980, two Nashville nurse-midwives who had a back-up physician applied for admitting privileges at three hospitals. At the first hospital, the pediatrics department refused to review their practice protocol (it's always a pleasure to deal with someone with an open mind) and refused to treat any baby delivered by a nurse-midwife. (This rather tends to create an inference that the midwives provided care of such impeccable standards that no improvement was possible. You'd think they'd be all over those babies like chickens on a June bug, trying to make up for defective care provided by midwives.) The second hospital said it was unsuitable for midwifery practice because it was a referral center for high-risk patients and couldn't handle normal births—although 75 percent of their patients in the preceding year had been low-risk patients. The third hospital threw a fit and changed its policies to make nurse-midwifery practice impossible. The hospital closed its birthing room, forbade laboring women to walk around, and required all maternity patients to have IV's, enemas, perineal shaving, and continuous fetal monitoring. Since, presumably, all these things were already being done when they were medically necessary, the hospital took it on itself to use unnecessary medical techniques to humiliate women in labor and cause them additional discomfort. It seems that all women in labor were to be punished for the presumption of some women who wanted to be assisted in labor by nurse-midwives, or the presumption of some women in wanting to *be* nurse-midwives. The use of psychiatry to punish dissidents is well documented in the Soviet Union, but the use of obstetrics for the same purpose in this country is unexpected.

As an additional pleasantry, the doctor who worked with the midwives had his malpractice insurance cancelled by the doctor-controlled carrier that covered about 80 percent of Tennessee physicians. Nurse Midwifery Associates sued the director of the insurance company. The District Court for the Middle District of Tennessee ruled that, if the doctor controlling the insurance carrier *did* have the policy cancelled, and if the insurance company director's motive was to limit competition in maternity practice, then he had violated the antitrust laws by engaging in an illegal boycott. The following year, the insurance company entered into a consent decree with the Federal Trade Commission. The insurer agreed to stop discriminating against doctors who supervise licensed midwives, particularly since they had no rational basis for believing that those doctors were more likely to lose malpractice suits than others.

Federal law (42 U.S.C. §1396d(a)(17)) says that Medicaid will pay certified nurse-midwives directly for their services (the fee doesn't have to be funnelled through a doctor)—but only if the services were legal in the state in which they were rendered. Several states (e.g., Alaska, Arkansas, California, Pennsylvania, Wisconsin) provide that Medicaid and/or private health insurance plans pay nurse-midwives directly for their services.

THE ROAD TO THE COURTHOUSE

• If medical actions or hospital routine injure a pregnant woman or an infant, a malpractice suit may be sustained against the doctors involved, the hospital, or both.

• The Pregnancy Discrimination Act is part of Title VII, and the routine of Title VII cases is no doubt familiar by now.

• The employer isn't the only possible defendant: a union violates Title VII by supporting an employer's policy of denying leaves of absence to pregnant employees. The state acts as an "employment agency"—and possible Title VII defendant—if it violates the unemployment pregnancy provisions and denies unemployment benefits for women who are denied reinstatement after pregnancy leave, while granting benefits to workers unable to return to work after temporary disability leave.

• If the employee doesn't disclose her pregnancy to the employer, but her doctor does, she may have a case against the doctor for invasion of privacy.

• A couple of plaintiffs have tried to sue school board members personally for their actions in firing pregnant workers. It didn't work: the courts said that the school board members acted in good faith and were immune from personal liability.

• What about a claim that the employer has breached a contract by failing to observe the maternity policy printed in its employee manual? The plaintiff in *White v. ITT* was told to study the employee manual when she was hired; she relied on the manual and the leave-of-absence form, believing that she would be reinstated after maternity leave. When she wasn't, she sued for fraud and breach of contract—and lost. The Eleventh Circuit said that Georgia law won't enforce a future promise made to an at-will employee (one who is hired for an indefinite amount of time and can be fired at the employer's pleasure).

• A unionized employee can use the contract's arbitration procedure. For example, a contract provided up to thirty days' non-medical leave "for any valid reason." The grievant was denied leave for nursing her baby. The employer said that its policy was to grant child-care leave only with a medical certificate. The arbitrator accepted that, but ruled for the grievant—because the employer had a history of interpreting "valid reason" liberally. The arbitrator granted the grievant 2/3 pay for the leave time she was improperly denied—less than full pay, because the employer acted in good faith.

THE SMOKING GUN

• An employee who is denied leave must be prepared to rebut the employer's claims by showing that her job *could* have been left unfilled while she was on leave, or that a temporary replacement could have been hired.

• An employee who is denied reinstatement must be prepared to rebut her employer by showing that the employer's circumstances did not change in a way that made reinstatement impossible. Two 1983 cases raise interesting questions about evidence and remedies:

• The defendant in *Goss v. Exxon Office Systems* needed to have a good sales territory available, because it had recruited a woman executive by promising a job to her salesman husband. There were two good territories: one handled by a man who was in the management's good graces; the other by the plaintiff, an excellent saleswoman who was described as a "wacko" and "pregnant and likely to leave anyway."

The plaintiff was removed from her sales territory and told to take an inferior sales territory or resign. She did resign, and the Eastern District of Pennsylvania found constructive discharge and sex discrimination based on her desire to combine motherhood and a career. The employer's explanation for removing a successful saleswoman from the territory ("we wanted to experiment and see if someone could get more out of it") was rejected as incredible and pretextual. The plaintiff was awarded $61,611.24 for lost commissions and back pay; the fringe benefits she would have received; and expenses of finding another job. She was also awarded "front pay" to compensate for lower earnings in her new job, but only for four months (the training program before she could go out in the field and earn commissions) rather than the four and a half years she asked for (time she estimated she would need to be re-established as a top saleswoman).

• *Beck v. Quiktrip Corp.* involved a woman who was thrown out of a sales training program when she became pregnant and later was fired after a telephone altercation with the sales manager on a day she took off because her older child was sick. The employer's evidence was that she was dropped from the training program because of unsatisfactory progress; she said she was learning slowly but was qualified to remain in the program. The employer said she was fired for absenteeism, misconduct ("being abusive to the store manager"), lack of cooperation (she called the area supervisor instead of the manager when she took off that day) and "verbal disrespect for manager." (It seems like a lot of accusations for one phone call, which involved ordinary hassling rather than death threats.) However, she was never given a written notice of unsatisfactory conduct, although the employer did give such notices to other employees.

The District Court agreed with the plaintiff that these claims were pretexts for firing her for pregnancy and/or motherhood, and the Tenth Circuit affirmed. More reluctantly, the Tenth Circuit upheld the District Court's decision to let the plaintiff introduce statistics showing the composition of the local work force and the percentage of women in sales in the Wichita area. It's true that these statistics did not show the treatment of pregnant women; but statistics that are not sufficient to make a prima facie case are not necessarily irrelevant. The moral: present statistical evidence if any is available—it may not be enough to win by itself, but it may influence a court or jury.

9

STERILIZATION AND STERILIZATION ABUSE

Depending on which psychological work-up you believe, Lucille Watson is of dull-normal intelligence, borderline, or mildly mentally retarded. She spent a few years in a regular public school, not learning much (but then, neither did many of her classmates who were considered normal), and some time in classes for the mentally retarded. She can read and write a little, and do some simple arithmetic. She lives in a halfway house for the retarded, which provides her with a single room and meals but has no facilities for children, and she sees men socially. Ms. Watson works part-time at a factory, packing boxes; a social worker visits her once a week to help her pay bills and make sure that she takes her birth control pills. Because Ms. Watson has difficulty managing money, her mother has been appointed guardian of her person and property.

Ms. Watson likes her job, likes traveling to work on the bus each day, enjoys going to the movies, holding hands, and what she calls "feeling good with a boy." She likes the halfway house but would rather have her own apartment. She knows that, unless she takes her pill every day, she could have a baby—but she thinks babies are fun. It would be nice to have a baby.

The social worker, Jeanne Cioffi, has suggested to Ms. Watson's mother that she file a petition for her daughter's sterilization.

When legal issues are discussed, various things are referred to as "slippery-slope" issues: that is, a debater claims that adoption of an opponent's morally dubious suggestion will lead right down the slippery slope to some inevitable and clearly undesirable destination. If the debater is a liberal, the destination is probably Nazism; if a conservative, Communism. But the legal issues of sterilization provide slippery slopes in both directions. Most people would agree that voluntary sterilization of women who wanted the operation and gave their informed consent is legitimate. (Although some people feel that interference with fertility, other than by abstinence, is immoral, and others feel that a woman's right to control her own body is limited to some extent by her husband's feelings in the matter.)

But when consent is given to a serious and probably irreversible operation like sterilization, is the consent truly voluntary? A woman may prefer to retain the option of having more children but choose sterilization anyway, because other methods of contraception failed for her or because she's afraid of cancer, a perforated uterus, or other contraceptive side-effects. If she's a practicing Catholic, she may opt for sterilization because she can confess and be forgiven for a single sin (which she is most unlikely to repeat) rather than confessing repeated use of contraceptives. (That's one reason why, in Puerto Rico, sterilization is simply called "La Operación," and it's been estimated that one-third of all women of childbearing age have been sterilized.) If she has to pay for birth control pills or barrier contraceptives out of her own pocket, but Medicaid will pay for sterilization, there's further incentive to choose the operation. If a woman is threatened with the loss of her job or welfare benefits unless she's sterilized, the incentive is even stronger. Finally, there are some circumstances under which sterilization without the woman's consent is legal: if she is so mentally handicapped that she can't give informed consent, and statutory or court-ordered guidelines are followed.

So one legal problem is to make sure that allegedly voluntary sterilizations really are voluntary; the other problem is to make sure that women who honestly want to be sterilized are not refused by hospitals or doctors and that doctors will perform tubal ligations for sterilization rather than hysterectomies. Hysterectomies involve more pain, longer recovery time, and more complications for the woman—but they're good practice for young surgeons, who will spend much of their careers removing uteri, which American medicine considers to be fairly dispensable organs. The major legal issue is the extent to which a woman will be permitted to make an individual decision, without intervention or approval by those who claim to know better.

VOLUNTARY STERILIZATION

In the bad old days, many hospitals refused to perform any voluntary nontherapeutic sterilizations (operations motivated by a desire to avoid pregnancy, not a danger to the mother's health posed by pregnancy), refused to perform them without a husband's consent (no husband, no operation) or established formulas (a woman could be sterilized if her age times the number of children she already had equaled 120, for example). Although it's never safe to be smug about modern progress, it's now not too difficult for a woman who wants to be sterilized to have the operation performed.

However, a private hospital doesn't have to perform sterilizations if

voluntary sterilizations are repugnant to the hospital administration's religious views, and doctors and nurses can't be fired or otherwise penalized
for refusing to participate in a voluntary sterilization that is offensive to
them on religious grounds. This is one of those situations calling for a
"balancing test": which of two constitutionally protected rights (freedom
of religion; right of privacy and control over one's own body) will be
favored. In this situation, freedom of religion wins out. The balancing test
is limited to religious objections: if the hospital provides general medical
care, it can't discriminate against sterilization operations.

The basic rule is that a person who is capable of informed consent, and
is over eighteen (or younger and married), can decide to be sterilized.
Sometimes hospitals require the husband's consent before sterilizing a
married woman. A New Jersey case says that a married woman, as a person,
has a right to control her own body, and therefore to make the decision
to be sterilized by herself; an Oregon state law and an Opinion of the
Attorney General from Iowa say much the same thing. An Arkansas case
says that public hospitals can't require a husband's consent for his wife's
sterilization, but the Ninth Circuit refused to order a private hospital to
stop requiring husbandly consent. The Ninth Circuit felt that, as no state
action was involved in the hospital's policy, courts had no right to tell the
hospital what to do.

South Carolina's Attorney General produced a say-nothing opinion, stating that it was unclear whether it was legal to sterilize a married woman
without her husband's consent. Getting the consent can be a little difficult
if the spouse disappeared years ago and has not been divorced in the
interim; so the Georgia and New Mexico statutes say that it isn't necessary
to get the consent of an unfindable spouse.

The reason a hospital might demand the husband's consent (apart from
free-floating paternalism) is fear of being sued by the unconsenting or
unconsulted husband. There's not much case law on this, but an Oklahoma
court pointed out that, as no man has a right to have a wife who can (or
will) bear children, no one can be liable for violation of a non-existent
right.

California and New Hampshire statutes forbid doctors and medical facilities from imposing restrictions on voluntary sterilizations (e.g., age,
spouse's consent, number of existing children) that would not be placed
on other non-emergency operations. In California (again) and Tennessee,
if a health insurance policy covers sterilization at all, it must cover voluntary sterilization for birth control as well as medically indicated sterilization. The Tennessee law also prevents the insurer from canceling
sterilization coverage unless the entire policy is canceled. And, to hark
back to sex discrimination in employment, the charge that an employer
provides benefits for disabilities caused by other non-emergency surgery,
but not for disability caused by tubal ligation, states a Title VII claim.

STERILIZATION ABUSE

One of the hazards of being a woman—especially a poor and/or nonwhite woman—is the prevalence of people who claim to know more about what's good for you than you do. Often the subject of these expert arias is "excessive" fertility: the bearing of more children than the expert thinks the woman wants, or more than she can care for adequately (by the expert's standards) or more than the welfare department wants to support. Sometimes this conflict eventuates in editorials, sermonizing, and compressed lips; sometimes the result is sterilization abuse.

There are various grades of sterilization abuse, from subtle manipulation of a woman who thinks she wants to be sterilized and isn't sure, to pressing a consent form and a pen into the hands of a woman in labor or recovering from a traumatic abortion, to the famous "Mississippi appendectomy" (a woman hospitalized for surgery requiring general anaesthetics wakes up with a surprise tubal ligation or hysterectomy). The problem is that sometimes the definition of "voluntary" sterilization is stretched pretty far: as long as the doctor consents and some relative or associate of the woman consents, the procedure is deemed voluntary. (I'm reminded of the old Wall Street saying: well, the company made money, the broker made money—two out of three ain't bad.)

Consider *Beck v. Lovell*, 361 So.2d 245 (Fla. 1978). The plaintiff's third child suffered from an Rh incompatibility (which is dangerous for the child but not for the mother). Her doctor suggested a hysterectomy; she refused. He suggested a tubal ligation. She said she'd think about it. She was probably looking for a tactful way of saying "get off my back"; the doctor assumed that she agreed. When she entered the hospital for the third child's birth, she had the sterilization provisions crossed off the consent form. While she was anaesthetized, one of the doctors participating in the delivery asked about the tubal ligation, and a nurse went into the hall and got the woman's *husband's* signature on the consent form. (There was some doubt as to whether he was the baby's father, so perhaps his motives were mixed.)

After finding out that she had been sterilized, the plaintiff suffered depression and emotional problems, and sued her obstetrician and his malpractice carrier for battery:

> He [the defendant] also stated in effect that while he did not recall appellant specifically agreeing to ligation, he understood that that is what she wished and since appellant was unable to consent while lying on the table, he felt he was doing her a favor by eliminating the need for subsequent surgery to ligate appellant's tubes, and the inconvenience and expense attending another operation.

One rather hopes that the defendant got a bonus lobotomy in the course of a hemorrhoid operation, but, alas, it wasn't to be. The plaintiff was awarded $25,000, but that's not much recompense for an unwanted and irreversible operation. It's hard to imagine what else she could have done (short of having "Do Not Ligate Here, Fool" tattooed on her abdomen) to indicate lack of desire to be sterilized. But then, in sterilization abuse, as in rape, the most unlikely things—including flat refusal—have been taken for consent.

Equally, consider *Downs v. Sawtelle*, 574 F.2d 1 (1st Cir. 1978), *cert. den.*, 439 U.S. 910. The plaintiff, a deaf-mute, was sterilized on her sister's consent and over the objections she made with her (limited) communications skills. She wrote to Dr. Curtis that she was getting married and that she and her fiancé wanted more children. (She had two.) "Dr. Curtis testified at trial that he treated the letter 'so lightly that I didn't attach much importance to it.' " (Opinion at p. 5.) Curtis also testified that he had no evidence that the plaintiff was feeble-minded or retarded and did not consider her to be either. But his hospital report recommended sterilization "based 90 percent on this girl's low mentality involving poor judgment and her lack of restraint on sex appetite and its consequences." No one even tried to get the plaintiff to sign the consent form, though obviously she could read and write; it was equally obvious that she knew that sterilization would prevent her from having the children she wanted.

A couple of issues emerge in the *Downs* case: first, the tendency to treat handicapped people as non-people, incapable of making decisions about their own lives. Second, the paranoid fear of the allegedly unbridled sexuality of groups perceived as inferior. The clichés change over time: at one time Jews were thought to be sexually insatiable (a statement sure to reduce any Jewish Prince or Princess to hysteria). In the early part of the twentieth century, the mentally retarded and mentally ill were supposed to have raging, uncontrollable libidos; and of course the white man's fear of allegedly superior black sexual prowess has existed as long as there has been any contact between the races. Third, there's the continuing difficulty women have in making themselves heard and understood by people in power, most of whom are men.

Sterilization abuse can also exist when the woman to be sterilized does sign the consent form—after someone makes her an offer she can't refuse. In 1979, for example, a county in Arizona agreed to provide maternity care for indigent women as well as sterilizations and abortions, and to stop conditioning the availability of medical care on birth control, sterilization, or abortion.

On a less cheerful note, a Georgia obstetrician was not held liable under any civil rights statute for his one-man campaign to reduce the welfare rolls: as Dr. Pierce testified,

> My policy was with people who were unable to financially support
> themselves, whether they be on Medicaid or just unable to pay their
> own bills, if they were having a third child, to request they voluntarily
> submit to sterilization following the delivery of the third child. If they
> did not wish this as a condition of my care, I requested that they seek
> another physician other than myself.

The opinion didn't say how many other doctors were available in the area
to care for indigent patients, but I surmise that Pierce was either the only
one, one of a few, or the best available; surely women on Medicaid didn't
seek him out for his bedside manner.

When this approach didn't work, he had other strings to his bow:

> After the delivery, Pierce requested his nurse to obtain Brown's [the
> plaintiff's] consent to sterilization. Brown refused. Upon word of her
> refusal, Pierce saw no necessity for further hospitalization and ordered
> her discharge and release from the hospital.

Ms. Brown, not unreasonably, brought a civil rights suit against Pierce;
less reasonably, she lost. "We perceive no reason why Dr. Pierce could
not establish and pursue the policy he has publicly and freely announced."
Because he wasn't acting as an agent of the state, the civil rights claim
failed. I think a malpractice claim might have been more successful, though
perhaps what Dr. Pierce did *was* standard medical practice for that time
and place.

For a decade, the federal laws have included (in several modified versions) provisions against sterilization abuse of Medicaid patients. Medicaid
will only pay for a sterilization operation if:

- The patient is at least twenty-one.
- S/he is capable of informed consent.
- S/he has voluntarily given informed consent by signing an approved
  form, at least thirty days, but not more than one hundred eighty days,
  before a sterilization (this requirement can be relaxed for emergency
  operations).
- The patient has been informed (in a language s/he understands) of
  the nature of the operation and the fact that it's probably irreversible.
- The person allegedly giving informed consent isn't intoxicated; in
  labor; or in the process of obtaining or having an abortion, when
  consent is sought.
- The person to be sterilized has been informed that s/he won't lose
  any benefits from the federal government if s/he refuses to be sterilized.

The Guidelines also forbid hysterectomies for sterilization if a tubal ligation (a less drastic, and therefore less dangerous, operation) is medically appropriate. But it's not difficult for a hospital, trying to find some hysterectomies for training purposes, to find something wrong with the cervix or uterus of a woman who wants to be sterilized and thus justify a "prophylactic" hysterectomy.

The age of twenty-one was chosen to balance the right of an adult to choose and consent to medical treatment against the repercussions of an immature person's premature decision to be sterilized. The age requirement has been upheld in court—once in a case that shows the difficulties inherent in any balancing test. The plaintiff in *Voe v. Califano* was a twenty-year-old woman who had been pregnant ten times and had had two children, a stillbirth, a miscarriage, and six abortions; she could not use birth control pills safely and other forms of contraception were unacceptable to her. While acknowledging that her case was indeed a tough one, the Connecticut District Court upheld the federal regulations, saying that the regulations represented a reasonable method of preventing sterilization abuse of minors.

The trouble with the federal regulations is that they don't penalize abusive sterilizations; they merely indicate the federal government's unwillingness to pay for them. That protects potential victims from most doctors, but not from ideologues like Dr. Pierce. Monitoring compliance with the guidelines has never been a high priority at HEW either.

Several states have laws against sterilization abuse: in California, for example, not only will an abusive procedure not be paid for out of public funds, but the doctor may lose his license for sterilization abuse. Kentucky doctors can be fined or jailed for noncompliance; Massachusetts doctors can be fined. In Maine, Maryland, and Oregon, it's illegal to condition any benefits (e.g., welfare; medical care) on sterilization. In Tennessee, sterilization abuse is a misdemeanor; in Utah, it's a felony.

INVOLUNTARY STERILIZATION

In the early part of this century, America was swept up in enthusiasm for eugenics: the scientific development of a better race. (Somewhat later, the Nazis gave eugenics a bad name—perhaps because of their definitions of inferior and superior races.) To a certain extent, eugenics was a well-meant attempt to create better human beings; but it was also a remarkably convenient "scientific" justification for prejudice. Eugenics "proved" that blacks, Orientals, and immigrants were "hereditary degenerates," inferior to white Anglo-Saxons. The same theory was trotted out to explain why women of superior racial stock were needed as breeders. Otherwise, the few racial superiors would be flooded out by a horde of promiscuously breeding racial inferiors.

The first step in eugenics is preventing the unfit from breeding. The controversy starts when the "unfit" must be defined. Most orthopedic handicaps and some instances of blindness and deafness are caused by accidents, so it's hard to claim that they're hereditary; anyway, people with those physical problems can usually speak for themselves. Further- more, people who accomplish a great deal in spite of physical limitations are usually seen as heroic, and it would be tactless (to say the least) to suggest that a wheelchair athlete or a blind lawyer would be an unfit parent. Though individual believers in eugenics may have believed (or believe) that being Irish, a Jew, black, or Hispanic is a sign of racial inferiority, they have never achieved enough of a consensus to get Nu- remberg laws enacted in this country.

Thus, eugenic fervor has usually centered on the mentally ill and men- tally retarded. As an example of eugenic enthusiasm (and bad legal rea- soning), consider *Buck v. Bell*, 274 U.S. 200 (1927), which ordered the involuntary sterilization of a retarded woman. This is the famous case in which Justice Holmes thundered, "Three generations of imbeciles are enough" (a proposition that has never been applied to politics, where it would be much more useful). But only the woman to be sterilized seems to have been what was then called an imbecile (now called "moderately retarded"). Her mother was less severely retarded, and her daughter, who died young, was said to have been very intelligent. Holmes said that a society that can conscript men to be killed in war can "conscript" retarded women and prevent them from having children; he also said that the principle that allows compulsory vaccination is broad enough to allow compulsory sterilization. But no one (even those with some sort of objec- tion to vaccination) wants to get smallpox or any other contagious disease; and the whole point of involuntary sterilization is to make sure that certain people who want children can't have them.

The federal government now won't pay for any sterilization of a retarded person (or anyone else incapable of informed consent). Colorado forbids all involuntary sterilization of retarded persons. Not all retarded persons are incapable of informed consent (though it's not hard to imagine ma- nipulation or undue influence being brought to bear).

The real legal and ethical issues come up when a retarded person isn't capable of informed consent or consistent use of birth control. Under those circumstances, s/he is probably not capable of caring for a child. So should the retarded person's parent or guardian (or the supervisor of the insti- tution in which s/he lives) try to stop the retarded person from having any kind of sexual activity, or make some provision for children, or for abor- tions, or sneak birth control pills into the cornflakes, or try to get the retarded person sterilized? None of the alternatives is particularly appealing. The most frightening part is that there are no objective methods of determining whether someone is mentally retarded. Imagine a Spanish-speaking kid with a severe hearing impairment and borderline autism being tested by a non-Spanish-speaking psychiatrist who has another appointment in twenty minutes. Some forms of retardation are genetic (e.g., Down's syndrome), others caused by poor maternal nutrition during pregnancy, the mother's drug or alcohol use, or brain injury during or after delivery. Any kind of retardation can affect a person's ability to be a good parent, but only types of retardation that affect the chromosomes can be inherited.

Anyway, there are fashions in racism just as in clothing. At one time, it was fashionable to describe Jewish immigrants as feeble-minded. As German Jewish immigrants began to prosper and establish themselves socially, the anti-Semitic cliché changed: now it was Eastern European immigrants who were feeble-minded. Current anti-Semitic cliché is that Jews are, on the contrary, exceptionally smart (or at least repugnantly clever). It is too unsubtle today to claim that the average black or Hispanic is feeble-minded and therefore should be precluded from having children; it's more fashionable to murmur regretfully about matriarchal homes and cultures of poverty.

At any given time, there will be *some* people who really are so mentally impaired that they can't care for children; I'm not denying that. Maybe it's even in their own best interests, and the best interests of society, that they be sterilized. But it's important to realize how easily this fact can be manipulated—often by sincere people with the best possible intentions.

Sixteen states have some kind of provision for sterilization of persons judged mentally incompetent, without the consent of the person to be sterilized. The details of the statutes vary enough to provide meat for many, many law review articles. Some of the statutes are based on "substituted consent": the parent or guardian consents for the incompetent person. Others are based on "parens patriae" power: the state acts as if it were a parent. Sometimes the best interest of the community, or of the incompetent persons, is invoked. Some of these statutes apply to all persons who have been judged incompetent; others only to those who have been institutionalized. Most of the laws require a court order for the sterilization: the retarded person's guardian or the director of the institution files a petition requesting the sterilization. Generally an independent "guardian ad litem" (trial guardian) is appointed for the retarded person. Independent experts are usually appointed and the hearing focuses on whether there is a real need for sterilization (i.e., the person involved is sexually active and can't use birth control) and whether it's in the subject's best interest (s/he could not cope with parenthood and is likely to regress).

The states without statutes authorizing involuntary sterilizations have reached two different solutions. One group of states says that, if there's no statute, courts have no jurisdiction to hear sterilization petitions. The other group allows sterilization petitions as long as they protect the due process rights of the person whose sterilization is sought. The criteria differ from state to state, but in general can be summed up:

- Clear and convincing proof (that is, real evidence, but not necessarily proof beyond a reasonable doubt)
- As much as possible, finding out what the retarded person wants
- A full hearing
- Appointment of an independent guardian and independent experts to review the situation
- Proof that the person whose sterilization is sought can't, and won't in the future, be able to give informed consent
- Proof that s/he is sexually active and can't use birth control
- Proof that s/he is unable to care for a child
- In short, that sterilization is in his/her best interests—not just in the best interests of those caring for him or her.

Either way, the problems are not insubstantial. You have to sympathize with a parent who is worn out caring for a severely retarded child, and who can't cope at all with grandchildren. In some of the cases, the person whose sterilization was sought was so handicapped that s/he couldn't even take care of personal hygiene and couldn't understand or deal with menstruation, much less pregnancy or delivery. (It's hard to imagine any man—other than one who was equally severely impaired—being attracted to such a woman, or if he were, being unscrupulous enough to exploit her sexually.)

But people labeled "retarded" are no more uniform than people labeled "normal"; some retarded people function fairly normally, hold jobs, and interact socially with other people. Consider *Stump v. Sparkman*. A mother petitioned for consent to have her "somewhat retarded" fifteen-year-old daughter sterilized because the girl stayed out all night with men. The request was granted without notice to the girl or appointment of an independent guardian for her. First she was told that she had had an appendectomy. She married at seventeen; she and her husband wanted children. When she did not conceive, she asked her mother, who said that her tubes had been tied but would come untied eventually. When she and her husband found out the truth, they brought a civil-rights suit against her mother, her mother's lawyer, the judge who granted the petition, and the doctor and hospital involved. She won at the trial and intermediate appeal levels (scaring some state judges, who feared liability if they granted a sterilization petition without a state law to back them up), but lost in the Supreme Court. According to the Supreme Court, the only state action involved was what the judge did; and, as he did not make his decision in the clear absence of jurisdiction, his actions were privileged (immune from suit), even if he was wrong. The judge could only be liable for acting entirely arbitrarily, with no grounding in law.

THE ROAD TO THE COURTHOUSE

• Most cases alleging sterilization abuse (or denial of access to voluntary sterilization) are brought as civil rights actions, alleging that doctors, hospitals, etc., violated the civil rights of the plaintiff or conspired to violate her civil rights (42 U.S.C.S. §§ 1983, 1986). The problem is that these laws require proof of state action. (See "The Smoking Gun," page 227.)

• Unfortunately, the federal Medicaid regulations don't include penalties for sterilization abuse, but at least payments are unavailable for abusive sterilizations.

• Failure to comply with a state or federal law or regulation against sterilization abuse is "negligence per se": if the plaintiff can prove that the law wasn't complied with, she does not have to prove other acts of negligence in a malpractice case.

• The doctor and hospital participating in sterilization abuse can be sued for battery, often with pretty good results.

• What about a botched sterilization that results in the birth of a child? Doctors are usually not dumb enough to guarantee the results, and any kind of surgery involves certain risks (including the risk of failure). But if the doctor says that sterility is 100 percent certain, or fails to test the patient's fertility after the operation, many states allow the unhappy parents to sue for "wrongful birth." Depending on the state, the slapdash medico may have to pay the mother's pregnancy and delivery expenses— or the entire anticipated cost of raising the child, minus the benefits of the new child's company and affection. In those states, unwilling parents are not required to mitigate their damages by abortion or surrendering the child for adoption. If the purpose of sterilization is to avert the birth of a child with a foreseeable birth defect, a negligent doctor may also be liable to the parents for their mental distress.

In a few states the doctor and/or parents may also be liable to a deformed child on the theory of "wrongful life"—only a few states, because of the logical paradox inherent in claiming that one should not have been born in the first place.

THE SMOKING GUN

• If the plaintiff has to prove state action, she may be able to do this by showing that the hospital in which the abusive sterilization was performed was the only available hospital; that the people involved in the sterilization were acting under "color of state law" (for example, social workers under pressure to reduce the welfare rolls); maybe the fact that a state agency appoints the hospital's Board of Directors will show state action. Some courts think that a hospital's accepting federal Hill-Burton hospital subsidies is a sign of state action; others disagree.

FOR UNTO (ALL OF) US A CHILD IS BORN: TECHNOLOGICAL PARENTHOOD

Dorothy L. Sayers's fans may recall that, when Lord Peter Wimsey married Harriet Vane, he insisted on using the old form of the Anglican marriage service. He said that he knew about the "procreation of children," but that the "increase of mankind" by any other method seemed too dangerous, and he preferred to stick to the old-fashioned way. Given the possibilities opened up by test-tube babies, artificial insemination, and surrogate motherhood, a lot of people are tempted to agree with him.

To switch genres for a moment, at least once per horror movie someone intones, "There are some things man wasn't meant to know." That point of view also has its attractions.

It is difficult, but not entirely impossible, to stop scientists from doing research in a particular area. It's easy to cut off government funding, which gets the message across. But the technology already exists for artificial insemination, *in vitro* fertilization ("test-tube babies") and surrogate motherhood. These things already exist, creating fodder for tabloid articles, dilemmas for theologians, and a severe knock to family law.

The legal system has always had trouble accommodating scientific advances, perhaps because the kind of people who become lawyers tend to be those who faint when frogs are dissected and call the repairman when the VCR gets unplugged. Anyway, reproductive technology raises questions of the most embarrassing sort: those that are so fundamental that no thought has been given to them. What is a "human being," anyway, and what does it take to be a mother or father for legal purposes? It has been said that it's a wise child who knows his own father; the way things are going, it takes discernment to recognize either parent.

There is a whole body of law dealing with paternity, because so much of law evolved to deal with inheritance. Many of the social controls on women evolved for the same reason: to spare the fathers of unmarried women the responsibility of supporting illegitimate children (a peculiar coinage—it's the parents' behavior that can be considered illegitimate; the kid didn't do anything wrong) and especially to protect men against the possibility that their property could pass to children fathered by another man. (Interestingly, Jewish law focuses only on the second of these objectives: an unmarried woman's child isn't illegitimate, but a married woman's child conceived outside the marriage is.) But the supply of legitimate heirs has always been chancy, and adoption (either of blood relatives or stepchildren, or even of strangers) has long been an accepted way of adding to the family. Adoption is also a way of providing loving and at least moderately prosperous homes for children who would otherwise be rejected or deprived (if they were carried to term in the first place). Viewed in either of those lights, adoption is unexceptionable. But even the noblest of institutions can be susceptible to abuse. It's usually considered appropriate (or at least necessary) to pay lawyers and some agencies for their services in connection with adoption. But why wait until the baby is born; why not make the arrangements so that the baby can be adopted at birth, or a few days later? Obstetricians and hospitals expect to get paid whether the baby is adopted or not, and the adoptive parents would probably be happy to assume this expense. As desirable babies are in short supply, the adoptive parents will also probably be happy to pay an agency or other intermediary quite a lot for locating a suitable infant. No doubt they'd provide a sum of money so the unfortunate mother can start a new life. I was going to say that it's a seller's market in babies for adoption; and at some point on the slippery slope, aid to a childless couple and unwed mother turns into outright sale of a human being. Nice people don't buy and sell babies, or at any rate don't talk about it. To prevent such abuses, all of the states have adoption laws, and some states make it illegal to pay anything (except for maternity expenses) for a person's consent to adoption of her (or his) child. This will become important when higher-tech surrogate motherhood is discussed.

In an adoption, the child is conceived and born by the usual, low-tech methods, then either the spouse of one of the child's parents adopts his or her stepchild or a couple (more rarely, a single person) adopts a child to whom they are not biologically related. In artificial insemination, a woman conceives when semen is introduced by other than the usual method. Usually artificial insemination is carried out by a doctor; in fact, some states make it illegal for anyone except a doctor to perform artificial insemination. These statutes are more than usually unenforceable, because artificial insemination is so easy: in 1980 the *Whole Earth Catalog* printed do-it-yourself instructions, calling for clean mason jars and turkey basters, that are enough to put you off turkey for life.

The challenge to the legal system is more substantial. Many, many law review articles go through the historically controversial nature of artificial insemination: is it legal? who is the father of the child? what, if any, are the rights of the sperm donor? is artificial insemination adultery? The controversy is now more or less a dead letter: about half the states have passed laws saying, more or less, yes; the husband of the woman inseminated (if he consented to the procedure); none; and of course not, don't be ridiculous.

Although some of the state statutes refer only to married couples, it's quite possible for single women to use artificial insemination, and it may even be the method of choice for lesbians or other women who want to be mothers but don't want to engage in the conventional methods of conception. One of the few cases on the issue—and one whose fact pattern is unlikely to be repeated—is New Jersey's *C.M. v. C.C.* Plaintiff and defendant were thinking about getting married. She wanted a child but did not believe in premarital sex. She inseminated herself with his semen and became pregnant; their relationship ended before the child was born. He petitioned for visitation rights, over her strenuous objections. The court did grant visitation, saying that he was, after all, the natural father. (Usually the sperm donor is anonymous; the mother never knows his identity, and he never knows if his contribution was used at all, or who conceived the child.) Sometimes the husband's semen is used: for example, if he is impotent but fertile, or if his sperm count is low so that several ejaculations are mixed for the insemination. Sometimes insemination is done with a mixture of the husband's and a donor's sperm—a tactful device to permit the couple to believe that perhaps the husband contributed the winning sperm cell.

A few states (e.g., Georgia) specify that the doctor who performs artificial insemination isn't liable to the child's legal parents, except for results of his own negligence. Otherwise, at least theoretically, the parents of a defective child conceived through artificial insemination might sue the doctor—and win. "Defective" child, in this context, suggests a manufactured object. Because the kid can't be returned within thirty days for a full refund, the parents' remedy would be a suit against the "manufacturer"—the doctor—for "breach of warranty" when they received a baby that wasn't up to specifications. The issue hasn't been litigated often, but I don't think courts would tend to see it that way. One Nevada case denied malpractice damages to a man whose wife was artificially inseminated without his consent; perhaps because the donor wasn't screened properly, the child was multi-handicapped and died in babyhood. The Nevada Supreme Court said that the doctor had no duty to the man, therefore could not have violated any duty. End of discussion, end of case.

Artificial insemination results in a child who is biologically related to at least one of its legal parents, and the technology involved is minimal, easily understood, and not subject to much manipulation. That could be why artificial insemination is fairly well accepted. It does create some legal problems, or more accurately some legal anxieties: whether a bequest to one's "children" includes those conceived twenty years post-mortem by use of frozen sperm, for example; whether the identity or medical records of sperm donors should ever be open to the children; and how, given the existence and relative prevalence of artificial insemination, one can ever be *entirely* sure one isn't committing incest. But these are minor worries, not sources of outright terror.

Adoption of an unrelated child is one way to deal with any problem of infertility or risk of genetic disease (for example, if both husband and wife are carriers of a serious genetic disease). Artificial insemination can deal with the husband's infertility or low fertility, or with genetic risks (though the donor may carry the same defect, or one even worse). With more medical intervention it may also be possible for a woman to have a child if she can carry a baby but can't conceive, if *in vitro* fertilization is used. If a woman doesn't produce eggs that can be fertilized or has a uterine or cervical problem that prevents carrying a baby to term, but her husband is fertile, they can have a baby if a surrogate mother can be found. A "test tube" baby is the child of both its legal parents, just like a child conventionally born; the child of a surrogate mother is biologically the child of its legal father and the surrogate mother. Theoretically, babies could be produced on order for infertile couples or women who want a child but don't want to be pregnant or who can't carry a child to term. Again theoretically, a kid can have as many as five parents: a sperm donor, an egg donor, a surrogate mother who carries the pregnancy to term, and the kid's legal parents. That's where the legal issues get really hairy.

In vitro fertilization is probably legal, simply because no one's taken the trouble to outlaw it. Illinois' child abuse law (of all things) says that anyone who intentionally causes the fertilization of an egg outside the human body legally assumes the care and custody of the child (like the Chinese belief that saving someone's life makes you responsible for him). But an Illinois District Court has ruled that *in vitro* fertilization is legal. Pennsylvania state law requires quarterly reports on *in vitro* fertilizations performed. If the test-tube soon-to-be baby is implanted in the uterus of the woman whose egg was fertilized, and whose husband donated the sperm, it's fairly straightforward who the parents are. Things get a bit more confusing if the fertilized egg is frozen for later implantation, or implanted in someone else; or if a woman is artificially inseminated and the embryo transferred to someone else's uterus. If embryos can be frozen, and a normal pregnancy carried to term by a woman in her forties, working women would be less threatened by the "biological clock" and could have babies at a more convenient time. This would certainly involve changes in society—and not, I suspect, a change that would be terribly popular.

Once again, it's the old debate about the end and the means. Does marriage consist of a (at least theoretically) monogamous heterosexual couple, raising whatever number of children God sees fit to bless them with (on the Divine schedule, not one chosen by the parents)? Or is it a couple having whatever number of children they want, when they want them? If a couple is infertile, to what extent may they legally—and morally—go to become parents? Kidnapping someone else's baby is obviously not acceptable. Repudiating a barren wife or passing off a concubine's child as a legitimate heir are unfashionable. Many of those who oppose nonprocreative sex on moral or religious grounds are equally condemnatory of nonsexual procreation.

The slope begins to get slippery about the point that embryos are produced, so to speak, for inventory. After all, any fertile woman has thousands of egg cells, and the process of removing a few is uncomfortable but does no lasting harm. The process of obtaining the odd few million sperm isn't even uncomfortable. Given enough Petri dishes (they don't really use test tubes) and enough time, quite a few of the egg cells are sure to be fertilized. Is it OK to freeze them and wait for a buyer to come along? Should the fertilized eggs be auctioned off to the highest bidder? Is it homicide if someone intentionally tips the contents of the Petri dish down the sink? Wrongful death if someone negligently deep-sixes the contents? If Mr. and Mrs. Jones have donated germ cells, five fertilizations have resulted, and they want only one child, is it licit to give away, sell—or destroy—the other four? Can unwanted embryos be reared artificially for research purposes?

Well, the answers are probably "no," although only the last question has been addressed by the legal system, and not even that fully. A number of states have laws against experimenting on fetuses unless the purpose is treatment of the fetus itself, rather than abstract research. But these statutes were probably motivated by a revulsion against the thought of aborted fetuses being used for experiments; it's not at all clear whether they apply to fetuses (or early embryos that haven't yet attained the status of fetuses) that are, so to speak, custom-made.

More than half of the conceptions that take place naturally are defective in some way and abort spontaneously—often before the woman is even aware that fertilization has taken place. What are the rights and obligations of the medical staff and the potential parents to such defective embryos? Is disposing of such an embryo the equivalent of an induced abortion?

At least one case says that the potential parents have some kind of interest in the fertilized egg. A New York jury awarded $50,000 for emotional distress to a woman whose fertilized egg was deliberately destroyed by one doctor before its scheduled implantation by another doctor. (Her husband was awarded nominal damages.) The doctor who destroyed the fertilized egg said he did it because the doctor who scheduled the procedure wasn't expert enough to perform it, and would have given the plaintiff a massive abdominal infection if he had been given the opportunity to try.

In June of 1983, a married couple from Los Angeles who had "conceived" three embryos in Australia by *in vitro* fertilization died in a plane crash in Chile. One embryo had been implanted but miscarried. A year later, the other two—and two hundred other frozen embryos at the same facility—were still the center of controversy. In October 1984, the Australian legislature decided that the two surviving embryos of the couple should be carried to term by a surrogate mother and adopted, rather than being destroyed (as had been proposed). The decision related specifically to those embryos, not the others; and the Attorney General of the Australian State of Victoria said future users of the surrogate motherhood process would have to designate "guardians" for the embryos.

Even if the sperm and egg come from someone other than the eventual child's legal parents, the donation—or sale—of these biological products isn't particularly controversial. Sperm and eggs can be separated from the human body but can't survive outside the body unless, of course, they combine. The participants in *in vitro* fertilization must rely on each other's good faith—that the doctor will take good care of the fertilized egg, and implant the right one—it's frustrating to go that far for biological parenthood and end up with the wrong kid. As the technology is new, and more or less experimental, there is no medical standard to which doctors can be held in malpractice cases.

For real reliance on other people's honor, you can't beat surrogate motherhood. If the husband is fertile and the wife entirely incapable of carrying a pregnancy to term, or if she doesn't produce eggs that could be used for *in vitro* fertilization, it's possible for another, fertile woman to be artificially inseminated with the husband's sperm (or implanted with the wife's egg fertilized by the husband's sperm, if this is possible for the particular couple). Then the surrogate mother bears the child and surrenders it to the husband (who doesn't have to adopt it—it's his child) and his wife (who then adopts the child).

People do make quite detailed contracts with surrogate mothers, specifying the payment to be made for the service, the prenatal care the surrogate is to receive, her agreement to abstain from sex with her own partner until she has become pregnant via artificial insemination (and perhaps later, if intercourse could be harmful to the fetus) and from smoking, drinking, and drugs; her consent, and the consent of her partner, to immediate adoption of the baby; and a specification that the surrogate mother assumes all the risks of pregnancy and birth, but the legal parents assume the risk that the baby will be defective. (Generally, only women with at least one healthy child are selected as surrogates, and married women are preferred—it looks better.) Some commentators suggest that the father be heavily insured so the deal won't be impaired by his untimely death; others suggest buying a policy that will provide for support of the child if it's so defective that it is rejected by both couples.

The practical problems are many: there's no way of ensuring that the baby will be healthy, or indeed that the surrogate mother won't miscarry. She could change her mind about the whole thing and have an abortion (and there's no way on God's grass-covered earth that a court will stop her), or the legal parents may change their minds (and no one will either order her to get an abortion or make them take the baby), or the surrogate may want to keep the baby (and no court will force her to surrender it).

So the law will probably leave the legal parents and the surrogate to sort things out among themselves and won't interfere. It's at least conceivable (excuse the expression) that the legal system will penalize those who get caught engaging in surrogate mother transactions. (And Surrogate, like Watergate, is a natural for headlines.) It's one thing to donate or sell sperm or egg cells; surrogate motherhood either approaches, or equals, selling a baby. One school of thought says of course the baby isn't sold— the surrogate just sells her *services*, as a sort of very early and conscientious babysitter. This seems awfully disingenuous to me—the same argument would apply in an illegal black-market adoption: the baby is free, only the childbearing services have to be paid for.

People involved in surrogate motherhood tend to keep it quiet, first of all to cut down on the number of reporters hanging around the bassinet, and second because of the legally unsettled nature of the proceedings. It's important to comply with the relevant state laws: some adoption laws require a waiting period after birth before a mother can relinquish her right to custody of the child. If the contract specifies an immediate adoption, these laws would be violated, thus making the contract illegal and even more unenforceable than usual.

I've only found cases on this topic from two states. The question has come up in Michigan three times: in effect, each time the courts have refused to touch it with a barge pole. I found two Kentucky cases, both from 1983. Once says that Kentucky law won't let the surrogate terminate parental rights (surrender the child for adoption) because the kid, at least theoretically, could have been fathered by her husband rather than the sperm donor. The Circuit Court didn't find that the testimony about artificial insemination settled the question; there was nothing in the record about her husband's blood type, or his sexual access (or non-access) during the time the child could have been conceived. (I can't prove it, but I think this was the court's alternative method of refusing to touch it with a barge pole.) But seven months later, the Circuit Court upheld a surrogate motherhood contract, saying that the legal father/sperm donor had not violated Kentucky's law against paying for an adoption—first, because it was his own child, and second, because the law forbade payments for *adoption*, not for termination of parental rights. (Now we're really splitting hairs.) The court also said that if the legislature thought such activities should be illegal, it was up to the legislature to pass a law to that effect.

The possibility of embryo transfer (Woman A conceives—or conception takes place in Petri Dish A—and the embryo is transferred to Woman B, who gives birth) opens up vistas of science fiction, hope, or paranoia. At the moment, the transfer can take place only when the fertilized egg has divided into a few cells—long before anything resembling a fetus has formed, and long before an unwanted pregnancy could be detected. But if this changes, will the definition of "viability" in the abortion laws change? It's already been argued that late abortions should be re-criminalized, because medical advances make a twenty-four-week, or even twenty-week, fetus viable outside the womb. Should a woman be forbidden to abort a fetus if some other woman wants it? Who pays the (enormous) cost of life support if a premature baby is abandoned because its mother wanted but was unable to obtain an abortion? How should the supply of transferrable fetuses be regulated—by computer matching service? raffles? auctions? (It's ironic that, at a time when much of the world confronts starvation and overpopulation, part of the industrialized West grapples with anorexia nervosa and artificial gestation.) Widespread infant mortality (or willingness to deprive one's own child of milk) made wet-nursing a potential job for many women; now it's possible for women to be pregnant for pay. This is hardly what feminists had in mind when calling for wider vocational opportunities for women. But the other side of the question is the real anguish felt by infertile couples, and their profound desire to raise children of their own.

THE ROAD TO THE COURTHOUSE

• Unless the state has a law forbidding such an action, a doctor who performs artificial insemination negligently, or who fails to screen the donors properly, can be sued for malpractice. The impaired child may also have a "wrongful life" action (see page 226).

• As I explained above, litigation involving *in vitro* fertilization is chancy. The technology is so new that no standards have evolved against which malpractice can be measured; and, unless the legal climate changes, courts are unlikely to get involved in a dispute between a surrogate and would-be legal parents.

• If a surrogate mother contract does get into court, and if the surrogate refuses to give up the baby, it's obvious that the court won't make her give up the baby. Probably she would be required to give back any money she had received; equally probably, the prospective legal parents are out any money they paid doctors or other people involved in the contract.

Maybe the surrogate would be ordered to reimburse them for these sums. But it's unlikely that anyone who would want to be a surrogate (unless she were altruistic or crazy about being pregnant) could afford substantial damages. (Maybe some enterprising insurance company will sell liability insurance for surrogate mothers.) It is also unlikely that the prospective parents would get any damages for emotional anguish or suffering. These types of damages are fairly common in tort actions, but not in contract actions.

THE SMOKING GUN

• Some commentators suggest that the surrogate contract include a provision that the baby be given a blood test after birth; if modern paternity testing (such as the Human Leukocyte Antigen—HLA—test) says that the legal father could not have fathered the child, the deal is off. But it takes a certain degree of cold-bloodedness to insist on this and go through with it.

11

ABORTION

It's June, both the kids will be in school next September, and there's an after-school program. Alice Lofgren saw a poster in the laundromat, offering job training for women with low incomes and at least one child. She fits the bill: she's on Welfare and has two children—and her period is late. Maybe it's another false alarm; if not, it's a souvenir of a few unplanned nights with a man she'd just as soon forget. She knows that her Medicaid benefits won't cover abortions unless someone will sign a paper that her health is at stake. The only thing that's at stake is whether she has a chance to get a job, or has a child she doesn't want and resents having to care for. She has sixty-two dollars saved in a coffee can in the kitchen, but somehow she suspects this won't be enough to get an abortion—even an illegal one.

Abortion is a profoundly emotional issue. An ordinary legal issue concerning the final resting place of some chunk of money or other can involve feelings of guilt, loss, anger, regret, shame, or rue. The stakes are even higher in criminal law, where someone has been victimized, and someone else may have to spend years of life (and quantities of the community's money) in jail. Depending on the speaker's or thinker's viewpoint, abortion either terminates a human life or prevents what would, if left alone, have become a human life from coming into independent existence.

Then, under ordinary circumstances, a pregnancy, wanted or unwanted, necessarily involves sex. (As we've seen in the preceding chapter, some wanted pregnancies depend on technology as well as conventional methods.) So a certain amount of the abortion controversy revolves around an attempt to substitute one set of mores—sex for reproduction only, or sex in marriage only—for another set: sex if and when the woman wants it, or if and when her husband or boyfriend demands it.

No one is really pro-abortion except in the sense of being pro-mastectomy or pro–leg amputation: the best of a number of horrible alternatives available to an unfortunate individual. (By the same token, some people, for religious or personal reasons, will choose death rather than have a mastectomy or a leg amputation.) But if abortion is legal, a woman who finds abortion morally unacceptable can cope with unwanted pregnancy in other ways. If abortion is made illegal, or made expensive or otherwise inaccessible, a woman who believes an abortion is the best solution for her can't get one, or can't get a safe abortion within her financial resources.

Part of the question is the proper characterization of the fertilized egg: as a human being or as part of a woman's body over which she has complete control. The other part is the appropriate relation between law and morality. Assuming for the moment that having an abortion is immoral behavior (it's certainly behavior that violates the teachings of some religions), should the behavior carry any legal sanctions, or should it be left to heaven?

The question of what a legal system should be—the extent to which it should protect people from the consequences of their own idiotic or immoral behavior—is unsettled and perhaps unsettlable. If law deals well with anything at all, it deals poorly with metaphysical questions. Baby boomers will no doubt remember kindly old Doctor Zorba intoning, week after week, "Man . . . woman . . . birth . . . death . . . infinity." This whole book proves that our legal system is designed by the first lot, not necessarily in the best interests of the second; that it's usually possible for the law to say whether someone has been born or not, but not when someone becomes alive and begins to accumulate legal rights; that it's no picnic determining when someone is dead; and infinity don't get no respect.

There are also political questions involved in the abortion controversy. In terms of electoral politics, the "right-to-lifers" are well organized, have lots of money, and number respectable churchmen as well as right-wing ideologues among their adherents. Some right-to-lifers arrive at their stance from pacifism and an abhorrence of killing; others favor a defense build-up and capital punishment—a stance rationalized by explaining that they are in favor of *innocent* life such as the life of the unborn. Those who believe that abortion should be illegal (or should be legal only to preserve the mother's life or health, or only in the aftermath of rape or incest) can be found in all parts of the political spectrum, but in general "right to life" gives you a bit of a hint.

Because of the conservative orientation of most right-to-lifers, they tend to oppose increases in Welfare benefits, socialized medicine, and children's allowances, leaving the right to life perilously close to that legal bugaboo, "a right without a remedy." It's been said—unfairly, but not without a grain of truth—that for right-to-lifers human life begins at conception and ends at birth.

Some right-wing libertarians believe abortion should be legal, or should not be illegal, because the government should not interfere in the personal lives of citizens; but in general, "pro-choice" voters tend to be more liberal or leftist than "right-to-life" voters. Because the United States is engaged in a swing to the right, things would look very bad indeed for abortion laws if it weren't for the second political current involved: sexual politics.

For a long time, the dividing line between "nice girls" and "sluts" was differential willingness to engage in premarital sex. A particular woman's moral scruples against what she had been taught was immoral behavior would be reinforced by the prospect of personal and family disgrace and an unpleasant sojourn in the Florence Crittenden home or perhaps a visit to an out-of-state aunt. The less scrupulous or more desperate might play Altar Roulette: unprotected premarital intercourse, premised on the belief that if she "got caught" her beau would "have to marry her"—and that having a husband and baby would make up for the neighbors' attention to the number of months between wedding and delivery. What made it a game of roulette was the fact that he didn't *have* to marry her; a situation emphasized by the fact that saying a girl was "in trouble" meant that she was pregnant, not that she had been caught shoplifting or attracted the attention of the House Un-American Activities Committee.

Some unknown genius of male suprematism—one who stands in the same relation to sexism that the inventor of the wheel does to transportation—figured out that sexual access to "nice girls" could be obtained on the same terms as sexual access to "sluts" (no continuing responsibility, minimal financial investment in candlelight dinners or six-packs, and minimal concern for the woman's sexual gratification—her lack of orgasm proved that she was frigid or unable to adjust to her feminine role), but only if the fear of illegitimate pregnancy could be removed. The stigma on unmarried motherhood has decreased significantly, and in many contexts birth control and abortion are legal and freely or relatively available. This is good news indeed for men who want free choice in sexual partners and women who have, or have reasonable expectations of, satisfying relationships; bad news for advocates of the double standard and those who believe that the monogamous family is not only morally correct but should be protected by legal and practical sanctions.

THIS YEAR'S ETERNAL VERITIES

Laws against abortion are a fairly recent development. Even religious condemnation of abortion is fairly recent, viewed against the time scale on which religions work. Some early and medieval Christian theologians taught that abortion was permissible either before quickening (the time at which fetal movements can be felt) or before "ensoulment"—set at forty days' gestation for a male fetus, eighty for a female. As there was no way to tell the sex until after the abortion, in practical terms this meant a first-trimester abortion.

The question of abortion is intimately involved with the development of the medical profession. The Hippocratic Oath obligates the doctor to refrain from giving anyone "an abortive remedy." This could mean several things: either that abortion is condemned as immoral; that doctors may perform abortions by surgery but not by giving drugs; or that a well-established group of abortionists had determined to keep doctors off their turf. In nineteenth-century America, there was a conflict between "regular" doctors (virtually all of them white men) and "irregulars" (more diverse in background, and ranging from outright con artists and sincere nut cases to what we would now call holistic practitioners). For a mixture of motives (driving the irregulars out of business; protecting women against very painful and dangerous operations) doctors supported the drive to make abortion illegal.

In the period 1860 to 1880, thirty-one states either enacted or revised their abortion laws, and by 1910, all the states except Kentucky forbade abortion. Abortion was a felony in each of these states except New Jersey, which made it a high misdemeanor. We don't have written legislative history, and it's too late to ask the legislators, so we can't tell if the legislation was designed to serve public morality or protect women against abortions that were noticeably more dangerous than childbirth—at a time when childbirth itself was extremely dangerous. After all, a safe abortion that minimizes physical trauma to the mother depends on sterile technique and an accurate knowledge of anatomy; anaesthetics, electric lights, and antibiotics help a lot. An abortion early in pregnancy creates less physical and emotional pain than a late abortion—but early abortion is premised on the ability to distinguish between pregnancy and a delayed period or menopause symptoms.

Most of these laws did not provide an absolute ban on abortion: nearly all permitted abortion to save the mother's life, and some permitted abortion to guard against endangering her health through continued pregnancy or delivery. By 1970, eleven states had enacted reform abortion laws, based on the Model Penal Code. The reform statutes permitted abortion if there was a substantial risk of permanent impairment to the mother's physical or mental health; if the pregnancy resulted from rape or incest; or if there was a substantial risk that the child would be born severely impaired (for example, if the mother had taken Thalidomide or been exposed to German measles). The typical procedure called for a group of doctors or a multi-disciplinary group of experts to consider the case, then certify that the applicant was in fact entitled to an abortion.

Like any procedure, this one was subject to abuses: wealthy women, for example, could usually round up a couple of tame psychiatrists to testify that bearing this child would damage their mental health. Even when the procedure operated according to its terms, the focus was on the experts, who decided whether there was a medical justification for the procedure. No provision was made for women who lacked the money, savoir faire, or willingness to go through the charade, or who were afraid to admit (perhaps even to themselves) that they were pregnant. The fact that a woman wanted an abortion because she was unmarried, too young or too poor to care for a baby (or another baby) or simply didn't want to have this (or any) baby didn't conform to the specifications. For women in these situations, a wide variety of illegal abortions was available, provided by practitioners ranging from back-alley butchers (not necessarily the least expensive) to genuine doctors, acting out of mercenary and/or compassionate motives.

The moral objection is the same whether an abortion is performed well or badly (unless the moral objection disguises sexual envy, so that a botched abortion is morally preferable as punishment). Those who find abortion morally acceptable naturally prefer that abortions be safe, affordable, and readily available. But there is a fundamental difference between a system in which access to abortion is controlled by doctors or social workers and one in which women decide to abort or maintain a pregnancy. Right now, what we have is a hybrid system, in which late abortions, government-funded abortions for indigent women and (sometimes) abortions for teenagers are rationed, and early abortions for women who can pay for them are more or less available on demand.

ROE AND DOE

On January 22, 1973 (a date which is extremely memorable to me, as it happens to be my birthday), the Supreme Court announced two decisions of enormous import: *Roe v. Wade*, 410 U.S. 113, and *Doe v. Bolton*, 410 U.S. 179.

Roe was a challenge to a state abortion law forbidding *all* abortions except those required to save the mother's life. The Court struck down the law, finding that it was overinclusive because it did not take into account the stage of pregnancy or other relevant factors, and therefore violated the privacy right derived from the Due Process clause of the Fourteenth Amendment.

> This right of privacy, whether it be founded in the Fourteenth Amendment's concept of personal liberty and restrictions upon state action, as we feel it is, or, as the District Court determined, in the Ninth Amendment's reservation of rights to the people, is broad enough to encompass a woman's decision whether or not to terminate her pregnancy . . . We, therefore, conclude that the right of personal privacy includes the abortion decision, but that this right is not unqualified and must be considered against important state interests in regulation.

As for the state interests in regulation, the Court set up (yet another) three-part scheme. (For judges, as for medieval alchemists, three is a magic number.)

- Approximately up to the end of the first trimester of pregnancy, the abortion decision must be left to the medical judgment of the pregnant woman's doctor. Note that the Court *did not* say that the decision is up to the woman.

- From the end of the first trimester to the time the fetus becomes viable (according to the Supreme Court, somewhere between the 24th and 28th week), states can regulate abortion, but only to preserve the pregnant woman's health.

- Once the fetus is viable, the state can regulate abortion to preserve the life or health *of the fetus*, and can even forbid abortion—unless a medical judgment has been made that the abortion is necessary to preserve the mother's life or health.

Doe v. Bolton clears up some related issues: first, that first-trimester abortions can legally be performed in free-standing clinics, because no proof was presented that only accredited hospitals could perform abortions safely. The state law, which required consent of three doctors and the approval of an abortion authorization committee, was unconstitutional because it was excessively restrictive of patients' rights—after all, the pregnant woman's own doctor would safeguard her rights.

The right of privacy is especially useful because, like Saran Wrap™, it stretches to fit anything a court wants it to cover, and shrinks back when it's no longer required. The Supreme Court has never found this useful right to include a right to ingest recreational drugs (or Laetrile) or have sex with members of one's own gender—arguably immoral actions that do not involve a fetus, which is arguably a human being and certainly nonconsenting.

The result was that states could no longer bar early abortions, could regulate second-trimester abortions only to protect the mother's health, and could regulate for the benefit of the fetus only after viability.

To call this decision "controversial" is understatement on a massive scale. Some people felt it didn't go far enough, because it maintained the expert-dominated medical model. Others saw the decision as a death warrant for millions of innocent lives, or objected to the Supreme Court telling the states what to do. Some states entered into a snit so enormous that they *still* haven't taken their pre–*Roe v. Wade* abortion laws off the books. Other states have amended their abortion laws to conform to *Roe* and *Doe*, but make it very clear that they do so unwillingly and will change their laws as soon as they can:

> Further, the General Assembly finds and declares that the longstanding policy of this State is to protect the right to life of the unborn child from conception by prohibiting abortion unless necessary to preserve the life of the mother is impermissible only because of the decisions of the United States Supreme Court and that, therefore, if those decisions of the United States Supreme Court are ever reversed or

modified, or if the United States Constitution is amended to allow
protection of the unborn, then the former policy of this State to prohibit abortions unless necessary for the preservation of the mother's
life shall be reinstated.

Unless the Supreme Court reverses itself, or unless the Constitution is
amended (see pages 259–260)—both possible, but unlikely—neither the
federal government nor the states can ban elective abortions (that is,
motivated by personal rather than medical concerns) entirely. However,
what they *can* do (and have done) is to bust hump to a greater or lesser
degree. They can require consent from, or notification to, someone that
woman doesn't want to know about the abortion. They can make performing abortions a nuisance for doctors by requiring sheaves of records or
long, heavily scripted counseling sessions. They can make abortion more
expensive by requiring elaborate facilities at abortion clinics. They can
make abortion virtually inaccessible to medically indigent women by refusing to provide Medicaid funds or the state equivalent. Some of these
restrictions have been upheld by courts, others invalidated or modified.
The need to litigate such restrictions definitely discourages a certain number of women from having abortions—or sends them to still-flourishing
illegal abortionists. The net result is that the safe, relatively inexpensive
abortions are less accessible, and perhaps the total number of abortions
decreases. This means, depending on your perspective, either that babies'
lives are saved or that women are condemned to compulsory childbearing.

CONSENT OR NOTIFICATION

It's fairly clear that husbands, estranged husbands, and unmarried fathers
of fetuses do not have veto power over pending abortions. This is true
both in the first trimester (when abortion is supposed to be a matter
between a woman and her doctor) and the second (when state intervention
is permissible only to protect the pregnant woman's health)—the pregnant
woman still has a unilateral right to decide to have an abortion. Although
the right to procreate does have constitutional standing (see the discussion
of sterilization on pages 216–227), a man's desire to procreate must be
subordinated to the pregnant woman's decision to have an abortion.

A few states do require notification of a married woman's husband (at
least if his whereabouts are known). A state's interest in promotion of
marriage, and husbands' interests in the procreative potential of marriage
have been held to justify a spousal *notice* requirement. But the most
common—and most litigated—consent and notice provisions are those
involving abortions for unemancipated minors.

Raising a child requires a great deal of intelligence, love, patience, and
sheer hard work. Becoming pregnant requires none of these, so it's in-

evitable that a certain number of teenage women (especially those who are uninformed about birth control, don't have access to professional advice, or who think birth control is unromantic) will become pregnant. Our tendency is to assume that bad things can't happen to us personally, and this tendency is strongest in teenagers.

For a variety of reasons—religious, ethical, practical, and emotional—parents tend to be opposed to their teenage offspring's (especially daughters') sexual activity, and it's virtually unimaginable that a parent would be *pleased* by a teenage daughter's unwed pregnancy. Parents can react with sorrowful compassion or extreme violence; at any point on the spectrum, a teenager can be excused for wanting to have an abortion quickly and in secret, before anyone else finds out that she is pregnant. As Robert B. Keiter points out in a 1982 article in the *Minnesota Law Review,* there are two aspects to the right of privacy: the right to do what you want, and not to have other people find out about it.

However, many states have laws requiring that a pregnant minor's parents be notified before her abortion; or that one or both parents must consent to the abortion. In theory, these are pure nuisance statutes, because a mere notice requirement won't do anything for the fetus. In practice, the prospect of their parents' finding out discourages some pregnant teenagers from having abortions.

For those who believe abortion is murder, the issue of teenage pregnancy is a simple one: abortion isn't justifiable, whatever the age of the pregnant woman. *Roe v. Wade*'s analysis is based on the stage of pregnancy, not the age of the woman seeking the abortion. However, *Roe v. Wade* explicitly states that the right to an abortion isn't absolute and can be qualified under certain circumstances. Some states and some courts have found that a limitation on minors' unqualified right to choose abortion is legitimate—based on "family privacy" or "parental authority." It's a hell of a note when privacy means squealing, or when states or courts intervene to protect parental authority that obviously has already broken down. It's interesting that many people who advocate greater government control of personal behavior involving sex and drugs advocate decreased governmental control over economic behavior. At the other end of the political spectrum, the opposite demand is made. Maybe people just like change.

The issues raised by teenagers' abortions are similar to those raised by involuntary sterilization (see pages 222–226). Some teenagers are capable of making informed, mature judgments; some are not (some adults aren't, either). But there's a paradox: if a teenager is too immature to decide whether or not to have an abortion, what kind of mother would she be? Can she make a mature decision to surrender the baby for adoption? (Assuming someone *wants* the baby—there are scores of prospective adoptive parents for the offspring of high-school cheerleaders and track stars, but they're not exactly lined up around the block to adopt a junkie prostitute's trick baby.) The question of whether it's *always* better to be alive than not alive is both obviously relevant here and insoluble, as we can't create a control group of aborted fetuses and ask *their* opinion.

The parallel between teenagers and mentally retarded or mentally ill people isn't perfect, of course. All the groups are legally limited in their capacity to consent to medical procedures, but teenagers will become adults and will gain the legal capacity to consent. But a pregnant teenager can't wait a couple of years to decide whether to have an abortion—she has to act fast.

If she does decide to have the baby (or waits until it's too late to have an abortion), some states allow her to give consent for her own prenatal care or delivery, or for medical care for her baby—but not necessarily for an abortion. What these states are saying is that *having* a baby makes a young woman mature enough to obtain medical care for herself and her child without the intervention of her own parents—but she's not necessarily mature enough to choose to have an abortion.

The Supreme Court has taken up the question of minors' abortions several times. In *Planned Parenthood v. Danforth,* the Court said that a blanket requirement of parental consent for first-trimester abortions was unconstitutional. No state interest (including the state interest in parental authority or safeguarding the family unit) is superior to a doctor's medical judgment that abortion is appropriate. (They did not say that the teenager, having gotten herself into this mess without parental guidance, had a right to get herself out of it the same way.)

Three years later, in *Bellotti v. Baird,* the Court explained what it meant by "blanket requirement." The Court found a distinction between mature minors—who can make an informed decision about abortion, and whose decisions should be given legal effect—and immature minors, who need parental or judicial guidance. *Bellotti* says that a teenage girl's parents can't be given absolute veto power over the abortion, and states can't require parental consent or notification in *every* instance. There must be an alternative procedure for young women to get consent: for example, a court hearing that can lead to a court order permitting the abortion if the young woman has been found sufficiently mature to make the decision about abortion, or if the court believes the abortion is in her best interests. This is an elegant theoretical formulation, but once again one wonders what the Supreme Court has been smoking. It's hard to imagine a pregnant teenager having the sophistication or resourcefulness to get a court order when she wants an abortion. Teams of Legal Aid lawyers certainly don't prowl the streets looking for unhappily pregnant clients. (In fact, the possibility that employees of the Legal Services Corporation might do something of the sort is one reason for President Reagan's hostility to the LSC.)

In 1983, the Supreme Court overturned a city ordinance requiring either parental consent or a court order for abortions to be performed on minors under fifteen—the ordinance made an impermissible class determination that all such minors lacked maturity to make an abortion decision. It's all right to require consent either of a parent or of a juvenile court— *if* the court has to grant all petitions showing good cause for the abortion unless the pregnant minor is too immature to make a valid decision.

However, a mere notice requirement was upheld in 1981's *H.L. v. Matheson* (450 U.S. 398), because the notice by itself does not create a parental veto power, and because the plaintiff did not allege maturity, emancipation, or a hostile home situation that would lead her to fear notice to her parents. An object lesson that *everything* that might come in handy should be pleaded.

Lower courts have come to various conclusions about minors' abortions and found various ways to distinguish inconvenient Supreme Court cases:

• Even if a girl is a Person in Need of Supervision, a juvenile court can't *order* her to take her mother's advice and have an abortion.

• A state statute giving a pregnant minor the right to consent to abortion supersedes an earlier statute requiring parental consent.

• Washington State's parental consent requirement is improper because it unduly infringes the privacy of pregnant minors—even though a Juvenile Court order can provide consent in exigent circumstances. None of the interests asserted by the state (making sure that abortion decisions are made thoughtfully, protecting the family unit, maintaining parental authority) can justify discrimination against minor women.

• *Wynn v. Carey* strikes down Illinois' former parental consent provision, saying it was both underinclusive (because it did not apply to married minors) and overinclusive (because it did apply to minors who were economically independent of their parents). A new provision was passed in 1983, presumably to take care of this problem.

LATE ABORTIONS

The states have pretty much given up trying to regulate first-trimester abortions: too much work for too little return. The Supreme Court has not budged from its position that the choice of a first-trimester abortion is a medical decision.

In the Supreme Court scheme, a state can regulate second-trimester abortions, but only to protect the pregnant woman's health. A first-trimester abortion, considered purely from the medical point of view, is a very minor operation—and much safer than childbirth. A second-trimester abortion carries more risk and is slightly more dangerous than childbirth.

Planned Parenthood v. Danforth invalidated a state law forbidding second-trimester saline abortions. This isn't too surprising a decision—first, because it's predictable that the Court would think that doctors, not legislators, should dictate abortion methods. Second, the saline method was the safest method of second-trimester abortion available in Missouri at that time, so that the state interest in protecting the pregnant woman's health would not justify forbidding this method.

A number of states provided, either by statute or by regulation, that all second-trimester abortions be performed in hospitals; numerous local ordinances regulating abortion took the same tack. The Supreme Court ruled on these requirements in June 1983. The ruling was that it's unconstitutional to require all second-trimester abortions to be performed in a hospital, as that term is conventionally defined. Such a requirement infringes on a pregnant woman's right to a safe, reasonably convenient, and reasonably inexpensive abortion. But a statute or ordinance that requires second-trimester abortions to be performed in a "hospital," if that term includes licensed outpatient abortion clinics, is constitutional, because it's a reasonable method of protecting the state's legitimate interest in women's health. (You'd think that if women were willing to take the risk, the state would feel its own interest in the women's health—which *has* to be less pressing than theirs—would be satisfied.) A free-standing abortion clinic costs a lot less to set up and run than a hospital does (in part because patients who are critically injured during an abortion can be sent to a hospital). As outpatient facilities, clinics aren't even tempted to require an expensive hospital stay as part of every second-trimester abortion. It makes a difference to patients, who probably pay less for clinic abortions (and are less likely to have to schedule—and explain to family and employers—a hospital stay). It makes a big difference to those who own abortion clinics, who naturally prefer to offer full-scale service.

It is a peculiarity of the debate over abortion that much of the debate—and a disproportionate number of statutes, ordinances, and court cases—deal with atypical abortions. Very few abortions are "therapeutic" (indicated to save the life or health of the mother), and most abortions, now that accurate early pregnancy tests are available, are performed in the first or second trimester. A late abortion is a serious operation, both physically and emotionally, and is also stressful for the medical personnel participating in the abortion. A woman who has an abortion five weeks after conception doesn't look or feel pregnant, and the products of conception don't look anything like a baby. If the abortion takes place twenty-five weeks after conception, the case is vastly different. In a few, but horrifying, cases, fetuses even emerge from the abortion procedure alive; the law has dealt extensively with this uncommon situation.

There are three main reasons why late abortions are performed: the pregnant woman is so dumb, ignorant, or out of it that she doesn't realize she is pregnant until pregnancy is well advanced; the abortion decision is so morally traumatic that it takes her a long time to decide; or she has reason to believe the fetus may be defective, and she has to wait for amniocentesis results to decide whether to abort. Although we're stretching pretty far into the unknowable here, it's possible that the availability of late abortion actually promotes childbearing: some high-risk would-be mothers might avoid pregnancy, or abort all fetuses as soon as pregnancy is confirmed, unless they have the option of amniocentesis and carrying normal fetuses to term.

THIRD-TRIMESTER AND POST-VIABILITY ABORTION

Roe v. Wade says that, once a fetus is viable (that is, could possibly survive outside the mother's body, with or without artificial support), the states can regulate abortion, or even forbid it unless there is a medical indication to preserve the woman's life or health. A dictum in *Roe v. Wade* says that viability occurs somewhere around twenty-four to twenty-eight weeks of gestation.

A bit later, in *Planned Parenthood v. Danforth*, the Supreme Court restressed its medical model of abortion, and indicated that viability isn't uniform, but varies for each pregnancy. "It isn't a proper legislative or judicial function to fix viability, which is essentially for the judgment of the responsible attending physician, at a specific point in the gestation period."

Many states have laws specifying the medical profession's duty to a viable fetus undergoing abortion: in general, doctors must perform life-support functions and keep the fetus alive, if possible. Some states require the presence of an additional doctor at a post-viability abortion, so that one doctor can take care of the pregnant woman while the other looks after the fetus. This is all very well in theory, but I wonder how a hospital or Welfare department, adjusting to cuts in spending for social services, can handle the extremely high cost of taking care of very premature infants.

It's permissible for a state to require doctors to file a pathology report on each aborted fetus. However, a law imposing liability on doctors for failure to preserve the lives of viable fetuses must be carefully drafted so it's specific, not overbroad, and doesn't impose liability on doctors without fault on their part.

In mid-1984, the Third Circuit ruled out Pennsylvania's requirement of a second physician and the requirement that the abortion method least dangerous to the fetus be used unless it increases risk to the pregnant woman. Both the requirements were held unconstitutional because they did not make the pregnant woman's safety the first priority.

The Eastern District of Louisiana upheld some parts of Louisiana's abortion law, ruled out others. The requirement that a second doctor be present at post-viability abortions was upheld, but a requirement that late abortions be performed by the method most likely to result in fetal survival wasn't (void for vagueness); neither was the requirement that the second doctor take all possible steps to preserve the fetus (sets up a conflict between the two doctors). A presumption of viability at twenty-four weeks was struck down; so was a requirement that three doctors certify the medical necessity of a post-viability abortion to prevent permanent impairment of the pregnant woman's health (because it infringes on a doctor's ability to practice medicine).

Some states indicate that doctors can be liable for negligence if a live-born fetus isn't given supportive care after the abortion; others even state that taking affirmative steps to kill a live-born fetus is some form of homicide. But these latter statutes are of little practical importance, because the cases are nearly impossible to prove. Probably the most famous case of this type is *Commonwealth v. Edelin,* 371 Mass. 497, 359 N.E.2d 4 (1976). Dr. Edelin was accused of killing an aborted fetus and was acquitted on appeal on a widely split decision. Some judges felt that there wasn't enough evidence that the fetus had survived the abortion procedure; others criticized the jury instructions about wanton and reckless conduct amounting to homicide. The patient said she was seventeen weeks pregnant; Dr. Edelin had a reasonable belief that the fetus was twenty-one to twenty-two weeks old and nonviable; other doctors estimated a twenty-four-week fetal age. Dr. Edelin testified that he did not feel a fetal heartbeat after the abortion, and another doctor corroborated. The pathology report was ambiguous, and could be interpreted to mean either that the fetus had breathed (and therefore was born alive) or that it had not.

The legal question of a doctor's duty in a late abortion is intimately related to the technological question of which fetuses are viable under what conditions. Spontaneously born premature babies that would inevitably have died a few years ago can now survive—at least if they're born in hospitals with equipment and expertise to keep them alive. The question of what happens to a premature baby (or live-born aborted fetus) in a less well-equipped hospital is unsettled; so is the question of rationing medical resources. If a hospital can give intensive care to only twenty-five infants, who has priority: a spontaneously born premature baby, a live-born abortus, or a severely handicapped newborn whose parents want treatment to be withheld?

INFORMED CONSENT

It's tough to be against informed consent; after all, informed consent is a kind of apple-pie issue for liberals, and even conservatives find it difficult to argue that people should have medical treatment without understanding it.

But the question of informed consent has a lot to do with who's writing the script. Patients are unlikely to consent to treatment if they're told, "There's no real scientific evidence for this, but it's convenient for us to do it this way," and "There may be some slight discomfort" arouses less anxiety than "It hurts like hell."

Because abortion has a moral dimension that other medical procedures lack, there's a further problem. A counselor who says, "You're doing the right thing. You shouldn't hesitate about having an abortion," will produce a different effect from one who says, "God will punish you for murdering your baby."

Most of the states that have post–*Roe v. Wade* abortion laws also require that the pregnant woman sign a statement indicating her informed consent to the abortion. Many of those states, in turn, require that women seeking abortion be counseled about alternatives to abortion and/or about the development of the fetus at various stages of pregnancy. (I suspect that the latter requirement sometimes backfires: although it's designed to make pregnant women think of their fetuses as babies—persons possessing a right of life—the effect may be to gross them out so much that they demand immediate abortions.)

These informed-consent requirements have had a rocky courtroom history.

• The Eastern District of Louisiana said in 1980 that a state can require abortion patients to be told about alternatives to abortion, because this was rationally related to informed consent. However, the court ruled that it was unconstitutional for a state to require the counselor to say that the fetus is a human life from the time of conception—or indeed to dictate a set script at all.

• In the same year, the District of North Dakota came to pretty much the same conclusion in *Leigh v. Olson*—that a requirement of disclosing alternatives to abortion was permissible (because it did not place an undue burden on the abortion decision) but counselors could not be required to explain the "probable anatomical and physiological characteristics" of the fetus.

• The Eighth Circuit, employing a favorite technique jurists use to build suspense, said that a requirement that women seeking abortions be advised of "reasonably possible medical and mental consequences resulting from abortion, pregnancy, and childbirth" was acceptable under the establishment of religion and free exercise clauses of the First Amendment, but was still unconstitutional because it could not stand up to the strict scrutiny required by a Due Process challenge.

• *Charles v. Carey* knocks out Illinois' informed consent rules and its requirement that the doctor performing the abortion provide the counseling. (Inability to delegate this duty makes performing abortions less attractive to doctors.)

• After 1980 (a banner year for informed-consent cases) things simmered down until 1982, when the District of Rhode Island found the requirement of delivering specified information (including the "psychological risks to the fetus") unconstitutionally vague. No compelling state interest was shown for the script, or for the requirement that the doctor performing the abortion do the counseling. Because they burdened the right of abortion without meeting a compelling state interest, the requirements were invalidated.

• The Supreme Court settled the matter in 1983, ruling that a state can neither proclaim that doctors are the only people qualified to give abortion counseling, nor dictate the script. Because the Supreme Court sees abortion as primarily a medical decision made by the pregnant woman in consultation with her doctor, not state can interfere with this doctor-patient relationship by substituting a formula for disclosure for the disclosure that the doctor thinks appropriate.

The Supreme Court also invalidated a requirement that there be a 24-hour waiting period between the counseling and giving of informed consent and the abortion. The Court's reasoning was that no evidence had been produced that the waiting period promoted either safety or informed consent. Several state laws do contain waiting-period provisions. An argument can be made either way: an abortion decision is a serious one, and should not be made hastily. But if a woman *knows* she's pregnant, and has decided to have an abortion before she approaches the clinic or hospital, the waiting period doesn't help her decide (she's already made up her mind); it just discourages her by requiring *another* day off from work, *another* baby-sitter, *another* long bus ride and hours in the waiting room. If the pregnancy is fairly well advanced, or if she must wait for amniocentesis results, the delay can be crucial. If the facility is heavily booked up, or if certain procedures are only performed on certain days, the waiting-period requirement may require scheduling at a time when a more dangerous abortion technique must be used—or may place the abortion post-viability, and thus make the abortion more distasteful or even illegal (if the state forbids post-viability elective abortions). After all, a woman who wants more time to make up her mind can always ask for a later appointment or leave the abortion facility when her pregnancy is confirmed, then return once she knows she wants to abort.

ZONING

One way to decrease the number of abortions is to increase the cost and/or inconvenience of getting an abortion. A very good way to do this is to place zoning restrictions that keep abortion clinics out of most of the city, or that require elaborate and prohibitively expensive equipment. Not unreasonably, then, anti-abortion groups have pressed for restrictive zoning laws. Courts have analyzed such laws in a number of ways.

• Out-and-out listing of abortion clinics as a "prohibited use" is invalid in Massachusetts because it discriminates against a woman's Constitutional privacy right to choose an abortion, and doctors' and health facilities' right to perform abortions. Neither public opposition to abortion nor the fact that the clinic was operated for profit outweighed this fundamental Constitutional right.

• In Ohio, the rule is more or less the opposite: doctors and clinics, it's held, have no fundamental right to perform abortions, and a city zoning law, keeping abortion clinics out of business districts, is legitimate because it has a rational relationship to a legitimate state interest (regulating health care, promoting childbirth). Furthermore, the zoning law did not "unduly burden" either the abortion decision or the doctor-patient relationship.

• New York came up with yet another formula: a state can set construction standards for abortion clinics that are different from those for other health facilities, even if these requirements make abortion more expensive. Under this theory, state regulation of abortion is invalid only if it places an undue burden on the abortion decision—not just the abortion process. (We'll see more of this kind of thinking in the discussion of public funding for abortion.)

• The Sixth Circuit turned thumbs down on an Ohio ordinance that required abortion clinics—but not other free-standing clinics—to have cardiac defibrillators, X-ray machines, full laboratories, and standard operating rooms, holding that these expensive provisions burdened women's right to choose abortion.

• The First Circuit, reasonably enough, said that a state can apply the *same* licensing standards to abortion clinics as to other clinics, as long as the regulation process doesn't impinge on a woman's right to get a first-trimester abortion.

• Sometimes it's the presence, not the absence, of operating rooms that causes the problem: a Louisiana zoning law allowed free-standing clinics as long as they did not have operating rooms. The zoning administrator denied a Certificate of Occupancy because the clinic's procedure rooms were considered "operating rooms for major surgery." The Western District of Louisiana allowed the administrator's decision to stand because it was made under the preexisting, valid zoning law. The decision might well have been to the contrary if the law had been passed specifically to exclude the abortion clinic.

• Illinois says that an ordinance requiring a clinic to get a license as an "ambulatory surgical treatment center" if *any* abortions were performed there, but only if it was *primarily* used for other procedures of comparable medical risk, is invalid. The ordinance is unconstitutional because it restricts women's privacy right to a first-trimester abortion, and doctors' Equal Protection right to have procedures of equal medical significance treated equally.

• The Fifth Circuit took a strong pro-choice stand in 1981, saying that a zoning decision excluding abortion clinics from business districts causes irreparable injury to the privacy rights of women seeking abortions. This is true even if other abortion facilities are available. The zoning decision is an affirmative government interference with the legally protected abortion decision (not just a refusal to remove existing restrictions on abortion). Any such interference has to be more than simply rational; it has to stand up to strict scrutiny. According to the Fifth Circuit, the ordinance did not pass this test.

The question of abortion clinic zoning, then, involves a patchwork of legal theories and standards of analysis; if there's a predictable pattern there, I can't find it. Matters are grimmer—if more explicable—when it comes to public funding for abortions for medically indigent women.

DR. JEKYLL AND MR. HYDE REVISITED

One of the basic clichés of legal discourse is that the power to tax is the power to destroy. For the indigent, there's a corollary: power to withhold funding is power to prevent. Given the inexorable march of medical costs, it's quite possible for a person who isn't indigent in the ordinary sense of the term to be medically indigent.

To help the medically indigent—and to provide established doctors a jackpot and novice doctors someone to practice on (the medical equivalent of an out-of-town tryout)—the Medicaid system has developed (or metastasized).

Those whose income (or, more accurately, lack of income) qualifies them for Medicaid can get virtually the full spectrum of medical care paid for by the state they live in; the state, in turn, is reimbursed by the federal government. One important exception is abortion.

The Hyde Amendment (which is an amendment to the "further continuing appropriations" passed each year for the Department of Health and Human Services) defines the extremely limited circumstances under which the federal government will reimburse the states for Medicaid abortions. The current version says that none of the Department of Health and Human Services' funds may be used for abortions unless the mother's life would be endangered if the pregnancy were carried to term. The Hyde Amendment also says that each state has discretion not to fund *any* abortion, even those for saving the mother's life. The implementing regulations for the Hyde Amendment and the Medicaid regulations are a little more liberal: federal funds can be used for abortion if a doctor certifies that the pregnant woman's life is at stake, or if the pregnancy is the result of rape or incest reported to a law enforcement or public health agency within sixty days of the incident. (In practical terms, this means if the pregnancy resulted from the rape or incestuous abuse of a woman not otherwise sexually active; there's no way for a pregnant married woman to know if the pregnancy is the result of rape or of marital sexual relations. The effect is to deny federal funding for abortions for women who choose to have voluntary sexual activity, based on the implicit assumption that it's appropriate for Congress to set moral standards for women who are eligible for Medicaid. It's the Golden Rule: the ones who have the gold make the rules.)

The Church Amendment (42 U.S.C. §300a-7) is related to the anti-sterilization-abuse guidelines discussed on pages 221–222 and to the abortion conscience provisions discussed below. The Church Amendment says that the receipt of public funds under the Public Health Services Act, Community Mental Health Centers Act, or the Developmental Disabilities Services and Facilities Construction Act doesn't authorize anyone to require a person or institution to perform abortions. (Because the Developmental Disabilities Act is involved, it protects against abortion abuse of the retarded, just as various cases and statutes protect against sterilization abuse. But the issues are similar: which retarded women are capable of being good mothers or making informed abortion decisions, and which are not?)

The Church Amendment also forbids discrimination on the basis of a person's refusal or *willingness* to participate in abortions or his or her history of performing legal abortions. Under the Church Amendment, then, a doctor or nurse's moral stance on abortion can't be used to make job decisions about him or her.

The Supreme Court, although it has been fairly pro-choice, has also been pro–Hyde Amendment. In 1976, the Court handled a case involving standing to challenge the refusal of state funding for indigents' abortions, and said,

> For a doctor who cannot afford to work for nothing, and a woman who cannot afford to pay him, the State's refusal to find an abortion is as effective an "interdiction" of it as would ever be necessary.

This makes perfect sense and has had very little influence on the Court's later decisions on Medicaid abortions.

There were two major Supreme Court decisions on this issue in 1977: *Beal v. Doe* and *Maher v. Roe*. Both cases say that a state has a strong legitimate interest in encouraging childbirth, even if state-paid childbirth is much more expensive than state-paid abortion. Therefore, states *can* decide to cover elective abortions in their Medicaid programs (even though federal reimbursement won't be available for what the state spends). But if the state chooses *not* to fund elective abortions, it does not violate the Equal Protection clause—the Medicaid laws don't oblige states to fund all medically necessary procedures for indigents, much less elective abortions.

Nineteen-eighty's *Harris v. McRae* (448 U.S. 297 (1980)) upholds the

Hyde Amendment and makes it clear that Medicaid law doesn't require any state to provide abortion funds for which it won't be reimbursed. *Harris* is notable for the verbal tap-dancing by which the Court avoids the obvious conclusion that refusal to fund Medicaid abortions makes poor women second-class citizens. Women who can pay for abortions can exercise their right to have an early abortion; medically indigent women can't.

> The Hyde Amendment, like the Connecticut welfare restriction at issue in *Maher,* places no governmental obstacle in the path of a woman who chooses to terminate her pregnancy, but rather, by means of unequal subsidization of abortion and other medical services, encourages alternative activity deemed in the public interest. [P. 315.]

Sure. And the law, in its majestic impartiality, forbids the rich as well as the poor to beg, sleep under bridges, and steal bread.

> Although government may not place obstacles in the path of a woman's exercise of her freedom of choice, it need not remove those not of its own creation. Indigency falls in the latter category. The financial constraints that restrict an indigent woman's ability to enjoy the full range of constitutionally protected freedom of choice are the product not of governmental restrictions on access to abortions, but rather of her indigency. Although Congress has opted to subsidize medically necessary services generally, but not certain medically necessary abortions, the fact remains that the Hyde Amendment leaves an indigent woman with at least the same range of choice in deciding whether to obtain a medically necessary abortion as she would have had if Congress had chosen to subsidize no health care costs at all. [Pp. 316–317.]

After all, if the woman's landlord decides to maximize his investment return by not providing heat in the winter, she's no worse off than Marie Antoinette, who didn't have central heating either.

After that impressive piece of reasoning, *Williams v. Zbaraz* is something of an anticlimax. It simply says that an Illinois statute precluding Medicaid payments for elective abortions, and restricting payment to life-saving medically necessary abortions, isn't in violation of the Equal Protection clause.

There's a split of authority in the lower courts. The Tenth Circuit and the Western District of Missouri say that states can avoid funding abortions for which they won't be reimbursed; the First Circuit says that states *must* fund abortions for which they will be reimbursed, and *may* fund other abortions. The Fourth and Eighth Circuits, Eastern District of Pennsylvania and Northern District of Georgia, New Jersey and Oregon state courts used various Constitutional theories to require the states within their jurisdiction to provide Medicaid funds for all medically necessary abortions for indigent women.

California is the one state that requires Medicaid funding of *elective* abortions. California's 1981, 1982, and 1983 budgets excluded funding for elective abortions, and three court cases in succession made them put it back in, on the theory that California Constitutional law requires an examination of every discriminatory program in light of the original purpose of the law it's supposed to implement—and restricting the procreative choice of poor women has nothing to do with the objectives of the Medi-Cal system.

Notice that, except for California's, all these cases involve funding of abortions that are at least assertedly medically necessary. On the level, very few abortions are medically necessary, but it's easier to get a doctor (for whatever motives) to swear that an abortion is essential to preserve a woman's mental or physical health (a comfortably elastic criterion) than to get one to swear that it's a matter of life and death. The routines that once were evoked to provide legal abortions for college co-eds can be polished up and used again for indigent women.

In a way it's surprising that so much effort should be invested in keeping poor women from having abortions (and thus forcing them to have unwanted children). Even if the emergence of a baby magically made a woman capable of supporting the new baby as well as herself and her older children, prenatal care and childbirth are much more expensive than abortion. (Economy efforts through eliminating prenatal care are common, if stupid, and create medical expenses for premature and handicapped children that are much higher than the savings.) One would tend to predict that just the opposite would be the case: that it would be necessary to protect poor women against right-wing zealots coercing women into having abortions, because said zealots were making a frontal assault on the welfare rolls.

CONSCIENCE PROVISIONS AND THE AVAILABILITY OF ABORTION

Several states have recognized that abortion coercion could be a problem and have enacted statutes making it clear that no public benefits (e.g., welfare payments) can be made contingent on having an abortion. This is one kind of conscience clause: it prevents women from having to have abortions they find morally unacceptable in order to retain benefits they need to live.

Most of the states have other kinds of conscience provisions. The less controversial kind protects doctors, nurses, and other medical personnel from retaliation if, for reasons of moral scruples, they refuse to participate in abortions. (The laws deal with moral objections to abortion in the abstract—not a belief that a particular patient is making a mistake by having an abortion.) It's difficult to oppose a statute of this type: many people have a strong religious or ethical belief that abortion is wrong, and they should not be forced to sacrifice their jobs or promotion possibilities because of these beliefs.

"Institutional" conscience provisions—provisions that allow hospitals, or private hospitals, to refuse to perform abortions—are more troublesome. A Pennsylvania statute forbids public hospitals and clinics to perform elective abortions—whatever the beliefs of the staff. People—including Boards of Directors—can have moral scruples, but buildings and equipment can't. Celia Gomes, R.N., has only one opinion about her own willingness or unwillingness to participate in abortion; the staff of Clear Brook Hospital can have a significant division of opinion on this important point.

More significantly, there may be women in the hospital's vicinity who want abortions, doctors who are willing to perform abortions, and medical staff who are willing to assist. If the hospital won't allow the abortion to be performed, and if there are no abortion clinics or more amiable hospitals nearby, the women are as effectively precluded from getting "mainstream" abortions as if elective abortions were illegal. (In either case, abortions might be available in more or less improvised circumstances.)

Several cases have dealt with the issue of hospitals' refusal to permit abortions on premises; the results are the usual mixed bag. Disappointingly, the Supreme Court has said that a policy choice not to perform abortions in public hospitals doesn't violate any Constitutional rights. Having an untrammeled right to a first-trimester abortion doesn't mean much if you can't afford it, or if you can and there's nowhere to have it performed.

The Sixth and Eighth Circuits see it a little differently. *Wolfe v. Schroering* holds that, while private hospitals can use conscience clauses to refuse to perform abortions, public hospitals can't; *Nyberg v. City of Virginia City* says a city can't prevent willing doctors from using the city hospital to perform abortions—at least if it's the only hospital in the community.

There have been several challenges to hospitals' refusal to perform abortions, challenges claiming "state action" as defined by 42 U.S.C.S. §1983. As we saw in the discussion of sterilization abuse, sometimes the fact that a hospital gets federal Hill-Burton construction money (taken by itself or in combination with other factors) is considered a sign of state involvement; sometimes it isn't. In *Jones v. Eastern Maine Medical Center*, the District of Maine would not grant an injunction requiring a hospital to perform second-trimester elective abortions. The court wasn't persuaded that the combination of Hill-Burton funds, provision of free medical assistance to indigents, and the fact that the hospital was the best-equipped in the area added up to state action for a §1983 case. But the Fourth

Circuit said that getting Hill-Burton funds, even by itself, was "state action," so a medical center *could* be sued under §1983 to challenge its refusal to perform elective abortions.

New Jersey came up with some highly quotable language to the effect that a private, non-profit, non-sectarian hospital that *has* the facilities to perform first-trimester abortions can't refuse to let the facilities be used for this purpose. The hospital is quasi-public, because its facilities are open to the public; the hospital is tax-exempt; and it gets financial support from the federal and local governments and from the public. The New Jersey court found it improper for a hospital that performed therapeutic abortions to refuse to perform elective abortions, and "Moral concepts cannot be the basis for a non-sectarian, non-profit eleemosynary [charitable] hospital's regulations where that hospital is holding out the use of its facilities to the general public."

In summary, it doesn't pay to hold your breath until St. Anybody's Hospital starts performing elective abortions; but an argument can be made that public, and perhaps private nonsectarian hospitals, must make their facilities available to medical staff who are willing to perform abortions.

ABORTION AND INSURANCE

The Pregnancy Discrimination Act, 42 U.S.C.S. §2000(k) and its implementing Guidelines make it an unfair employment practice for an employer to discriminate based on the fact that a woman has had an abortion. Employers may, if they wish, provide health insurance benefits for elective abortions (fat chance); if they do provide health insurance, they must provide coverage for therapeutic abortions and for abortion complications (e.g., hemorrhage, infection). The Guidelines say that the employer must provide fringe benefits other than health insurance (e.g., sick leave) for abortions on the same terms as they are provided for other medical conditions.

But the Guidelines, after all, are Guidelines, and states can and do have their own opinions on the matter; a few of them place restrictions on the employers' and/or insurers' abortion coverage. Kentucky and Rhode Island say that insurance policies may only cover elective abortions through a separate rider at extra cost (rather like a "floater" on one's homeowner's insurance policy to cover silverware and furs); Pennsylvania insurers must provide optional, cheaper health insurance policies that don't cover elective abortions.

THE HLA: GOING TOO FAR?

Right-to-life advocates haven't given up on the possibility of the Supreme Court's reversing its position, and several state laws make it obvious that they will be changed as soon as this happens; but anti-abortion advocates are also trying to amend the Constitution to give states the power to regulate and forbid elective (or all) abortions.

A number of Human Life Amendments have been knocking around Congress. Their purpose is to make it the law of the land that life begins at conception. Some versions also try to relocate control of abortion to the individual states rather than the Supreme Court or other agencies of the federal government. A number of state statutes already declare that life begins at conception.

There are a couple of problems with this approach. Not everyone would agree that government agencies have the right to decide when life begins. Some would say it's an unsolvable, metaphysical question; others that it's a question perfectly within the competence of medicine, or of religion.

The practical problems are pretty close to insuperable. More than half of all fertilized eggs miscarry, many of them because of genetic abnormalities so massive that the conceptus aborts before a pregnancy is confirmed, or even suspected. A state can close down abortion clinics, but how can it find out if doctors are giving hormone shots to bring on "late" periods? How can a state distinguish between authentic menstrual irregularity and the miscarriage of an early embryo, or between an early miscarriage greeted with regret and one that provides profound relief? Can a state require (or, more to the point, enforce a requirement of) regular pregnancy tests so that women will be aware that they have conceived? What kind of pregnancy tests would be used—tests that require two months' gestation, the instant pregnancy tests that require about a month's gestation, or state-of-the-art tests that can detect pregnancy a few days after fertilization? Once a woman is pregnant, can a state order her to stop smoking, ingesting potential mutagens, lose weight, exercise more, stop lifting heavy objects, quit her hazardous job, or take other steps to preserve the pregnancy? At least in New York, restaurants and bars can be compelled to nag all patrons that alcohol consumption during pregnancy is dangerous to fetal health; can Prohibition be re-instituted for pregnant women (or women of childbearing age)? (See pages 191–196 for a discussion of industrial fetal protection programs.) Will all the government interventions be punitive to women, or will every woman (and her fetus) be given the right to free prenatal care? And where's the money going to come from for these massive monitoring programs?

Some birth control methods, like "morning after" pills and certain IUDs, work by preventing implantation of the fertilized egg. Under a Human Life Amendment, these birth control methods might be banned (unless the amendment, like the Oklahoma and Pennsylvania state laws, specifically exempts birth control devices).

Anyway, if a fertilized egg *is* a person, it necessarily has legal rights of some kind (though it's hard to imagine it having any legal obligations). Identical twins develop from the division of a single fertilized egg, fraternal twins from the fertilization of two eggs—does that mean, during gestation, each identical twin is only half a person?

As Professor David Westfall of the Harvard Law School pointed out, something will have to be done to settle fetal property rights. If a will leaves something to "my children" or "my descendants," are fetuses included? Can a woman be sued for having a miscarriage? Is the fetus a dependent providing a tax deduction from the moment of conception? (If so, the IRS won't be happy; it doesn't even have the facilities to check whether allegedly *born* dependents really exist and really are dependent.) Apportionment of Congressional districts is based on the number of *people* in the district, not the number of registered voters or people of voting age. The Nixon clone in Philip Roth's *Our Gang* campaigned on a promise of giving fetuses the vote; should they be represented in Congress?

As it stands now, the basic rule in tort law is that a baby born alive (or his or her estate, if the baby dies after birth) has a right to sue for injuries sustained during gestation. Most states also permit a wrongful-death claim arising out of injuries causing the stillbirth of a viable fetus. Pro-choice commentators criticize such decisions. Some recent fetal wrongful-death decisions emphasize that they do not limit voluntary abortions.

If an anti-abortion Congressional amendment is to be passed at all (perhaps it has crossed your mind that I don't think this is a great idea) it would make much more sense to limit it in scope. Something like, "Each state, as of (effective date) shall be free to regulate or prohibit induced abortions within the state. Any provision of the United States Constitution to the contrary is hereby amended for this purpose only."

THE ROAD TO THE COURTHOUSE

• Although state laws haven't really come to grips with the question, it may be possible to use state paternity laws to sue for abortion expenses. But unless paternity is admitted, it would be difficult or impossible to prove paternity, as paternity is usually established by comparing the blood group or other biological markers of the baby and putative father.

• Because abortion patients can travel to other states to have abortions, it's at least possible that a conspiracy to monopolize and restrain trade in abortions (for example, a group of clinics agreeing to keep abortion prices comfortably high rather than competing on price) could violate the Sherman Act.

- The more responsible anti-abortion advocates try to provide women with counseling, financial help, adoption assistance, and other alternatives to abortion, and/or use the courts and legislative methods to change the law. The least responsible are outright terrorists, using arson, kidnapping, and threats of violence against clinics, staffs, and abortion patients. The Justice Department has declined to use the Ku Klux Klan Act or other civil rights acts to undertake an investigation of such violence (the modern equivalent of destroying the village in order to save it), but local police and Attorneys General may be less blasé.

- An intermediate harassment technique is to hassle women entering clinics, or to get access to abortion records and notify the patient's relatives. A victim of the latter tactic has filed suit in the Superior Court of Orange County (California), asking for $5 million in damages against the hospital where the abortion was performed and against the National Right to Life Committee, charging invasion of privacy, infliction of emotional distress, negligence, and unauthorized release of medical information.

THE SMOKING GUN

- Because, for all practical purposes, abortion law is a subdivision of Constitutional law, Constitutional techniques of analysis are useful. On one side is the Constitutionally protected right of privacy, which allows women to choose abortion at least until viability. When a state limits abortion and is challenged, it claims interests such as protection of women's health (which can be refuted by showing that the regulation doesn't really promote health), parental authority, family harmony, or promotion of childbirth. Which side wins depends on the relevant court's interpretation of the Bill of Rights.

- A state's refusal to fund therapeutic abortions on Medicaid can be challenged as discrimination against poor women or against abortion as opposed to other medically necessary procedures. Once again, the result is a toss-up. Except in California, I haven't found any cases requiring funding of elective abortions.

- Even if there is a conscience provision, a facility's refusal to perform abortions can be challenged under 42 U.S.C.S. §1983. Victory depends on being able to show state action—perhaps by showing a combination of federal and local government funds, the facility being open to the public, and the absence of other facilities.

- I haven't seen anyone try it, but perhaps a case could be premised on a "bona fide seniority system"—that is, whatever the rights of the fetus, the rights of the living woman should prevail.

NOTES

CHAPTER 1

SEX DISCRIMINATION IN EMPLOYMENT: SUBSTANTIVE LAW

Note: If racial, religious, or national-origin discrimination is also involved in a case, the victim may be able to use other federal civil rights laws (e.g., 42 U.S.C. §1981, 1983, 1985) but I'm not going to open that can of worms here.

p. 22 The cite for Title VII is 42 U.S.C. §2000e–2(a).
"Not necessarily fifteen full-time employees" *Thurber v. Jack Reilly's Inc.*, 32 FEP Cases 1511 (1st Cir. 1983).
"Job applicants can use . . ." EEOC Dec. No. 71–1325 (1971).
". . . but independent contractors . . ." *Smith v. Dutra Trucking Co.*, 410 F.Supp. 513 (D. Cal. 1976), *aff'd* 580 F.2d 1054, *cert.den.*, 439 U.S. 1076; *Jenkins v. Travelers Ins. Co.*, 436 F.Supp. 950 (D. Ore. 1977).

p. 23 "An odd 1981 decision . . ." *Backus v. Baptist Medical Center*, 510 F.Supp. 1191 (E.D. Ark. 1981).
"In any situation that does not involve a bona fide occupational qualification . . ." *Kohne v. Imco Container Co.*, 480 F.Supp. 1015 (W.D. Va. 1979).
Being a woman is not a BFOQ for a flight attendant: *Wilson v. Southwest Airlines Co.*, 517 F.Supp. 292 (N.D. Tex. 1981); being a man is not a BFOQ for waiting on tables at dinner in a "continental cuisine" room: *EEOC v. Sky King Inc.*, 34 FEP Cases 1644 (D. N.M. 1982). The employer's sincere, good-faith belief that the male purser's job is different from the female stewardess's job is no defense to Title VII and EPA suits: *Laffey v. Northwest Airlines, Inc.*, 35 FEP Cases 508 (D.C. Cir. 7/20/84).
On "sexiness" as a BFOQ: *Wilson v. Southwest Airlines Co.*, 517 F.Supp. 292 (N.D. Tex. 1981); *Guardian Capital Corp. v. NYS Division of Human Rights*, 46 A.D.2d 832, 360 N.Y.S.2d 937 (1974) (restaurant); *Craft v. Metromedia Inc.* 572 F.Supp. 868 (D. Mo. 1983) (television station).

pp. 23–24 EEOC Guidelines are at 29 C.F.R. §1604.2(a)(1) (on BFOQs), 1604.5

(help-wanted ads). By the way, the New York case of *Carey v. Binghamton Press Co. Inc.*, 415 N.Y.S.2d 523 (1979), says that newspapers can be held liable for publishing an obviously discriminatory ad. However, if the newspaper questions the ad and the employer claims that there is a BFOQ involved, the newspaper can't be expected to conduct an independent investigation and is legally entitled to take the employer's word for it.

p. 24 "In this case, the height requirement . . ." *Costa v. Markey*, 706 F.2d 1 (1st Cir. 1983).
Malarkey v. Texaco Inc., 31 EPD ¶33,491 (2d Cir. 1983).
Phillips v. Martin Marietta Corp., 400 U.S. 542 (1971).
"An action that has several motives . . ." *Slotkin v. Human Development Corp.*, 454 F.Supp. 250 (D. Mo. 1978).

pp. 24–25 The Guidelines are at 29 C.F.R. §1604.3. Title VII only preempts state laws that are *less* protective of women and minorities. Therefore, *Grann v. City of Madison*, 53 LW 2028 (7th Cir. 6/25/84), holds that an employer is exempt from reverse-bias suits from male employees if it obeys a state Fair Employment agency and raises the salary of woman employees to equal that of male employees with more seniority.
On protective laws, see *LeBeau v. L-O-F Co.*, 33 FEP Cases 1700 (7th Cir. 1984), allowing an employer to follow the EEOC's 1965 Guidelines and abide by a state law forbidding overtime by woman employees, for the period of time before the law was found unconstitutional.

p. 25 *Hishon v. King & Spaulding*, 52 LW 4627 (1984). Settlement: *Nat. L.J.*, 6/25/84, p.2.

p. 26 The EEOC's affirmative action Guidelines are at 29 C.F.R. §1608; the OFCCP version is printed at 41 C.F.R. Part 60–1.

p. 27 "A recent Illinois case . . ." *Ende v. Board of Regents*, 32 FEP Cases 390 (N.D. Ill. 1983).
The *Wall Street Journal* article is "Battle of the Sexes Isn't Much of a Fight in the Salary Area" (no by-line), 3/14/83, p. 18.

p. 28 ". . . so a woman college professor's claim . . ." *Berry v. Board of Supervisors of Louisiana State University*, 715 F.2d 971 (5th Cir. 9/26/83); remand ordered, see *Nat. L.J.*, 11/28/83, p. 31.
"A year earlier, a Florida District Court . . ." *Lancaster v. Holt, Rinehart & Winston*, 32 EPD ¶33,744 (N.D. Fla. 1982).
"For instance, a Detroit health club . . ." *Bence v. Detroit Health Corp.*, 32 FEP Cases 434 (6th Cir. 1983).
"However, a bank . . ." *EEOC v. First Citizens Bank of Billings*, 31 EPD ¶33,508 (D. Mont. 1983).

p. 29 ". . . when a hospital paid orderlies more . . ." *Odomes v. Nucare Inc.*, 653 F.2d 246 (6th Cir. 1981).
DiSalvo v. Chamber of Commerce, 416 F.Supp.844 (W.D. Mo. 1976), *aff'd* 568 F.2d 593 (8th Cir.).

Rinkel v. Associated Pipeline Contractors, 17 FEP Cases 224 (D. Alaska 1978). The EEOC can't enforce the EPA: *EEOC v. Allstate Insurance Co.,* 570 F.Supp. 1224 (S.D. Miss. 1983), *app. dism.,* 52 LW 3885; *EEOC v. Martin Industries, Inc.,* 581 F.Supp. 1029 (N.D. Ala. 1983), *app. dism.,* 53 LW 3205; *EEOC v. Westinghouse,* 33 FEP Cases 1232, *app. dism.,* 53 LW 3205.
It can so: *EEOC v. Hernando Bank, Inc.,* 52 LW 1133 (5th Cir. 2/13/84); *EEOC v. Dayton Power & Light,* 35 FEP Cases 401 (S.D. Ohio 7/10/84).

p. 30 ". . . but it's now fairly well settled"   *Gerlach v. Michigan Bell Telephone Co.,* 501 F.Supp. 1300 (E.D. Mich. 1980); *County of Washington v. Gunther,* 452 U.S. 161 (1981).
Corning Glass Works v. Brennan, 417 U.S. 188 (1974).
". . . well, functionally identical work . . ."   *Shultz v. Wheaton Glass Co.,* 421 F.2d 259 (3d Cir. 1970), *cert. den.,* 398 U.S. 905 (1970).

p. 31 *Christensen v. Iowa,* 563 F.2d 353, 356 (8th Cir. 1977). *Tacoma-Pierce County Public Health Association v. Tacoma-Pierce County Health Department,* 586 P.2d 1215, 22 Wash. App. 1 (1978), makes a similar point. It holds that an employer isn't guilty of sex discrimination if it pays more for predominantly male jobs than for predominantly female jobs of equal, or even of greater, value to the employer—provided that the employer conforms to prevailing wage standards, doesn't exclude qualified women from the "male" jobs, and pays the "man's" wage to any woman holding one of these jobs.
Lemons v. City & County of Denver, 620 F.2d 228 (10th Cir. 1980), *cert.den.,* 449 U.S. 888.
Futran v. Ring Radio Co., 501 F.Supp. 734 (N.D. Ga. 1980).
IUE v. Westinghouse, 631 F.2d 1094 (3d Cir. 1980). Also see the EEOC Guidelines, 29 C.F.R. §1604.8, and *Morgado v. Birmingham-Jefferson County Civil Defense Corps,* 706 F.2d 1184 (11th Cir. 1983), which makes the sensible point that the mere existence of written job descriptions (especially if the ink is still wet) doesn't constitute a "merit system" justifying unequal pay. The employer must be able to demonstrate superior performance and/or greater responsibility for the higher-paid employee.

p. 32 *County of Washington v. Gunther,* 452 U.S. 161 (1981).
"As a case in point . . ."   *Plemer v. Parsons-Gilbane,* 32 EPD ¶33,817 (5th Cir. 1983).

p. 33 *Spaulding v. U. of Wash.,* 35 FEP Cases 168 (W.D. Wash. 1981), *aff'd,* 35 FEP Cases 217 (9th Cir. 7/3/84).

p. 34 "Almost all of the states . . ."   AK §18.80.210; AZ §41–1463 (B)(2); CA Gov't §12940(a); CO §24–34–402(1)(a); CT §46–58(a); DE T19 §711(a)(1); FL §23.167(1)(a)(b); HI §378–2(1); ID §67–5909(1); IL ch 68 §1–103(Q); IN §22–9–1–3(1); IA §601A–6(1)(a); KS §44–1030(a)(1); KY §344.010(4); LA EPD ¶23,550; ME T5§4571; MD T49B §16(a)(1); MA ch 151B §4(1); MI §37.2102(1); MN §363.12(2); MO §296.020(1); MT §49–1–102(1); NB §48–1104; NV §613.330(1); NH §354–A:2; NJ §10:5–4; NM §28–1–7(A) NY Exec §296(1)(a); NC §143–422.2; ND §34–01–19; OH §4112.02(A); OK §1302(A)(1)(2); OR §659.030(1)(a); PA T43 §953; RI

§28–5–5; SC §1–13–80(a); SD §20–13–10; TN §4–21–105(a)(1); UT §34–35–6(1)(a); VT T21§495(a); WA §49.60.030(1)(a); WV § 5–11–3(h); WI §111.321; WY §27–9–105(a)(1).

"Forty-two states . . ." AK §18.80.220; AZ §41–1463(B)(1); AR §81–333; CA Labor §1197.5; CO §24.34.402(1)(a); CT §46a–62; DE T19 §711(a); FL §23.167(1)(a); HI §378–2(1); ID §67–5909(1); IL ch 48 §4a; IN §22.2–2.4; KS §44–1009(a)(1); KY §344.010(4); ME T5 §4572(1)(A); MD T100 §55A; MA ch 149 §105A; MI §37.2202 (1)(a); MN §181.66; MO §290.410; MT §49–2–303(1)(a); NB §48–1104(1); NV §613.330(1); NH §354–A:8; NJ §10:5–12; NM §28–1–7(A); NY Labor §194; ND §34–06.1–03; OH §4111.17(a); OK §1302(A)(1) (2); OR §659.030(1)(b); PA T 42 §955(a); RI §28–5–7(A); SC §1–13–80(h); SD §20–13–10; TN §4–21–105(a)(1); UT §34–35–6(1)(a); VA §40.1–28.6; WA §49.60.180(3); WV §5–11(3)(h); WI §111.36 (1)(a); WY §27–4–302.

"Six states have tackled . . ." KY §337.420; MN Laws 1982 ch 634; OR §652.220; SD §60–12–15; TN §50–321(a); WV §21–5B–2.

pp. 35–36 The *Manhart* case is *Los Angeles Dep't of Water & Power v. Manhart*, 435 U.S. 702 (1978); *Norris* is *Arizona Governing Committee v. Norris*, 103 S.Ct. 3492 (1983). Also see *Spirt v. TIAA*, 52 LW 2688 (2d Cir. 5/21/84), re retroactivity of unisex actuarial tables.

p. 36 The letter to the *Wall Street Journal* is from B. Kipp Franklin, not otherwise identified, printed 6/1/83.

p. 37 The EEOC fringe benefit Guidelines are at 29 C.F.R. §1604.9. Note that discrimination in benefits may also violate the Equal Pay Act, so it's worth adding an EPA claim to the complaint. State laws dealing with health and disability insurance are preempted by ERISA (the federal pension and benefit law): *Shaw v. Delta Airlines*, 51 LW 4968 (S. Ct. 1982).

"The Supreme Court said no . . ." *Newport News Shipbuilding Co. v. EEOC*, 32 FEP Cases 1 (1983).

p. 38 The EEOC Guideline on discrimination against married women is at 29 C.F.R. §1604.4.

"In mid-1983, the Ninth Circuit . . ." *Wambheim v. JC Penney Co.*, 705 F.2d 1492 (9th Cir. 1983), *cert.den.*, 103 S. Ct. 2890.

". . . men and only men . . ." *EEOC v. Fremont Christian School*, 52 LW 2609 (N.D. Cal. 4/13/84).

p. 39 Two good general references on nepotism rules: Catherine R. Lazuran, "Distinctions Based on Marital Status as Constituting Sex Discrimination," 34 *A.L.R. Fed.* 648; and Henry Ben-Zvi, "(Mrs.) Alice Doesn't Work Here Anymore: No-Spouse Rules and the American Working Woman," 29 *U.C.L.A.L. Rev.* 199 (October 1981).

Nepotism and full-time work: *Kraft, Inc. v. State*, 284 N.W.2d 386 (Minn. 1979). *Sprogis v. United Air Lines*, 444 F.2d 1194 (7th Cir. 1971); *Stroud v. Delta Air Lines Inc.*, 544 F.2d 892 (5th Cir. 1977); followed in *EEOC v. Delta Air Lines Inc.*, 578 F.2d 115 (5th Cir. 1978).

p. 41 "In general, a company can maintain . . ." EEOC Dec. No. 70–453, 2 FEP Cases 429 (1970).

"The Fifth Circuit, though . . ." *Georgi v. Farmers Electric Cooperative Inc.*, 32 EPD ¶33,816 (5th Cir. 1983).

Linebaugh v. Auto Leasing Co., 18 FEP Cases 752 (W.D. Ky. 1978).

"In 1976, New York State's highest court . . ." *Sanbonmatsu v. Boyer*, 39 N.Y.2d 914, 386 N.Y.S.2d 404 (1976).

"New Yorkers have to watch out for . . ." *Pizza Hut, Inc. v. NYS Human Rights Appeal Board*, 51 N.Y.2d 506, 434 N.Y.S.2d 961 (1980).

p. 42 "Shooting for the foot department . . ." *Vuyanich v. Republic National Bank*, 409 F.Supp. 1083 (D. Tex. 1976).

"Union women may . . ." see Irving Kosarsky and Vern Hauck, "The No-Spouse Rule, Title VII and Arbitration," 32 *Lab. L. J.* 366 (June 1981).

Citations for state laws forbidding discrimination on basis of marital status: AK §18.80.220, CA Gov't §12940(a)(3); CT §46a–60(a)(1); FL §23.167(1)(a); HI §378–2(1); IL ch 68§§1–103(Q): ME T5 §553; MD T49B §16(a)(1); MI §37.2202; MN §363.12(1); MT §49–2–303(1)(a); NB §48–1111; NH §354–A:8(i); NJ §10:5–12; NY Exec §291(1); OR §659.020(2); WA §49.60.180(2); WI §111.321.

p. 43 ". . . a clear instance of sex discrimination based on stereotypes . . ." *Michigan Department of Civil Rights ex rel Cornell v. Edward A. Sparrow Hospital Association*, 326 N.W.2d 519, 119 Mich. App. 387 (1982).

"An Illinois bank . . ." *Carroll v. Talman Federal Savings and Loan*, 604 F.2d 1028 (7th Cir. 1979).

"At least one case upholds . . ." *Lanigan v. Bartlett & Co. Grain*, 466 F.Supp. 1388 (W.D. Mo. 1979).

p. 44 "The EEOC found . . ." EEOC Dec. No. 77–36 (1977), EEOC Dec. (CCH) ¶6,588.

"The Southern District of New York agreed . . ." *EEOC v. Sage Realty*, 87 FRD 365 (1980).

"A Michigan District Court . . ." *Marentette v. Michigan Host Inc.*, 24 FEP Cases 1665 (E.D. Mich. 1980).

CHAPTER 2

SEX DISCRIMINATION IN EMPLOYMENT:
PROCEDURAL LAW

---

p. 46 The legal encyclopedia is 21 *Am.Jur. Trials*, Russell Specter and Paul J. Spiegelman's article, "Employment Discrimination Under Federal Civil Rights Acts," starting on page 1. In general, see Barbara Lindeman Schlei and Paul Grossman, *Employment Discrimination Law*, 2d ed., (BNA 1983), a telephone-book-sized tome that will tell you more about Title VII than you care to know.

p. 47 "In those states (e.g., Pennsylvania)" *Douglas v. Red Carpet Corp. of America*, 31 EPD ¶33,509 (E.D. Pa. 1982).

State adjudication is *res judicata: Buckhalter v. Pepsi-Cola General Bottlers Inc.*, 53 LW 2124 (N.D. Ill. 8/13/84).
About the EEOC complaint: 29 C.F.R. §1601.7–1601.14.

p. 48 "If new allegations *are* added later . . ." 29 C.F.R. §1601.12.
Statements to EEOC privileged: *Thomas v. Petrullis* (Ill. App. 1984), see *Nat. L.J.*, 7/30/84, p. 9.
"Once a charge has been filed . . ." 29 C.F.R. §1601.10.
"providing a copy of the charge . . ." 29 C.F.R. §1601.14.
"bell the cat . . ." *Universal Restaurants Inc. v. Fellows*, 701 F.2d 447 (5th Cir. 1983).

p. 49 "Title VII directs . . ." 42 U.S.C.S. §2000e–5(b).
"The EEOC's no-cause determination is not binding . . ." 42 U.S.C.S. §2000e–5(f)(1); *Alexander v. Gardner-Denver Co.*, 415 U.S. 36 (1974); *Glorator Corp. v. EEOC*, 592 F.2d 765 (4th Cir. 1979).
"that the claim has sufficient merit . . ." EEOC Compliance Manual §40.1.
"if the appropriate EEOC official certifies . . ." 29 C.F.R. §1601.28(a)(2), Compliance Manual §6.2. If you care, the appropriate officials are the Area Director, District Director, Director of the Office of Field Services and the Director of the Office of Systemic Programs.
The systems and programs are outlined in the EEOC Compliance Manual §2.1(e), 2.3(d), 21.1, 22.2.

p. 51 "offices should be on the lookout for retaliation cases . . ." Compliance Manual §13.3.
Thomas quotes: Joann S. Lublin, "EEOC Switches Emphasis to Litigation from Fast Settlements in Job-Bias Cases," *Wall Street Journal*, 10/28/83.
"Fact-finding conference" 29 C.F.R. §1601.15–.18.

p. 52 Negotiated settlement: 29 C.F.R. §1601.20.
"digging up the precious nuggets . . ." EEOC Compliance Manual §83.3.
"The EEOC will also close its file . . ." 29 C.F.R. §1601.19; Compliance Manual §4.2–4.9.

p. 53 "If an employer is the subject of several charges . . ." Compliance Manual §16.8.
Preconciliation conference: Compliance Manual §62.4(c).
"According to the Compliance Manual, the desired outcome . . ." Compliance Manual §64.1. Sample clauses for conciliation agreements are found in §62 Appendix A and §1100 of the Compliance Manual.
"If the EEOC does not bother . . ." *Hall v. EEOC*, 456 F.Supp. 695 (N.D. Cal. 1978); see Jerald J. Director, "Necessity and Sufficiency of Conciliation Proceedings by EEOC as Prerequisite to Civil Action," 5 *A.L.R. Fed.* 334.

p. 54 "the charging party cannot benefit by the conciliation agreement . . ." 29 C.F.R. §1601.24(c).
"The Fourth Circuit says yes . . ." *Adams v. Procter & Gamble Mfg. Co.*, 678 F.2d 1190 (4th Cir. 1982).
Suit by the EEOC: 29 C.F.R. §1601.27.

Right-to-sue letter: 29 C.F.R. §1601.28.

p. 55 ". . . the trial takes place in Federal District Court." State courts don't have jurisdiction over Title VII claims: *Valenzuela v. Kraft, Inc.*, 53 LW 2091 (9th Cir. 7/31/84).
"only Title VII claims . . ." sometimes (e.g., if the plaintiff is asking for an injunction) the case will be heard by a three-judge panel instead of a single judge.
"A jury will hear and decide on . . ." *Davis v. Burlington Industries Inc.*, 30 EPD ¶33,312 (D. Ga. 1983).
Standards for appointed counsel: *Poindexter v. FBI*, 53 LW 2040 (D.C. Cir. 6/26/84).
Preliminary relief: 29 C.F.R. §1601.23.
"Four Circuits and two District Courts . . ." 1st Cir., *Hochstadt v. Worcester Foundation for Experimental Biology Inc.*, 545 F.2d 222 (1976); 2d Cir., *Sheehan v. Purolator Courier Corp.*, 676 F.2d 877 (1981); 5th Cir., *Drew v. Liberty Mutual Insurance Co.*, 480 F.2d 69 (1973), *cert.den.*, 417 U.S. 935; 9th Cir., *Berg v. Richmond Unified School District*, 528 F.2d 1208 (1975), *vacated on other grounds*, 434 U.S. 158; D. MN, *Mead v. US Fidelity & Guaranty Co.*, 442 F.Supp. 102 (1977); D. OH, *Hyland v. Kenner Prods. Co.*, 10 FEP Cases 367 (1974). The nay-sayers are: D. AL, *McGee v. Purolator Courier Corp.*, 430 F.Supp. 1285 (1977); D. AR, *Hunter v. Ward*, 476 F.Supp. 913 (1978); D. MI, *Troy v. Shell Oil Co.*, 378 F.Supp. 1042 (1974), *app.dism.*, 519 F.2d 403 (6th Cir.); D. OK, *Collins v. Southwestern Bell*, 376 F.Supp. 979 (1974); D. WI, *Nottleson v. A.O. Smith Corp.*, 397 F.Supp. 928 (1975).

p. 56 Use of statistical breakdown: *Donaldson v. Pillsbury Co.*, 554 F.2d 825 (8th Cir. 1977), *cert.den.*, 434 U.S. 856.
Interrogatories are covered by Federal Rules of Civil Procedure (FRCP) 33; de-mands to produce by Rule 34; depositions by Rule 30b.

p. 57 Re timing requirements: 29 C.F.R. §1601.13.

p. 58 On timeliness of state charge and 300-day period:
Charge OK even if not timely under state law: 6th CIR., *Jones v. Airco Carbide Chemical Co.*, 691 F.2d 1200 (1982); 10th CIR., *Smith v. Oral Roberts Evangelistic Association*, 34 FEP Cases 1640 (1984); S.D. FL, *Platts v. Cordis Dow Corp.*, 558 F.Supp. 114 (1983); S.D. OH, *Jackson v. Ohio Bell Tel. Co.*, 555 F.Supp. 80 (1982); W.D. OK, *Morris v. UPS*, 515 F.Supp. 1317 (1981); M.D. TN, *Russell v. Belmont College*, 554 F.Supp. 667 (1982).
No good unless timely under state law: N.D. IL, *Lowell v. Glidden-Durkee*, 529 F.Supp. 17 (1981) and *O'Young v. Hobart Corp.*, 35 FEP Cases 275 (1983); N.D. IN, *Battle v. Clark Equipment*, 524 F.Supp. 683 (1981); S.D. IN, *Gunn v. Dow Chemical*, 522 F.Supp. 1172 (1981); D. KS, *Stewart v. MBPXL*, 34 FEP Cases 1667 (1982) and *Gutierrez v. Boeing Co.*, 34 FEP Cases 1666 (1982).

p. 59 ". . . asking the District Court to appoint counsel . . ." see *Millard v. La Pointe's Fashion Store, Inc.*, 34 FEP Cases 1335 (9th Cir. 1984).
Continuing violations: *Berlitz School of Languages of America v. Bartelt*, 698 F.2d 1003 (9th Cir. 1983), *cert. den.*, 104 S.Ct. 277 (1984); *Rinkel v. Associated Pipeline Contractors, Inc.*, 17 FEP Cases 224 (D. Alaska 1978).

"Another exception . . ." *Reeb v. Economic Opportunity Atlanta, Inc.*, 516 F.2d 924 (5th Cir. 1975).

pp. 60–61 "All the employer has to . . ." *Burdine v. Texas Dep't of Community Affairs*, 450 U.S. 248 (1981).

p. 61 "*all* women, or *substantially* all women . . ." *Weeks v. Southern Bell Tel. & Tel.*, 408 F.2d 228 (5th Cir. 1969).
"expert testimony that a substantial percentage of women . . ." *Cheatwood v. South Central Bell Tel. & Tel.*, 303 F.Supp. 754 (D. Ala. 1969).
Canty v. Olivarez, 452 F.Supp. 762 (D. Ga. 1978); *Anderson v. City of Bessemer City*, 717 F.2d 149 (4th Cir. 1983).
East v. Romine Inc., 518 F.2d 332 (5th Cir. 1975).
Kennedy v. Godwin, 437 F.Supp. 447 (D. Va. 1977).
Academic tenure is different from other employment decisions: for one thing, tenure is more or less lifetime employment; for another, tenure for one professor doesn't preclude tenure for another—but hiring one person keeps everyone else out of the job. So the prima facie case is different, and requires proof that a significant percentage of the departmental faculty or scholars in the field favored tenure for the plaintiff: *Zahorek v. Cornell University*, 52 LW 2517 (2d Cir. 1984).
". . . the various language schools owned by Berlitz . . ." *Berlitz School of Languages of America, Inc. v. Bartelt*, 698 F.2d 1003 (9th Cir. 1983), *cert. den.*, 104 S.Ct. 277 (1984).
"The plaintiff has to prove that her job was equal . . ." *Dunlop v. General Electric*, 401 F.Supp. 1353 (D. Va. 1975).
"Maybe a *woman's* salary . . ." *Roesel v. Joliet Wrought Washer Co.*, 596 F.2d 183 (7th Cir. 1979).
Prima facie in letter: *EEOC v. Maricopa City College District*, 35 FEP Cases 234 (9th Cir. 6/28/84).

pp. 61–62 ". . . as evidence of the employer's *intent* to discriminate . . ." *Connecticut State Employees' Association v. Connecticut*, 31 FEP Cases 191 (D. Conn. 1983).
Wilkins v. University of Houston, 654 F.2d 388 (5th Cir. 1981).

p. 62 Strategy in promotion cases: see 21 *Am.Jur. Trials* 1.

p. 63 "If the plaintiff's skills are fairly modest . . ." *Abron v. Black & Decker Mfg. Co.*, 439 F.Supp. 1095 (D. Md. 1977).
". . . just based on raw numbers . . ." *Frockt v. Olin Corp.*, 344 F.Supp. 369 (D. Ind. 1972); *Olson v. Philco-Ford*, 531 F.2d 474 (10th Cir. 1976); *Hazelwood School District v. US*, 433 U.S. 299 (1977); *Molthan v. Temple University*, 83 FRD 368 (D. Pa. 1979).
". . . relate to the employer's existing work force . . ." *James v. Stockham Valves & Fitting Co.*, 559 F.2d 310 (5th Cir. 1977), *cert. den.*, 434 U.S. 1034.
"An employer can use statistics to bolster its defense . . ." *Lieberman v. Gant*, 630 F.2d 60 (2d Cir. 1979).
"all bets are off in a small company . . ." *Harper v. TWA*, 11 FEP Cases 1074 (8th Cir. 1975).

pp. 63–64 The quote comes from Finkelstein, "The Judicial Reception of Multiple Regression Studies in Race and Sex Discrimination Cases, 80 *Columbia L. Rev.* 737 (1980); *EEOC v. McCarthy,* 32 FEP Cases 815 (D. Mass. 1983), and *Craik v. Minnesota State University Board,* 34 FEP Cases 649 (8th Cir. 1984), are recent cases approving the use of multiple-regression analysis for this purpose.

p. 64 On preliminary relief, see *Cruise v. Capital International Airways Inc.*, 8 FEP Cases 623 (E.D. Pa. 1974).

For an example of a case in which reinstatement is inappropriate, see *Bellissimo v. Westinghouse,* 34 FEP Cases 1498 (W.D. Pa. 1984). The plaintiff—a lawyer, of all things—was fired because she couldn't get along with her supervisor. She won her case by proving that the source of the friction was the supervisor's prejudice against women. But the hostility would continue if she were reinstated, and could impair her effectiveness as a lawyer—so instead of reinstatement she got a year's front pay; the court assumed she could find another job in a year.

Back pay includes overtime, health insurance, shift pay, bonuses, and raises as well as straight salary: *Pettway v. American Cast Iron Pipe Co.*, 494 F.2d 211 (5th Cir. 1974); *Amalgamated Meat Cutters v. Safeway,* 4 FEP Cases 510 (D. Kan. 1972).

Front pay: see Russell J. Davis, "Appropriateness of Particular Forms of Nonmonetary Relief," 38 *A.L.R. Fed.* 27.

p. 65 Bumping permissible: D. AR, *Cross v. Board of Education,* 394 F.Supp. 531 (1975); D. DC, *Griffiths v. Hampton,* 12 EPD ¶11,038 (1975).

Bumping not allowed: 2d CIR., *Acha v. Beame,* 531 F.2d 648 (1976); 4th CIR., *Shortt v. County of Arlington,* 589 F.2d 779 (1978); 5th CIR., *Gamble v. Birmingham S.R. Co.*, 514 F.2d 678 (1975); 6th CIR., *Thornton v. East Texas Motor Freight,* 497 F.2d 416 (1974); 8th CIR., *Reed v. Arlington Hotel Co.*, 476 F.2d 721 (1973), *cert.den.*, 414 U.S. 854.

". . . defendant has to prove mitigation of damages . . ." *Sprogis v. United Air Lines Inc.*, 517 F.2d 387 (7th Cir. 1975); *Di Salvo v. Chamber of Commerce,* 568 F.2d 593 (8th Cir. 1978); *Goodwin v. Pittsburgh,* 480 F.Supp. 627 (W.D. Pa. 1979). Just because the employer acted in good faith is no defense—the plaintiff can still get back pay: *Albemarle Paper Co. v. Moody,* 422 U.S. 405 (1975); *United Transportation Union v. Norfolk & W.R. Co.*, 532 F.2d 336 (4th Cir. 1975).

Pay discrimination doesn't constitute discharge: *Bourke v. Powell Elec. Mfg. Co.*, 617 F.2d 61 (5th Cir. 1980); *Heagney v. University of Washington,* 642 F.2d 1157 (9th Cir. 1981).

Unemployment compensation subtracted from back pay: Yes: 7th CIR., *Bowe v.Colgate-Palmolive,* 489 F.2d 896 (1969); D. CT, *Association Against Discrimination in Employment Inc. v. Weiks,* 454 F.Supp. 758 (1978); D. FL, *Diaz v. Pan American World Airways Inc.*, 346 F.Supp. 1301 (1972).

No: 3d CIR., *Craig v. Y & Y Snacks,* 33 FEP Cases 187 (1983); 4th CIR., *EEOC v. Ford Motor Co.*, 645 F.2d 183 (1981), *rev'd on other grounds,* U.S. No. 81–300 (6/28/82); 6th CIR., *Maben v. Lear Siegler Inc.*, 457 F.2d 806 (1971); 9th CIR., *Kauffman v. Sidereal Corp.*, 695 F.2d 343 (1982); 11th CIR., *Brown v. A.J. Gerrard Mfg. Co.*, 694 F.2d 1290 (Cir. 1983).

Employer ordered to remove derogatory references from employee's records:

Bellissimo v. Westinghouse, 34 FEP Cases 1498 (W.D. Pa. 1984); employer ordered to publish ads: *EEOC v. Sky King Inc.*, 34 FEP Cases 1644 (D. N.M. 1982).

p. 66 "A few cases do allow . . ." *Claiborne v. Illinois C. Railroad*, 401 F.Supp. 1022 (D. La. 1975), *aff'd in part, vacated in part on other grounds*, 583 F.2d 143; *Williams v. Owens-Illinois Inc.*, 469 F.Supp. 70 (N.D. Cal. 1979), *aff'd in part and rev'd in part on other grounds*, 665 F.2d 918; *Humphrey v. Southwestern Portland Cement Co.*, 369 F.Supp. 832 (W.D. Tex. 1973), *rev'd on other grounds*, 488 F.2d 691; *Carey v. Greyhound Lines Inc.*, 380 F.Supp. 467 (E.D. La. 1973); *Freeman v. Kelvinator*, 469 F.Supp. 999 (E.D. Mich. 1979).
". . . but most courts say no." e.g., *Harrington v. Vandalia-Butler Board of Education*, 585 F.2d 192 (6th Cir. 1978), *cert.den.*, 99 S.Ct. 2053; *Pearson v. Western Electric Co.*, 542 F.2d 1150 (10th Cir. 1976); *Evans v. Meadow Steel Prods. Inc.*, 32 EPD ¶33,935 (D.Ga. 1983); *Putterman v. Knitgoods Workers' Union*, 33 EPD ¶33,964 (D.NY. 1983). See Annotation, "Punitive Damages in Actions for Violations of Title VII," 43 *A.L.R. Fed.* 338.
Brown v. Blue Cross, 33 FEP Cases 317 (E.D. Mich. 1983).

pp. 66–67 Details of settlement and Thomas quote from 114 *Labor Relations Reporter* (BNA) 144; *Wall Street Journal* quote from Joann S. Lublin, "GM Settles Job-Bias Case for $42.5 Million," 10/19/83, p. 8.

p. 67 Liquidated damages under the EPA (unlike back pay) are unavailable if the employer acted in good faith: *Bellissimo v. Westinghouse*, 34 FEP Cases 1498 (W.D. Pa. 1984).
Definition of willfulness: *Sinclair v. Auto Club of Oklahoma*, 34 FEP Cases 1206 (10th Cir. 1984).
"EPA plaintiffs are not entitled . . ." *Altman v. Stevens Fashion Fabrics*, 441 F.Supp. 1318 (N.D. Cal. 1977); *Postemski v. Pratt & Whitney Aircraft Co.*, 443 F.Supp. 101 (D.Conn. 1977).
"Plaintiff cannot get Title VII and EPA damages . . ." *Putterman v. Knitgood Workers' Union*, 33 EPD ¶33,964 (D.NY. 1983).

pp. 67–68 "in all except 'very unusual' or 'special' circumstances . . ." *Christiansburg Garment Co. v. EEOC*, 434 U.S. 412 (1978).
"The plaintiff has 'prevailed' . . ." *Miller v. Staats*, 31 FEP Cases 976 (D.C. Cir. 1983).

p. 68 "To 'prevail' the plaintiff does not have to get everything she asks for . . ." *City of Los Angeles v. Manhart*, 51 LW 3852 (S.Ct. 1983).
"The fees involved can include . . ." *Fischer v. Adams*, 572 F.2d 406 (1st Cir. 1978); *NY Gaslight Club, Inc. v. Carey*, 100 S.Ct. 2024 (1980).
Fee award for paralegals: *Richardson v. Byrd*, 32 FEP Cases 603 (5th Cir. 1983).
Pro se fees: see Vincent M. Waldman, "Pro Se Can You Sue? Attorney Fees for Pro Se Litigants," 34 *Stanford L. Rev.* 659 (February 1982); *Laffey v. Northwest Airlines*, 32 FEP Cases 770 (D. D.C. 1983).
"The general rule . . ." but see *Laffey v. Northwest Airlines*, 53 LW 2181 (D.C. Cir. 9/28/84), which uses the firm's own rates, not the going rates, as a standard.

Factors in fee award: see *Johnson v. Georgia Highway Express Inc.*, 488 F.2d 714 (5th Cir. 1974). Contingent fee isn't necessarily a ceiling: *Sisco v. J.S. Alberici Construction Co.*, 52 LW 2677 (8th Cir. 4/24/84).

p. 69 Fee awards: Austin Wehrwein, "$1.4 M Fee in Sex Bias Case," *Nat. L. J.*, 2/21/83, p. 14.
". . . (relatively) easy to bring a civil rights class action . . ." see *Nance v. Union Carbide Corp.*, 540 F.2d 718 (4th Cir. 1976); *Rich v. Martin Marietta Corp.*, 522 F.2d 333 (10th Cir. 1975).

p. 70 "A Title VII case can be based . . ." *Universal Restaurants, Inc. v. Fellows*, 701 F.2d 447 (5th Cir. 1983).

pp. 70–71 On (b)(2) and (b)(3) class actions, see Larry W. Bridgesmith, "Representing the Title VII Class Action: A Question of Degree," 26 *Wayne L. Rev.* 1413 (September 1980). If you really want to dig in, try chapter 34 of the Schlei & Grossman treatise on employment discrimination law, and Richard Alpert, "Federal Civil Rights Class Actions," in *Federal Civil Rights Litigation 1982* (Practicing Law Institute Litigation Course Handbook #194).

p. 71 The *Am.Jur. Trials* quote is on page 164 of the Specter and Spiegelman article.
Bifurcated trial: *Mims v. Wilson*, 514 F.2d 106 (5th Cir. 1975); see 21 *Am.Jur. Trials* 157, and James L. Hughes et al., "Back Pay in Employment Discrimination Cases," 35 *Vanderbilt L. Rev.* 893 (May 1982).

CHAPTER 3

SEXUAL HARASSMENT: HEAVEN WON'T PROTECT THE WORKING GIRL

---

p. 74 The NOW definition is quoted in Marvin F. Hill, Jr., and Curtiss K. Behrens, "Love in the Office: A Guide for Dealing with Sexual Harassment under Title VII of the Civil Rights Act of 1964," 30 *DePaul L. Rev.* 581 (Spring 1981). For background, also see John B. Attanasio, "Equal Justice Under Chaos: The Developing Law of Sexual Harassment," 51 *U. Cinn. L. Rev.* 1 (1982); Alice M. Montgomery, "Sexual Harassment in the Workplace: A Practitioner's Guide to Tort Actions," 10 *Golden Gate U. L. Rev.* 879 (Summer 1980).

p. 75 The EEOC Guidelines are at 29 C.F.R. §1604.11; the quote is §1604.11(a). See EEOC Dec. No. 84–1, CCH EEOC Decisions ¶6,839: unwelcome sexual jokes, comments, and gestures aimed only at women constitute sexual harassment if they interfere unreasonably with the woman's job performance.
Barnes v. Costle, 561 F.2d 983 (D.C. Cir. 1977).

pp. 76–77 *Bundy v. Jackson*, 19 FEP Cases 828, 831 (D. D.C. 1979) and 641 F.2d 934 (D.C. Cir. 1981).

p. 77 *Neeley v. American Fidelity Assurance Co.*, 17 EPD ¶8395 (W.D. Okla. 1978).

Smith v. Rust Engineering Co., 20 FEP Cases 1172 (N.D. Ala. 1978).
". . . a 1979 case from the Southern District of Texas . . .", *Smith v. Amoco Chemical Corp.*, 20 FEP Cases 724; *Hill v. BASF Wyandotte Corp.*, 27 FEP Cases 66 (E.D. Mich. 1981) is similar.
Fisher v. Flynn, 598 F.2d 663 (1st Cir. 1979).

p. 78 *Clark v. World Airways*, 24 FEP Cases 305 (D. D.C. 1980).
Halpert v. Wertheim, 24 EPD ¶31,243 (S.D.N.Y. 1980). After all, coarse language can offend men as well as women; and, as EEOC Decision #70401, 2 FEP Cases 427 (1970), says, it's not actionable harassment if men are treated just as badly as women.
Walter v. KFGO Radio, 518 F.Supp. 1309 (D. N.D. 1981).
". . . harassment by a female supervisor . . ." *Huebschen v. Department of Health and Social Services*, 32 EPD ¶33,812 (7th Cir. 1983).
Sexually provocative uniform: EEOC Dec. No. 77–36 (1977), CCH EEOC Dec. ¶6588, *aff'd, EEOC v. Sage Realty*, 87 FRD 365 (S.D.N.Y. 1980).
Heelan v. Johns-Manville Corp., 451 F.Supp. 1382 (D. Colo. 1978).
"A 1981 Tennessee case . . ." *Morgan v. Hertz Corp.*, 542 F.Supp. 123 (W.D. Tenn. 1981).

p. 79 *Koster v. Chase Manhattan Bank*, 554 F.Supp. 283 (S.D.N.Y. 1983).
". . . an environment heavily charged with discrimination . . ." *Rogers v. EEOC*, 454 F.2d 234 (5th Cir. 1971), *cert.den.*, 406 U.S. 957 (1972)—though an impartially offensive atmosphere with equal racism for all, where the Spic's colleagues are referred to as the Polack, Yid, Wop, and Mick, is the equivalent of no harassment: *Bradford v. Sloan Paper Co.*, 383 F.Supp. 1157 (D. Ala. 1974).
Brown v. City of Guthrie, 22 FEP Cases 1627 (W.D. Okla. 1980).
Henson v. City of Dundee, 682 F.2d 897 (11th Cir. 1982).

p. 80 *Robson v. Eva's Super Market, Inc.*, 538 F.Supp. 857 (N.D. Oh. 1982).
Phillips v. Smalley Management Services, 32 FEP Cases 975 (11th Cir. 1983).
Katz v. Dole, 31 FEP Cases 1521 (4th Cir. 1983).
Ferguson v. Du Pont, 560 F.Supp. 1172 (D. Del. 1983); semble *Cummings v. Walsh Construction Co.*, 561 F.Supp. 872 (D. Ga. 1983). EEOC Guidelines: 29 C.F.R. §1604.11. Also see EEOC Dec. No. 84–3, EPD ¶6841, holding a restaurant owner liable for harassment committed by a frequent customer against the waitresses. The theory was that the harasser was a friend of the owner's and would have improved his behavior if admonished.
"The Guidelines are entitled to deference . . ." *Ferguson v. Du Pont*.

p. 81 *Martin v. Norbar, Inc.*, 537 F.Supp. 1260 (S.D. Ohio 1982).
Meyers v. ITT Diversified Credit Corp., 527 F.Supp. 1064 (E.D. Mo. 1981); *Davis v. Western-Southern Life Ins. Co.*, 34 FEP Cases 97 (N.D. Ohio 2/14/84).
Munford v. James T. Barnes & Co., 441 F.Supp. 459 (E.D. Mich. 1977).
Barnes v. Costle, 561 F.2d 983 (D.C. Cir. 1977).
Craig v. Y & Y Snacks, Inc., 33 FEP Cases 187 (3d Cir. 1983).
On liability of the employer for harassment in violation of policy: *Cummings v. Walsh Construction Co.*, 561 F.Supp. 872 (D. Ga. 1983).

p. 82 *Zabkowicz v. West Bend Co.*, 35 FEP Cases 610 (E.D. Wis. 7/23/84).

Fisher Foods, Inc., 80 LA 133 (1983); *University of Mississippi Health Sciences Center*, 78 LA 417 (1982). See Marmo, "Arbitrating Sex Harassment Cases," 35 *Arbitration J.* 35 (1980).

p. 83 "Courts are split . . ." Arbitration or other internal grievance procedure required: *Meyers v. ITT Diversified Credit Corp.*, 527 F.Supp. 1064 (E.D. Mo. 1981); arbitration not required, *Cummings v. Walsh Construction Co.*, 561 F.Supp. 872 (D. Ga. 1983).

". . . the entire Title VII song and dance . . ." see, e.g., *Stringer v. Pennsylvania*, 446 F.Supp. 704 (M.D. Pa. 1978), and *Shaffer v. National Can Corp.*, 565 F.Supp. 909 (D. Pa. 1983), on timeliness of sexual harassment charges.

". . . the victim has to sue the employer . . ." and on pendent jurisdiction: *Guyette v. Stauffer Chemical Co.*, 518 F.Supp. 521 (D.N.J. 1981).

On pendent jurisdiction, see *Rogers v. Loew's L'Enfant Plaza Hotel*, 526 F.Supp. 523 (D. D.C. 1982), and *Phillips v. Smalley Maintenance Services*, 32 FEP Cases 975 (11th Cir. 1983).

"However, even an at-will employee . . ." *Monge v. Beebe Rubber Co.*, 114 N.H. 130, 316 A.2d 549 (1974).

Suit for battery: *Brown v. Winn-Dixie Montgomery Inc.*, 31 EPD ¶33,577 (Fla. 1983).

"Only five states . . ." CT §46a–60(8); IL, see EPD ¶22,422.01; MI §37.2103(h); MN §363.01(1)—see *Continental Can Co. v. State*, one of the few cases making the employer responsible for actions of nonsupervisory co-employees; WI §111.321.

". . . used in much the same way . . ." see, e.g., *Robles v. Bear, Stearns & Co.*, 30 EPD ¶33,221 (N.Y. 1982); *SUNY v. State Human Rights Appeals Board*, 438 N.Y.S.2d 643 (N.Y. 1981).

On constructive discharge: *Young v. Southwestern Savings & Loan Ass'n*, 509 F.2d 140 (5th Cir. 1975); *Continental Can Co. v. State*, 297 N.W.2d 241 (Minn. 1980). However, there is no constructive discharge if the employee welcomes the comments, contributes to them, and doesn't indicate until the suit is filed that such comments were intolerable or caused her to quit her job: *Gan v. Kepro Circuit Systems, Inc.*, 28 FEP Cases 639 (E.D. Mo. 1982).

New York Human Rights Law: *Rudow v. NYC Comm'n on Human Rights*, 34 EPD ¶34,359 (N.Y. 1984).

Caldwell v. Hodgeman, 25 FEP Cases 1647 (D. Mass. 1981).

p. 84 No unemployment benefits for harasser: *Rivera v. Adm'r*, 34 FEP Cases 894 (La. 1984).

Conspiracy action by state employees: *Skadegaard v. Farrell*, 33 FEP Cases 1528 (D.NJ. 1984).

On elements of a prima facie case, see John B. Attanasio, "Equal Justice Under Chaos," 51 *U.Cinn.L.Rev.* 1 (1982); John F. Major, "Wrongful Discharge of At-Will Employee: Sexual Harassment," 29 *Am.Jur. POF2d* 335; *Neidhart v. D.H. Holmes Co.*, 21 FEP Cases 452 (E.D. La. 1979); *Hosemann v. Technical Materials Inc.*, 554 F.Supp. 659 (D. R.I. 1982); *Henson v. City of Dundee*, 682 F.2d 897 (11th Cir. 1982); *Phillips v. Smalley Maintenance Services*, 32 FEP Cases 975 (11th Cir. 1983); *Lamb v. Drilco Division*, 32 FEP Cases 105 (S.D. Tex. 1983).

p. 85 "The District Court for the Northern District of California . . ." *Priest v. Rotary*, 52 LW 2137 (N.D. Cal. 8/19/83).

Injunctions against further harassment: see, e.g., *Morgan v. Hertz*, 542 F.Supp. 123 (D. Tenn. 1981); for back pay, see, e.g., *Coley v. Consolidated Rail Corp.*, 561 F.Supp. 645 (D. Mich. 1982); *Kyriazi v. Western Electric Co.*, 476 F.Supp. 335 (D. N.J. 1979).

On damages in general, see Note, "Legal Remedies for Employment-related Sexual Harassment," 64 *Minn. L. Rev.* 151 (1979).

". . . and a penitent employer offers . . ." *Davis v. Western-Southern Life Ins. Co.*, 34 FEP Cases 97 (N.D. Ohio 1984).

CHAPTER 4

NON-EMPLOYMENT DISCRIMINATION

---

p. 88 References on state ERAs: Paul M. Kurtz, "The State Equal Rights Amendments and Their Impact on Domestic Relations Law," 11 *Fam. Law. Q.* 101 (1977); Dawn-Marie Driscoll and Barbara J. Rouse, "Through a Glass Darkly: A Look at State Equal Rights Amendments," 12 *Suffolk U. L. Rev.* 1282 (1978); G. Alan Tarr and Mary Cornelia Porter, "Gender Equality and Judicial Federalism: The Role of State Appellate Courts," 9 *Hastings Con. L. Q.* 919 (1982); Judith I. Avner and Kim E. Greene, "State ERA Impact on Family Law," 8 Fam. L. Rep. 4023 (1982); Francis J. Flaherty, "Wins Grow Under State ERAs," *Nat. L. J.*, 9/19/83; p. 3; special section on state constitutional law, *Nat. L. J.*, 3/12/84, p. 30.

The seventeen state ERAs are (all references are to the state Constitutions): AK art. 1 §3; CO art. 2 §29; CT art. 1 §20; HI art. 1 §4; IL art. 1 §18; LA art. 1 §2; MD art. 46; MA Part I, art. 1; MT art. 2 §4; NH Part 1, art. 2; NM art. 2 §18; PA art. 1 §28; TX art. 1 §3a; UT art. 4 §1; VA art. 1 §11; WA art. 31 §1; WY art. 6 §1.

p. 89 ". . . typical, just typical . . ." *Fluker v. State*, 248 Ga. 290, 282 S.E.2d 112 (Ga. 1981), is an interesting case upholding a state law that defined a "pander" as a man who obtained clients for a female prostitute. The luckless Mr. Fluker's lawyer challenged the statute on equal-protection grounds. The court was unsympathetic, stating that, since women bore all the risk of pregnancy and much of the risk of violence and venereal disease, the statute wasn't unconstitutional even though it spared male prostitutes and their madams.

On the ECOA see Gail R. Reizenstein, "A Fresh Look at the Equal Credit Opportunity Act," 14 *Akron L. Rev.* 215 (Fall 1980), and Susan Smith Blakely, "Credit Opportunity for Women: The Equal Credit Opportunity Act and its Effects," 4 *Wisconsin L. Rev.* 655 (1981).

The Equal Credit Opportunity Act is 15 U.S.C.S. §1691–1691f; Regulation B is 12 C.F.R. Part 202.

ECOA applies to consumer leases: *Brothers v. First Leasing*, 724 F.2d 789 (9th Cir. 1/24/84), *cert.den.*, 53 LW 3210.

p. 90 12 C.F.R. §202.5 gives these as possible factors in determining the probability that alimony or child support payments will be made consistently:

- written agreement or court order
- enforcement mechanisms available
- length of time payments have been received
- reliability of payments
- payor's creditworthiness.

Miller v. American Express 688 F.2d 1235 (9th Cir. 1982).
About the applicant's husband: the Federal Trade Commission has published an advisory opinion (which isn't binding on creditors) that a creditor is entitled to request a credit report on a credit applicant's husband in only four situations:

- The husband is also liable on the account
- He's entitled to use the account
- The applicant lives in a community-property state
- She relies on his income in whole or in part to justify granting credit.

p. 91 ". . . can bring private suits against the malefactors . . ." ECOA cases are always—and necessarily—jury trials because of the way the statute is written: *Vander Missen v. Kellogg-Citizens National Bank,* 83 FRD 206 (E.D. Wis. 1979). Damages for embarrassment and harm to reputation: *Shuman v. Standard Oil of California,* 453 F.Supp. 450 (N.D. Cal. 1978).
Disparate impact analysis: Reizenstein article cited above.
Markham v. Colonial Mortgage Service Ass'n Inc., 605 F.2d 566 (D.C. Cir. 1979). Plaintiffs don't always win: in *Haynes v. Bank of Wedowee,* 434 F.2d 266 (5th Cir. 1981), the bank relied on a couple's joint checking account in lending money to the wife; when the husband declared bankruptcy, it wasn't a violation of ECOA for the bank to find that she was in default on the loan, or to accelerate maturity (declare the entire amount due) and apply funds in the joint checking account to the debt.

p. 92 References on sex discrimination in education: Jeffrey F. Ghent, "Application of State Law to Sex Discrimination in Sports," 66 *A.L.R.*3d 1262; June E. Jensen, "Title IX and Intercollegiate Athletics: HEW Gets Serious About Equality in Sports?" 15 *New England L. Rev.* 573 (Summer 1979); Nancy Peterson, "*Lieberman v. University of Chicago:* Refusal to Imply a Damages Remedy under Title IX," 1983 *Wis. L. Rev.* 181 (Jan–Feb); Kathleen Sylvester, "Ruling Sets Stage for Further Bias Policy Change," *Nat. L. J.,* 3/12/84, p. 5.
". . . all applications for federal funds . . ." 34 C.F.R. §106.4(a).

p. 93 "At the high-school level . . ." *Newberg v. Board of Public Education* (Pennsylvania Common Pleas No. 5822, 8/30/83).
Grove City College v. Bell, 52 LW 4283 (S.Ct. 2/28/84).
"The Third Circuit held . . ." *Haffer v. Temple University,* 524 F.Supp. 531 (E.D. Pa. 1981), *aff'd,* 688 F.2d 14. The athletic regs also appear in the Department of Health and Human Services Regulations, at 45 C.F.R. Part 86.

"In 1983, the Fifth Circuit . . ." *Iron Arrow Honor Society v. Schweiker*, 702 F.2d 549 (5th Cir. 1983). The court did not apply the fraternity/sorority exemption because the court's reading of the legislative history shows that the exemption was designed to reach only "social" clubs, not those with implications for students' later professional careers. (But don't people network with their fraternity brothers or sorority sisters?)

p. 94 ". . . it doesn't recompense *victims* of discrimination in education . . ." *Lieberman v. University of Chicago*, 660 F.2d 1185 (7th Cir. 1981); *Cannon v. University of Chicago*, 441 U.S. 677 (1979) (private right of action exists); *on remand*, 710 F.2d 351 (7th Cir. 1983) (but not for damages).
"But a school *employee* . . ." *Strong v. Demopolis County Board of Education*, 515 F.Supp. 730 (S.D. Ala. 1981). She probably wouldn't have an Equal Pay Act claim, because male coaches of boys' teams probably coached different sports, with larger teams and more practice sessions—so the two jobs would not be considered equal. Also see *Erickson v. Bd. of Ed., Proviso Township*, 120 Ill.App.3d 264, 458 N.E.2d 84 (1984).
"The Court of Appeals, New York's highest court . . ." *Matter of Estate of Wilson*, 465 N.Y.S.2d 900, 452 N.E.2d 1228, 52 N.Y. 461 (1983).
"A few months earlier, an intermediate appeals court . . ." *Matter of Johnson*, 93 AD.2d 1, 460 N.Y.S.2d 932 (1983).

p. 95 "In 1982, an Illinois District Court . . ." *O'Connor v. Board of Education*, 545 F.Supp. 376 (D. Ill. 1982).

p. 96 "But the next year . . ." *Force by Force v. Pierce City School Dist.*, 570 F.Supp. 1020 (D. Mo. 1983).
"New York upheld . . ." *Forte v. Board of Education*, 105 Misc.2d 36, 431 N.Y.S.2d 321 (1980); semble *Petrie v. Illinois High School Assoc.*, 75 Ill.App.3d 980, 394 N.E.2d 855 (1979).
"In Washington—an ERA state . . ." *Darrin v. Gould*, 85 Wash.2d 859, 540 P.2d 882 (1975).
"A similar decision has been reached . . ." *Commonwealth v. Pennsylvania Interscholastic Athletic Association*, 334 A.2d 839 (1975).
". . . has struck down a proposed bill . . ." *Opinion of Justices*, 374 Mass. 836, 371 N.E.2d 426 (1977).
". . . and a rule keeping boys . . ." *Attorney General v. Mass. Interscholastic Athletic Ass'n*, 393 N.E.2d 284 (Mass. 1979).
". . . one found that separate girls' and boys' basketball leagues . . ." *Michigan Dep't of Civil Rights ex rel Forton v. Waterford Township Department of Parks and Recreation*, 335 N.W.2d 204 (Mich. 1983). The court also applied Michigan's statute forbidding sex discrimination in public accommodations.
"The other case did not find an equal protection violation . . ." *Striebel v. Minnesota State High School League*, 321 N.W.2d 400 (Minn. 1982).
". . . they can recover from a teachers' union . . ." *United Teachers of Seaford v. New York State Human Rights Appeals Board*, 68 A.D.2d 907, 414 N.Y.S.2d 207 (1979).

". . . if the female coaches' lower salary . . .." *Kings Park Central School District v. State Division of Human Rights*, 74 A.D.2d 570, 424 N.Y.S.2d 293 (1980).

p. 97 "Private clubs are also exempt . . ." 42 U.S.C.S. §2000e(b)(2); *Kemerer v. Davis*, 520 F.Supp. 256 (D. Mich. 1981); EEOC Dec. No. 83–10, CCH EEOC Dec. ¶6837, found that there was no actionable sex discrimination in the employment practices of an organization created to support medical research, because it was a bona fide private club with only one, tax-exempt purpose (ack: owledgment of medical research); it was entirely owned and controlled by members who were medical researchers; there were no public advertisements to attract new members; the organization did not earn profits or pay dividends to investors; and all surplus funds were applied to advance medical research.

"The Civil Rights Act of 1964 . . ." 42 U.S.C.S. §2002(a)(3).

". . . thirty-two states have civil rights laws . . ." AK §18.80.230; CA Civ §51; CO §24–34–501; CT §53–35; DE T6 §4504; FL §509.101; ID §67–5909; IL ch 68 §5–101; IA §601A.2(10); KS §44–1002; KY §344.145; LA Const. art. 1 §2; ME T5 §4591; MD T49B §5; MA ch. 272 §98; MI §28.343; MN §363.03(3); MT §49–1–102; NB §20–133; NH §354–A:8(IV); NJ §10:1–2; NM §4–33–7(F); NY Civ. Rts. §40; ND §12.1–14–04; OR §30.675; PA T43 §953; RI §11–24–4; SD §20–13–29; TN §4–21–111; UT §13–7–3; WV §5–11–9(f); WI §942.04.

p. 98 "New York ruled . . ." *U.S. Power Squadron v. State Human Rights Appeal Board*, 465 N.Y.S.2d 871 (N.Y. 1983).

". . . therefore need not become the Boy's and Girl's Club . . ." *Isbister v. Boy's Club of Santa Cruz Inc.*, 192 Cal.Rptr. 560, 144 Cal. App.3d 360 (1983).

"A man belonging to a Connecticut club . . ." *Cross v. Midtown Club*, 33 Conn. Sup 150, 365 A.2d 1227 (1976).

p. 99 ". . . was not a place of public accommodation . . ." *U.S. Jaycees v. Mass. Comm. Against Discrimination* (Sup.Jud.Ct. M–3078, 4/3/84); *U.S. Jaycees v. Richardet*, 666 P.2d 1008 (Alaska 1983); *U.S. Jaycees v. Bloomfield*, 434 A.2d 1379 (D.C. 1981).

"The Eighth Circuit reversed . . ." *U.S. Jaycees v. McClure*, 709 F.2d 1560 (8th Cir. 1983); Supreme Court argument No. 83–724, 52 LW 3785 4/18/84, decision, 52 LW 5076 7/3/84.

Strategies come from Michael M. Burns, "The Exclusion of Women from Influential Men's Clubs: The Inner Sanctum and the Myth of Full Equality," 18 *Harvard Civil Rights/Civil Liberties L. Rev.* 321 (Summer 1983).

". . . because the club has a liquor license . . ." *Moose Lodge v. Irvis*, 407 U.S. 163 (1972); ". . . some courts will add up . . ." *Citizens Council on Human Relations v. Buffalo Yacht Club*, 438 F.Supp. 316 (W.D.N.Y. 1977) ($1 a year lease of city property, restaurant and liquor licenses issued by city, club's assumption of state function by controlling access to adjacent park).

p. 100 "Maryland did this . . ." no by-line, "Maryland Acts to End Tax Exemption for Male Country Club," *New York Times*, 8/4/83.

"One state . . ." South Carolina §11–9–15.

Unisex insurance references: Jeanette Blevins, "Challenges to Sex-Based Mortality

Tables in Insurance and Pensions," 6 *Women's Rights L. Rep.* 59 (Fall–Winter 1980); Stephen R. Kaufman, "Banning 'Actuarially Sound' Discrimination: The Proposed Nondiscrimination in Insurance Act," 20 *Harv. J. Legislation* 631 (Summer 1983); Burke A. Christensen, "Reasonable Sex Discrimination," 122 *Trusts and Estates* 57 (October 1983).

p. 101 "Figures from the American Council of Life Insurance . . ." Daniel Seligman, "Insurance and the Price of Sex," *Fortune,* 2/21/83, p. 84.

p. 102 "The first state . . ." MT Laws 1983 ch 531.
"Four states . . ." HI §294.33; MA ch 175 §113B, 175E §4; MI §500. 2109; NC §58–30.4.
"Pennsylvania's Insurance Commissioner . . ." *Hartford Accident and Indemnity Co. v. Insurance Commissioner,* 442 A.2d 382 (Pa. 1982). See Tamar Lewin, "Equal Rights Ruling for Auto Insurance Expected to Spread," *New York Times,* 10/23/84, p. A18.
On the other hand, a Louisiana court upheld sex-based auto insurance rates: *Insurance Services Organization v. Commissioner of Insurance,* 381 So.2d 515 (1979). On Pennsylvania consent decree, see Francis J. Flaherty, "The 'Unisex' Policy Uproar," *Nat. L. J.* 2/28/83, p. 1. You win some, you lose some: the Ninth Circuit said that sex-based disability insurance rates did not violate the Ku Klux Klan Act—the claim of discriminatory motive wasn't strong enough—and the insurance commissioner's cursory application review didn't constitute "state action": *Life Insurance Co. of North America v. Reichardt,* 591 F.2d 499 (9th Cir. 1979).
"The IRS now uses . . ." Prop. Regs. §20.2031–7, 25.2512–5.

p. 103 On surnames: Ronald A. Case, "Right of Married Women to Use Maiden Surname," 67 A.L.R.3d 1266.

p. 104 "A number of courts have ruled . . ." AZ: *Malone v.Sullivan,* 124 Ariz. 469, 605 P.2d 447 (1980); FL: *Petition of Hooper,* 436 So.2d 401 (1983); NB: *Simmons v. O'Brien,* 201 Neb. 778, 272 N.W.2d 273 (1978); NJ: *In re Application of Lawrence,* 133 N.J. Super. 408, 337 A.2d 49 (1975); OH: *Ball v. Brown,* 450 F.Supp. 4 (D. Ohio 1977); VA: *In re Miller,* 218 Va. 939, 243 S.E.2d 464 (1978).
"Requiring a married employee . . ." *Allen v. Lovejoy,* 553 F.2d 522 (6th Cir. 1977). Mote in your neighbor's eye, beam in yours department: the plaintiff's birth name is Hill; Allen is her husband's name.
". . . allowed to register to vote . . ." *State v. Taylor,* 415 So.2d 1043 (Ala. 1982).
"Regulation B . . ." 12 C.F.R. §202.7(b).
Information on tax returns and Social Security is from Julian Block, "Name dropping . . . self-help guide," *Vogue,* March 1983, p. 176.

p. 105 "Several state laws requiring . . ." FL: *Sydney v. Pingree,* 565 F.Supp. 412 (D. Fla. 1982); HI: *Jech v. Burch,* 446 F.Supp. 714 (D. Hawaii 1979); NC: *O'Brien v. Tilson,* 523 F.Supp. 494 (D. N.C. 1981).
"Other states have case law . . ." MA: *Secretary of Commonwealth v. City Clerk of Lowell,* 373 Mass. 178, 366 N.E.2d 717 (1977); NB: *Cohee v. Cohee,* 210 Neb. 855, 317 N.W.2d 381 (1982).

"Changing an existing kid's name . . ."   e.g., *Application of Saxton*, 309 N.W.2d 298 (Minn. 1981).

"It's fairly well settled that Title VII does not apply . . ."   see Donna L. Wise, "Challenging Sexual Preference Discrimination in Private Employment," 41 *Ohio St. L. J.* 501 (Fall 1980), and Russell J. Davis, "Refusal to Hire, or Dismissal from Employment, on Account of Plaintiff's Sexual Lifestyle . . ."   78 *A.L.R.3d* 18, for citations.

Society for Individual Rights, Inc. v. Hampton, 6 EPD ¶8934 (D. Cal. 1973).

p. 106 *Acanford v. Board of Education*, 359 F.Supp. 843 (D. Md. 1973), *aff'd on other grounds*, 491 F.2d 498, *cert.den.*, 419 U.S. 836.

Gay Law Students Association v. Pacific Tel. & Tel., 24 Cal.3d 458, 156 Cal.Rptr. 14, 595 P.2d 592 (1979).

Statute void for vagueness: *Burton v. Cascade School District*, 512 F.2d 850 (9th Cir. 1975); the statute is from Oregon.

Advocacy of homosexuality: *National Gay Task Force v. Board of Education of Oklahoma City, cert. granted*, from 34 EPD ¶34,357 (10th Cir. 1984).

Discharge for homosexual conduct: *Beller v. Middendorf*, 632 F.2d 788 (9th Cir. 1980), *cert.den.*, 452 U.S. 905—see Becky Morrow, "Military Ban on Homosexuals Widely Litigated," 106 *New Jersey L. J.* 449 (11/20/80).

Reinstatement of reservist: *Ben Shalom v. Sec'y of the Army*, 489 F.Supp. 964 (E.D. Wis. 1980).

Valdes v. Lumbermen's Mutual Cas. Co., 507 F.Supp. 10 (S.D. Fla. 1980).

pp. 106–107 Graduate student: *Naragon v. Wharton*, 33 FEP Cases 61 (M.D. La. 9/30/83).

p. 107 Housing discrimination: *Hubert v. Williams*, 184 Cal.Rptr. 161 (Superior Ct. 1982)—though A.B. 1, a bill forbidding sexual preference discrimination in employment, was vetoed by Governor Deukmejian on 3/13/84. In New York City, since 1983, tenants have had the right to have one person not named on the lease living with them—regardless of the sex of the other person, or the nature of the relationship, and regardless of whether the lease forbids apartment-sharing. But before that, the case of *Avest 7th Corp. v. Ringelheim*, 458 N.Y.S.2d 903 (A.D. 1982), forbade a landlord from evicting a lesbian tenant on the grounds that the lover who lived with her wasn't a member of her "immediate family," in violation of the lease.

Cohabitation with a woman: *Kenney v. Kenney*, 78 Misc.2d 927, 352 N.Y.S.2d 344 (Sup. 1974).

Lesbian mothers: e.g., *Nadler v. Superior Court*, 255 Cal.App.2d 523, 63 Cal.Rptr. 352 (1967); *DiStefano v. DiStefano*, 401 N.Y.S.2d 636, 60 A.D.2d 976 (1978); *Bezro v. Patenaude*, 410 N.E.2d 1207 (Mass. 1980); *Hall v. Hall*, 291 N.W.2d 143, 95 Mich.App. 614 (1980); *Kallas v. Kallas*, 614 P.2d 641 (Utah 1980); *D.H. v. J.H.*, 418 N.E.2d 286 (Ind.App. 1981); *Jacobson v. Jacobson*, 314 N.W.2d 78 (N.D. 1981).

"Convicted defendants appeal . . ."   sometimes this approach works, sometimes it doesn't: e.g., *Tucker v. State*, 417 So.2d 1006 (Fla. 1982); *State v. Baker*, 636 S.W.2d 902 (Mo. 1982); *State v. Taylor*, 643 S.W.2d 14 (Mo. 1982). A similar argument is sometimes raised—with even less success—about the number of women serving as jury or grand jury forepersons.

p. 108 ". . . to *forbid* women from serving on juries at all . . ." The first quote is from *Ballard v. U.S.*, 329 U.S. 187, 195 (1946); the second, from *Taylor v. Louisiana,* 419 U.S. 522,537 (1974).
"It isn't permissible . . ." *U.S. v. Zirpolo,* 450 F.2d 424 (3d Cir. 1978).
"Federal and some state laws . . ." Jury Selection and Service Act, 28 U.S.C.S. §1861; e.g., New Jersey §2A:72–2, 10:1–7.
"It's no good either . . ." *Duren v. Missouri,* 439 U.S. 357 (1979).
"You think *you* have problems . . ." *Machetti v. Linahan,* 679 F.2d 236 (11th Cir. 1982).
"Virginia and Georgia . . ." *Archer v. Mayes,* 213 Va. 638, 194 S.E.2d 707 (1973); *U.S. v. Rosenthal,* 482 F.Supp. 867 (M.D. Ga. 1979).
". . . but Florida found . . ." *Anthony v. Alachua County Court Executive,* 418 So.2d 264 (Fla. 1982).

pp. 108–109 *Porter v. Freeman,* 577 F.2d 329 (5th Cir. 1978).

p. 109 "Many states excuse lawyers . . ." Katherine Bishop, "A Question of Bias?" *Nat. L. J.,* 3/28/83, p. 2, 7/11/83, p. 34.
"Which obligated a married woman . . ." *Crosby v. Crosby,* 434 So.2d 162 (La. 1983).
"A department store's practice . . ." *Becnel v. City Stores Co.,* 675 F.2d 731 (5th Cir. 1982).
". . . consortium . . . to men . . ." *Conser v. Biddy,* 625 S.W.2d 457 (Ark. 1981).
". . . allowing widows but not widowers . . ." *Hall v. McBride,* 416 So.2d 986 (Ala. 1982).
"But an Arkansas law . . ." *Swafford v. Tyson Foods Inc.,* 621 S.W.2d 862 (Ark. 1981).
"Washington State limitation . . ." *Maxwell v. Department of Social Services,* 30 Wash.App. 591, 636 P.2d 1102 (1981).

p. 110 A Louisiana policy . . ." *McMurry v. Phelps,* 533 F.Supp. 742 (D. La. 1982).
"But Kentucky was allowed . . ." *Canterino v. Wilson,* 546 F.Supp. 174 (D. Ky. 1982) and 562 F.Supp. 106 (D. Ky. 1983).
"A consent decree that sets standards . . ." *Eldredge v. Koch,* 118 Misc.2d 163, 459 N.Y.S.2d 960 (1983).
"Woman runners and organizations of runners . . ." *Martin v. International Olympic Commission,* 53 LW 2047 (9th Cir. 6/21/84).

CHAPTER 5

SELF-DEFENSE AND DOMESTIC VIOLENCE

p. 113 "Most states further refine this . . ." for an interesting discussion that relates domestic violence to the law of self-defense, see Note, "Intramarital As-

saults," 10 *Rutgers-Camden L. J.* 643 (1979). Sixteen states (AL, AZ, CO, CT, FL, IL, IO, MN, NB, NC, OR, PA, SC, TX, UT, WV) don't require retreat when a person is attacked at work—see 41 *A.L.R.*2d 584.
"Several state statutes . . ."   AZ §13–411(A); CO §18–1–704(2)(C); HI §703–304(2); KY §503.050(2); NJ §2A:113–6; NY Penal §35.15(2); TX Penal T2 §9.32(3)(B); UT §76–2–402; VT T13 §2305(2).
". . . while other statutes say . . ."   e.g., AR §41–507(a), NM §40A–2–8; ND §12.1–05–07; WA §9A.16.050.

p. 114 "But it's permissible for a person . . ."   see, e.g., *People v. Lenzi*, 41 Ill.App.3d 825, 355 N.E.2d 153 (1976); *People v. Harding*, 29 Ill.App.3d 1053, 331 N.E.2d 653 (1975).

p. 115 *People v. Shields*, 18 Ill.App.3d 1080, 331 N.E.2d 212 (1974).
State v. Wanrow, 559 P.2d 548,558; 88 Wash.2d 221,231 (1977).

p. 116 For general reference, see Lisa G. Lerman, Franci Livingston and Vicki Jackson, "State Legislation on Domestic Violence," 6 *Response to Violence in the Family* No. 5 (September/October 1983), and Lisa G. Lerman, "Mediation of Wife Abuse Cases: The Adverse Impact of Informal Dispute Resolution on Women," 7 *Harv. Women's Law J.* 57 (Spring 1984). Anything in the present tense ("Lerman says" "Lerman warns") is a paraphrase from an interview on 11/8/83, during a very pleasant lunch in a Washington Chinese restaurant. See also Barbara K. Finesmith, "Police Responses to Battered Women: A Critique and Proposals for Reform," 14 *Seton Hall L.Rev.* 74 (1983).

p. 119 "However, the statutes of twenty-one states . . ."   AK §18.65.510; AZ §13.3601; HI §709–906(3); IL §2304–41; ME T15 §301(D); MD art. 27 §11F(C); MA ch 209A §1; MO §455.080; NB §42–927; NH §173–B:1; NJ §2C:25–1; ND §14–07.2–01; OH §3113.31; OK T22 §40.2; OR §108.620(d); RI §11–5–9; UT §30–6–8; VA §9–109(3); WA §10.99.020; WI §165.85(4)(b); WY §35–21–101.
State laws on shelter funding: AL §30–6–6; AK §18.65.510; AZ §25.311.01; CA Welfare & Institutions §18291; CO 1983 Session Laws HB 1050; CT §17–31K; FL §409.607; GA §19–13–20; ID §39–5201; IL ch 40 §2401; IN §4–23–17.5; KS §23–108; KY §209.160; LA §46:2121; ME T22 §8501; MD art. 88A §101; MI §400.1501; MN §241.61; MS 1983 Session Laws HB 670; MO §455:200; MT §40–2–401; NB §42–907; NH §773–B:12, 457:29; NJ §30:14–1; NY Social Services §2–31(a); NC 1982 Session Laws HB 1148; ND §4–03–21; OH §3113.33; OK 1983 Session Laws SB 47; OR §106.045; PA 1982 Session Laws 851; SD 1983 Session Laws HB 1086; TX Human Resources §51.001; UT §30–6–9; VT T32 §1712(1); VA §63.1–316; WY §35–21–101.
"Connoisseurs of gallows humor . . ."   the states are AL, AR, CA, FL, ID, IL, IN, KS, KY, MD (imposed by county), MI, MN, MO (county), MT, NV, NH, NJ, ND, OH, OR, SD, VT, VA, and WV. See Lerman, Livingston & Jackson at pp. 12–13.
"Seven states (Arkansas . . .)"   AR §41.1653; CA Penal §273.5; IN §35–42–2–1(2)(D) (second offense); OH §2919.25; RI §11–5–9; TN §39–2–105; TX Penal T5 §22.01(a)(C).

"Forty-three states have laws of this type . . ." AL §30–5–1; AK §09.55.600; AZ §13.3602; CA Civil §4359, Civil Procedure §527.6; CO §14–4–101; CT §46B–15; DE T10 §902; FL §741.30; GA §19–13.2; HI §580–1; IL ch 40 §2301–1; IN 1983 Session Laws SB 295; IA §236–1; KS §60–3101; KY §403.710; LA §46:2134; MA ch 209A §1; ME T19 §761; MD Courts §4–404; MN §518B.01; MS §93–21–1; MO §455.010; MT §29–19–201; NB §42–901; NV §33.020; NH §173–B:1; NJ §2C:25–1; NY Family Court §800; NC §50B–1; ND §14–07.1; OH §3113.31; OR §133.055; PA T35 §10182; SD §25–10–1; TN §36–1201; TX Family T4 §71.01; UT §30–6–1; VT T15 §1101; WA §10.99.020; WV §48.2A–1; WI §813.025(2)(a); WY §35–21–101.

"In about half the states . . ." AL (common-law spouses), AK, CO, CT, GA, HI, IL, IA, KS, ME, MN, MS, MO, NH, NJ, OH, OR (cohabiting one year or more), PA (living as spouses), RI, TX, UT, WA, WY (living as spouses).

"The statutes are tricky . . ." The Tennessee statute is especially convoluted. Tenn. Code Ann. §36–1203 says, "Any and all who have been subjected to or threatened with abuse by a present adult family or household member may seek relief under this chapter by filing a sworn petition alleging such abuse by the respondent." The *next* paragraph says, "It is declared to be the legislative intent of this chapter that it shall apply only to husbands and wives who have been and are at the time of the seeking of the relief, legally married." Go figure it.

p. 121 Order of Protection provisions: a recent New York case, *Karten v. Stanger, N.Y.L.J.*, 7/26/84, p. 15, is unusual in that it allows an Order of Protection to dictate a property distribution.

"The Alaska and Colorado statutes obligate . . ." AK §25.35.010; CO §14–4–104.

p. 122 The information about the Seattle 1979–80 study came from Lisa G. Lerman, "Criminal Prosecution of Wife Beaters," in 4 *Response to Violence in the Family* No. 3 (January/February 1981); information on no-drop policies, from that article and from John Riley, "Spouse-Abuse Victim Jailed After No-Drop Policy Invoked," *Nat. L. J.*, 8/22/83, p. 4. The Alaska case is *Municipality of Anchorage v. Wall*, 3 ANM–82–8496 Crim.

p. 124 Warrantless arrest in domestic violence cases: AK §12.25.030; AZ §13–3601(B); CT §54–1F; GA §17–4–20; HI §709–906(2); ID §19–603(6); KY §431.005(2); LA Criminal Procedure art. 213; NV §171.124(1)(f); NH §594–10–1; NJ §2C:25–5; NM §31–1–7; NC §15A–401(b)(3); ND §14–07.1–06; OH §2935.03(B); RI §11–5–9; VA §12.2–81; WA §10.99.030(3)(a). Enforcement of order of protection: e.g, AK §25.35.050; CO §14–4–104; ME T19 §770, MA ch 276 §28. The Oregon law (§133.310(3)) says the police officer "shall" arrest the violator of an order of protection.

"A class action suit was filed . . ." the case is *Bruno v. Codd*, 47 N.Y.2d 582, 393 N.E.2d 976, 419 N.Y.S.2d 901 (1979); the consent order is discussed in Lorraine Patricia Eber, "The Battered Wife's Dilemma: To Kill or To Be Killed," 32 *Hastings L. J.* 895 (March 1981).

"The Oregon law says . . ." the case is *Nearing v. Weaver* (Ore. Sup.Ct. 10/4/83), discussed in John Riley, "Police Duty to Protect Widened," *Nat. L. J.*, 10/24/83.

p. 125 *State v. Brown,* 145 N.J. Super. 571, 364 A.2d 27 (1976).
Intrafamily immunity: *Moran v. Beyer,* 52 LW 2692 (7th Cir. 1983).
Two interesting articles about state of mind in homicide cases: Joshua Dressler, "Rethinking Heat of Passion," 73 *J. Criminal Law & Criminology* 421 (Summer 1982) and Dolores A. Donovan and Stephanie M. Wildman, "Is the Reasonable Man Obsolete? A Critical Perspective on Self-Defense and Provocation," 14 *Loyola U. L. Rev. (Los Angeles)* 435 (1981).

p. 128 "If the defense theory is self-defense . . ." see *State v. Finley,* 290 S.E.2d 808 (S.C. 1982); state has to rebut self-defense argument: *People v. Reeves,* 47 Ill.App.3d 406, 362 N.E.2d 9 (1977); *People v. Stallworth,* 364 Mich. 528, 111 N.W.2d 742 (1961); *Commonwealth v. Gillespie,* 434 A.2d 781 (Pa. 1981).
"A finding of justifiable homicide . . ." *Easterling v. State,* 267 P.2d 185 (Okla. 1954); *Kiess v. State,* 17 Tenn. 478, 144 S.W.2d 735 (1940); *People v. Reeves,* 47 Ill.App.3d 406, 362 N.E.2d 9 (1977); *People v. Bush,* 84 Cal.App.3d 294, 148 Cal.Rptr. 430 (1978); *People v. Lucas,* 160 Cal.App.2d 305, 324 P.2d 933 (1958); *Commonwealth v. Watson,* 431 A.2d 949 (Pa. 1981); *State v. Lamb,* 71 N.J. 545, 366 A.2d 981 (1976).
"The courts are split . . .": *State v. Amaya,* 438 A.2d 892 (Me. 1981); *Turner v. State,* 428 N.E.2d 1244 (Ind. 1981); *State v. Thomas,* 66 Oh.St.2d 518, 423 N.E.2d 137 (1981). Also see *People v. De Rushia,* 109 Mich. App. 419, 311 N.W.2d 374 (Mich. 1981).

p. 129 "However, the violent acts . . ." *People v. Lyle,* 613 P.2d 896 (Colo. 1980).
"According to a 1981 law review article . . ." the article is Karen McKinnie, "The Use of Expert Testimony in the Defense of Battered Women," 52 *U. Colo. L. Rev.* 587 (1981); the cases are *State v. Carrethers.* Crim. No. 100359 (Ariz. 1979), *State v. Wendy Jones,* Crim. No. 93879 (Ariz. 1976), and *State v. Ida Mae Jones,* Crim. No. 98666 (Ariz. 1978).
On the duty to retreat: CT, *State v. Shaw,* 441 A.2d 561 (Conn. 1981); MI, *People v. McGrandy,* 9 Mich. App. 187, 156 N.W.2d 48 (1948), *People v. Lenkevich,* 394 Mich. 117, 229 N.W.2d 298 (1975), *People v. Mroue,* 315 N.W.2d 192 (Mich. 1981); NJ, *State v. Lamb,* 71 N.J. 545, 366A.2d 981 (1976), *State v. Felton,* 434 A.2d 1131, 180 N.J. Super. 361 (1981); PA, *Commonwealth v. Eberle,* 474 Pa. 548, 379 A.2d 90 (1977); SC, *State vs. Grantham,* 224 S.C. 41, 77 S.E.2d 291 (1953); FL, *Rippie v. State,* 404 So.2d 160 (Fla. 1981).
"Carolyn Wilkes Kaas . . ." the article is, "The Admissibility of Expert Testimony on the Battered Woman Syndrome in Support of a Claim of Self-Defense," 15 *Conn. L. Rev.* 121 (Fall 1982).

p. 130 "Some courts will allow . . ." DC, *Ibn-Tamas v. U.S.,* 407A.2d 626 (1979); GA, *Smith v. State,* 247 Ga. 612, 277 S.E.2d 678 (1981); WA, *State v. Kelly,* 655 P.2d 1201 (1982); OH, *State v. Thomas,* 66 Ohio St.2d 518, 423 N.E.2d 137 (1981); WY, *Buhrle v. State,* 627 P.2d 1374 (1981).

CHAPTER 6

RAPE

p. 132 ". . . hundreds of cases . . ." for example, *State v. Hines*, 296 N.C. 377, 211 S.E.2d 201 (1975); *Beard v. State*, 323 N.E.2d 216 (Ind. 1975); *State v. Gallup*, 520 S.W.2d 619 (Mo. 1975).

"now the usual requirement . . ." the 50 state statutes are: AL §13A–6–61; AK §11.41.410; AZ §13–1406; AR §41–1803; CA Penal §261; CO §18–3–402; CT §53a–65; DE T 11 §763; FL §794.011; GA §16–6–1; HI §707–30; ID §18–6101; IL ch. 38 §11–1; IN §35–42–4–1; IA §709.1; KS §21–3502; KY §510.010; LA §14:41; ME T 17A §252; MD art. 27 §463; MA ch. 265 §22; MI §750.520b; MN §609.342; MS §97–3–65; MO §566.030; MT §45–5–503; NB §28–319; NV §200.366; NH §632:1; NJ §2C:14–2; NM §30–9–11; NY Penal §130.25; NC §14–27.2; ND §12.1–20–01; OH §2907.02; OK T 21 §1111; OR §163.375; PA T 18 §3121; RI §11–37–2; SC §16–3–651; SD §22–22–1; TN §39–2–603; TX Penal art. 2 §21.01; UT §76–5–402; VT T 13 §3252; VA §18.2–61; WA §9.79.010; WV §61–8B–3; WI §940.225; WY §6–2–302.

"either to the victim or to another person . . ." e.g., AL, NY, VT.

"present violence or future retaliation . . ." e.g., CA, CO, OR, SC.

"if she was too frightened . . ." e.g., AL, ID, KS, KY, LA, ME, MN, MT, NY, OH, OR, PA, RI, SC, TX, VT, VA, WV.

p. 133 "The defendant argued . . ." *People v. Clarke*, 50 Ill.2d 104, 277 N.E.2d 866 (1971).

"Corroboration has been demanded . . ." see Vivian Berger, "Man's Trial, Woman's Tribulation: Rape Cases in the Courtroom," 77 *Columbia L. Rev.* 1 (1977), or, if you want to get really angry, F. Lee Bailey & Henry B. Rothblatt, *Crimes of Violence: Rape and Other Sex Crimes* (1973; 1978 pocket part).

The rape shield statutes are: AK §12.45.045; AR §41–1810.1; CA Evidence §782; CO §18–3–407; DE T 11 §763; FL §794.022; GA §24–2–3; HI Rules of Evidence 412; KY §510.145; LA §15:498; MD art. 27 §461A; MA ch. 233 §21B; MI §750.520j; MN §609.347; MS §97–3–68; MO §491.015; MT §94–5–503(5); NB §28–321–323; NV §48.069; NH §623–A:6; NJ §2C:14–7; NM §30–9–16; NY Crim.Proc. §60.42; NC §8–58:6; ND §12.1–20–14; OH §2907.02(D); OK T 22 §750; PA T 18 §3106; RI §11–37–13; SC §16.3–659.1; TN §40–17–119; TX Penal T 5 §21.13; VT T 13 §3255; VA §18.2–67.7; WA §9A.44.020; WV §61–8B–12; WI §971.31(11); WY §6–2–312.

Many cases have found these rape shield laws constitutional: see, e.g., *People v. McKenna*, 196 Co. 369, 585 P.2d 275 (1978); *State v. McCoy*, 274 S.C. 70, 261 S.E.2d 159 (1979).

p. 134 *People v. Smith*, 340 N.W.2d 855 (Mich.App. 1983), holds that a defendant who neither complies with the notice provisions of the rape shield law, nor raises the issues of consent, can't cross-examine the victim on her prior sexual activities with the defendant. In the same year, New York's *People v. Westfall*, 469 N.Y.S.2d 162, holds that evidence of the victim's sexual history was inadmissible. One defendant denied participation in the rape at all; the other denied previous sexual intercourse with the victim. It was uncontested that the victim was the girlfriend of the defendant's father, but testimony of sexual history with the father wasn't admissible because he was not accused of participation in the rape.

p. 135 Information on the Hale charge comes from 92 *A.L.R.3d* 866. Montana disallowed the Hale charge in 1984 in *State v. Liddell*, No. 83–276 (Sup.Ct. 7/10/84), see *Nat. L. J.* 9/10/84, p. 23.

p. 137 *Beard v. State*, 323 N.E.2d 216 (Ind. 1975); *People v. Wilcox*, 33 Ill.App.3d 432, 337 N.E.2d 211 (1975); *State v. Gallup*, 520 S.W.2d. 619 (Mo. 1975); *Johnson v. U.S.*, 426 F.2d 651 (D.C. Cir. 1970), *cert.den.*, 401 U.S. 846.

p. 138 Rape-trauma syndrome: KS *State v. Marks*, 647 P.2d 1292 (Kan. 1982); CA *People v. Bledsoe*, 53 LW 2039 (Cal.Sup.Ct. 6/14/84); MN *State v. Saldana* 324 N.W.2d 227 (Minn. 1982); MO *State v. Taylor*, 663 S.W.2d 235 (Mo. 1984).

p. 139 The statutes are gender-neutral except AL, DE, GA, ID, IL, KS, ME, MD, MS, MT, NY, OR, TX, VA, WA.
"In five states . . ." see the citations for rape statutes given on page 285.

p. 140 *State v. Myers*, 606 P.2d 250 (Utah 1980).
People v. Edmond, 32 Ill.Dec. 159, 395 N.E.2d 106 (1979).
State v. Herzog, 610 P.2d 1281 (Utah 1980).
Commonwealth v. Gouveia, 358 N.E.2d 1001, 371 Mass. 566 (1976).

p. 141 *People v. Thompson*, 76 Mich.App. 705, 257 N.W.2d 268 (1977).
Milenkovic v. State, 272 N.W.2d 320, 86 Wis.2d 272 (1978).

p. 142 The Freeman article is, " 'But if You Can't Rape Your Wife, Who(m) Can You Rape?': The Marital Rape Exception Re-Examined": 15 *Family L. Q.* 1 (1981).
" . . . not married to the perpetrator." See citations for rape statutes given on page 285; see Freeman on the common-law exception.
"Florida jury . . ." no by-line, "Jurors in Florida Convict Man of Raping His Wife," *New York Times*, 9/2/84, p. A34.

p. 143 "The technical details vary . . ." see Freeman again.
The Burrows article is "Abolishing the Marital Exception for Rape: A Statutory Proposal," 1983 *U.Ill. L. Rev.* 201. Also see *Weishaupt v. Commonwealth*, 52 LW 2639 (Va.Sup.Ct. 4/17/84).
"There are exceptions . . ." CA Penal §262(a); CT §53a–70b; MA *State v. Chretien*, 417 N.E.2d 1203 (1981); NH §632–A:5; NJ §2C–14–5(b); WI §940.225(b); WY §6–2–307.

p. 144 *Vasquez v. State*, 623 P.2d 1205 (Wyo. 1981).
People v. De Stefano, N.Y.L.J., 8/31/83, p. 14 (Suffolk County).

p. 145 *Kline v. 1500 Massachusetts Avenue Apartment Corp.*, 439 F.2d 477 (D.C. Cir. 1970).
Ponticas v. KMS Investment, 331 N.W.2d 907 (Minn. 1983).

p. 146 *Virginia D. v. Madesco Investment Corp.*, 648 S.W.2d 881 (Mo. 1983).
Garzilli v. Howard Johnson's Motor Lodges, 419 F.Supp. 1210 (E.D.N.Y. 1976).

Anderson v. Malloy, 700 F.2d 1208 (8th Cir. 1983).

Gail Ballou's Spring 1981 article, "Recourse for Rape Victims: Third Party Liability," in 4 *Harvard Women's L.J.* 105, gives cites for more cases in which rape victims won civil cases against third parties: *Lyon v. Carey,* 533 F.2d 649 (D.C. Cir. 1976); *Applewhite v. City of Baton Rouge,* 380 So.2d 119 (La. 1979)—a case calculated to make you feel really safe—the rapist was a cop; *Weeks v. Feltner,* 297 N.W.2d 679 (Mich. 1980); *Kenny v. Southeastern Pennsylvania Transit Authority,* 581 F.2d. 351 (3d Cir. 1978), *cert.den.,* 439 U.S. 1073 (1979); *Robilotto v. State,* 429 N.Y.S.2d 362 (Ct.Cl. 1980). In the case of *Holley v. Mount Zion Terrace Apartments Inc.* 382 So.2d 98 (Fla. 1980), a summary judgment for the landlord was reversed, but *Smith v. ABC Realty Co.,* 336 N.Y.S.2d. 104 (1972), holds against the tenant, on the ground that the landlord's negligence wasn't the proximate cause of the rape.

In general, it's hard to sue the rapist's employer, because rape is by no means in the scope of employment, but some plantiffs have succeeded in overcoming this obstacle: *Meyer v. Graphic Arts Internat'l Local Union 63–A,* 88 Cal.App.3d 176, 151 Cal.Rptr. 597 (1979); *Kane v. Hartford Accident & Indem. Co.,* 98 Cal.App.3d. 350, 159 Cal.Rptr. 446 (1979); *Williams v. Feather Sound, Inc.,* 386 So.2d 1238 (Fla. 1980).

The victim may also be able to collect Workers' Compensation if she is raped at work, and the nature of her job makes her vulnerable to attack: *Commercial Standard Ins. Co. v. Marin,* 488 S.W.2d 861 (Tex.Civ.App. 1972); *B & B Nursing Home v. Blair,* 496 P.2d 796 (Okla. 1972); *Tredway v. District of Columbia,* 403 A.2d 732 (D.C. 1979), *cert.den.,* 444 U.S. 867. But a servicewoman who sued her "employer"—the United States—for the rape and beating she suffered while serving as an Army reservist had her case dismissed by a California District Court. The rapists were on our side—they were also reservists. The court's rationale is that being raped is "incident to service" in the military, and therefore not an appropriate subject for suit: *Galusha (Buckmiller) v. U.S.,* D. Cal. 9/17/84, discussed in Mary Ann Galante, "Rape is Held 'Incident to Service,'" *Nat.L.J.,* 10/15/84, p. 10.

p. 146 "A long shot . . ." *Tarasoff v. Board of Regents,* 17 Cal.3d 425, 551 P.2d 334, 131 Cal.Rptr. 14 (1976).

CHAPTER 7

WOMEN'S HEALTH ISSUES

---

p. 149 For general reference on DES: Romualdo P. Eclavea, "Products Liability: Diethylstilbestrol," 2 *A.L.R.* 4th 1091; Melissa A. Turner, "Bearing the Burden of DES Exposure," 60 *Oregon L. Rev.* 309 (1981); Frank M. McClellan, Thomas H. Tate, Allen T. Eaton, "Strict Liability for Prescription Drug Injuries: The Improper Marketing Theory," 26 *St. Louis U. L.J.* 1 (December 1981); Timothy J. Langella, "*Bichler v. Eli Lilly:* An Improper Use of Conscious Parallelism as Evidence of Concerted Action," 62 *Boston U.L.Rev.* 633 (March 1982); Harlan S.

Abrahams and Bobbie Joan Musgrave, "The DES Labyrinth," 33 *South Carolina L.Rev.* 663 (1982); Glen O. Robinson, "Multiple Causation in Tort Law: Reflections on the DES Cases," 68 *Virginia L.Rev.* 713 (1982); Warren E. Platt, Sara E. Staebill, Preston H. Longino Jr. and Stephen Swinton, "Design Defect: Definition and Proof," in *Product Design Litigation* at 141 (PLI Litigation & Administrative Law Series #205) (1982); Judi Scott, "Products Liability," 1982 *Annual Survey Am. Law* 709 (June 1983); Barry S. Roberts and Charles F. Royster, "DES and the Identification Problem," 16 *Akron L.Rev.* 447 (Winter 1983); Sheila L. Birnbaum and Barbara Wrubel, "Agent Orange Class Certification and Industry-Wide Liability for DES," *Nat.L.J.*, 2/27/84, p. 38. The "Shainwald interview" is a personal interview with Sybil Shainwald, New York City malpractice litigator and chair of the National Women's Health Network, on March 23, 1984.

p. 153 *Abel v. Eli Lilly & Co.*, 289 N.W.2d 22 (Mich. App. 1979); *aff'd*, 2/6/84, Mich. Sup.Ct. No. 64712, *cert.den.*, 53 LW 3226. The innumerable later references to this defendant will simply be to "Lilly."
Erlich v. Abbott Laboratories, Pennsylvania Court of Common Pleas No. 4331 (2/2/81).
Namm v. Charles E. Frosst & Co., 178 N.J. Super. 19, 427 A.2d 1121 (1981); *Morton v. Abbott*, 538 F.Supp. 593 (M.D. Fla. 1982).
". . . judges refusing to apply enterprise liability . . ." e.g., *Abel v. Lilly; Morton v. Abbott; Ferrigno v. Lilly*, 175 N.J. Super. 551, 420 A.2d 1305 (1980); *Sindell v. Abbott*, 26 Cal.3d 588, 607 P.2d 924, 163 Cal.Rptr. 132 (1980), *cert.den.*, 449 U.S. 912.
Bichler v. Lilly, 55 N.Y.2d 571, 450 N.Y.S.2d 776 (1982); for an illustration of contribution, see *Helmrich v. Lilly*, CCH Products Liability Reporter ¶9529 (N.Y. A.D. 1983).

p. 154 ". . . private individuals are not allowed to sue the FDA . . ." *Gray v. U.S.*, 445 F.Supp. 337 (S.D. Tex. 1978); *Kiel v. Lilly*, 490 F.Supp. 479 (E.D. Mich. 1980).
". . . to prove they couldn't have manufactured the drug . . ." But, in California at least, it's no defense to prove that the manufacturer sold DES only for use in treating prostate cancer—because druggists dispensed all kinds of DES more or less indiscriminately: *Miles v. Superior Court*, 133 Cal.App.3d 587, 184 Cal.Rptr. 98 (1982); also see *Mertan v. Squibb*, 190 Cal.Rptr. 349 (1983).
". . . two later New Jersey cases . . ." *Namm v. Frosst*, 178 N.J. Super. 19, 427 A.2d 1121 (1981); *Pipon v. Burroughs-Wellcome*, 532 F.Supp. 637 (1982), *aff'd*, 696 F.2d 984.
FL: *Morton v. Abbott*, 538 F.Supp. 593 (M.D. Fla. 1982). MA: *Payton v. Abbott*, 83 F.R.D. 382 (D.Mass. 1979); 512 F.Supp. 1031 (D.Mass. 1981); 386 Mass. 540, 437 N.E.2d 171 (1982). MO: *Zafft v. Lilly*, CCH PLR Reports No. 583, p. 10 (Mo.Sup. 9/11/84), *aff'd*, 53 LW 2175. SC: *Ryan v. Lilly*, 514 F.Supp. 1004 (D.S.C. 1981). TX: *Gray v. U.S.*, 445 F.Supp. 337 (S.D. Tex, 1978).
McElhaney v. Lilly, 564 F.Supp. 265 (D.S.D. 1983), 575 F.Supp. 228 (D.S.D. 1983) *aff'd*, CCH PLR ¶10,125 (8th Cir. 1984).

p. 155 *Collins v. Lilly*, CCH PLR ¶9871 (Wis.Sup.Ct. 1984) *cert.den.* 53 LW

3226; the criticisms came from Sheila L. Birnbaum and Barbara Wrubel, "Agent Orange Class Certification and Industrywide Liability for DES," *Nat. L.J.*, 2/27/84, p. 38.

p. 157 ". . . express sympathy for the victim but still close her out of the court-house . . ." NY: *Manno v. Levi*, CCH PLR ¶9741 (1983), *aff'd*, ¶10,181 (N.Y. Ct.App. 1984); *Fleishman v. Lilly*, 465 N.Y.S.2d 735 (App. 1984). TN: *Mathis v. Lilly*, CCH PLR ¶9798 (6th Cir. 1983).
". . . can be brought by that minor . . ." *Tate v. Lilly*, 522 F.Supp. 1048 (M.D. Tenn. 1981). All the states except Arizona, Florida, and Pennsylvania "toll for minority"—that is, the statute of limitations is tolled (suspended) until a potential plaintiff reaches majority.
"A Florida court simply refused . . ." *Diamond v. Squibb*, 397 So.2d 671 (Fla. 1981).
The quote is from *Yustick v. Lilly*, CCH PLR ¶9859 (E.D. Mich. 1983).
IL: *Needham v. White Labs*, 639 F.2d 394 (7th Cir. 1981), *cert.den.*, 50 LW 3276. OH: *Harper v. Lilly*, 575 F.Supp. 1359 (N.D. Ohio 1983). PA: *O'Brien v. Lilly*, 668 F.2d 704, 717–18 (3d Cir. 1981).

p. 159 *Mizell v. Lilly*, 526 F.Supp. 589 (D.S.C. 1981).
Trahan v. Squibb, 567 F.Supp. 505 (M.D. Tenn. 1983); also see *Kirk v. Emons Industries*, *N.Y.L.J.*, 9/10/84 (Sup.Ct.), for a less favorable outcome for the plaintiff, and *Bruck v. Lilly*, 523 F.Supp. 480 (S.D. Ohio 1981), for choice of law problems when a case is transferred from one District Court to another.
". . . doctors and nurse-midwives providing prenatal care . . ." New York Public Health §2503.

p. 160 "(. . . California, Maine, New York) nip this tactic in the bud . . ." CA Health & Safety §1367.9; ME Title 24A §2540; NY Insurance §174–b.
". . . state-funded programs to inform the public . . ." ME Title 22 ch. 267; NJ §26:2–113; NY Public Health §2500c.
"If the manufacturer can't be identified . . ." To be on the safe side, the plaintiff had better sue every plausible defendant and add "John Doe" to the complaint as a defendant if local law permits it. The plaintiff in *Swiss v. Lilly*, CCH PLR ¶9757 (D.R.I. 1983) developed cancer in 1977. She sued all the eventual defendants but one in 1978. Because the Rhode Island statute of limitations is three years from the date of discovery, the suit was timely. But in 1981, she amended her complaint to add another defendant. The Federal Rules require that a new party be notified of the suit before the original statute of limitations runs—so the plaintiff was out of luck.

p. 161 "DES daughters can sue . . ." *Mink v. University of Chicago*, 460 F.Supp. 713 (N.D. Ill. 1978); *Plummer v. Abbott Laboratories*, 568 F.Supp. 920 (D.R.I. 1984). See Lynne Reaves, "Fear Not Enough," 69 *A.B.A. J.* 725 (1983); Corey Scott Cramin, "Emotional Distress Damages for Cancerphobia: A Case for the DES Daughter," 14 *Pacific L.J.* 1215 (July 1983).
"On the other hand . . ." *Mink v. University of Chicago*, 460 F.Supp. 713 (N.D. Ill. 1978); *Wetherill v. University of Chicago*, 565 F.Supp. 1553 (N.D. Ill. 1983).

The university can demand that the manufacturer pay part or all of the damages: *Helmrich v. Lilly,* CCH PLR ¶9529 (NY 1983).
"A 1979 California case . . ." *Rawlings v. Abbott Laboratories,* 97 Cal.App.3d 890, 159 Cal.Rptr. 119 (1979).

p. 162 ". . . it had no connection with the plaintiff's mother . . ." *Lemire v. Garrard Drugs,* 95 Mich.App. 520, 291 N.W.2d 103 (1980).
"California says DES mothers . . ." *Murphy v. Squibb* CCH PLR ¶10,141 (Cal.App. 1984).
Evidence of improper marketing: *Toole v. Richardson Merrell Inc.,* 60 Cal.Rptr. 398 (1967); *Lewis v. Baker,* 413 P.2d 400 (Ore. 1966); *McDaniel v. McNeil Labs Inc.,* 241 N.W.2d 822 (Neb. 1976). Frank M. McClellan, Thomas H. Tate, and Allen Eaton, in their article, "Strict Liability for Prescription Drug Injuries: The Improper Marketing Theory," 26 *St. Louis U. L.J.* 1, suggest that a prescription drug should be considered defective if the FDA wasn't given all the information it would have needed to make an informed judgment about the drug's safety and effectiveness.
Ferrigno v. Lilly, 175 N.J. Super. 551, 420 A.2d 1305 (1980); *Needham v.White Labs,* 639 F.2d 394 (7th Cir. 1981), *cert.den.,* 50 LW 3276.
"Two years later, a Louisiana court . . ." *Schneider v. Lilly,* 556 F.Supp. 809 (D.La. 1983).

p. 163 *Kaufman v. Lilly,* N.Y.L.J., 2/14/84, p. 13 (Appellate Division). Also see *Katz v. Lilly,* 84 F.R.D. 378 (E.D.N.Y. 1978), which allows the defendant to try to fight off collateral estoppel by getting testimony from the jurors in the earlier case. The defendant can't impeach (challenge) the earlier verdict, but it can establish that it was a compromise verdict that should not be given collateral estoppel effect. To back up a little, theoretically a jury verdict is supposed to be agreed on by all the jurors. If half of them want to award the plaintiff a dollar and the other half vote for giving her a million dollars, theoretically they're supposed to keep arguing until everyone agrees on a figure. (In some places, jury verdicts can be made by a majority, not necessarily unanimous.) In the real world, they often bring in a verdict of $500,000 so they can go home. This is a compromise verdict and is strictly non-kosher.

p. 165 "The general rule . . ." e.g., *Dunkin v. Syntex Labs,* 443 F.Supp. 121 (W.D. Tenn. 1977); *Lindsay v. Ortho Pharmaceuticals,* 637 F.2d 87 (2d Cir. 1980); *Brochu v. Ortho Pharmaceuticals,* 642 F.2d 652 (1st Cir. 1981).
"learned intermediary" *Sterling Drug, Inc. v. Cornish,* 370 F.2d 82 (8th Cir. 1966); *Goodson v. Searle Labs,* 471 F.Supp. 546 (D.Conn. 1978); *Reeder v. Hammond,* 336 N.W.2d 3 (Mich.App. 1983).
". . . to keep up with medical knowledge . . ." *Lindsay v. Ortho Pharmaceuticals,* 637 F.2d 87 (2d Cir. 1980).
On overpromotion: see Janet Fairchild, "Promotional Efforts Directed Toward Prescribing Physician as Affecting Prescription Drug Manufacturer's Liability for Product-Caused Injury," 94 *A.L.R.3d* 1080; *Mahr v. Searle,* 72 Ill.App.3d 540, 390 N.E.2d 1214 (1979).
Chambers v. Searle, 441 F.Supp. 377 (D. Md. 1975), *aff'd,* 567 F.2d 269.

p. 166 *Spinden v. Johnson & Johnson,* 427 A.2d 597, 177 N.J. Super. 605 (1981).
". . . a 1983 Michigan case . . ." *Reeder v. Hammond,* 336 N.W.2d 3 (Mich. App. 1983).
"Two years earlier, the First Circuit . . ." *Brochu v. Ortho Pharmaceuticals,* 642 F.2d 652 (1st Cir. 1981).
The requirements for the Patient Package Insert (PPI) are at 21 CFR §310.501.
". . . it is automatically considered negligent . . ." *Keil v. Lilly,* 490 F.Supp. 479 (E.D. Mich. 1980); *Lukaszewicz v. Ortho Pharmaceuticals,* 532 F.Supp. 211 (D.Wis. 1981).
Hamilton v. Hardy, 37 Colo. App. 375, 549 P.2d 1099 (1976); but *Batiste v. American Home Products,* 32 N.C. App. 1, 231 S.E.2d 269 (1977), says the doctor isn't liable if there is no negligence or intentional misconduct and can't be blamed for the manufacturer's breach of implied warranties.
Klink v. Searle, 26 Wash.App. 951, 614 P.2d 701 (1980).

p. 167 "Unfortunately, these theories don't always work . . ." *Chambers v. Searle,* 441 F.Supp. 377 (D.Md. 1975), *aff'd,* 567 F.2d 269; *Seley v. Searle,* 423 N.E.2d 831, 67 Oh.St.2d 192 (Ohio 1981); *Cobb v. Syntex,* 444 So.2d 203 (La.App. 1983).

pp. 167–168 "At least in New Hampshire . . ." *Brochu v. Ortho Pharmaceuticals,* 642 F.2d 652 (1st Cir. 1981).

p. 168 "In Illinois, the statute of limitations . . ." *Witherill v. Weimer,* 85 Ill.2d 146, 421 N.E.2d 869 (1981). On the statute of limitations and choice of law, see *Steele v. Searle,* 428 F.Supp. 646 (S.D. Miss. 1977).
"The manufacturer can get off the hook . . ." *Chambers v. Searle,* 441 F.Supp. 377 (D.Md. 1975), *aff'd,* 567 F.2d 269.
"If the patient withholds information . . ." *Seley v. Searle,* 423 N.E.2d 831, 67 Oh.St.2d 192 (Ohio 1981).
Smoking and the Pill: *Skill v. Martinez,* 91 F.R.D. 498 (D. N.J. 1981).
Res ipsa in Pill cases: *Oresman v. Searle,* 321 F.Supp. 449 (D. R.I. 1971). See James L. Rigelhaupt, Jr., "Liability of Manufacturer or Seller for Injury or Death Allegedly Caused by Use of Contraceptive," 70 *A.L.R.*3d 315 (1976).

p. 169 IUD warnings given to doctors: *Terhune v. A.H. Robins Co.,* 90 Wash.2d 9, 577 P.2d 975 (1978); *McKee v. Moore,* 648 P.2d 21 (Okla. 1982).
FDA regs on "new-drug" IUDs: 21 CFR §310.502.
On the discovery rule: 5th Cir.: *Timberlake v. Robins,* 52 LW 2579 (3/9/84); *Mann v. Robins* CCH PLR ¶10,188 (3/9/84). NB: *Condon v. Robins* CCH PLR ¶10,038 (4/20/84). PA: *Caldwell v. Robins,* 577 F.Supp. 796 (W.D. Pa. 1984).
"In Wisconsin, the statute starts to run . . ." *Hansen v. Robins,* CCH PLR ¶9761 (1983).
New York rule: *Ooft v. City of N.Y.,* 104 Misc.2d 876, 429 N.Y.S.2d 376 (1980); *Melstein v. Ortho Pharmaceutical Corp.,* CCH PLR ¶9523 (D. N.Y. 1983); *Kristeller v. Robins,* CCH PLR ¶9733 (N.D.N.Y. 1983); *Lindsey v. Robins,* 91 A.D.2d 150 (1983); *Fitzpatrick v. Robins,* CCH PLR ¶9915 (A.D. 1984); *Davis v. Robins,* 99 A.D.2d 342 (1984).

p. 170 California rule: *Tresemer v. Burke,* 86 Cal.App.3d 656, 150 Cal.Rptr. 384

(1978). Oregon's rule is similar: *Dortch v. Robins*, 59 Or.App. 310, 650 P.2d 1046 (1982).

Martinez v. Rosenzweig, 70 Ill.App.3d 155, 387 N.E.2d 1263, 1265, 1268 (1979).

Philpott v. Robins, CCH PLR ¶9713 (9th Cir. 1983).

"A Michigan plaintiff ran into a different problem . . ." *Blaha v. Robins*, CCH PLR ¶9623 (6th Cir. 1983).

p. 171 "The Indiana plaintiff . . ." also see *Tolen v. Robins*, CCH PLR ¶10,117 (D. Ind. 1984); more bad news for a plaintiff who learned the reason for the injury long after she had been injured.

p. 172 "A group of California cases . . ." *Re Northern District of California Dalkon Shield Litigation*, 503 F.Supp. 194 (N.D. Cal. 1980), *aff'd sub nom Sidney-Vinstein v. Robins*, CCH PLR ¶9522 (9th Cir. 1983).

Miller v. Mobile County Board of Health, 409 So.2d 420 (Ala. 1981). Also see the similar case of *McMillen v. Robins*, CCH PLR ¶10,074 (Neb. 1984).

Sellers v. Robins CCH PLR ¶9771 (11th Cir. 1983).

". . . doctor neither told her . . ." Another plaintiff tried to argue that the statute of limitations was tolled by a continuing failure to warn, in *Doyle v. Planned Parenthood*, 31 Wash.App. 126, 639 P.2d 240 (1982), but the court didn't agree. The clinic tried to reach her and warn her about the danger of her Majzlin Spring IUD, but couldn't contact her. Rather than exculpating the clinic on the ground that it had, after all, given it the old college try, the court simply said that the plaintiff was time-barred, and that the attempt to contact her did not re-start the doctor-patient relationship.

Tresemer v. Burke, 86 Cal.App.3d 656, 150 Cal.Rptr. 384 (1978).

p. 173 "(e.g., $15,000 in one Oregon case . . ." no by-line, "Settlement Ends a Suit Against Dalkon Shield," *New York Times*, 1/18/84. The Colorado case is *Palmer v. Robins*, CCH PLR ¶10,085 (Colo.Sup.Ct. 1984); Minnesota's case is *Strempke v. Robins*, No. 3–80–168 (D.Minn.). On the Florida case, see "4.9 Million Award in IUD Suit" (no by-line), *New York Times*, 12/18/83, p. 23.

"At the end of 1984 . . ." see Martha Middleton, "Robins Mounts Drive to Settle Dalkon Suits," *Nat.L.J.*, 12/24/84, p.1; Mary Williams Walsh, "Lawyers Share Tips for Suing Robins on Dalkon Shield," *Wall St.J.*, 11/19/84, p. 43.

"Robins made tort law (and accounting) history . . ." Richard W. Stevenson, "Robins Sets up Dalkon Shield Payments Fund," *New York Times* 4/3/85, p. A1; Francine Schwadel, "Robins Sets $615 Million Pool to Cover Dalkon Shield Claims, Halts Dividend," *Wall St.J.*, 4/3/85 p. 2; David Ranii, "Makers Move on IUDs, Tampons," *Nat.L.J.*, 4/15/85, p. 3.

Hilliard v. Robins, CCH PLR ¶9828 (Cal.App. 1984).

"In February, 1985, special masters . . ." *Hewitt v. Robins*, No. 3–83–1291 (D. Minn.) See Martha Middleton, "Dalkon Makers Cited for 'Ongoing Fraud,' " *Nat.L.J.* 3/11/85, p. 8.

p. 174 "Evidence of further wrongdoing . . ." Francine Schwadel, "Witness for Robins Probed for Perjury on Dalkon Shield," *Wall St. J.*, 4/9/85, p. 46.

Express warranty theory: *Palmer v. Robins*, CCH PLR ¶10,085 (Colo. 6/4/84).

Declaratory judgment and recall suit: *National Women's Health Network v. Rob-*

ins, 545 F.Supp. 1177 (D. Mass. 1982). Robins warning to users: no by-line, "Dalkon Shield Removal Urged," *New York Times*, 10/30/84, p. A21.

p. 175 Dalkon Shield trials in Minnesota: David Ranii, "Simultaneous Dalkon Trials Keep Judges Busy in Minn.," *Nat.L.J.*, 11/14/83, p. 4, and "Judge Blasts Dalkon Maker," *Nat.L.J.*, 3/19/84, p. 3. On judicial misconduct charges: *Gardiner v. Robins*, No. 84–5061 (Judicial Council of the 8th Circuit, 12/26/84); see *Nat. L.J.*, 1/14/85. p.2.

p. 176 The National Women's Health Network Litigation Information Service's address is PO Box 5055, FDR Station, New York, N.Y. 10150. Attorneys interested in Dalkon Shield groups can write to Paul D. Rheingold, Esq., Trustee, Dalkon Shield-IUD Group, 200 Park Avenue, New York, N.Y. 10166. In March 1984 it cost $250 to join the basic group and $350 per case for state court materials. For more information on plaintiffs' lawyers' information clearing-houses, see David Ranii, "How the Plaintiffs' Bar Shares Its Information," *Nat.L.J.*, 7/23/84, p. 1. Case on attorney's ad: *Zauderer v. Office of Disciplinary Counsel*, No. 83–2166 (Sup.Ct. 1984).

p. 177 Doctor's affidavit not needed: *Davis v. Robins*, N.Y.L.J., 3/8/84, p. 3 (N.Y. A.D. 1984).
Contributory negligence is jury issue: *Ooft v. City of N.Y.*, 104 Misc.2d 879, 429 N.Y.S.2d 376 (1980).
Hilliard v. Robins, CCH PLR ¶9828 (Cal.App. 1984).
Palmer v. Robins, CCH PLR ¶10,085 (Colo.Sup. 6/4/84).

p. 178 Information booklet for Depo-provera: 21 CFR §310.501a.
The class-action suit is *NWHN et al. v. Upjohn Lab and Does 1–100* (Cal.Sup.).

p. 179 $10.5 million verdict against Johnson and Johnson: Carrie Dolan and Paul Ingrassia, "Toxic Shock Victim Awarded $10.5 Million in Jury Verdict Against Johnson & Johnson," *Wall Street Journal*, 12/24/82. Also see *Moran v. Int'l Playtex*, N.Y.L.J., 10/2/84, p. 1 (N.Y. 1984), on the timing of discovery as it relates to punitive damages.
Recall of Playtex and Tampax tampons: Playtex advertisement on page A19 of *New York Times*, 4/3/85; "Tambrands, Inc. Halts Tampons With Fiber Tied to Toxic Shock," *Wall St. J.*, 4/3/85, p. 22; David Ranii, "Makers Move on IUDs, Tampons," *Nat.L.J.* 4/15/85, p. 3.

p. 180 *Kehm v. Procter & Gamble*, CCH PLR ¶9873, 52 LW 2346 (8th Cir. 1983).
"The Fourth Circuit has taken a similar position." *Ellis v. Int'l Playtex*, 53 LW 2202 (4th Cir. 9/25/84), discussed in David Lauter, "TSS Studies Admissible," *Nat.L.J.*, 10/15/84, p. 10.
University of Wisconsin studies: a summary of the study results is printed in Paul Wenske, "The Secrets of TSS," *Nat.L.J.*, 3/5/84, p. 1. On the work product issue, see *Procter & Gamble v. Howard*, Kansas Sup.Ct. 83–55818–5 (1983); John Riley, "Are More TSS Cases Likely to Settle?" *Nat.L.J.*, 12/19/83, p. 6, and Paul Wenske, "Judge Seals Data on TSS Research," *Nat.L.J.*, 6/4/84, p. 7, for a discussion of *Rogers v. P & G*. On a related issue—whether P & G can use discovery to get

names and addresses of participants in the Center for Disease Control's study of TSS, see David Ranii, "TSS Data Ruling Argued," *Nat.L.J.*, 11/22/82, p. 4. The underlying case of *Lampshire v. Procter & Gamble*, 11th Cir. 82–8164, was settled.

An Iowa attorney was found guilty of contempt of court for selling packets of evidence that he had compiled for the *Kehm* case—but the offense wasn't the sale by itself, but violation of a court-approved agreement with P & G not to disclose confidential documents. See David Ranii, "Lawyer Cited in Document Sale," *Nat.L.J.*, 7/18/83, p. 10. On the Missouri settlement: no by-line, "Procter & Gamble Co. to Settle Tampon Suit for at Least $625,000," *Wall Street Journal*, 12/7/83; Phillip H. Wiggins, "FDA Inquiry Jars VLI Stock," *New York Times*, 12/7/83.

p. 181 Dow spokesman quoted in unbylined article, "Dow Chemical Stops Making Nausea Drug for Pregnant Women," *Wall Street Journal*, 6/10/83.

p. 182 ". . . a case filed in 1977 . . ." *Mekdeci v. Richardson-Merrell*, 11th Cir. 77–255; see Edward J. Burke, "The Brawl Over Bendectin," *Nat.L.J.*, 4/6/81, p. 1.
Oxendine case: *Oxendine v. Merrell Dow* (D.C. Super. 1245–82); David Lauter, "Bendectin Award May Spur Suits," *Nat.L.J.*, 6/13/83, p. 3, and "Bendectin Award Nixed by D.C. Judge," *Nat.L.J.*, 9/19/83. (Bendectin was a product of the Richardson-Merrell Co., which was bought by Dow in 1980.)
Koller v. Richardson-Merrell, CCH PLR ¶9523, 9583 (both D.D.C. 1983).
The FDA bulletin: David Lauter, "New Bendectin Studies, Ruling May Affect Cases," *Nat.L.J.*, 9/5/83, p. 4.
Dismissal of 1,100 consolidated Bendectin claims: *In Re "Bendectin" Products Liability Litigation*, 53 LW 2480 (S.D. Oh. 3/12/85).
Also see *Barson v. Squibb*, CCH PLR ¶10,020 (Utah Sup.Ct. 1984), articulating a manufacturer's duty to keep informed of potential birth defects caused by an anti-miscarriage drug, and to warn doctors of the dangers.
Bupivocaine: no by-line, "FDA Issues Warnings on Use of Anesthetic for Pregnant Women," *Wall Street Journal*, 8/23/83.

p. 183 "The statute of limitations starts to run . . ." *Klein v. Dow Corning Corp.*, 661 F.2d 998 (2d Cir. 1981).
The Texas case is *Coniss v. McGhan Medical Corp.*, D.C. Tex. 81–4062, discussed in David Lauter, "Is 3-M Rethinking Breast Implant Cases?" *Nat.L.J.*, 1/2/84, p. 9.

CHAPTER 8

PREGNANCY, CHILDBIRTH, AND MOTHERHOOD

---

p. 184 On pregnancy, motherhood, and Title VII in general, see 1 FRES §§2:350–357, 4:45, for a nice, lucid discussion; also see Paul A. Fischer, "Pregnancy leave or maternity leave policy, or lack thereof, as unlawful employment practice," 27 *A.L.R. Fed.* 537.

Andrew Weissman's April 1983 article, "Sexual Equality Under the Pregnancy Discrimination Act," 83 *Columbia L. Rev.* 690, discusses three approaches to the questions raised by pregnancy: the sex-blind "assimilationist" approach, which stresses the similarity between the sexes; the "pluralist" model, which stresses the differences; and a "hybrid" model, which says that different treatment of the sexes may, in some cases, be necessary to provide equality of result.

p. 187 The *Tranquilli* court chose not to follow 29 C.F.R. §1601.10a, which holds that an employment policy excluding pregnant applicants or employees is a prima facie violation of Title VII.
"So far, the Guidelines . . ." see, e.g., *Kansas Association v. EEOC*, 22 FEP Cases 1343 (D.Kan. 1980).

p. 188 "The PDA . . ." see 123 *Congressional Record* 29,644 (1977); 124 *Congressional Record* H6863 (1978).
". . . to fire an employee for becoming pregnant out of wedlock . . ." *Jacobs v. Martin Sweets Co.*, 550 F.2d 364 (6th Cir. 1971).
". . . or to refuse to grant maternity leave . . ." EEOC Dec. No. 71–562, CCH EEOC Dec. ¶6184 (1970); *Doe v. Osteopathic Hospital of Wichita, Inc.*, 333 F.Supp. 1357 (D.C. Kan. 1971).
"On the other hand . . ." *Willett v. Emory & Henry College*, 427 F.Supp. 631 (D.C. Va. 1977), *aff'd*, 569 F.2d 212 (4th Cir.).
State statutes on pregnancy discrimination: CT §46a–51(17); HI §378–1; KY §344.030(6); MD T 49B §17; MI §37.2201(d); MN §363.01(29); OH §4112.01(B); OR §659.029; SC §1–13–30(1). AK §18.80.220; ME T 49B §17.

p. 189 The Montana law has been upheld by *Mountain States Tel. & Tel. Co. v. Comm'r of Labor & Industry*, 608 P.2d 1047 (Mont. 1979), *app.dismissed*, 445 U.S. 921, which says that these provisions are not preempted by ERISA (the federal pension law) or the National Labor Relations Act. Furthermore, the right to maternity leave is uniquely personal and can't be taken away by a collective bargaining agreement.
Miller-Wohl Co. v. Comm'r, 515 F.Supp. 1264 (D. Mont. 1981), *vac. on other grounds*, 685 F.2d 1088 (9th Cir.), also upholds the Montana law, this time against a claim that it was an illegal protective law (the court said it wasn't violative of equal protection, but simply places men and women on a more equal footing and gives families the possibility of raising children without permanent loss of the mother's income) and that it was preempted by the Pregnancy Discrimination Amendment (the court pointed out that an employer could comply with both the Montana law and the PDA by offering reasonable leaves of absence to temporarily disabled employees of both sexes).
"Since the Pregnancy Discrimination Act . . ." see Introduction, Questions and Answers on the PDA, 29 CFR Appendix at page 138.
". . . a 1979 case from the Fourth Circuit . . ." *Mitchell v. Board of Trustees of Pickens County School District*, 599 F.2d 582 (4th Cir. 1979).
"Two early EEOC decisions . . ." EEOC Dec. No. 70–600, CCH EEOC Dec. ¶6122 (1970); No. 71–1897, CCH EEOC Dec. ¶6268 (1971).

p. 190 ". . . a maternity leave policy that presumes . . ."   *Paxman v. Campbell*, 612 F.2d 848 (4th Cir. 1980), *cert.den.*, 449 U.S. 1129.
". . . violates the Due Process clause . . ."   *Cleveland Board of Education v. LaFleur*, 414 U.S. 632 (1974).
"Some cases allow mandatory—and unpaid—maternity leave . . ."   e.g., *Condit v. United Air Lines, Inc.*, 558 F.2d 1176 (4th Cir. 1977), *cert.den.*, 435 U.S. 934; *Re National Airlines Inc.*, 434 F.Supp. 249 (D. Fla. 1979); *Harriss v. Pan Am*, 649 F.2d 670 (9th Cir. 1980).
Burwell v. Eastern Air Lines Inc., 633 F.2d 361 (4th Cir. 1980), *cert.den.*, 450 U.S. 965.

p. 191 *De Laurier v. San Diego Unified School District*, 588 F.2d 674 (9th Cir. 1978).
"Therefore, an airline's maternity leave policy for its ground crew . . ."   *Maclennan v. American Airlines, Inc.*, 440 F.Supp. 466 (E.D. Va. 1977).
"Similarly, it was permissible for an insurance company . . ."   *Langley v. State Farm Fire & Casualty Co.*, 644 F.2d 1124 (5th Cir. 1981).
Conners v. University of Tennessee Press, 31 EPD ¶33,521 (D. Tenn. 1982).
For general reference on fetal protection programs: Hannah Arterian Furnish, "Prenatal Exposure to Fetally Toxic Work Environments," 66 *Iowa L.Rev.* 65 (Oct. 1980); Nothstein and Ayres, "Sex Based Considerations of Differentiation in the Workplace: Exploring the Biomedical Interface Between OSHA and Title VII," 26 *Villanova L.Rev.* 239 (Jan. 1981); Wendy W. Williams, "Firing the Woman to Protect the Fetus: The Reconciliation of Fetal Protection with Employment Opportunity Goals Under Title VII," 69 *Georgetown L.J.* 641 (Feb. 1981); Linda G. Howard, "Hazardous Substances in the Workplace: Implications for the Employment Rights of Women," 129 *U.Pa.L.Rev.* 798 (1981); Mark A. Rothstein, "Employee Selection Based on Susceptibility to Occupational Illness," 81 *Michigan L.Rev.* 1379 (May 1983).

p. 192 "A very early case . . ."   *Cheatwood v. Southern Bell*, 303 F.Supp. 754 (D. Ala. 1969).
In re National Airlines Inc., 434 F.Supp. 249 (D. Fla. 1979); *Zuniga v. Kleberg County Hospital*, 692 F.2d 986 (5th Cir. 1982).
The quote is from 46 *Federal Register* 3916 (1981).

p. 193 The EEOC Guidelines can be found in the CCH *EEOC Compliance Manual* ¶4301–4320.
"Flying bunny" image: see Jacqueline H. Lower, "The Pregnant Employee's Appearance as a BFOQ Under the Pregnancy Discrimination Amendment," 14 *Loyola U.L.J. (Chicago)* 195 (Fall 1982).
NRC guidelines: Nuclear Regulatory Guide §8.13 (1975).
EEOC Dec. No. 75–055, CCH EEOC Dec. ¶6443 (1974); EEOC Dec. No. 75–072, CCH EEOC Dec. ¶6442 (1974).

p. 194 *Hayes v. Shelby Memorial Hospital*, 546 F.Supp. 259 (N.D. Ala. 1982); *Zuniga v. Kleberg County Hospital*, 692 F.2d 986 (5th Cir. 1982).

p. 195 ". . . but it could be argued . . ." see the Furnish article cited above; but also see the discussion of the *American Cyanamid* case on pp. 195–196.
OSHA lead standards: 29 CFR §1910.1025(j)(3)(c); 1025 (k)(1)(ii).
OSHA DBCP standard: 29 CFR §1910.1044.
"OSHA's Review Commission (qualifying for the Pontius Pilate Award of 1981) . . ." *American Cyanamid*, 9 OSH Cases 1599, 1981 CCH OSH Dec. ¶25,338.
The D.C. Circuit agreed with OSHA: *Oil, Chemical and Atomic Workers Int'l Union v. American Cyanamid*, 53 LW 2125 (D.C. Cir. 1984).
Christman v. American Cyanamid, 92 FRD 441 (N.D. W.V. 1981); on settlement, see *Civil Liberties* (ACLU) No. 348 (Winter 1984), p.7.

p. 196 Connecticut statute is §46a–60(a)(7)(E), (a)(9), (a)(10). A recent Connecticut case, *Wroblewski v. Lexington Gardens, Inc.*, 32 EPD ¶33,791 (1982), says that an employer can't restrict questions about genito-urinary health to woman employees. It's no defense to make an unsupported claim that woman employees object to complete physical exams—or to mention potential fetal harm from certain insecticides when there is no evidence that the employer uses those insecticides. "The Fifth Circuit found . . ." *Meyer v. Brown & Root Construction Co.*, 661 F.2d 369 (5th Cir. 1981).

p. 197 ". . . replaced by another, non-pregnant woman . . ." see *Harper v. Thiokol Chemical Corp.*, 619 F.2d 489 (5th Cir. 1980).
"The case went to arbitration." *Stauffer Chemical Co.*, 78 *Labor Arbitration Reports* 1276 (1982).
Doerr v. B.F. Goodrich Co., 484 F.Supp. 320 (N.D. Ohio 1979).
Salazar v. Marathon Oil Co., 90 *Labor Cases* ¶33,985 (S.D. Tex. 1980).

pp. 197–198 *Fancher v. Nimmo*, 549 F.Supp. 1324 (E.D. Ark. 1982).

p. 198 *Wright v. Olin*, 697 F.2d 1172 (4th Cir. 1982).

p. 199 ". . . so can employees disabled by pregnancy . . ." *TWA v. City of Philadelphia*, 403 A.2d 1057 (Pa. 1979).
Harriss v. Pan Am World Airways, 437 F.Supp. 413 (D. Cal. 1977); but Questions and Answers 18 says the employer can't force the employee to exhaust her vacation benefits before maternity leave.
". . . no obligation to continue the salary of employees on maternity leave . . ." *Somers v. Aldine Independent School District*, 464 F.Supp. 900 (D. Tex. 1979), *aff'd*, 620 F.2d 298.

p. 200 *Barone v. Hackett* 28 FEP Cases 1765 (D.R.I. 1982).
Newport News Shipbuilding Co. v. EEOC, 32 FEP Cases 1 (1983).
"Even before the Pregnancy Discrimination Act . . ." *Nashville Gas Co. v. Satty*, 434 U.S. 136 (1977); also see *Burwell v. Eastern Air Lines Inc.*, 633 F.2d 361 (4th Cir. 1980), *cert.den.*, 450 U.S. 965 (violation of Title VII to require pregnant stewardesses to forfeit seniority when they transfer to ground positions).
". . . her seniority must be computed . . ." *McArthur v. Southern Airways, Inc.*, 404 F.Supp. 508 (N.D. Ga. 1975).

p. 201 "When the Federal Unemployment Tax Act (FUTA) . . ." 26 U.S.C.A. §3304(a)(12). Andrew Weissman, writing in the April 1983 issue of the *Columbia L.Rev.*, points out that, in this instance, pregnancy is *not* treated like other disabilities; unemployment benefits are available every time an employee is fired for pregnancy.

". . . was legitimately denied unemployment benefits . . ." *Wincek v. Commonwealth Unemployment Compensation Board of Review*, 439 A.2d 890 (Pa. 1982).

". . . to play the game before collecting unemployment benefits . . ." *Dohoney v. Director of Division of Employment Security*, 377 Mass. 333, 386 N.E.2d 10 (1979); *Garrow v. Levine*, 52 A.D.2d 708, 382 N.Y.S.2d 588 (1976).

". . . her job must be held open . . ." also see *In Re Southwestern Bell Tel Co. Maternity Benefits Litigation*, 602 F.2d 845 (8th Cir. 1979).

". . . to fire all employees who do not return . . ." *Mason v. Continental Insurance Co.*, 32 EPD ¶33,778 (D. Ala. 1983).

"A business-necessity defense is available . . ." *Satty v. Nashville Gas Co.*, 522 F.2d 850 (6th Cir. 1975); *Newmon v. Delta Airlines*, 374 F.Supp. 238 (D. Ga. 1973); *Burton v. School Committee of Quahoag Regional School District*, 432 N.E.2d 725, 13 Mass. App. 989 (1982).

"The same defense is available . . ." *McGaffney v. Southwest Mississippi General Hospital*, 5 FEP Cases 1312 (D. Miss. 1973); *Newmon v. Delta Airlines*, 374 F.Supp. 238 (D. Ga. 1973); EEOC Dec. No. 71–2309, 7 FEP Cases 454 (1971).

". . . unless the time limit . . ." EEOC Dec. No. 74–68, 8 FEP Cases 428 (1973); EEOC Dec. No. 75–095, 10 FEP Cases 813 (1974); *Fabian v. Independent School District*, 409 F.Supp. 94 (D. Okla 1976).

p. 202 The quote is from *Wetzel v. Liberty Mutual Insurance Co.*, 511 F.2d 199, 208 (3d Cir. 1975); also see *Cleveland Board of Education v. LaFleur*, 414 U.S. 632 (1974).

". . . she is entitled to collect unemployment benefits . . ." *Swavely v. Industrial Relations Commission*, 345 So.2d 399 (Fla. 1977); *Whitehead v. Mississippi Employment Security Commission*, 349 So.2d 1048 (Miss. 1977); *Trail v. Industrial Comm.*, 540 S.W.2d 179 (Mo. 1976); *Allegretti v. Commonwealth Unemployment Compensation Board of Review*, 324 A.2d 860 (Pa. 1974).

"One creative employer . . ." *Harper v. Thiokol Chemical Corp.*, 619 F.2d 489 (5th Cir. 1980).

p. 203 "A 1978 Seventh Circuit case . . ." *In re Consolidated Pretrial Proceedings in the Airline Cases*, 582 F.2d 1142.

". . . a request for discretionary non-medical leave . . ." EEOC Dec. No. 78–41, CCH EEOC Dec. ¶6724 (1978); No. 78–50, CCH EEOC Dec. ¶6732 (1978); *Board of School Directors of Fox Chapel Area School District v. Rossetti*, 411 A.2d 486, 488 Pa. 125 (1979); *Northern Indiana Public Service Co.*, 80 LA. 41 (1982); *Kansas Association v. EEOC*, 33 FEP Cases 589 (D. Kan. 1983).

". . . giving male teachers a day of paid leave . . ." *Byrd v. Unified School District #1*, 453 F.Supp. 621 (D. Wis. 1978).

"Just because a union contract provides . . ." *Chaleff v. Board of Trustees, Teachers' Pension & Annuity Fund*, 457 A.2d 33, 188 N.J. Super. 194 (1983). "A 1975 opinion that never mentions Title VII . . ." *Martin v. Dann*, 10 FEP Cases 944 (D.D.C. 1975).

p. 204 "The Supreme Judicial Court of Massachusetts ruled . . ." *Manias v. Director of Division of Employment*, S–2885 (Mass. 2/16/83); *Nat. L.J.* 3/28/83.

p. 205 ". . . courts don't like to interfere with hospital policies . . ." see Mary F. Forrest, "Natural Childbirth: Rights and Liabilities of the Parties," 17 *J. Fam.L.* 309 (1979); *Baier v. Women's Hospital Foundation*, 340 So.2d 360 (La. 1976).
Williams v. Lallie Kemp Charity Hospital, 428 So.2d 1000 (La.App. 1983).
"A 1983 New York case . . ." *Hughson v. St. Francis Hospital*, 459 N.Y.S.2d. 814 (1983).
". . . the common or garden malpractice suit . . ." e.g., *Register v. Wilmington Medical Center Inc.*, 377 A.2d. 8 (Del. 1977); *Friel v. Vineland OB/GYN PA*, 400 A.2d 147, 166 N.J. Super. 579 (1979); *Bunch v. Mercy Hospital of New Orleans*, 404 So.2d 520 (La.App. 1981).
The quote comes from 2 *Professional Bulletin*, American Society for Psychoprophylaxis in Obstetrics 4 (1977).

p. 206 "One woman gave birth in the parking lot . . ." *Campbell v. Mincey*, 413 F.Supp. 16 (N.D. Miss. 1975); *Hill v. Ohio County*, 468 S.W.2d. 306 (Ky. 1971).
"On the other hand, hospitals do have a duty . . ." *Hernandez v. Smith*, 552 F.2d 142 (5th Cir. 1977).
". . . fathers should be pacing the corridor or buying rounds . . ." *Hulit v. St. Vincent's Hospital*, 164 Mont. 168, 520 P.2d 99 (1974); *Fitzgerald v. Porter Memorial Hospital*, 523 F.2d 716 (7th Cir. 1975), *cert.den.*, 425 U.S. 916 (1976).
Whitman v. Mercy-Memorial Hospital, 52 LW 2287 (Mich. App. 9/16/83).

p. 207 ". . . Orthodox Jewish parents . . ." *Oliner v. Lenox Hill Hospital*, 431 N.Y.S.2d. 271, 106 Misc.2d. 107 (Sup.Ct. 1980).
On malpractice, etc., in home birth, see the Mary F. Forrest article cited above, and Ron Collins, "Midwife Indicted for Boy's Death," *Nat. L.J.*, 7/18/83, p. 3.

pp. 207–208 Information on regulation of birth centers from the National Association of Childbearing Centers, RD 1, Box 1, Perkiomenville, PA 18074. AK Health & Social Services ch. 12, art. 14; AZ §9–10–101; CA Licensing and Certification of Health Facilities T22 ch. 7 art. 9; GA Dep't Human Resources ch. 290–5–41; IN Regulations for General and Specific Hospitals HHL §1; KS §28–4–370; KY 902 Administrative Register 20:150; MA ch. 111 §3, 51–56; ch. 112 §80C; NC Diagnostic and Birth Center Regulations; NH Code of Administrative Rules Part He-P 801; NM Regulations for Maternity Homes; NY Administrative Code Title 10, Chapter V, Subchapter B Part 600, Subchapter C Parts 700, 710, 715, 750–752; UT Department of Health Rules and Regulations §26–21–1; WA Administrative Code chs. 18.46, 248.29.

p. 209 Blue Cross plan for shorter hospital stays: *Wall Street Journal*, 11/15/83, p. 1 (untitled news item).
"A 1984 New York case . . ." *New York Hospital v. Josil*, N.Y.L.J., 1/19/84, p.11.

p. 210 "Nebraska, North Dakota, and Oregon . . ." NB §71–1405; ND §23–07–10; OR §432.205. TN §63.6.204.
"sixteen will grant licenses to lay midwives . . ." AZ §36–751; AR §72–2207 (72–2201 licenses certified nurse-midwives); CT §20–75; DE T16 §122; FL §467.001; GA §31–26–1; IN §25–22.5–5–5; MN §148.30; NH §326:D–2; NJ §45:10–1; NM §9–7–6; PA T63 §171; RI §23–13–9; SC §40–33–50; TX Health & Safety §4477 rule 49(a); WA §18.50.010.
"twenty restrict licenses to certified nurse-midwives . . ." AL §34–19–4; AK §47.07.900; CA Bus. & Prof. §2505; CO §12–36–106; HI §321–13(a)(1); KY §211.180; MD HO §7–603; MA ch. 112 §80C; MI §333.17210; MO §334.120; MT §37–8–409; NY Public Health §2560; NC §90.178.1; OH §4731.30; OK T59 §577.1; SD §36–9A; UT §58–44–1; VA §32.1–145; WV §30–15–1; WI §441.15.

p. 211 On unlicensed midwives: *Bowland v. Municipal Court,* 18 Cal.3d. 479, 559 P.2d 1081, 134 Cal.Rptr. 630 (1976), denies the right of unlicensed midwives to challenge the statute forbidding unlicensed practice of medicine. The court's rationale is that pregnancy isn't a "sickness or affliction" but is a "physical condition" as defined by the statute, which isn't vague, unconstitutionally broad, or a violation of a prospective mother's right of privacy.

p. 212 On the Nashville nurse-midwives: the case is *Nurse Midwifery Associates v. Hibbett,* 549 F.Supp. 1185 (M.D. Tenn. 1982); the FTC consent decree is *State Volunteer Mutual Insurance Co. Inc.*, CCH Trade Cases ¶22,030 (5/31/83). See *Wall Street Journal,* 2/22/83, p. 1 (unsigned news item); Michael deCourcy Hinds, "Midwives Seek Delivery from Discrimination," *New York Times,* 8/7/83, p. E9; Barbara McCormick, "Childbearing and Nurse-Midwives: A Woman's Right to Choose," 58 *N.Y.U. L.Rev.* 661 (June 1983).

p. 213 Direct payment of midwives: e.g., AK §21.42.355, 47.07.900; AR §72–2202; CA Welfare & Institutions §14132.4; PA T40 §3001; WI §441.15.
". . . a union violates Title VII . . ." EEOC Dec. No. 70–600, CCH EEOC Dec. ¶6122 (1970).
"The state acts as an 'employment agency' . . ." EEOC Dec. No. 78–46, CCH EEOC Dec. ¶6729 (1978).
"a case against the doctor for invasion of privacy . . ." *Drake v. Covington County Board of Education,* 371 F.Supp. 974 (M.D. Ala. 1974).
". . . the school board acted in good faith . . ." *Paxman v. Campbell,* 612 F.2d 848 (4th Cir. 1980), *cert.den.,* 449 U.S. 1129; *Clanton v. Orleans Parish School Board,* 649 F.2d 1084 (5th cir. 1981).

p. 214 *White v. ITT,* 114 LRRM 3132 (11th Cir. 1983).
". . . up to thirty days' non-medical leave . . ." *Northern Indiana Public Service Co.,* 80 LA 41 (1982).
Goss v. Exxon Office Systems, 33 FEP Cases 21 (E.D. Pa. 1983).

p. 215 *Beck v. Quiktrip Corp.,* 32 EPD ¶33,643 (10th Cir. 1983).

CHAPTER 9

STERILIZATION AND STERILIZATION ABUSE

p. 216 For general reference: Emily Diamond, "Coerced Sterilization Under Federally Funded Family Planning Programs," 11 *New England L. Rev.* 589 (1976); Robert and Marcia Pearch Burgdorf, "The Wicked Witch Is Almost Dead: *Buck v. Bell* and the Sterilization of Handicapped Persons," 50 *Temple L. Q.* 995 (1977); Deborah DuBois Davis, "Addressing the Consent Issue Involved in the Sterilization of Mentally Incompetent Females," 43 *Albany L. Rev.* 322 (1979); Jo Ellen Diehl, "*Ruby v. Massey:* Sterilization of the Mentally Retarded," 9 *Capital U. L. Rev.* 191 (1979); Rosalind Pollack Petchesky, "Reproduction, Ethics, and Public Policy: The Federal Sterilization Regulations," 9 *Hastings Center Reports* 29 (Oct 1979); Dick Grosboll, "Sterilization Abuse: Current State of the Law and Remedies for Abuse," 10 *Golden Gate U. L. Rev.* 1147 (Summer 1980); Stephen L. Isaacs, "The Law of Fertility Regulation in the United States: A 1980 Review," 19 *J. Fam. Law.* 65 (Nov 1980); Deborah Harden Ross, "Sterilization of the Developmentally Disabled: Shedding Some Myth-Conceptions," 9 *Florida State U. L. Rev.* 599 (1981); Robert J. Cynkar, "*Buck v. Bell:* " 'Felt Necessities' v. Fundamental Values?" 81 *Columbia L. Rev.* 1418 (Nov 1981); Denise Lachance, "*In re Grady:* The Mentally Retarded Individual's Right to Choose Sterilization," 6 *Am. J. Law & Medicine* 559 (Winter 1981); Richard K. and Robert D. Sherlock, "Sterilizing the Retarded: Constitutional, Statutory, and Policy Alternatives," 60 *North Carolina L. Rev.* 943 (June 1982); P. Marcos Sokkappa, "Sterilization Petitions: Developing Judicial Guidelines," 44 *Montana L. Rev.* 127 (Winter 1983).

p. 218 ". . . if voluntary sterilizations are repugnant . . ." *Chrisman v. Sisters of St. Joseph of Peace*, 506 F.2d 308 (9th Cir. 1974). KS §65–446; MD HG §20–214; MA ch 272:21B; PA T43 §955.2; RI §23–17–11 (doctors and nurses only—not hospitals); WV §16–11–1; WI §441.06, 441.08 (personnel only—not hospitals). See *Swanson v. St. John's Lutheran Hospital*, 615 P.2d 883 (Mont. 1980), on damages for a nurse fired for refusing to participate in a tubal ligation.
". . . it can't discriminate against sterilization operations . . ." *Hathaway v. Worcester City Hospital*, 475 F.2d 701 (1st Cir. 1973).
"The basic rule . . ." AR §59–501(M), 82–3105; GA §31–20–1; KY §212.341; NC §90–271; OR §435.305; TN §56–7–1006; UT §64–10–1.
"A New Jersey case . . ." *Ponter v. Ponter*, 135 N.J. Super. 50, 342 A.2d 574 (1975); Iowa Opp. A.G. 10/28/75; OR §435.305.
"An Arkansas case . . ." *Sims v. University of Arkansas Medical Center*, No. 1-r–76–C–67 (E.D. Ark. 3/4/77).
". . . but the Ninth Circuit . . ." *Taylor v. St. Vincent's Hospital*, 523 F.2d 75 (9th Cir. 1975).
"South Carolina's attorney general . . ." 1976–7 Op. A.G. No. 77–110.
". . . so the Georgia and New Mexico statutes . . ." GA §31–20–1; NM §24–1–14. Also see *Holton v. Crozer-Chester Memorial Center*, 560 F.2d 575 (3rd Cir. 1977), allowing a class action against a group of private hospitals that required the husband's consent to sterilization of married women. The hospitals were

generous enough to sterilize women who had been separated for two years. One named plaintiff had been separated for twenty-three months; the other's husband was, as usual, at an unknown location.

". . . as no man has a right . . ." *Murray v. Vandevander,* 522 P.2d 302 (Okla. 1974).

"California and New Hampshire statutes . . ." CA Health & Safety §1258 (doctors and health facilities) §1232 (clinics) §1459 (county hospitals) §32128.10 (public hospitals). NH §460:21–a.

"In California (again) and Tennessee . . ." CA Insurance §10120; TN §56–7–1006 (health insurance policy), §56–27–133 (medical service plans).

". . . but not for disability caused by tubal ligation . . ." *Grogg v. General Motors Corp.,* 444 F.Supp. 1215 (D.N.Y. 1978).

p. 220 "In 1979, for example, a county in Arizona agreed . . ." Consent judgment in *Harris v. Karam* (D. Ariz. 1979, Civ 78–601–PHX VAC) a class action brought under 42 U.S.C.S. §1983 against the county and county officials.

pp. 220–221 "On a less cheerful note . . ." *Walker v. Pierce,* 560 F.2d 609, 611, 612 (4th Cir. 1977).

p. 221 Federal anti–sterilization abuse regulations: 42 C.F.R. §50.201; *Relf v. Weinberger,* 372 F.Supp. 1196 (D.D.C. 1974); *Relf v. Mathews,* 403 F.Supp. 1235 (D.D.C. 1975).

p. 222 "The age requirement has been upheld in court . . ." *Peck v. Califano,* 454 F.Supp. 484 (D. Utah 1977); *Voe v. Califano,* 434 F.Supp. 1058 (D.Conn. 1977). Also see *Gooley v. Moss,* 398 N.E.2d 1314 (Ind.App. 1979), on statute of limitations problems in sterilization-abuse cases.

State statutes against sterilization abuse: CA Welfare & Institutions §14191; *California Medical Ass'n v. Lackner* (Cal.App. 9/30/81); KY §212.341, 212.990; ME T34–B §7001; MD HG §20–214; MA ch 112 §12W; MN §149.925; NC §90–271; OR §435.305; TN §68–34–108; UT §64–10–1; VA §54–325.9; WA §1.92.100; WV §16–11–1; WI 4 Admin. Code ch HSS §101.03 (168).

See pages 195–196 for a discussion of sterilization and fetal protection programs. California Gov't §12945.5 makes it an unlawful employment practice for an employer to require an employee to be sterilized as a condition of employment.

p. 223 "Colorado forbids . . ." §27–10.15–12.

p. 224 "Sixteen states have some kind of provision . . ." AR §59–501; CT §45–78p; DE T16 §5701; ID §39–3901; ME T34–B §7001; MN §252A.13; NH §464–A:25I(c); NJ §30:4–24.2(d); NC §35–36, modified by *NC Ass'n for Retarded Children v. North Carolina,* 420 F.Supp. 451 (M.D. N.C. 1976); OR §436.010 (referred to as "sterilization for social protection"); SC §44–47–10; UT §64–10–1; VT T18 §8701 (state policy is prevention of procreation when this is in the best interest of the public and the retarded person); VA §54–325.11; WV §27–16–1.

p. 225 ". . . courts have no jurisdiction to hear sterilization petitions . . ." AL *Hudson v. Hudson,* 373 So.2d 310 (Ala. 1979); CA *Guardianship of Tulley,* 83 Cal.App.3d 698, 146 Cal.Rptr. 266 (1978); DE *In re S.C.E.,* 378 A.2d 144 (1977) (noninstitutionalized person); IN *A.L. v. G.R.H.*, 163 Ind. App. 636, 325 N.E.2d 501 (1971), *cert.den.*, 425 U.S. 936 (1976); MO *In the Interest of M.K.R.*, 515 S.W.2d 467 (Mo. 1974); New York is split: *In re D.D.*, 90 Misc.2d 236, 394 N.Y.S.2d 104—but see the next note; TX *Frazier v. Levi*, 440 S.W.2d 393 (Tex.Civ.App. 1979); WI *In re Guardianship of Eberhardy*, 102 Wis.2d 539, 307 N.W.2d 881 (1981).

"The other group allows . . ." AL *Wyatt v. Aderholt*, 368 F.Supp. 1383 (M.D. Ala. 1974); AK *C.D.M. v. State*, 627 P.2d 607(1981); CO *In re A.W.*, 637 P.2d 366 (1981); CT *Ruby v. Massey*, 452 F.Supp. 361 (D. Conn. 1978); MD *Wentzel v. Montgomery General Hospital*, 449 A.2d 1244 (Md. 1982); MA *In re Mary Moe*, 385 Mass. 555, 532 N.E.2d 712 (1982); NH *In re Penny N.*, 120 N.H. 269, 414 A.2d 541 (1980); NJ *In re Grady*, 85 N.J. 235, 426 A.2d 467 (1981); NY *In re Sallmaier*, 85 Misc.2d 295, 378 N.Y.S.2d 989 (Sup.Ct. 1976); PA *Matter of Terwilliger*, 450 A.2d 1376 (1982); WA *In re Guardianship of Hayes*, 93 Wash.2d 228, 608 P.2d 635 (1980).

Stump v. Sparkman, 435 U.S. 347 (1978); see Martha O. Shoemaker, "*Stump v. Sparkman:* The Scope of Judicial and Derivative Immunity Under 42 U.S.C. §1983," 6 *Women's Rights Law Reporter* 107 (Fall-Winter 1980).

p. 226 Wrongful birth: I'm not going to open this can of worms—it would take a chapter to discuss it thoroughly—but see, e.g., the Health Law Center's *Hospital Law Manual* (Aspen, 1982) ¶5–7, pp. 44–6; Amy Norwood Moore, "Judicial Limitations on Damages Recoverable for the Wrongful Birth of a Healthy Infant," 68 *Va. L. Rev.* 1311 (Sept. 1982); cases such as *University of Arizona Health Services Center v. Arizona Superior Court*, 52 LW 2090 (Ariz. Sup.Ct. 7/20/83); *Jones v. Malinowski* (Md.Ct.App. No. 29, 4/6/84), and Robert C. Schwenkel, "Wrongful Life: An Infant's Claim to Damages," 30 *Buffalo L. Rev.* 587 (Summer 1981); and cases such as *Curlender v. Bio-Science Labs*, 106 Cal.App.3d 811, 165 Cal.Rptr. 477 (1980).

"If the purpose of the sterilization . . ." e.g., *Speck v. Finegold*, 439 A.2d 110 (Pa. 1981).

p. 227 State action: *Downs v. Sawtelle*, 574 F.2d 1 (1st Cir. 1978), *cert.den.*, 439 U.S. 910; see the Grosboll article listed under "general reference."

CHAPTER 10

FOR UNTO (ALL OF) US A CHILD IS BORN: TECHNOLOGICAL PARENTHOOD

---

p. 229 ". . . and some states make it illegal to pay . . ." e.g., AZ §8–126(c); CA Penal §273; CO §19–4–115; DE T13 §928; FL §72.40; ID §18–1511; IL ch 40 §1526; IA §600.9; KY §199.590; MA ch 210 §11A; MI §710.54; NV §127.290; NC §48–37.

". . . for anyone except a doctor to perform artificial insemination . . ." e.g., GA §43–34–42; OK T10 §551; OR §677.365(4).

p. 230 "Many, many law review articles . . ." a representative selection: Paula Deane Turner, "Love's Labor Lost: Legal and Ethical Implications in Artificial Human Procreation," 58 *U. Det. Urban L. J.* 459 (1981); Lindsey E. Harris, "Artificial Insemination and Surrogate Motherhood: A Nursery Full of Unresolved Questions," 17 *Willamette L. Rev.* 913 (1981); Lisa J. Greenberg and Harold Hirsh, "Surrogate Motherhood and Artificial Insemination: Contractual Implications," 29 *Med. Trial Technique Q.* 149 (1983 Annual).

". . . about half the states have passed laws . . ." AK §25.20.405; CA Civ §7005; CO §19–6–106; CT §45–69f–n; FL §742.11; GA §19–7–21; KS §23–128; LA Civ. art. 188; MD Estate & Trust §1–206(b); MA ch 46 §4B; MI §700.111(2); MN §257.56; MT §40–6–106; NV §126.061; NY Dom.Rel. §73; NC §49A–1; OK T10 §551; OR §109.239, 677.355; TN §53–446; TX Fam. §12.03; VA §64.1–7.1; WA §26.26.050; WI §891.40; WY §14–2–103.

C.M. v. C.C., 152 N.J. Super. 160, 377 A.2d 821 (1977).

"A few states (e.g., Georgia) . . ." GA §43–34–42. Sample consent forms are given in *Am. Jur. Legal Forms* 2d, *Physicians*, §202:81–88.

"One Nevada case . . ." *Fitzgerald v. Rueckl* (Nev. Sup. Ct. No. 11433, 1982): see David Ranii, "Future Shock for Family Law," *Nat. L.J.*, 3/26/84, p. 1.

p. 231 "*In vitro* fertilization is probably legal . . ." *Smith v. Hartigan*, 83–C–4324 (D.Ill. 2/4/83); see the Ranii article cited above. The statute is IL ch. 38 §81–26(7); cf. MN §145.421(2), (3), §145.422.

Reports: PA T18 §3213(e)—oddly, part of the Abortion Control Act.

". . . if the fertilized egg is frozen . . ." I'm not making this stuff up: see "First Baby Born of Frozen Embryo" (no by-line), *New York Times*, 4/11/84, p. A16.

p. 232 ". . . laws against experimenting on fetuses . . ." CA Health & Safety §25956; IL ch. 38 §81–26(3); KY §436.026; LA §40:1299.35.13; ME T22 §1593; MA ch 112 §12J(a)I, IV; MI §333.2685; MN §145.422(1); OK T 63 §1–735; PA T35 §6605(b); TN §39–308(b); UT §76–7–310; WY §35–6–115.

Law review articles about *in vitro* fertilization: Dennis M. Flannery, Carol Drescher Weisman, Christopher P. Lipsett & Alan M. Braverman, "Test Tube Babies: Legal Issues Raised by In Vitro Fertilization," 67 *Georgetown L. J.* 1295; Kathryn Venturatos Lorio, "In Vitro Fertilization and Embryo Transfer: Fertile Areas for Litigation," 35 *Southwestern U. L. J.* 973 (Feb 1982); Margaret I. Lane et.al., "In Vitro Fertilization: Hope for Childless Couples Breeds Legal Exposure for Physicians," 17 *U. Richmond L. Rev.* 311 (Winter 1983).

". . . potential parents have some kind of interest . . ." *DelZio v. Columbia Presbyterian Medical Center* (S.D.N.Y. No. 74–3588, 4/12/78).

p. 233 "A married couple from Los Angeles . . ." David Margolick, "Legal Rights of Embryos," *New York Times*, 6/27/84, p. A12, and no by-line, "Australians Reject Bid to Destroy 2 Embryos," *New York Times*, 10/24/84, p. A18.

"People do make quite detailed contracts . . ." e.g., Elizabeth A. Erickson, "Contracts to Bear a Child," 66 *Cal. L. Rev.* 611 (1978); Katie Marie Brophy, "A Surrogate Mother Contract to Bear a Child," 20 *J. Fam. L.* 263 (1981–2). Other law review articles on surrogate motherhood: John W. and Susan D. Phillips, "In Defense of Surrogate Parenting: A Critical Analysis of the Recent Kentucky Experience," 69 *Kentucky L.J.* 877 (1980–1); Ellen Lassner Van Hoften, "Surrogate Motherhood in California: Legislative Proposals," 18 *San Diego L. Rev.* 341 (1981); Perry J. Vieth, "Surrogate Mothering: Medical Reality in a Legal Vacuum," 8 *J. Legislation* 140 (1981); Robert C. Black, "Legal Problems of Surrogate Mother-hood," 16 *New England L. Rev.* 373 (1981); Walter Wadlington, "Artificial Con-ception: The Challenge for Family Law," 69 *Virginia L. Rev.* 465 (April 1983); Kelly L. Frey, "New Reproductive Technologies: 465 (April 1983); Kelly L. Frey, "New Reproductive Technologies: The Legal Problem and a Solution," 49 *Tenn. L. Rev.* 303 (Winter 1982).

p. 234 "One school of thought . . ." e.g., the Frey article cited above.
". . . some adoption laws require a waiting period . . ." e.g., Kentucky (see opinion of Attorney General Beshear, quoted in 16 *Family L. Q.* 297 (Winter 1983); *Anonymous v. Anonymous,* 7 *Family Law Reporter* 2459 (N.Y. 1981).
"The question has come up in Michigan three times . . ." *Doe v. Kelley,* 106 Mich.App. 169, 307 N.W.2d 438 (1981); *Syrkowski v. Appleyard,* 8 *Family Law Reporter* 2139 (Mich. 1981), *aff'd,* 9 *Family Law Reporter* 2260 (Mich. App. 1983). The District of Columbia, citing these cases, said that "further information" is required before a woman can adopt the surrogate-mothered baby: *In re RKS,* 52 LW 2648 (D.C. Sup. 4/13/84).
"One says that Kentucky law . . ." *In re Baby Girl,* 9 *Family Law Reporter* 2348 (Ky. Cir. Ct. 1983).
"But seven months later . . ." *Kentucky v. Surrogate Parenting Association Inc.,* 52 LW 2363, 10 *Family Law Reporter* 1105 (1983).

CHAPTER 11

ABORTION

---

p. 237 References on abortion: Don F. Vaccaro, "Right of a Minor to Have Abortion Performed Without Parental Consent," 42 *A.L.R.*3d 1406; W.E. Shipley, "Woman's Right to Have an Abortion Without Consent of, or Against Objections Of, Child's Father," 62 *A.L.R.*3d 1097; Wanda Ellen Wakefield, "Validity of State Statutes and Regulations Limiting or Restricting Public Funding for Abortions Sought by Indigent Women," 20 *A.L.R.*4th 1166; Linda Robinson, "Abortion Clinic Zoning: The Right to Procreative Freedom and the Zoning Power," 5 *Women's Rights Law Reporter* 283 (Summer 1979); Jean Gray Platt, ed., "Survey of Abortion Law" (Special Project), *Arizona State L.J.* 73 (Winter 1980); John R. Schaibley, III, "Sex Selection Abortion: A Constitutional Analysis of the Abortion Liberty and a Person's Right to Know," 56 *Indiana L.J.* 281 (Winter 1981); S. Stockwell Stoutamire, "The Effect of Legalized Abortion on Wrongful Life Ac-tions," 9 *Florida State U. L. Rev.* 137 (Winter 1981); Rosamond A. Barber, "Note: Criminal Liability of Physicians: An Encroachment on the Abortion Right?" 18 *Am. Crim. L. Rev.* 591 (Spring 1981); Ken Martyn, "Technological Advances and *Roe v. Wade:* The Need to Rethink Abortion Law," 29 *UCLA L. Rev.* 1194 (June–Aug 1982); Elizabeth Buchanan, "The Constitution and the Anomaly of the Preg-nant Teenager," 24 *Ariz. L. Rev.* 553 (Summer 1982); Susan A. Bush, "Parental

Notification: A State-Created Obstacle to a Minor Woman's Right of Privacy," 12 *Golden Gate U. L. Rev.* 579 (Summer 1982); Brian D. Shore, "Marital Secrets: The Emerging Issue of Abortion Spousal Notification Laws," 3 *J. Legal Med.* 461 (September 1982); Gina Schacter, "A Private Cause of Action for Abortion Expenses Under State Paternity Statutes," 7 *Women's Rights Law Rep.* 63 (Winter 1982); Robert B. Keitler, "Privacy, Children, and Their Parents: Reflections on and Beyond the Supreme Court's Approach," 66 *Minn. L. Rev.* 459 (1982); Martha Christine Foley, "Hospitalization Requirements for Second Trimester Abortions: For the Purpose of Health or Hindrance?" 71 *Georgetown L. J.* 991 (February 1983); Curt S. Rush, "Genetic Screening, Eugenic Abortion, and *Roe v. Wade*," 50 *Bklyn. L. Rev.* 113 (Fall 1983); Nancy Ford, "The Evolution of a Constitutional Right to an Abortion," 4 *J. Legal Med.* 271 (September 1983).

p. 240 On "regular" physicians, evolution of state abortion law: see Platt article cited above. The eleven states were AR, CA, CO, DE, GA, KS, MD, NM, NC, SC, and VA.

p. 241 Quote is from pp. 153–4 of the *Roe v. Wade* majority opinion. However, as *Roe* is written in terms of women acting on doctors' advice, a state law *can* forbid performance of abortions by anyone except physicians: *Connecticut v. Menillo*, 423 U.S. 9 (1975). It would be possible—and cheaper—for abortions to be performed safely by trained paramedics, but, as we've seen in the discussion of midwives, independent paraprofessionals in health care get short shrift.

p. 242 ". . . could no longer bar early abortions . . ." see *Friendship Medical Ctr. Ltd. v. Chicago Board of Health*, 505 F.2d 1141 (7th Cir. 1974), *cert.den.*, 420 U.S. 997 (woman's fundamental right of privacy includes freedom from regulations that limit first-trimester abortions); *Emma G. v. Edwards*, 434 F.Supp. 1048 (E.D. La. 1977) (state can't require all first-trimester abortions to be performed in hospitals).
". . . they *still* haven't taken their pre–*Roe v. Wade* abortion laws off the books." AL §13A–13–7; AZ §13–3603; AR §41–2551, –2554; CA Health & Safety §25951; CO §25–1–667; DE T11 §651, T24 §1790; IA §707.7; KS §21–3407; MI §750.14; MS §97–3–3; NH §585.12; NM §30–5–2; OR §435.15; VT T13 §101; WA §9.02.070; WV §61–2–8 (found unconstitutional in 1975 but not replaced); WI §940.04.
The quote is from IL ch 38 ¶81–21; cf ID §18–613, MT §50–20–102; NB §28–325; ND §14–02.1–01; PA T18 §3202(c); SD §34–23A–21.

p. 243 ". . . do not have veto power . . ." *Coe v. Gerstein*, 376 F. Supp. 695 (D. Fla. 1973); *Doe v. Rampton*, 366 F. Supp. 189 (D. Utah 1973); *Doe v. Doe*, 314 N.E.2d 128 (Mass. 1974); *Planned Parenthood v. Danforth*, 428 U.S. 52 (1976).
". . . still has a unilateral right . . ." *Wolfe v. Schroering*, 541 F.2d 523 (6th Cir. 1976).
". . . must be subordinated . . ." *Jones v. Smith*, 278 So.2d 339 (Fla. 1973), *cert. den.*, 415 U.S. 958; *Rothenberger v. Doe*, 149 N.J. Super. 478, 374 A.2d 57 (1977).
Spousal notification statutes: FL §390.001(4)(a); IL ch 38 ¶81–23.4; MT §50–20–107 (unless they are separated); NV §442.254 (unless separated); ND §14.02.1–

02 (third-trimester abortions); SC §44–41–10 (third-trimester); SD §34–23A–7 (married minor); UT §76–7–304; WA §9.02.070. See *Fritz v. Coleman,* 53 LW 3017 (Md.App. 3/6/84); *Eubanks v. Collins,* 10 FLR 1659 (W.D.Ky. 9/11/84). ". . . have been held to justify a spousal *notice* requirement . . ." *Scheinberg v. Smith,* 659 F.2d 476,485 (5th Cir. 1981). The Fifth Circuit said, "absent such a right the marital relationship between a couple could be maintained without a band ever discovering why or how his aspirations for a family have been frustrated. This is surely a perversion of the institution of marriage, as conceived in our society and as instituted by the state." While I agree that having an abortion without consulting one's husband is a rotten thing to do, the remedy seems to me to be in the divorce court rather than the abortion statute. Compulsory child-bearing seems to me a much more serious perversion of the marriage relationship, but they didn't ask me.

p. 244 State laws requiring *notice* to parents: AZ §36–2152; IL Acts 1983 SB No. 521; FL §390.025 (abortion referral or counseling service must make good-faith effort to explain effects of and alternatives to abortion to parents of minor client); ME T22 §1597; MD HG §20–103; NB §28–3333 (minor must sign a statement that she has consulted her parents—and if you believe that, you may be interested in this bridge . . .); NB §23–333 (similar to MD); NV §442.255; ND §14–02.1–02 (disapproved by *Leigh v. Olson,* 497 F. Supp. 1340 (D. N.D. 1980); UT §76–7–304.
Parental *consent* requirements: AK §18.16.010; FL §390.001(4)(a); IN §35–1–58.5–2.5; KY §311.732; LA §1299.35.5 (upheld by *Re Application of Doe,* 407 So.2d 1190 (La. 1981)); MA ch 112 §12S; MO §188.028; MT §50–20–107; ND §14.02.1–03.1; OH §2919.11; PA T18 §3206; SC §44–41–30; SD §34–23A–7; WA §9.02.070 (disapproved by *State v. Koome,* 94 Wash.2d 901, 530 P.2d 260 (1975).

p. 245 Consent to prenatal care: e.g., AK §09.65.100, CO §13–22–102, IL ch 111 §4501.2; MD art 43 §135(a)(1); MA ch 112 §12S, NY Pub Health §2504(1); UT §78–14–5(4)(f).
Bellotti v. Baird ("Bellotti II") 443 U.S. 622 (1979). Also see *Women's Services v. Thone,* 636 F.2d 206 (8th Cir. 1980) (applies *Bellotti II* to invalidate parental consultation requirement), and *Leigh v. Olson,* 497 F. Supp. 1340 (D. N.D. 1980) (requirement of notice to all parents of minors—even mature minors—is invalid).

pp. 245–246 ". . . overturned a city ordinance . . ." *City of Akron v. Akron Center for Reproductive Health,* 51 LW 4767 (6/15/83).
"It's all right . . ." *Planned Parenthood v. Ashcroft,* 51 LW 4783 (6/15/83).

p. 246 ". . . can't *order* her to take her mother's advice . . ." *Re Smith,* 16 Md. App. 209, 295 A.2d 238 (1972).
". . . giving a pregnant minor the right to consent . . ." *Re Diane,* 318 A.2d 629 (Del. 1974).
"Washington State's parental consent requirement . . ." *State v. Koome,* 84 Wash.2d 901, 530 P.2d 260 (1975).
Wynn v. Carey 599 F.2d 193 (7th Cir. 1979).
". . . too much work for too little return." e.g., *Women's Medical Center of*

Providence v. Cannon, 463 F. Supp. 531 (D. R.I. 1978), tossing out a Department of Health rule that all doctors performing first-trimester abortions must have full privileges at a nearby hospital, because the rule violated patients' equal-protection rights, and because the patients had a right to an early abortion free of state interference.

p. 247 "A number of states . . ."   according to the 1983 Foley article cited above, the states were Connecticut, Hawaii, Idaho, Illinois, Massachusetts, Montana, New York, North Dakota, Oklahoma, Pennsylvania (held unconstitutional by *ACOG v. Thornburgh*, 52 LW 2713 (3d Cir. 1984)).
"The Supreme Court rules on these requirements . . ."   *City of Akron v. Akron Center for Reproductive Health*, 51 LW 4767 (6/15/83); *Simopoulos v. Virginia*, 51 LW 4791 (6/15/83).

p. 248 *Planned Parenthood v. Danforth*, 428 U.S. 52, 63(1976)—which hasn't stopped some states from so determining: e.g., MA ch 112 §12M (24 weeks), MN §145.411 (halfway through gestation period), OK T63 §1–732 (24 weeks).
". . . laws specifying the medical profession's duty . . ."   AZ §36–2301 (preserve live-born fetus); CA Health & Safety §25955.9 (live-born fetus entitled to medical treatment); DE T24 §1795 (preserve live-born fetus); FL §390.001(4)(a); ID §18–608(2); IL ch 38 ¶81–25, –26 (doctor must certify fetus is non-viable before performing elective abortion; must use all medical skill to preserve life of viable fetus unless this would increase risk to the mother); IN §35–1–58.5–7 (post-viability abortions restricted to hospitals with Neonatal Intensive Care units); IA §707.7; LA §40:1299.35 (requirement of ultrasound to assess fetal development; second doctor must be present at post-viability abortion to help fetus); ME T22 §1591; MA ch 112 §12M; MN §145.411; MO §188.030, .035 (intentional killing of live-born fetus is second-degree murder); MT §50–20–109; NB §28.330, .331; NV §442.270; NY Penal §125.05 (second doctor at post-viability abortion); ND §14–02.1–05, –08 (second doctor required; killing live-born fetus is Class C felony); OH §2919.13 (killing live-born fetus is manslaughter); OK T63 §1–730, –734 (same); PA T18 §3210, –3212 (held unconstitutional by *ACOG v. Thornburgh*); RI §11–9–18; SD §34–23A–206; UT §76–7–307, –309; WA §18.71–240 (medical treatment for live-born fetus mandatory); WY §35–6–104.
"It's permissible for a state . . ."   *Planned Parenthood v. Ashcroft*, 51 LW 4783 (6/15/83).
"However, a law imposing liability on doctors . . ."   e.g., *Colautti v. Franklin*, 439 U.S. 379 (1979), striking down part of the former Pennsylvania statute. The revised Pennsylvania statute didn't do much better; the Third Circuit tossed out most of it in *ACOG v. Thornburgh*, No. 82–1785, 52 LW 2713 (5/31/84).
"The Eastern District of Louisiana upheld . . ."   *Margaret S. v. Edwards*, 488 F. Supp. 181 (E.D. La. 1980).

p. 249 ". . . because the cases are nearly impossible to prove."   e.g., *State v. Waddill*, Cal. Super. Ct. No. C37815 dismissed 6/11/79, and Minneapolis Grand Jury's 1974 refusal to indict: see Rosamond A. Barber, "Note: Criminal Liability

of Physicians: An Encroachment on the Abortion Right?" 18 *Am. Crim. L. Rev.*
591 (1981).

p. 250 ". . . sign a statement indicating her informed consent . . ." (* indicates
statutory script for the conference) DE T24 §1794*; FL §390.025*; ID §18–608(2),
–609*; IL ch 38 ¶81–23.2* (requirement that doctor performing the abortion do
the counseling knocked out by *Charles v. Carey*, 627 F.2d 772 (7th Cir. 1980));
KY §311.720* (invalidated by *Eubanks v. Collins*, 10 FLR 1659 (W.D. Ky. 9/11/
84); ME T22 §1599*; MD HG §20–211*; MA ch 112 §12Q, 12S*; MN §145.411;
MO §188.010, 188.039*; MT §50–20–102*; NB §28–326(8)*; NV §442.240*; ND
§14–02.1–02* (invalidated in part by *Leigh v. Olson*, 497 F. Supp. 1340 (D. N.D.
1980)); OH §2919.12; PA T18 §3205* (invalidated by *ACOG v. Thornburgh*, 52
LW 2713 (1984)); RI §23–4.7–1; SD §34–23A–10.1*; TN §39–4–202*; UT §76–
7–305*; WA §9.02.070.
"The Eastern District of Louisiana . . ." *Margaret S. v. Edwards*, 488 F. Supp.
181 (E.D. La. 1980).
Leigh v. Olson, 497 F. Supp. 1340 (D. N.D. 1980).
". . . employing a favorite technique jurists use to build suspense . . ." *Women's
Services v. Thone*, 636 F.2d 206 (8th Cir. 1980). In this case, the state is Nebraska.
Charles v. Carey, 627 F.2d 772 (7th Cir. 1980).
". . . when the District of Rhode Island found . . ." *Women's Medical Center
of Providence v. Roberts*, 530 F. Supp. 1136.
"The Supreme Court settled the matter . . ." *City of Akron v. Akron Center
for Reproductive Health*, 51 LW 4767 (6/15/83). Also see *ACOG v. Thornburgh*,
52 LW 2713 (3d Cir. 1984).

p. 251 "Several state laws do contain waiting-period provisions." IL ch 38 ¶81–
23.2 (24 hrs); ME T22 §1599 (48 hrs); NB §28–327 (48 hrs); NV §442.240 (at least
one, not more than 30, days between consent and abortion); PA T18 §3205 (24
hrs); TN §39–4–202 (48 hrs).
". . . if the state forbids post-viability elective abortions" FL §390.001(4); GA
§16–12–141; HI §453–16; ID §18–608(2); IL ch 38 ¶81–25; IA §707.7; KY §311.780;
LA §40:1299.35; ME T22 §1598; MA ch 112 §12M; MN §145.411; MT §50–2–
109; NB §28–329; NV §442.240; NC §14–45.1; OK T63 §1–732; PA T18 §3210;
SC §44–41–10; SD §34–23A–5; UT §78–7–301; VA §18.2–71; WY §35–6–102.

p. 252 "Courts have analyzed such [zoning] laws in a number of ways . . ." also
see *Planned Parenthood v. Citizens for Community Action*, 558 F.2d 861 (8th
Cir. 1977), on standards for granting injunctions against enforcement of zoning
laws forbidding abortion clinics.
". . . is invalid in Massachusetts . . ." *Framingham Clinic v. Board of Select-
men*, 367 N.E.2d 606 (Mass. 1977).
"In Ohio, the rule is more or less the opposite . . ." *West Side Women's Services
Inc. v. City of Cleveland*, 450 F. Supp. 796 (N.D. Ohio 1978), *aff'd* 582 F.2d
1281, *cert. den.*, 439 U.S. 983.
"New York came up with yet another formula . . ." *Westchester Women's Health
Org. Inc. v. Whalen*, 475 F. Supp. 734 (S.D.N.Y. 1979).

"The Sixth Circuit turned thumbs down . . ." *Mahoning Women's Center v. Hunter*, 610 F.2d 456 (6th Cir. 1979).

"The First Circuit, reasonably enough . . ." *Baird v. Department of Public Health*, 599 F.2d 1098 (1st Cir. 1979).

". . . allowed free-standing clinics . . ." *Bossier City Medical Suite, Inc. v. Bossier City*, 483 F. Supp. 633 (W.D. La. 1980).

". . . get a license as an 'ambulatory surgical treatment center' . . ." *Village of Oak Lawn v. Marcowitz*, 427 N.E.2d 36 (Ill. 1981).

pp. 252–253 "The Fifth Circuit took a strong pro-choice stand . . ." *Deerfield Medical Center v. City of Deerfield Beach*, 661 F.2d 328 (5th Cir. 1981).

p. 253 "The current version . . ." PL 97–377 §204, 96 Stat. 1830, 1894 §204. "The implementing regulations for the Hyde Amendment . . ." are at 42 CFR §411.201; the Medicaid regulations are at 42 CFR §50.301. The provisions for grants for Family Planning services (42 CFR Part 59) deny grants to organizations that provide abortions as a means of family planning. (Also see *Planned Parenthood v. Arizona*, 718 F.2d 938 (9th Cir. 1983).) In July 1984 the United States threatened to cut off foreign aid to countries in which abortion was used as a means of family planning—a neat demonstration of chauvinism in both its primary and secondary meanings.

p. 254 "In 1976, the Court handled a case involving standing . . ." *Singleton v. Wulff*, 428 U.S. 106, 118 (1976).
Beal v. Doe, 432 U.S. 438 (1977), *Maher v. Roe*, 432 U.S. 464 (1977). States forbidding public funding of abortions except for preservation of the mother's life: NJ §40:4D–6.1 (but see *Right to Choose v. Byrne*, discussed below); ND §14–02.3–01; PA T18 §3215; TN Acts 1983 ch 403 §15; WI §20.927.

p. 255 *Williams v. Zbaraz*, 448 U.S. 358 (1980).
Split of authority: 10TH CIR *D.R. v. Mitchell*, 645 F.2d 852 (10th Cir. 1981). WD MO *Frieman v. Walsh*, 481 F. Supp. 137 (W.D. Mo. 1979). 1ST CIR *Preterm v. Dukakis*, 591 F.2d 121 (1st Cir. 1979), *cert. den.*, 99 S. Ct. 2182 (1979); on certification of class to protest refusal to fund Medicaid therapeutic abortions, see *Moe v. Sec'y of Admin. & Finance*, 417 N.E.2d 387 (Mass. 1981). 4TH CIR *Doe v. Kenley*, 584 F.2d 1362 (4th Cir. 1978). 8TH CIR *Reproductive Health Services v. Freeman*, 614 F.2d 585 (8th Cir. 1980). ED PA *Roe v. Casey*, 464 F. Supp. 487 (E.D. Pa. 1978). ND GA *Doe v. Bushee*, 471 F. Supp. 1326 (N.D. Ga. 1979). NJ *Right to Choose v. Byrne*, 91 N.J. 287, 450 A.2d 925 (N.J. 1982). OR *Planned Parenthood v. Oregon Dep't of Human Resources*, No. CA–A–20856 (Or. 5/11/83). CA *Committee to Defend Reproductive Rights v. Myers*, 172 Cal. Rptr. 866, 625 P.2d 779 (Cal. 1981); *Same v. Cory*, 132 Cal. App. 3d 852, 183 Cal. Rptr. 475 (1982); *Same v. Rank*, 198 Cal. Rptr. 630 (1984).

p. 256 "Several states have recognized that abortion coercion could be a problem . . ." AR §41–2554; KY §311.810 (no coercion to abort or refrain from aborting); MD HG §20–214; MN §145.925; PA T18 §3201; UT §76–7–312.
State conscience laws: AK §18.16.010 (institutional and individual); AZ §36–2151 (both) CA Health & Safety §29555 (individual; not-for-profit religious hospital);

DE T24 §1790 (both) FL §390.001 (both) GA §16–12–142 (both); HI §453–16 (both); IL ch 38 ¶81–33 (both); IA §146.1 (individual); KS §65.443 (individual); KY §311.800 (individual, private hospital); ME T22 §1591 (both); MD HG §20–214 (both); MA ch 112 §12I (both); MN §145.414 (both); MT §50–2–111 (individual, private hospital); NB §28–337, –338 (both); NM §30–5–1, 30–5–2 (both); NJ §2A:65A–1 (both); NC §14–45.1 (both); OK T63 §1–741 (individual, private hospital); PA T43 §955.2 (both); SD §34–23A–12, –14 (both); TN §39–4–204, –205 (both); TX Civ §4512.7 (individual, private hospital); UT §76–7–306 (individual, private hospital); VA §18.2–75 (both); WI §441.06, 448.06 (both); WY §35–6–105, –106 (both).
"A Pennsylvania statute . . ." T18 §3215.

p. 257 ". . . a policy choice not to perform abortions . . ." *Poelker v. Doe,* 432 U.S. 519 (1977).
Wolfe v. Schroering, 541 F.2d 523 (6th Cir. 1976).
Nyberg v. City of Virginia City, 667 F.2d 754 (8th Cir. 1982).
Jones v. Eastern Maine Medical Center, 448 F. Supp. 1156 (D. Me. 1978).

p. 258 "But the Fourth Circuit said . . ." *Doe v. Charleston Area Medical Center Inc.,* 529 F.2d 638 (4th Cir. 1975).
"New Jersey came up with some highly quotable language . . ." *Doe v. Bridgeton Hospital Ass'n,* 71 N.J. 478, 485, 366 A.2d 641, 647 (1976), *cert. den.,* 433 U.S. 914.
Abortion Guidelines: Questions and Answers on the Pregnancy Discrimination Amendment, Questions 34–37, 29 CFR Appendix at p. 142. Religious organizations (even if they are employers) lack standing to challenge the abortion provisions of the PDA and Guidelines: *National Conference of Catholic Bishops v. Bell,* 490 F. Supp. 734 (D. D.C. 1980).
State statutes on abortion and insurance: KY §304.5–160; RI §27–18–28; PA T18 §3215(e).

p. 259 ". . . already declare that human life begins at conception." IL ch 38 ¶81–21; KY §311.720 (invalidated by *Eubanks v. Collins,* 10 FLR 1659 (W.D. Ky. 9/11/84); MA ch 112 §12K; MO §188.010; NB §28–326(4); OK T63 §1–730 (excludes IUD and other birth control devices); PA T18 §3203 (ditto).

p. 260 "As Professor David Westfall of the Harvard Law School pointed out . . ." "Beyond Abortion: the Potential Reach of a Human Life Amendment," 8 *Am. J. Law. & Medicine* 97 (Summer 1982). Professor Westfall was my Estate Planning teacher, but that's not his major claim to fame.
Fetal wrongful death: cf. *Kuhnke v. Fisher,* 52 LW 2703 (Mont. Sup. Ct. 5/24/84); *Harman v. Daniels,* 525 F. Supp. 798 (D. Va. 1981) (fetus isn't a "person" and has no right of recovery for attack made on mother during her pregnancy) with *Hopkins v. McBane,* 11 FLR 1146 (N.D. Sup. 1984); *see* Amy Tarr, "More States Back Wrongful-Death Fetus Claims," *Nat.L.J.,* 5/13/85, p. 7.
Paternity suits: see Gina Schacter, "A Private Cause of Action for Abortion Expenses Under State Paternity Statutes," 7 *Women's Rights Law Reporter* 63 (Winter 1982).

Sherman Act: *Feminist Women's Health Center v. Mohammed*, 586 F.2d 530 (5th Cir. 1978), *cert. den.*, 444 U.S. 924.

p. 261 "The Justice Department has declined . . ."   no by-line, "Clinic Terrorism Continues, Reagan Justice Department Refuses to Act," *National NOW Times*, May/June 1984, p. 1.
"A victim of the latter tactic . . ."   Ann Japenga, "Abortion Suit Brought on by Privacy Issue," *National NOW Times*, May/June 1984, p. 4 (reprinted from the *Los Angeles Times*).

FEDERAL COURTS

	CIRCUIT (Federal)	DISTRICT COURTS* (Federal)	REGIONAL REPORTER
ALABAMA	5th (pre-1980)/11th	N,M,S	SO2d
ALASKA	9th	①	P2d
ARIZONA	9th	①	P2d
ARKANSAS	8th	E,W	SW2d
CALIFORNIA	9th	N,E,C,S	P2d
COLORADO	10th	①	P2d
CONNECTICUT	2d	①	A2d
DELAWARE	3d	①	A2d
D.C.	D.C.	①	A2d
FLORIDA	5th (pre-1980)/11th	N,M,S	SO2d
GEORGIA	5th (pre-1980)/11th	N,M,S	SE2d
HAWAII	9th	①	P2d
IDAHO	9th	①	P2d
ILLINOIS	7th	N,C,S	NE2d
INDIANA	7th	N,S	NE2d
IOWA	8th	N,S	NW2d
KANSAS	10th	①	P2d
KENTUCKY	6th	E,W	SW2d
LOUISIANA	5th	E,M,W	SO2d
MAINE	1st	①	A2d
MARYLAND	4th	①	A2d
MASSACHUSETTS	1st	①	NE2d
MICHIGAN	6th	E,W	NW2d
MINNESOTA	8th	①	NW2d
MISSISSIPPI	5th	N,S	SO2d

*① = one federal judicial district in the state
N = north, E = east, W = west, S = south, C = central, M = middle

MISSOURI	8th	E,W	SW2d
MONTANA	9th	①	P2d
NEBRASKA	8th	①	NW2d
NEVADA	9th	①	P2d
NEW HAMPSHIRE	1st	①	A2d
NEW JERSEY	3d	①	A2d
NEW MEXICO	10th	①	P2d
NEW YORK	2d	N,E,W,S	NE2d
NORTH CAROLINA	4th	E,M,W	SE2d
NORTH DAKOTA	8th	①	NW2d
OHIO	6th	N,S	NE2d
OKLAHOMA	10th	N,E,W	P2d
OREGON	9th	①	P2d
PENNSYLVANIA	3d	E,M,W	A2d
RHODE ISLAND	1st	①	A2d
SOUTH CAROLINA	4th	①	SE2d
SOUTH DAKOTA	8th	①	NW2d
TENNESSEE	6th	E,M,W	SW2d
TEXAS	5th	N,E,W,S	SW2d
UTAH	10th	①	P2d
VERMONT	2d	①	A2d
VIRGINIA	4th	E,W	SE2d
WASHINGTON	9th	E,W	P2d
WEST VIRGINIA	4th	N,S	SE2d
WISCONSIN	7th	E,W	NW2d
WYOMING	10th	①	P2d

*① = one federal judicial district in the state
N = north, E = east, W = west, S = south, C = central, M = middle

GLOSSARY

A.L.R. *American Law Reports.* A multivolume collection of articles on legal topics. Now in its fourth series (A.L.R. 4th), but you may see cites to A.L.R. (the first series), A.L.R.2d or A.L.R.3d.

Am.Jur.2d: *American Jurisprudence, Second Series*—a legal encyclopedia.

app.den. (or dism.): The U.S. Supreme Court (or a state's highest court) refuses to hear the appeal of a case, usually because there is something improper about the application.

B.F.O.Q.: Bona fide occupational qualification. An employer can defend against a sex-discrimination charge by proving that being male (or female, depending on who's doing the charging) really is a prerequisite to doing the job properly.

BNA: Bureau of National Affairs. A legal publisher.

CCH: Commerce Clearing House. A legal publisher.

cf.: Compare with. Used in cites to indicate cases or materials that should be read because they take a different position than the materials originally cited.

C.F.R.: *Code of Federal Regulation.* A series of paperbacks (updated annually) in which federal agency regulations are published.

cert.den.: certiorari denied. The U.S. Supreme Court, or a state's highest court, has the discretion to hear or refuse to hear a case, and refuses.

choice of law: a legal discipline concerned with deciding which system of law (e.g., U.S. or Scottish law; Maine or South Carolina state law) should be applied in a particular case. Choice of law is important if the parties to the case live in different jurisdictions, or if the case involves events occurring in several places.

collateral estoppel: a legal doctrine that keeps parties to one case from re-litigating a point that was settled in another case.

consortium: the right to a person's society, companionship, and help; a spouse's consortium includes sexual and reproductive elements. If a personal injury results in a loss of consortium, the spouse or child of the injured person can sue the party causing the loss for damages equalling the value of the lost consortium.

Δ: lawyers' symbol for "defendant."

e.g.: Latin abbreviation for "for example": "Americans love movie stars (e.g., Clark Gable)."

EPD: *Employment Practices Decisions*—a CCH looseleaf service.

FDA: the federal Food and Drug Administration, responsible for licensing prescription and over-the-counter drugs.

FEP Cases: *Fair Employment Practices Cases*—a looseleaf service published by BNA.

F.L.R.: *Family Law Reporter*—a looseleaf service published by BNA.

F.R.: The *Federal Register*—a daily publication of the federal government, containing regulations and proposed regulations of federal agencies.

F.R.D.: Federal Rules Decisions—a reporter printing decisions interpreting the Federal Rules of Civil Procedure and Federal Rules of Evidence.

F.2d: Federal Reporter, Second Series—the reporter in which U.S. Court of Appeals decisions are printed.

F.Supp.: Federal Supplement (still in its first series)—the reporter in which U.S. District Court Decisions are printed.

forum: the appropriate place (both geographical and legal) for hearing a particular case. For example, the correct forum might be the state courts of Minnesota or the federal District Court for the Central District of California.

forum non conveniens: a defendant can object to the forum in which a case is brought on the grounds that it's inconvenient—for example, the defendant, most of the witnesses, and the physical evidence are somewhere else.

j.n.o.v.: judgment *non obstante veredicto,* or "in spite of the verdict": a trial-court judge overrules a legally incorrect verdict of the jury that has heard the case and substitutes his or her own judgment.

K: lawyers' symbol for "contract."

k: lawyers' symbol for "thousand," as in, "They offered sixty-five k, but we turned it down."

looseleaf service: a law book sold in the form of a binder with replaceable pages. The subscriber gets weekly or monthly supplements with additional pages or replacement pages updating the text and explaining recent legal developments.

N.Y.L.J.: *New York Law Journal,* a daily newspaper. Many cases are published first in the *Law Journal;* some are never published anywhere else.

Nat.L.J.: *National Law Journal,* a weekly newspaper.

negligence: a tort law concept; negligence means failing to act as carefully and intelligently as an ordinary, reasonable person in the same situation. That is, doctors are required to act as ordinary, prudent doctors; drivers, as ordinary, reasonable drivers. In some jurisdictions and cases, if the plaintiff is *contributorily* *negligent* (that is, if the plaintiff's negligence contributed to the harm at all) the plaintiff can't recover any damages. In other circumstances, the standard is comparative negligence: the plaintiff's recovery of damages is reduced to account for his, her, or its negligence.

π: lawyers' symbol for "plaintiff."

P-H: Prentice-Hall. A legal publisher.

P.L.R.: *Products Liability Reporter*, a looseleaf service published by CCH.

P.P.I.: Patient Package Insert. Informational material that the FDA requires to be provided with certain drugs.

per se: Latin for "by itself." *Per se* negligence is an action so heavily disapproved of (e.g., failing to give required warnings to drug buyers) that a plaintiff can prove negligence by proving this action and nothing else.

pretextual: a term often used in employment discrimination cases. The plaintiff charges that a practice constitutes illegal discrimination. The employer defends itself by claiming there was a legitimate, nondiscriminatory reason for the practice. The plaintiff can then charge that the employer's explanation is pretextual—that is, it has no real existence and is a cover-up for discrimination.

probative: testimony or other evidence tending to prove the point it's offered for is probative.

qv.: Latin abbreviation for "which see"—indicates that the item will be discussed more fully elsewhere.

regional reporters: the West Publishing Company collects state court cases and arranges them by region:

> A.2d Atlantic (Second Series) NE2d Northeastern (Second Series) NW2d Northwestern (Second Series) P2d Pacific (Second Series) So2d Southern (Second Series) SE2d Southeastern (Second Series) SW2d Southwestern (Second Series).

remittitur: if a jury finds damages that are excessive by legal standards, the judge can order *remittitur,* giving the plaintiff a choice between accepting lower damages and having a new trial.

res ipsa loquitur: Latin for "the thing speaks for itself." *Res ipsa* is a tort law doctrine holding that some things are too obvious to require proof. The classic example is the severed toe found in a package of chewing tobacco, obviously as a result of poor quality control by the tobacco company.

res judicata: Latin for "a thing decided": a point that has been settled and can't be re-litigated in the same case.

semble: Latin for "it resembles." If the citation reads, *Jenkins v. Paulmier,* 308

A.2d 719 (Ct. 1981), *semble Arkway v. Rambeau,* 422 P.2d 835 (Co. 1982), it means the *Arkway* case is similar to the *Jenkins* case.

standing: short for "standing to sue." In general, American courts can't give opinions in the abstract or answer general questions ("Is school segregation constitutional?"): they must decide a "case or controversy" involving real people and institutions. Therefore, to bring a case, there must be at least one plaintiff with standing to sue (e.g., a pregnant stewardess in a case involving airline maternity-leave policies).

strict liability: a tort-law doctrine holding the manufacturer of a dangerous product liable for harm caused by the product even if the manufacturer wasn't negligent.

Title VII: the federal law forbidding discrimination in employment on the basis of sex, race, religion, or national origin.

Title IX: the federal law forbidding sex discrimination in educational programs receiving federal funds.

tort: any wrongful act (whether careless or intentional) that causes injury, and for which the party suffering the damage can sue the party alleged to have caused the damage. Negligence, libel, slander, wrongful death, and abusive discharge are examples of torts.

tortfeasor: a party committing a tort.

U.S.C.: United States Code, a compilation of federal statutes. It's published in three versions: U.S.C. just has the text of the statutes; U.S.C.A. (U.S. Code Annotated) and U.S.C.S. (U.S. Code Service) also have legislative history, case cites, and other explanatory material added by the publisher.

voir dire: "to see [them] say"—spoken examination of potential jurors to see which ones should be seated as jurors in that particular case.

INDEX